DAYANAND COMMEMORATION VOLUME

DAYANAND COMMEMORATION VOLUME

A HOMAGE TO MAHARSHI DAYANAND SARASWATI
FROM INDIA AND THE WORLD
IN CELEBRATION OF THE
DAYANAND NIRVANA ARDHA SHATABDI

EDITED BY

HAR BILAS SARDA

GYAN

Published by

Gyan Publishing House
5, Ansari Road
Daryaganj, New Delhi-110002
Phone: 011-47034999, 9811692060
E-mail: books@gyanbooks.com

Distribution Network
gyanbooks.com
India, USA, Canada, UK, Australia

ISBN: 978-93-6208-014-1 (HB)
First Published, 1933

2nd Impression 2024

Printed at: Gyan Press, Delhi.

DAYANAND COMMEMORATION VOLUME
Editor: HAR BILAS SARDA

SWAMI DAYANAND SARASWATI

DAYANAND COMMEMORATION VOLUME

A HOMAGE TO MAHARSHI DAYANAND SARASWATI

FROM INDIA AND THE WORLD

IN CELEBRATION OF THE

DAYANAND NIRVANA ARDHA SHATABDI

EDITED BY HAR BILAS SARDA, M.L.A.

AJMER 1933.

ॐ

To the

Sacred Memory

of

Maharshi Dayanand Saraswati

The world is fettered by the chain forged by superstition and ignorance. I have come to snap asunder that chain and to set slaves at liberty. It is contrary to my mission to have people deprived of their freedom.

DAYANAND SARASWATI

Though I was born in Aryavarta (India) and live in it, yet just as I do not defend the falsehoods of the faiths and religions of this country, but expose them fully; in like manner, I deal with the religions of other countries. I treat the foreigners in the same way as my own countrymen, so far as the elevation of the human race is concerned.

DAYANAND SARASWATI

FOREWORD

The Paropkarni Sabha published a Centenary edition of Swami Dayanand's works, which included all his books except the voluminous Commentary on the Vedas, on the occasion of the Centenary of his birth which was celebrated at Muttra in February, 1925. As Swami Dayanand Saraswati died at Ajmer on 30th October, 1883, the Paropkarni Sabha decided at its meeting held on 24, December, 1925, to hold the bi-centenary celebrations of his demise at Ajmer. The idea came into my mind that the Paropkarni Sabha might appropriately bring out on that occasion a Commemoration Volume in honour of Dayanand Saraswati. The Dayanand Nirvāna Ardha Shatābdi Sabha, at its meeting held on 21st March 1932 approved of my proposal. In February-March, 1933, I issued invitations to a number of Indian, European and American scholars and savants to contribute articles to the volume. The short time available precluded response from scholars from Europe on a very generous scale; and, though the volume falls short of the greatness of the occasion, the response from scholars in India has been very gratifying, and it has become possible to bring out a fairly presentable volume. I must acknowledge with gratitude the ready response which the learned scholars and eminent ladies and gentlemen who have contributed papers or appreciations to the volume have given to my invitation, and on behalf of the Dayanand Nirvāna Ardha Shatābdi Sabha, I offer them sincere thanks.

The facilities available in Ajmer for printing and binding a volume like the present are very limited, and the resources of the local Vedic Yantralaya have been strained to the utmost to allow of this volume to be brought out in time for the Dayanand Nirvāna Ardha Shatābdi Celebrations. It has not been found possible to use diacritical marks in all articles.

I must apologise for not being able to print the contributions in any particular order, as some of them were received after a large part of the volume was in print. They have been placed as the exigencies of printing the whole volume within the short time available demanded.

I must take this opportunity to express my sincere thanks to Prof. P. Seshadri, the well-known educationist and learned Principal of the Government College, Ajmer, for the help he has ungrudgingly given me in correcting the proofs. I am also obliged to him for valuable suggestions and help in seeing the book through the Press. My obligations are also due to Mahamahopadhyaya Pandit Gaurishankar Hirachand Ojha, the historian of Rajputana and Pandit Rameshvar G. Ojha, Professor of Sanskrit, Government College, Ajmer, for correcting the proofs of the Hindi articles in the volume.

AJMER HAR BILAS SARDA

CONTRIBUTORS

CONTENTS

REPRINTS

HINDI

URDU.

LIST OF PLATES

To face page

SWAMI DAYANAND SARASWATI

INTRODUCTION

"GREAT men are the fire-pillars in this dark pilgrimage of mankind: they stand as heavenly Signs, ever-living witnesses of what has been, prophetic tokens of what still may be, the revealed, embodied possibilities of human nature"—Thomas Carlyle.

Great men are pillars of light to light up the path of man in this life: their lives and their work serve as guides to men to enable them to traverse the passage of life in this world in safety and peace. They are the divine and never-failing embodiments of knowledge of the good that there was in the Past, and they reveal in an unmistakeable manner what mankind in future may be, and to what height of greatness every man may rise. Great men are the living illustrations of the noble elevation to which humanity will eventually rise in the future.

A Great Man, is an unfailing guide of mankind and embodies in himself the nobility and perfection of human nature. Dayanand Saraswati was, in this sense of the term, a perfect example of a great man.

"Great men seem to be part of the Infinite, brothers of the Seas and the Mountains," says Colonel Ingersoll, the greatest of the American orators. Humanity is infinite. Great men, possessing in a greater measure the qualities that distinguish man from animals, help us to realise infinity in their greatness. As the skies, the seas and the mountains transcend our physical vision and appear to us to have no end, so do great men transcend our mental vision and their proportions fade into infinity. The seas and the mountains determine on the physical plane, the settlement of people, the growth of cities and towns, and the flow of trade; so do great men not only elevate the moral and spiritual life of man, but bring into being, ideas and forces, that control and regulate in a great measure, the ordinary day to day life of peoples, and permanently affect their out-look and their ideals. The influence of great men is lasting, as the influence of the seas and the mountains.

Great men are not all fashioned after one pattern. Every one has an individuality of his own. There is no single standard by which to measure them all. No one in this world can remain uninfluenced by the environment in which he grows up: and the environment never being the same, different people develop different qualities and in different measures.

One generally accepted standard used in judging great men, however, is the good they have done to the world, the extent to which they have helped the masses, the level of happiness and prosperity to which they have raised mankind, the intellectual and spiritual advancement of the peoples of the world they have brought about. It is this standard that reminds one of the dictum that great men are part of the infinite.

Sri Rama Chandra, Bhishma, Sagara, Asoka, Samudragupta, Vikramaditya, Harsha, Alexander, Cæsar, Akbar, Charlemagne, Napolean were all great men each in his own way. Great poets like Valmiki, Kalidas, Homer, Virgil, Shakespeare, Goethe; philosophers and thinkers like Vyas, Gautama, Kanāda, Śaṅkarāchārya, Plato, Aristotle, Kant, Herbert Spencer have brought much light and joy to the world and have helped in raising the intellectual and spiritual level of mankind, and added to their happiness and contentment. Patriots like Pratap, Sivaji, William Tell, Washington, Garibaldi, Robert Bruce, Kamal Pasha have served humanity through their own countries, raised the moral level of mankind and have established landmarks which are a never-failing source of strength and inspiration to men in every country and clime. Greater than all these, however, are men, who, having known Truth and received the light not vouchsafed to ordinary men, love mankind; who, burning with the desire to promote human welfare, themselves lead lives of absolute purity and self-denial, and devote themselves to revealing fundamental truths of life, forgotten or long hidden; who hold aloft high ideals of conduct for people to follow, and ceaselessly work to lighten their burdens and to remove the injustices, the sufferings, the sorrows of the world by banishing ignorance, and guiding them towards truth, light and happiness. While heroes extort admiration and furnish inspiration; poets, thinkers, and philosophers win gratitude and affection, mankind offer their reverence, love, homage and adoration to the Regenerators of people like Krishna, Buddha and Jesus. Dayanand Saraswati belonged to this small number of the Elect.

These men represent the highest and the noblest in humanity; they have reached the summit of human glory and greatness.

The Vedas

According to Hindu belief, when God created man, he revealed the Vedas for his guidance. The Vedas radiated the light that illumined the world by teaching those eternal truths and principles that help us to realise the nature and the co-relation of God and man—of *Parmātmā*, *Atmā* and *Prakriti*—of humanity and Divinity.

Professor Max Muller says:—"In the history of the world, the Vedas fill a gap which no literary work in any other language could fill." Guigault says:—"The Ṛig Veda is the most sublime conception of the great highways of humanity." Mons Leon Delbos says:— "There is no monument of Greece or Rome more precious than the Ṛig Veda." When the Yajur Veda was presented to Voltaire, he expressed his belief that "the Veda was the most precious gift for which the West had ever been indebted to the East."

Sriyut Aurovindo Ghosh, one of the greatest living Indians says:—"The ancient civilization did possess secrets of science, some of which modern knowledge has recovered, extended and made rich and precise, but others are even now not recovered.

There is then nothing fantastic in Dayanand's idea that the Veda contains truth of science as well as truth of religion. I will even add my own conviction that the Veda contains other truths of science, the modern world does not at all possess, and in that case Dayanand has rather *understated* than overstated the depth and range of the Vedic wisdom.

"In the matter of Vedic interpretation, I am convinced that whatever may be the final complete interpretation, Dayanand will be honoured as the first discoverer of the right clues. Amidst the chaos and obscurity of old ignorance and age-long misunderstanding, his was the eye of direct vision that pierced to the truth and fastened on that which was essential. He has found the key of doors that time had closed, and rent asunder the seals of the imprisoned fountain. The essential is that he seized justly on the Vedas as the Indian rock of ages and had the daring conception to build on what his penetrating glance perceived in it a whole nationhood. Ram Mohan Roy, that great soul and puissant worker, who laid his hand on Bengal and shook her out of her long indolent sleep by her rivers and her rice fields, stopped short at the Upanishads. Dayanand looked beyond and perceived that our true or original seed was the Vedas. He had the national instinct and he was able to make it luminous—an intuition in place of an instinct. Therefore the works that derive from him, however they depart from received traditions, must needs be profoundly national........ If the character given by the Vedic Ṛishis to their goal is admitted, we are bound whenever the hymns speak of Agni or some other god, to see behind that name what was present always to the thought of the Ṛishi, the One Supreme Deity, or else one of His powers with its attendant qualities and attributes. Immediately the whole character of the Vedas is fixed in the sense Dayanand gave to it, the merely ritual, mythological and polytheistic interpretation of Sayaṇāchārya collapses, the naturalistic and historical interpretation of Europeans also vanishes. We have instead a real scripture, one of the world's sacred books and the divine word of a lofty and noble religion."

The Hindu Race

The Indians were thus the original teachers and leaders of mankind. They gave civilization and religion to the world, and their country, Aryavarta (now called India) became the sacred land of civilized humanity. The Aryas carried *dharma*, truth and enlightenment to the remotest corners of the world, all over Asia, Europe, Africa and America. With the lapse of time, after reaching the highest meridian of earthly prosperity, decline set in amongst them, and gradually, they lost the knowledge of the Vedas and the sciences based on their teachings. They forgot the Dharma their forefathers had taught the world. Their spiritual light, their moral grandeur, their physical prowess and their purity of life deteriorated, till those eternal truths of Being that underlie true Dharma, fell in danger of disappearing. The knowledge of Sanskrit (देव वाणी) declined; true Dharma became rare. And the term *Arya*, once a term which connoted nobility, culture and greatness, gave place to "Hindu" which, with the progress of time became synonymous with "the weak and the feeble".

The people who taught philosophy and science to the Greeks and the Egyptians, and religion to the whole world, fell a victim to foreign invaders inferior to them in civilization, culture and refinement. So great was the fall that even a correct copy of the Vedas—the most precious heritage bequeathed by their ancestors to mankind was not easily available in India. The Hindu nation became a byword for an inefficient, helpless and subject people.

The people that first preached to the world the brotherhood of man, and the unity of mankind became hopelessly divided into innumerable castes — watertight compartments. They even began to regard it a sin for a member of one caste to marry into another caste, to take food cooked by a member of another caste even to dine with him. Nay, in some parts of this sacred land, they even now regard it a pollution to be within a certain distance of a member of certain castes. Owing to this ignorant, narrow, exclusive and iron bound caste-system resulting in disunity, the country fell a prey to the greed, oppression and domination of backward tribes, who, from time to time invaded the hospitable, fertile and rich land of India from the West or the North-West. The people who had reached the summit of spiritual glory, and the pinnacle of worldly prosperity, who carried their messages of peace, good-will, enlightenment and happiness to every part of the world, who taught arts and sciences to the ignorant and un-enlightened nations of both the hemispheres, who were justly celebrated as the greatest, the richest and the wisest people on earth, were found in the beginning of the nineteenth century A. D. hopelessly divided, weak and ignorant, strangers to their sublime language and their superb literature, unable to defend themselves against foreign invasion; unable to protect their arts and sciences, their noble culture, their magnificent civilization and their divine religion. Such was the state of affairs in this land when Swami Dayanand Saraswati was born in Vikrama Samvat 1881 (A. D. 1824-25).

The Hindu Śastras inculcate that truth reasserts itself, that when the salvation of mankind is in jeopardy, a great soul appears and leads men again towards those eternal springs which give life and vigour.

> यदा यदा हि धर्मस्य ग्लानिर्भवति भारत ।
> अभ्युत्थानमधर्मस्य तदात्मानं सृजाम्यहम् ॥ ७ ॥
> परित्राणाय साधूनां विनाशाय च दुष्कृताम् ।
> धर्मसंस्थापनार्थाय सम्भवामि युगे युगे ॥ ८ ॥ (गीता अ० ४)

This *sloka* of the Gita merely gives expression to the eternal truth that whenever the eternal truths of life are in danger of disappearance, whenever the race through which these truths were revealed to mankind is in danger of forgetting them, the Divine Mercy begins to operate and a great soul appears to re-unfold those truths and teach people anew the true faith that leads to life and happiness.

Dayanand saw the world steeped in ignorance and superstition, torn asunder by prejudice and selfishness, and without light to guide the path of man and of nations to salvation. Life-long study and contemplation based on careful observation drove him to the conclusion that the prime cause of degeneration was the neglect of those eternal truths taught in the Vedas, which govern humanity and which properly understood and practised, will elevate mankind and bring prosperity and happiness to the world. He determined to revive their study.

Finding also that the evils that ate into the vitals of Hindu society were multifarious and manifold, he resolved to tackle them all; and in order to throw the light of Vedic teachings on all important matters that concerned the life of the people—religious, social and economic—he began to write books containing those teachings, all in Hindi for the use and benefit of all classes of society — for the Hindus as well as the non-Hindus. He travelled all over the country, spreading the light of truth wherever he went, preaching Vedic religion and ideals, giving public lectures, holding private discourses and friendly discussions with Christian missionaries, Muslim maulvis and the protagonists of other religions as well as with the learned Brahmins.

He knew that the Brahmins, who were the law-givers of India, accept without question, the supreme authority of the Vedas in all things and at all times— they hold that the Vedas, being divine wisdom, override all Śastras and none may question their authority. As Aurovindo Ghosh says:— "Even, when the Vedas were no longer understood, even when their traditions were lost behind Pauranic forms, they were still held in honour, though without knowledge, as authoritative revelation and inspired Book of knowledge, the source of all sanctions and standard of all truth." He therefore decided that the best way to redeem his people was to teach them what the Vedas contained. He resolved to show them that the Vedas, the Revelation, the source of Hindu religion and its highest authority, did not support superstition, idolatry, class privilege, sex and caste disqualifications, pernicious customs, emasculating and degrading practices that had reduced the Hindu nation to a state of helpless decrepitude and weakness.

Dayanand, a World-Teacher

Swami Dayanand Saraswati was not a mere Reformer. He was a World Teacher. His mission was to uplift all mankind. Some people, while fully admitting Dayanand's greatness and the great work he did for the Hindus, while also appreciating that his teachings would help to uplift mankind, find it difficult to reconcile their idea of his great and noble aim with his exposure and criticism of the doctrines and practices prevalent in Islam and Christianity and other religions. They think that the great man that he was, that his aim being the progress and unity of human race, he should not have denounced the religious beliefs or condemned the practices followed by the followers of those faiths. They approve of his denunciation of idol-worship, the caste-system, untouchability, child-marriage, enforced widowhood, class-privilege—evils prevalent amongst the Hindus. They do not mind the unrest and the disturbance he created amongst the Hindus by his ceaseless campaign against the evils that rent Hindu society asunder; but they would not, dare not, expose or condemn the falsehoods and the evils prevalent in Islamic or Christian society. A high-placed Englishman, while expressing his admiration for his noble character and the great work Swamiji had done, said to me that great men like him should not condemn or denounce the beliefs and practices of the followers of other religions.

Those who hold such opinions, judge of the greatness of others by their own smallness. They fail to understand Dayanand's aim, his character or the work he had set before himself. They betray their ignorance of his mission. They fail to comprehend the real greatness, the high nobility of purpose which inspired his work.

They only look upon him as a *Hindu* Reformer, as one whose work was to purge Hindu Society of what they think are the evils and falsehoods in Hinduism. They only see a part of the man, not the whole of him. They fail to see that he was not a mere Hindu Reformer, but a lover of humanity, a World Redeemer. His mission was to purge human society—not Hindu Society only—of the evils from which it suffered owing to wrong beliefs whether those beliefs and doctrines were inculcated by Hinduism or Christianity or Islam. He made no difference between faith and faith. He was a World Teacher and his task was to uplift mankind, whether it lived in India and followed Hinduism, or in Persia or Arabia and followed Islam, or in Europe and America and followed Christianity. He loved all mankind, and his aim was to save from degradation and falsehood all men whether they lived in this country or that, or followed this faith or that. He says in the *Satyarth Prakash*:—"Though I was born in Aryavarta (India) and still live in it; yet just as I do not defend the falsehoods of the religions prevailing in this country but expose them fully; in like manner I deal with the religions of other countries and thier supporters. *I treat the foreigners in the same way as my own countrymen so far as the elevation of the human race is concerned.* It behoves all men to act likewise."

This declaration of his, clearly shows that when he criticised Hinduism or Islam or Christianity, it was not in a carping spirit, not as an antagonist, but in a spirit of love and philanthropy. A father anxious to secure the happiness and prosperity of all his sons who have gone astray does not confine himself to guiding and warning the eldest son, leaving the others to their fate; but loving all of them, points out to them all, the wrong paths they had taken, warns them all against the evils they suffer from; shows them all, the right path they should follow. So did Dayanand. His aim was not to save Hindus only; he looked upon Hindus, Muslims, Christians, Buddhists, Zoarastrians, all as his kith and kin, all as his sons; and as he loved them all, he could not but point out the falsehoods and the evils of the various faiths they followed. He would not have been the World Redeemer that he was, had he not done so.

Dayanand, a Product of Hinduism

A remarkable thing about Dayanand Saraswati is that he and his teachings are the products solely of Hindu Śastras and Hindu culture. Foreign culture, Western civilization had not the slightest influence in making him what he was. He did not know English and was in no way influenced by European culture or European thought.

English-educated people in India began to condemn idolatry, class privilege, caste-system, evil customs and practices like the child marriage, and enforced widowhood, in consequence of the English education they had received. And because they thought that these practices constituted Hinduism, they began to reject Hinduism too. Dayanand without receiving any Western education or coming under Western influence, by a study of the real Hindu Śastras found that these practices were against the teachings of Hindu Śastras and therefore rejected them. He shewed that the Vedic religion (true Hinduism) was free from all these evils that now go under the name of Hinduism.

His Distinguishing Features

A study of Dayanand's life and work brings out prominently his three distinguishing features. They are:—

1. Love of truth and absolute rejection of untruth.
2. The dedication of his life to the service of mankind. He set to work to free India from untruth, superstition, and the worship of false gods in all matters, religious, social, economic and political, and *through India*, the whole human race.
3. His love of mankind.

Love of Truth

From his childhood he was a seeker after Truth. His

discriminating mind accepted truth as soon as he found it and instantly rejected untruth. Born in a rich, high class Brahmin family in a town which has since been identified as Tankārā in the Morvi State in Kathiawar, when only eight years old, Mulshankar, for such was the name given to him by his parents, was invested with the sacred thread which marks the initiation of a child into Brahmacharya—a life of celebacy, purity, acquisition of knowledge and search after truth.

During a vigil at night, on the Shivrātri day, in a temple of Siva, he saw mice play on the idol and eat the food placed before it, which he had been taught to worship as God. The truth flashed on his mind that the idol which was unable to prevent mice from running about on it and eating up its food, could not be God, who is the Creator and all powerful Ruler of the world. He woke up his father, who had fallen asleep during the vigil, and asked him to explain the phenomenon he had witnessed. The father's attempt to explain away the occurrence proved futile and Dayanand lost faith in idol-worship.

Dayanand Saraswati had an insatiable appetite for knowledge as he was determined to know the truth in every matter—the real substance of things. He was not only a most diligent student, but had expressed his determination to devote his life to acquisition of knowledge, and to go for study to Benares, the chief seat of Sanskrit learning in India. Finding his parents resolved to prevent this by forcing him to enter into wedlock, he made up his mind to flee from the uncongenial atmosphere which stifled truth. He took the earliest opportunity to leave the environment where life moved in a narrow, false and artificial circle. He left home and his parents, and began to prepare himself for a life of service to truth, service to his country and service to humanity. He went wherever he could find a teacher to impart him knowledge. He spent a number of years going from place to place regardless of bodily discomforts, gladly suffering hardships and privations, leading a life of strenuous, unceasing toil and wholeheartedly devoted himself to the study of ancient Sanskrit learning. He went to Mount Abu, the Satpura Hills, to the distant Himalayas, explored hermitages, lonely caves, and mountain retreats in search of sages, teachers of truth, *yogis* and Mahatmas who would initiate him into the realms of the highest knowledge which man can acquire in order that he may become fully fitted to lead a life devoted to the service of humanity. He underwent strict discipline, led a life of true Brahmacharya to find the Truth. He found it at last in Muttra, where he became a disciple of Swami Virjanand Saraswati, from whom he acquired perfect proficiency in Sanskrit learning, in order to be able to hold. his own against the most learned in the land, whose opposition he was sure to encounter in his campaign against untruth.

Dayanand early realised that untruth leads to error and sin, and entails sorrow and suffering. He also realised that the world was full of sorrow and suffering because it had accepted untruth, and that it could be saved only by bringing it back to the citadel of truth. He went to Benares, stormed the chief citadel of prejudice and privilege and demolished it. He challenged the most learned of the Pandits there to accept truth, and give up untruth and superstition. He told them that the Vedas, the Revelation, the sole authority on religion, condemned idol-worship, caste by birth, child-marriage and untouchability, that they taught pure monotheism, equality of man and the sexes, and challenged them to prove the contrary. The Pandits failed to do so: orthodoxy was beaten in its own stronghold. Vested interests, class privileges and life-long habits and beliefs, but chiefly caste bondage, stood in the way of an open acceptance of truth and a complete change. But Hindu society was convulsed; its sleep disturbed. People began to think—a habit which they had long given up so far as religion was concerned. His teachings have borne fruit. The fifty years that have passed since his death have witnessed a great and vital change. The doctrines he preached, the truths he taught are now generally accepted by the masses who begin to look upon him as the Redeemer, the Saviour of Hindu society. Swami Dayanand's life is the vindiction of truth. It is an embodiment of truth. It illustrates the triumph of Truth.

Dedication of life to service of Mankind

Having realized truth, he determined to carry it first to everyone in the country high or low, rich or poor, and then through India to the whole world. He dedicated his life to the service of mankind by fighting untruth, and planting the banner of Truth, Righteousness and Dharma on a pedestal visible and accessible to all. He gave up all thought of marriage or a career. His one burning desire was to free mankind from error and sin. He kept himself free from all bonds and impediments which might stand in his way.

As he held that the Vedas contained the Truth, a correct and true interpretation of the Vedic texts became an essential condition to a proper understanding of their teachings. He decided to bring this fountain of nourishing, revivifying and revitalizing *amrit* to the door of every one. The Vedas had become sealed books to the Hindus generally. They had become the precious and the exclusive possession of a privileged and exclusive caste who, in order to perpetuate their dominant position in Hindu society, had forbidden its study by any one but themselves, and went so far as to inflict penalties on certain castes if they would even hear them recited. He taught them to every one who wished to learn them. He declared that the Vedas were the gift of God to mankind and it was the birthright of every person to read them and act according to their teachings. He therefore took up the work of translating them into Hindi—the *lingua franca* of India—the *lingua Indica*—so that every one may have access to them and understand them. Dayanand believed that the acceptance of the Vedas and acting according to their teachings will bring salvation to mankind; and he set to work to achieve that object. He took to propagating the truth as taught by the Vedas by lectures, discourses, debates, discussions, conversation and by writing books, and pamphlets. He went round the country taking the banner of Truth to every important town in India where Hindi was understood, every sacred place where large masses of people gather together to perform religious ceremonies, to celebrate festivals and to bathe in the sacred waters of the Ganges, the Jumna, the Narbada, the Tapti, e.g. the *Kumbha* at Hardwar, the *Ardha Kumbhis* at Allahabad and Ujjain. He visited every place of pilgrimage, small or great, Pushkar, Benares, Gaya, Muttra, Ajodhia, Allahabad, Nasik, Badrinarain etc. He had no headquarters, no place to go to for rest or recuperation. Day and night, night and day, he devoted himself to the service of the people writing, preaching, debating, advising, counselling.

Not content to do what he would be able to accomplish during his own life, which he foresaw would not be long, and convinced that it was necessary to carry the message of Truth to all countries of the world, he created a Trust—the Paropkarini Sabha—and appointed 23 Trustees to continue his work after him and carry the Banner of Truth to every country in the world, in Europe, America and Asia and thus free men from superstitions, falsehoods and shackles of all kinds. He enjoined upon them the duty:—

(1) To propagate and spread the knowledge of the *Vedas* and the *Vedāngas*, i. e. to say, to expound them and get them expounded, to read and hear them read, to recite and get them recited, and to publish them.

(2) To establish Missions and send missionaries to all countries of the world to teach men the Vedic Faith, and to preach that Truth should be accepted and Untruth rejected.

(3) To give protection and right education to the orphans and the poor people of India.

Love of Mankind

The philosopher Helvetius says:—"Don't expect too much from men if you would love mankind." Dayanand knew that the evil in the world was due to ignorance, want of knowledge of Truth. As his heart was full of love for mankind, he had only pity for the wrong-doing, even the wickedness of men. He denounced untruth, often in strong terms, but had no hatred for any one, not even for the wrong doer, the criminal and the wicked. The infinite love and compassion that filled his heart left no room there for feelings of recrimination or revenge.

Several incidents in his life illustrate how a wrong committed by a person against him instead of exciting hatred or anger invoked pity and compassion in him. Once when he was in Anupshahar (U. P.) carrying on his crusade against untruth, a Brahmin, enraged by Swamiji's denunciation of idol worship resolved to kill him, and gave him poison in a *pān* (betel leaf). Swamiji came to know of it in time, and saved himself by performing a *yogic* act, *Neoli Kriya*. He, however, said nothing to the man. Somehow or other the news of this reached the ears of the Tahsildar and Magistrate of the place, Sayad Muhammad, who arrested and imprisoned the Brahmin. Thinking that Swamiji would appreciate his action, he went to Swamiji to inform him of it. The Swami would not speak to him. The Tahsildar was surprised and asked him the reason of it. Swamiji said to him "I have not come to this world to imprison people, but to free them from shackles. If men do not give up evil doing why should we leave our nobleness and higher purpose." Swamiji then got the culprit released.

When we think of Dayanand Saraswati, we see the sublime spectacle of a Superman, who, knowing the Truth, and also knowing that the world is full of sorrow because it has left the path of Truth, stands before it with a heart full of pity and compassion for erring mankind; with no resources except his own dominant intellect, his superb courage and his indomitable will; with only a piece of cloth round his loins and a stick in his hand; convinced that it was his duty to save mankind and determined to do so; conscious that he possessed the strength to free it from falsehood, superstition and sin which had taken a firm hold of it and were dragging it lower and lower down the slough of despondency and degradation.

Dayanand's Place in History

It is not possible at the present time to assign Swami Dayanand Saraswati his true place in history. We are too near him yet to get a full view of his proportions. True perspective is wanting. If you stand at the foot of a mountain, or fifty yards away from it you can only say that it is a great big thing, but you cannot say where it stands in the grade of mountains. You must stand at a great distance from a mountain and be able to get a comprehensive view of its length and height, of the space it occupies in the landscape as compared with the others, before you can give it its rank amongst the mountains of the world. So with great men. A century or two must pass before even the best informed can form a tolerably clear idea of a great man's proportions. You have to wait till the forces generated and set to work by a great personality have fully developed and adjusted themselves not only to the forces at work when that personality appeared on the horizon, but have also met and come to some adjustment with the reactions to the disturbing forces brought into being by that great man. You have to wait till this is done; for it is then that you can get a true perspective of the man and can assign him his true place amongst great personalities.

Dayanand, as stated before, was one of the great teachers and redeemers of the world like Krishna, Buddha and Jesus. Time, however, is not yet for assigning Dayanand his true place among them. Could any one, fifty years after Buddha's death, or the Crucification of Christ, declare the position Buddha or Christ was to occupy in history? Could any one even so late as the conversion of Emperor Asoka have assigned Buddha the place he now occupies in human history; or even a thousand years after his death assign Jesus the position he now holds amongst mankind? It took centuries to bring to fruition the seeds sewn by them. It was several centuries before Buddha and Jesus were recognised as great benefactors of mankind. As a matter of history, within fifty years of their deaths no one assigned to Buddha or Jesus even that position amongst men, which, according to the informed people all over the world, Dayanand occupies to-day. And if the logic of things and human experience are any guide, there is no doubt that a couple of centuries hence, the world will accept Dayanand as as great a benefactor of mankind as Jesus or Buddha.

The heart of Jesus like that of Dayanand was full of pity for the sufferings of men. Intellectually, however, Dayanand was far superior to him. Dayanand was a profound scholar. His supreme place in the field of knowledge of Vedic Literature was undisputed and unquestioned. Both Jesus and Dayanand tried to redeem the people. Both loved them and served them. Both had to give up their lives at the altar of the service of humanity. Jesus was crucified: Dayanand was poisoned.

Buddha, one of the noblest of men, is nearer Dayanand than Jesus. Both spent a large part of their lives in search of truth, and at last finding it, gave up the rest of their lives to proclaiming it and making it accessible to all. Both were equally pure in their lives, and gave up the world to serve mankind. Both loved humanity and were full of pity and compassion for the faults, the follies, the foibles, the fatalities of men. Both were incarnations of mercy and forgiveness. Buddha's mission, born as he was in the India of the sixth century B.C., was to do away with superstition, ritualism run riot, and to teach men simplicity and brotherhood. Dayanand declared that he had come to the world to break the chains of slavery, and free mankind from error, superstition, ignorance, domination of all kinds, ecclesiastical, social, economic. Dayanand was equipped for the purpose with a cultivated intellect of the highest order, and knowledge of the Vedic literature, unrivalled and supreme. In this, Dayanand had an advantage over Buddha. Then, Buddha had only to deal with the Brahmin priesthood: Dayanand had to meet and overcome not only the Brahmin orthodoxy but the prejudices and errors of the votaries of Islam, Christianity, Jainism, Sikhism and others.

Both Buddha and Dayanand were products of pure unadultrated Hindu culture and Hindu thought, and owed nothing to alien civilizations, cultures or religions. In Buddha's time, little of the world outside India was known: Dayanand had a pretty clear idea of the great world outside India. Buddha found his people politically independent but suffering from excessive ritualism and presumption, and given to excessive self-indulgence. Dayanand found his people weaklings, steeped in ignorance and superstition, helpless and degraded, bound hand and foot, slaves politically, economically and socially. He had a harder task to perform to redeem them and, through them, the rest of mankind. Yet he has sown the seed which will bear the fruit of World Redemption. Time will show that he was one of the greatest benefactors of humanity—true Redeemer and Deliverer, true Regenerator of mankind.

AJMER

Har Bilas Sarda

SWAMI DAYANAND

(A Sketch)

SWAMI DAYANAND was born sometime in the *Samvat* year 1881 in an Audich Brahmin family of Tankara a village in the State of Morvi in Kathiawar. His name given by his parents was Mulshankar. His father Karsanji was a rich zamindar and banker and a State Official. At the age of five Mulshankar had acquired a knowledge of Devnagri and had committed several sacred texts to memory. At the age of eight he was invested with the sacred thread as also the *Gayatri Mantra* and taught *Sandhya*. He had memorized Rudradhyaya and the *Yajurveda Sanhita*. The family followed the Shaiva faith and Mulshankar or Mulji as he was called, was taught to worship Shiva with obligations to undertake fasts. In *Samvat* 1894 (A. D. 1837) during the Shivratri vigil, finding mice playing on the idol and eating its food he woke up his father and asked for an explanation and not getting a satisfactory answer lost faith in idol-worship. The death of his younger sister and the uncle who was also his tutor caused him great grief and he began to consider how to alleviate human suffering. In order to avoid matrimony which his father was forcing on him he left home in his twenty-first year in *Samvat* 1903 (A.D. 1846). His father's attempt to bring him back to the family proved unsuccessful.

He visited several places and at last went to Parmanand Paramhansa and read Vedanta with him. Finding that preparing food for himself was an impediment to study, he resolved to become a *sannyasi*. After some difficulty, a Deccani Swami Purnanand initiated him into the fourth order and gave him the name of Dayanand Saraswati at Chanoda Kanyali. He learnt *Yoga* from Jwalanand Puri and Shivanand Giri. He then went to Mount Abu and Arvada Bhawani and finally to the Kumbha Fair at Hardwar in *Samvat* 1911 (A. D. 1854) and continued practicing *Yoga*. He mixed freely with *sannyasis*, also devoting intervals of time to *Yogic* practice in the hills of Chandi. He then visited Rishikesh, Tehri, Garhwal, Kedarghat, Rudra Prayag, Guptakashi, Trijuginarayan and the heights of Tunganath and Okhimath, where a little halt was made for rest. Kedarnath was next climbed as also Joshimath and Badrinath.

At Joshimath having learnt from the learned Rawalji that certain Mahatmas resided in those parts, Swami Dayanand undertook several difficult and dangerous trips, having incidentally travelled the path which the Pandavas had taken in old days and passed the cold weather at Dronasagar.

In Samvat 1913 (1856 A.D.) Dayanand went to Benares *via* Mirzapur. After a brief stay there in the beginning of *Samvat* 1914, Swami Dayanand went to the forest regions of the Central Provinces and spent three years there employing his time in communion with Nature and converse with *sannyasis*.

In *Samvat* 1917 (1860 A.D.) he went to Muttra where Swami Dayanand read the sacred books with Swami Virjanand Saraswati who though blind was an intellectual giant. Finding in him a true Guru and guide, Swami Dayanand became his disciple and read with him for nearly four years, at the end of which, he took leave of Swami Virjanand. Swami Virjanand charged Dayanand with the duty of devoting himself to the mission of uplifting the country, the rescue of the sacred books, the removal of sectarianism and finally, the promulgation of Vedic religion throughout the world. Leaving Muttra in the Baisakh of *Samvat* 1921 (A.D. 1864) Swami Dayanand came to Agra where he taught the virtues of *Sandhya* and the supreme importance of self-control and continence. Then followed a tour along Dholpur, Lashkar, Gwalior, Karauli and Jaipur, culminating in Pushkar in *Samvat* 1926 (A.D. 1869) where a great stir was made by Swami Dayanand's vigorous attacks on the Bhâgvat and practice of idol-worship. The next place to visit was Ajmer, where a long halt was made and many discussions held with Christian missionaries and Muhammadan Maulvis. It was at Ajmer that the question of cow-protection was first taken up in a series of articles and the attention of the British authorities drawn towards this beneficial measure.

Swami Dayanand again went to the Kumbha Fair at Hardwar in the company of several *Brahmcharis and Sannyasis* and a fairly good equipment of books; for, by this time, the texts of the Vedas had been secured. He pitched a camp there with a banner on which was inscribed पाखंड खंडनी पताका. Hardwar was convulsed and the agitation spread throughout the country. His call for co-operation was in vain, and in despair, having distributed all his books and furniture, Swami Dayanand entered on a life of renunciation. For seven years clad in a loin-cloth, he undertook a vigorous denunciation of the Pauranic corruption, visiting Anupshahr, Belon, Ramghat, Chhalesar, Soron, Harganj, Farrukhabad, Kanauj and Cawnpore, finally arriving at Kashi where in a public discussion held under the presidency of the Maharaja of Benares, he vanquished the entire learning of Benares representated by Swami Vishuddhanand, Bal Sastri and 300 other Pandits. The *Pioneer*, in its notice, characterised Swami Dayanand as the Luther of India. Swami Dayanand paid six successive visits to Benares at this time and it was here that he started the experiment of founding Sanskrit Pathshalas. Again it was at Benares that he first started issuing his translation of the Vedas from the *Lazarus Press.*

Having thus practically finished with Kashi, Swami Dayanand reached Calcutta *via* Monghyr and Bhagalpur, where he came in special contact with the leaders of the Brahmo Samaj. So far, his medium of speech was Sanskrit. Finding however, that one of his Calcutta addresses was not truly interpreted by Pandit Mahesh Chandra Vidyaratna, he adopted the Hindi language in his discourses. After an open discussion with Pandit Taraknath

Tarkavachaspati, Swami Dayanand returned to Cawnpore *via* Bhagalpur, Patna, Chhapra, Arrah, and Dumraon. His favourite exhortation to the public at this time was the throwing of idols into the Ganges.

Swamiji then went to Allahabad where *the Satyarth Prakash* was dictated. It was published under the auspices of Raja Jaikishendas, C.S.I. Leaving Allahabad and going *via* Jubbulpur and Nasik in the *Kartik* of *Samvat* 1931 (A.D. 1874) Swami Dayanand arrived in Bombay. From this centre, brief visits were paid to various places in the Gujarat and Kathiawar, and on Saturday the 5th of *Chaitra Shukla* of *Samvat* 1932 (A.D. 1875) the first Arya Samaj was established in Bombay. Then came the turn of Poona where a series of fifteen powerful public addresses were given and a few discussions held.

Samvat 1933 (A.D. 1876) was spent in visiting Farrukhabad Benares, Jaunpur, Ayodhya, Lucknow, Shahjahanpur, Bareilly and Karnavas, the journey terminating in Delhi about the time of Lord Lytton's Darbar in January, 1877 A.D. Here an attempt was made to organize a concerted programme of reforms by the principal Hindu and Muslim reformers but without success. Swamiji then went to the Punjab *via* Meerut and Saharanpur and an Arya Samaj was established at Lahore on *Jeth-Shukla* 13 in *Samvat* 1934 (1877 A.D.). Returning from the Punjab, several places in the United Provinces were again visited, also Ajmer, whence the tour through the U. P. and Bihar was resumed and several discussions held with the people of other faiths.

In *Samvat* 1936 (1879 A. D.) Swamiji again visited the Kumbha Fair held that year. Swamiji then went to Udaipur on an invitation from His Highness the Maharana Sahib. Here he made a Will, constituting a Trust with 23 Trustees and got it registered in the State Council office. Thus was established the Paropkarini Sabha. Maharana Sri Sajjan Singhji Bahadur received Swami Dayanand and his teachings with sincere reverence. Shahpura was the next place

RAJA JAIKISHANDAS, C.S.I.

visited where Rajadhiraj Sir Nahar Singhji read the *Manusmriti* with Swami Dayanand. On the 31st of May, 1883, A. D. (*Jeth Samvat* 1940) at the invitation of His Highness the Maharaja Jaswant Singhji of Jodhpur, Swamiji went there. Here Swami Dayanand was taken ill on 29th September. He went to Mount Abu, but as no improvement took place he came to Ajmer on 27th October. He became worse and breathed his last at 6 p. m. on the *Amavas* of *Kartik* of *Vicrama Samvat* 1940 (30th October 1883 A.D). His principal works are:—

Commentaries on Rigveda and Yajurveda
Ashtadhyayiabhashya
Introduction to the Commentary on Rigveda.
Satyarthprakash
Aryabhivinaya
Satyadharmavichar
Sanskarvidhi
Panchmahayagyavidhi
Kashiśastrath
Aryoddeshyaratnamala
Vyavaharabhanu
Vedavirudhmata-khandan
Bhramochchhedan
Gokarunanidhi
Bhranti-nivaranam
Śastrarth Ferozabad
Anubhramochchhedan
Vedantdhwanta-nivaran
Swami-narayana-mata khandan
Vedangaprakash, fourteen parts (complete)
Sanskrit-vakya-prabodh

MAHATMA GANDHI

Dear Diwan Bahadur,

I have your letter. Among the many rich legacies that Swami Dayanand has left to us, his unequivocal pronouncement against untouchability is undoubtedly one.

7-5-33 p.m.

Yours sincerely,
M. K. Gandhi

Diwan Bahadur
Har Bilas Sarda
Har Niwas
Civil Lines
Ajmer

I offer my homage of veneration to Swami Dayananda, the great path-maker in modern India, who through bewildering tangles of creeds and practices — the dense undergrowth of the degenerate days of our country — cleared a straight path that was meant to lead the Hindus to a simple and rational life of devotion to God and service for man. With a clear-sighted vision of truth and courage of determination he preached and worked for our self-respect and vigorous awakenment of mind that could strive for a harmonious

Dr. RABINDRANATH TAGORE

adjustment with the progressive spirit of the modern age and at the same time keep in perfect touch with that glorious past of India when it revealed its personality in freedom of thought and action, in an unclouded radiance of spiritual realisation.

Rabindranath Tagore

July 15. 1933

Santiniketan

THE ETERNAL QUEST

ALTHOUGH science is neither of the East nor of the West, but international in its universality, yet India by her habit of mind and inherited gifts handed down from generation to generation, is specially fitted to make great contributions in furtherance of knowledge. The burning Indian imagination which can extort new order out of a mass of apparently contradictory facts, can also be held in check by the habit of concentration; it is this restraint which confers the power to hold the mind in pursuit of truth in infinite patience. The specific requirements for making great discoveries are vivid imagination, clear inner vision, great faculties of invention and experimental skill of the highest order. In order to discover the life-mechanism in the interior of the tree, one has to become the tree and feel throbbings of its pulsating life. This inner vision is, however, to be continuously tested by results of experimentation, for otherwise it is apt to lead to wildest speculation subversive of all intellectual sanity. A true inquirer has to compare at every step his thought with objective reality, abandoning remorselessly all in which these are not agreed; he has with unflinching courage and persistence to fight his way for establishing truth for which he has dedicated himself. It is no easy life that lies before the investigator; he has to steel his body to the utmost. There is to be for him no life of ease, but one of unending struggle. Even after all this, there is no assurance whatever of success to reward him for his ceaseless toil. He has to cast life as an offering, regarding gain or loss, success or failure, as one. But the lure that draws heroic souls is not success that can be easily attained, but defeat and tribulation in the pursuit of knowledge. What sustains him in hours of deepest depression is the consciousness that both in the East and in the West, there is an undying spirit for the spread of knowledge and for the removal of ignorance. We shall pass away, even nations and kingdoms will disappear, Truth alone will survive, for it is Eternal.

CALCUTTA

J. C. BOSE

MAHATMA HANSRAJ

SWAMI DAYANAND

SWAMI DAYANAND was a great Ṛishi. Ṛishis are those who can see truth face to face. By austerity, knowledge and communion with the Supreme-spirit, they develope their Soul-power to such an extent, that they can pry into the secrets of what surrounds them. Their vision clearly sees through the misty past, the tangled present and mysterious future. Intuition reveals to the Ṛishis the truth which scientists and philosophers try to find out by the laborious process of experiment and reasoning. Such were the Ṛishis of old and Swami Dayanand, though born in the 19th century, was one of them. It is not given to us to know the process of evolution by which Ṛishi Dayanand had attained such a high perfection of mental, moral and spiritual life, but when we come to understand the importance of what he thought and acted, we at once realise the elevated position which he occupies among the great men of the world.

Like the ancient sages of India, Ṛishi Dayanand had supreme faith in God and His word. His faith in the Supreme Being was not the belief of a Savant, who weighs arguments for or against the existence of God and declares that He probably exists; it was the faith of a Ṛishi, who had felt God and seen him as if with his own eyes. He further believed that God himself was the source of light that was vouchsafed to man. The Father of man had manifested His love towards him, not only in looking to the needs of his physical life, but also to those of his spiritual being. His word of wisdom was the fountain-head of all religious life in the world. The mission of the great Swami was to lay open this word of wisdom to men of different faiths; but this was a most difficult task. For the last three thousand years and even before, the Vedas had become a sealed book even to Indians, not to speak of other nations who had migrated from India and settled in other countries. Indian scholars had come to believe that Vedic *mantras* were meant merely for chanting on the occasions of the performance of various *yagyas* (यज्ञ), that their meanings were of no importance in themselves as compared with their spiritual efficacy in securing some gain to the worshipper, and that Vedic prayers were addressed to various gods and goddesses, not to one Supreme Being. The root cause of the mistake lay in the fact that many a Vedic word had on passing into Sanskrit of later times changed its sense, and medieval interpreters of the Vedas had never come in contact with the teachers who had received Vedic knowledge from ancient Ṛishis and Munis. In Vedic times, the etymological sense of a word with its wide significance was more important than the narrow sense, which had come to be attached to it in later times. European scholars followed the lead of Puranic commentators and fell into the same error. Prof. Max Muller had a glimpse of the truth as regards the meaning of the Vedic words, when he said that in the Vedic age words were in a 'fluid state of meaning'. He, however, did not follow the light, which he had sighted and translated the Vedas in the ways of Sāyaṇa. Swami Dayanand saw the truth in its full light and with the key of truth in his hand, he unlocked the hidden meanings of Vedic *mantras*. His task was supremely difficult and any scholar of less undaunted courage, weaker faith and less towering intellect would have shrunk from this self-imposed Herculean enterprise. But Swami Dayanand was not made of ordinary stuff. He interpreted the Vedas in the light which had come to him from his inner soul and writings of ancient Ṛishis and proved to the world how high and noble were the teachings of sacred scriptures. Thousands of years before, the great Ṛishi Vyas had in his *Sharirik-Sutras*, explained that such words as *Pran* and *Akash* ordinarily translated as the sky and the vital breath by ignorant pandits, did mean Brahma—the Great God—in the Vedas. Swami

Dayanand followed the very lines adopted by Maharshi Vyas and translated Indra, Varuna, Saraswati etc., as the various names of one Supreme Being whose praises are sung under different names in the Vedic *mantras*. Thus he refuted the charge that the Vedic religion was not a monotheistic faith. The orthodox pandits disbelieved him and ridiculed his translation, but, I find that now they are gradually drifting to his mode of interpretation and in their mode of explanation of Vedic *mantras*, they have very often to depend on the etymological sense of the Vedic words. Swami Dayanand completed the stupendous task of clearing the debris which had accumulated over the Vedas and hidden their light. Others will come after him and beautify the ground which has been cleared. Swami Dayanand believed that the message of the Vedas was meant for the amelioration of humanity in all lands and climes and that it was his duty to proclaim it everywhere. All glory to the great Ṛishi who realised such a great ideal and worked for it day and night during the whole of his life.

Swami Dayanand was a great world-teacher but his high position did not prevent him from working as a lover of his country. He himself was an Indian and as such he could not but feel for his country which had fallen from a high pedestal of glory to the lowest depths of degradation. It was his duty to lift it up to the pinnacle of glory from which it had fallen. He felt that the Hindūs of India were the prey of bad customs and wrong beliefs and that as long as they were not weaned away from them they would never improve. He moved from place to place and, in his thundering voice and inimitable eloquence, denounced the evils into which his people had fallen. Fifty years ago when his voice was raised in favour of reforms he pointed out to his countrymen the evils of child-marriage, enforced widowhood, female ignorance, untouchability of submerged classes, idolatry and the caste-system. He preached against the close-door policy of Hindus and impressed upon them the need of following the true *Varna Ashrama* system.

The seeds which he had sown have grown into saplings, but time will come when these saplings will grow into strong trees offering refreshing shade and sweet fruits to our people. The movement started by the Ṛishi will spread over the whole country and bring strength, peace and comfort to the millions of this ancient land.

In all humility and reverence, I bow down to Ṛishi Dayanand, the great World-Teacher, earnest patriot, far-sighted reformer and unique scholar.

DHARMSALA

HANSRAJ

TRIBUTE

IN the few hours now at my disposal, I can only send by way of an humble offering, a few lines in memory of Swami Dayanand Saraswati, *the first great architect of modern India.* His learning was stupendous and his character great. But, above all, *his vision was clearer and broader than is generally given to nation-makers.* In the neo-Hinduism of to-day, in Indian Nationalism, in the vigour of the Hindu Mahāsabhā mentality, in the methods of Mahātmā Gandhi, we can trace the influence of Swamiji's unerring vision and statesmanship. His memory, undoubtedly, will enrich the heritage of future India.

BOMBAY

KANHAIYALAL M. MUNSHI

SWAMI DAYANAND SARASWATI

His place in India's Life-history

HE is a true statesman who can legislate for the future, who can set a force at work which will go on influencing the lives and thoughts of unborn generations. When the history of India's growth comes to be written, that high rank will be adjudged to the "naked fakir", Dayanand Saraswati. He rescued the heart of Hinduism from atrophy; he linked it with the spirit of eternal progression ruling the outer world; he proved that whatever is best and truest in the legacy of the ancient sages of Āryāvarta is a possession open to the entire human race, and not confined to any "twice-born" caste or sacred soil.

The true test of every religion is its influence upon conduct, for "the faith that is without work is dead". That test, the church of Dayanand has passed most triumphantly. Its performance is writ large over the face of the Punjab and much of the classic land of Madhyadeśa, and is not unknown elsewhere in India.

Mr. Ramsay Macdonald, during his first visit to India, observed, "the Punjab is dour." This dourness, which we owe mainly to Dayanand, supplied the correct antidote to the malady that was eating into the vitals of Hindu society at the end of seven centuries of Muslim domination. It is the much-needed antithesis to the emotional effervescence of Bengal and the frothy wordiness of Madras, and the hopeless, helpless, shrinking attitude of the general Hindu mind as it was at Dayanand's birth.

Dayanand has proved by word and deed alike that a career of activity, of progress, of aggression (if one may call it so) is not incompatible with the spirit of Hinduism when rightly understood. He has established the absolute equality of the brethren. Hence, wherever the Arya Samaj is a reality, there has been a marvellous elevation of the masses. It is essentially a democratic religion; its work is the fruit of middle-class and lower middle-class guidance and the hearty co-operation of all ranks. The energy of the new faith has overflown into the broad fields of education, relief of distress, reclamation of backward classes, and training in handiwork, no less than in scriptural scholarship and propaganda writing. Its contribution to the intellectual and moral life of New India is almost incredible for such a numerically small body.

It was not such a very dim and distant past when a portion of Hindu society, miscalled the Sanātana Samāj, everywhere stood up in arms against the Arya Samaj, and theological questions at issue between the Sanātanists and the Aryas were sought to be decided—as I have known in Degu Sarai and Dinapur in Bihar, and in Benares—not by the dry light of reason, but by the quarter-staff and the criminal court. That stage is over. To-day the Arya Samaj has vindicated itself by its service to our country and people. To-day Hinduism calls upon it as its best ally. To-day Hinduism has paid the Arya Samaj the highest tribute, that of imitation by stealing its programme.

May the invisible spirit of Dayanand continue to watch silently over his Church! May that Church never come to the end of so many other Churches in India and elsewhere by ignoring the supreme efficacy of moral character and substituting a new superstition and a new rigid ritualism in the place of the older ones that it had at its birth set out to destroy!

CALCUTTA

JADUNATH SARKAR

SWAMI DAYANAND SARASWATI—A NATION BUILDER

SWAMI DAYANAND SARASWATI was, undoubtedly, one of the great gifts of Providence to India in the last century.

Though born and brought up in simple circumstances in his home in Kathiawar, (Gujarat Province), he, in course of time, developed qualities of head and heart that make men great and entitle them to a place of honour in the pages of the history of their times. It is stated that, when barely 21 years of age, Swami Dayanand, in response to an urge from within, decided to leave the parental roof in search of religious knowledge. One fine morning he left home quietly for good. He wandered from place to place and temple to temple throughout Northern India, studying the Hindu Śāstras with a voracious appetite. He devoted over 20 years to serious study and meditation and visited even many of the out-of-the-way places of pilgrimage in his quest of ancient learning. The roaming life he led, naturally brought him in contact with men in all walks of life from priests to princes. But he felt deeply disappointed at what he saw. The degraded condition of the so-called custodians of the Hindu traditions and learning simply lacerated his heart. He found Hindu society divided into numerous castes and fractions. He saw that the noble teachings of the great Arya Ṛishis were trampled under foot, and that superstition and dogma, the inventions of selfish priesthood, held sway over the minds of the people. He observed Hindu India lying prostrate, with all her pristine glory gone and her religion, arts and science dishonoured and vilified. He noticed that hundreds and thousands of Hindus were forsaking their noble religion and traditions and were espousing with pride the cause of foreign religions and civilization. He saw all this and, like a true patriot, at once made up his mind to sacrifice himself in the service of the motherland.

'India must be saved', thought he, 'and at all costs'. He formed his plan in no time and, after pondering over it for a few days while roaming on the banks of the sacred Ganges near Hardwar, he set himself to work.

And his plan was simple. The fortresses of idolatry must be stormed and destroyed and a net-work of institutions to inculcate the true Vedic religion established; the blessings of the Vedic age be glorified and national pride roused in the mind of the Hindu masses. Discarding all his scanty belongings—books, clothes etc.—with a *kaupīna* round his loins and a *kamaṇḍala* in his hand, and resigning himself to Divine protection and guidance, he left Hardwar single-handed to launch his compaign. He travelled on foot along the course of the river Ganges, stopping at every important village and town; haranguing people and dissuading them from the worship of idols. In the course of his itinerary, he reached Farrukhabad where the leading citizens arranged for a public discussion. The representative of the orthodox religion was, however, unable to stand the brunt of his attack and the result was that several of the audience, soon after the discussion, consigned their idols to the waters of the Ganges and one of the leading citizens who was about to instal a *Sivalingam* in his newly-built temple, offered the building to the Swamiji for opening a *pathashala* in it and undertook to bear the recurring expenses of the institution. The signal victory at Farrukhabad naturally raised high hopes in his mind and, like a conqueror, he marched on to Benares, the citadel of orthodoxy. His fame as the opponent of idol-worship and caste had, however, preceded him to the place and, within a day or two of his arrival, the population of Benares was raised to such a pitch of frenzy that His Highness the Maharaja of Benares was compelled to arrange a public discussion with him.

The public discussion or *Shastrartha* was attended by thousands of men, and every notable Pandit of the place made it a point to be present on the occasion. Although nothing definite was settled in it and the meeting ended in tumult and uproar, it undoubtedly had the effect of bringing the Swamiji into prominence and establishing his reputation as a great Vedic scholar throughout the country. Swami Dayanand soon after received an invitation from Calcutta which he accepted, and repaired to the place. There he came in close touch with the leaders of the Brahmo Samaj like Devendra Nath Tagore and Keshab Chandra Sen and delivered a series of lectures under their auspices. The Brahmos, however, did not agree with him in assigning to the Vedas the exalted position he wanted and Swami Dayanand would not agree to attach any importance to the Christian teachings which the Brahmos held dear. But it appears that association with them suggested to him the idea of founding an institution similar to the Brahmo Samaj for the propagation of the Vedic religion. In the meantime, he received a pressing invitation from some of the leading citizens of Bombay and left for that place. The orthodox gentry of Bombay soon arranged for a public discussion on idol-worship, but their representative failed to show any authority from the Vedas in support of the doctrine. This meant another signal victory for the Swamiji. The intelligentia of the town thronged round him and he delivered lecture after lecture expounding the real teachings of the Vedic religion. The Hindu young men who did not know anything about their religion beyond the mythological tales they had heard from their priests and *āchāryas* and who found their convictions incapable of standing the light of reason or the onslaughts of the Christian missionary, hailed Swami Dayanand as a great Saviour of their ancient religion. The Swamiji made full use of the opportunity and started to organize them by founding the first Arya Samaj there on the 10th April, 1875. A Sanskrit Pāṭhaśhālā was also opened and plans were made for the spreading of the gospel of the Vedas throughout the length and breadth of the country.

If India was really as great and prosperous in the past as is claimed by Swami Dayanand and many other distinguished

Indian patriots, the question arises what has led to its present degraded condition. The Swamiji believed that the unfortunate war of Mahābhārata was responsible for all this. The devastating effects of this Great War are undoubtedly acknowledged on all hands. All the great men of the country perished in it and hardly any able-bodied person was left in the land. The subsequent generation, born mainly of old and decrepit men, who survived the Great War, and bred and brought up in an atmosphere of misery and destitution— the after-effects of the Great War— quite naturally consisted of inferior sort of men and women, incapable of cherishing the high Aryan ideals. The Hindus thus put on the downward grade, gradually sank lower and lower and fell an easy prey to the foreign invaders. The foreign conquerors, one after the other, in their desire to establish permanent sway over the land, made short work of what was left of the Aryan nobility and culture and the result has been that the Hindus find themselves to-day reduced to their present condition. They are lost to their religion, to their culture and to their traditions. And we have frankly to acknowledge that Swami Dayanand was the first to raise his powerful voice against this denationalisation and to think of openly fighting the causes responsible for it. All men, taught he, are children of one common Father and differences of caste represented only the differences of professions. The Brahmin, Kshattriya, Vaiśya and Śūdra were members of one common brotherhood and India was their motherland. They must turn their attention to the glorious past once again. They should discard the worship of gods and goddesses which had rent up the society into pieces and take to the worship of the One Formless Supreme Being. They should have one common language and make Sanskrit their *lingua franca*. They should revive the ancient Gurukula system of education and look up to the Vedas for guidance and help for advancement in arts and sciences, for the Vedas represented the store-house of learning—both spiritual and temporal—which God gave to humanity in the beginning of creation and which comprise the *alpha* and *omega* of all wisdom.

We may not agree with the Swamiji in all his beliefs, but, as time has shown, the result of his teachings was simply magical. The rising tide of the influence of western civilization was stemmed. The proselytising activities of the Christian missionary received a rude shock and hundreds of schools and colleges owned and managed by the Hindus sprang up in the country and the study and exposition of the ancient Vedic literature commenced on a scale and in a manner that its repercussions were felt even in distant Europe and America. And every Hindu now feels proud of the teachings of the Upanishads and the Bhagavadgītā and even the savants of the West willingly pay tributes of praise to the achievements of the ancient Hindu Ṛishis. In a word, India is now awakened to the consciousness of its past glory and the Hindu mind is passing through the transition stages leading to the awakening of the national consciousness. All praise to Swami Dayanand Saraswati, the great patriot and nation-builder.

As has been mentioned above, Swami Dayanand came in contact with a number of Indian princes. A perusal of his Will by which he constituted a public body known as the Paropkāriṇī Sabhā for the purpose of carrying on his work after his death, shows that their number was not inconsiderable. The rulers of Udaipur, Shahpura and Jodhpur were the principal ones among the Ṛajputana princes to come under his spiritual influence, and unfortunate to say that his success with these princes resulted in creating for him a number of mortal enemies. One of these enemies took her revenge by having slow poison administered to him, which acted and brought the precious life of the great patriot to a premature close on the 30th October, 1883.

Besides the great qualities of head and heart, Swami Dayanand possessed a strong and handsome physique. He was a stout and squarely-built man, of amiable disposition and pleasant ways. The writer of this note has had occasion to come in contact with several people who had the good fortune of knowing him personally and, from the impression left on them, in spite of the lapse of so much time, it was not difficult for him to realise what a powerful personality the Swamiji possessed. In purity of character, in fearlessness of expression, in the acuteness and comprehensiveness of intellect, in devotion to the Vedas and his love for the country he was an outstanding figure of his time.

Swami Dayanand was 59 years of age when he departed from this world. During his life he wrote a number of important and voluminous books which are read and appreciated by thousands of Indians. The chief among these are the *Satyarth Prakāsh* and the *Commentary on the Vedas*.

DAYALBAGH, AGRA — ANAND SWARUP

SINCE six years I have been too busy with my great expedition of exploration in the very heart of Asia for being able to study carefully and follow the different kinds of social work in India.

But every son of your great charming and admirable country who by his life, his teaching and his work contributes to the happiness prosperity, progress and peace of the peoples of India, has my sincere sympathy and my admiration. The only thing I can do is to send my heartiest greetings to the beloved country that has given birth to so many great and wonderful leaders and teachers, thinkers and poets.

PEKING, CHINA — SVEN HEDIN

HARMONISING HINDUISM WITH MODERN KNOWLEDGE

ANCIENT wisdom should not be treated as a thing apart from modern Truth. Just as the material wealth of our forefathers has merged into our own resources, so also must the moral wealth inherited from them flow into and become one with modern truth and wisdom. Ancient and modern are not like two different valleys divided by an impassable ridge, but one continuous territory, the one imperceptibly passing into the other.

There is no reason, whatever, why the religion of the Hindus should in any respect be unsuitable for modern times. Our forefathers could not provide for all time. They gave us more than the forefathers of any other people ever gave to them. They left a tradition of wise conservatism for ensuring continuity of culture, and to provide against destruction, but not to prevent adjustment or progress and help decay itself. It is our own fault, if we mis-interpreted this conservatism into a death-trap for Truth.

Our religion was founded by, and added to, from time to time, by some of the greatest souls that the world ever saw. Their one passion was the quest of Truth and they dug into the mysteries of HEAVEN and EARTH with a Will and an Energy, a poise of Reason and Emotion unsurpassed by any other nation in the world. It is our special good fortune to be born to such a rich inheritance. If instead of using it, we have made it a millstone round our neck, none but ourselves are to blame.

Truth is eternal, but by reason of the natural limitations of the human mind, it is discovered only in parts. A continuous readjustment is necessary, so that the sum of Truth in our possession may be combined into a whole. Previous conquests over darkness will serve as a stepping stone and not hinder, if only we are not misled into raising impassable barriers between old and new. To integrate ancient truth and modern knowledge is the only way to life in the fullness to which we are entitled.

The Hindus have bowed their heads to the current tide of Truth. They are not going to be ascetics in the world's march. They have opened the door of their life in all respects to modernity. How then can they imprison only their religion in a harem apart? Segregation is as hurtful to our religion as to our womenfolk.

Swami Dayanand's soul rebelled against the idea of Hinduism being relegated to a status of unsuitability to modern times. He strove, by a process of merciless chopping off, to make the ancient forest habitable for modern life. Let us not convert his great labour into another obstinate sect, but understanding the purpose and the meaning of his noble effort, strive to fulfil it as he wanted it, viz., to make Hinduism a habitable tenement for progressive modern life, a religion whose culture, tradition and tenets make no compromise with evil, but offer no impediment to human progress.

If there is one religion that aimed at being rigorously consistent with science that is Truth, it is the religion of our fathers. Other religions have to be 'harmonised' with science, but Hinduism is Science itself in the highest and truest sense.

Truth is automatically self-effacing. This is in its very nature. If any reforming school resists this self-effacement and seeks to live apart from that which it is its function to reform, thenceforward it begins to rot and decay. Swami Dayanand's teachings have permeated wide and a stage is being reached when they can no longer form a denomination apart, but must live in the soul of Hinduism itself.

The coming period of Hinduism is bound to be a period of great assimilation. The re-absorption and integration of all reforming sects will proceed with increasing pace and will necessarily mean the self-effacement of these denominations. Swami Dayanand's aim can be fulfilled only by re-absorption of his reform into Hinduism as a whole.

TIRUCHENGODU, S. I. C. RAJGOPALACHARI

SĀṀKHYA: REALISM OR IDEALISM?

THE term "Idealism", in common usage, denotes the view which reduces the world of sense to a realm of ideas. The orange is merely a bundle of sensations and perceptions and has no existence in itself as apart from its perception. Its *esse* is *percipi*. "Realism", on the other hand, signifies the doctrine which believes in the real existence of things, independently of the ideas of not only percepient A or percepient B, but of all percepients as such, including "God" the Eternal Percepient. The absolute opposition between thought and things, familiarly expressed by—"What is mind?—No *matter*"; "What is matter?—Never *mind*"—which the above distinction between Idealism and Realism implies has however no meaning in the Sāṁkhya System according to which the so-called "Idea" *suo generis* is not a distinct entity from the object which evokes it, seeing that the trial of Buddhi-Ahaṁkāra—Manas (which is responsible for the Idea) and the Viśayas (objects) of the different organs-of-sense are alike the *vikāras* or the evolutes of the Prakṛti, Nature or Matter, and as such must be assigned the same grade of reality, in spite of the fact that the former has the dominance of the Sattva quality within it and the latter that of the Tamas (cp. Sāṁ. Kārikā 25). We cannot therefore speak of the Idealism or the Realism of the Sāṁkhya in the sense which is familiar to Modern European Philosophy which (with the exception of some types of "Faculty" Psychology which approach in that respect the Indian point of view) makes no distinction between Soul, Mind and Consciousness. The Mind is Soul functioning in a particular mode, and so is memory and joy and fear and conscience and determination and all the other forms of thinking, feeling and willing. Not so the Sāṁkhya, according to which the mental and moral "Faculties" of man are capable of growth and decay and cannot for that reason constitute any part of the Soul—Cit or Puruṣa—who is assumed to be serene and immutable, unconcerned with everything fleeting and transient. The Soul or Puruṣa however supplies the light or illumination which, working so-to-say through the lense of the organs of sense, helps to produce the "images" of the objects. To speak in the technical terms of the Sāṁkhya Philosophy, Buddhi-Ahaṁkāra-Manas function with a view to produce the knowledge of the external world, simply because the soul or Puruṣa appears to be interested in the results of the process and suffers himself to be reflected into the mirror of the Buddhi. The *danseuse* will cease to practise her blandishments the moment the spectator closes his eyes in sleep or in the superior discriminative knowledge of *Viveka*. The interest of the Puruṣa supplies in other words the electric current which illumines the bulb or sets the dynamo in motion; but the current *qua* current has nothing in common with the apparatus which it vivifies. Thus it is that in the Sāṁkhya system thought and things, ideas and matter, cannot be placed in opposition. If things be unreal, so must be their ideas; if the ideas be real, so also must be the things to which they refer.

2. The question as to whether the Sāṁkhya is Realism or Idealism can however be put from a slightly different point of view. An idealistic system believes that nothing else really exists but the ideas or consciousness (*cit*). It is thus normally a form of Monism, either believing in the existence of only one Subject (the so-called Subjective Idealism), or when, as a concession to actual experience, an infinite number of knowing subjects is posited, it puts forth the hypothesis of an Absolute Intelligence to guarantee the uniformity of experience (the so-called Absolute Idealism). Now the Classical Sāṁkhya believes in the existence of the Prakṛti (=Pradhāna=Kṣara=Avyakta) or Nature as being coeval with the Soul or Puruṣa. It is in fact a pronounced and incurable Dualism (Dvaita-vāda) and cannot in any ordinary sense

be classified as Idealism. Nay, more: the Sāṁkhya is even Pluralistic, as believing in an infinite number of Puruṣas.

3. If this be all that there is to say on the point, the question proposed at the beginning of the essay need not have arisen at all. But there are a few disturbing factors imbedded in the System which cannot be satisfactorily explained that way. According to the Classical Sāṁkhya of Iśvarakṛṣṇa's Kārikās the Prakṛti, prior to the act of evolution, remains in a state of equipoise (guṇasāmya) of its three constituents. At the sight of the Puruṣa or the Soul this equipoise is disturbed, some one or the other of the three Guṇas gets the better of the other two, the Prakṛti is thrown into an agitation and begins to flow out like the milk in the udder of the cow at the sight of her calf (Kārikās 56-60). From the nature of the case it seems clear that the exact line of evolution which the Prakṛti is to take will depend, let us say, upon the nature of the sympathetic current established between the Prakṛti and the Puruṣa: it will have the dominance of the Sattva in one case, of the Rajas in the other and of the Tamas in the third in varying proportions. There can thus be as many lines of evolution, as many worlds in fact, as there are Puruṣas. This is something like the position of "Subjective Idealism". An ancient Jain Commentator—I have mislaid the reference—informs us that the original Sāṁkhya view believed in the existence of as many Pradhānas as there are Ātmans (*Pratyātma-Pradhāna-vādino Maulika-Sāṁkhyāh*). The Early Christians believed that the Earth was the centre of the Universe, and that the Sun, the Moon and the Stars—in fact, the whole terrestrial and cosmic creation—was for Man. The Sāṁkhyas likewise make the experience and knowledge of the Puruṣa the only purpose of Prakṛti's evolution, the Prakṛti being ready to evolve separately for each Puruṣa. Modern Science refuses to endorse such a homo-centric view of the Universe, which, according to the scientists, existed long before Man was born. To think of the Sāṁkhya as a scientific theory of world-creation according to the doctrine of

Evolution or Pariṇāma is therefore not only uncritical but absolutely misleading. For, no strictly physical or scientific theory of world-creation would ever dream of bringing in the psychological categories of Buddhi and Ahaṁkāra as some of the earliest steps in cosmo-genesis. In this sense then the Sāṁkhya can be classified as Idealism.

4. An attempt has been recently made by an Indian scholar[1] to prove that the true Sāṁkhya of the Kārikās is a Theory of Reality, a sort of "a dynamic Order" and a "triune-unity of differentiated aspects." Kārikās 56 to 60 which form the main basis of the argument in Para 3 above are included by Prof. Mukerji amongst the "added Kārikās", but no convincing philological reasons are put forth for the fact of the interpolation. That the concluding Kārikās involve self-contradiction is known from the time of Śaṅkara onwards; and the contradiction is so flagrant that it is impossible to suppose that the author himself could have been ignorant of it. But as a cosmological theory Sāṁkhya could not well avoid it, and it is a perversion of history to assert that the Sāṁkhyas accepted the Mīmāṅsā doctrine of "*Na kadācid anīdṛśam jagat,*" had no interest in finding out when and how the process of world-creation began or is going to end, or that they did not care to preach any doctrine of Salvation by means of knowledge. All documentary evidence goes to prove that the Sāṁkhya was nothing else if not a doctrine of Salvation by knowledge. Even Buddhism that had little interest in purely cosmological or metaphysical questions did preach the Way to Nirvāṇa. That change and motion logically imply permanence and rest was too obvious a conclusion to escape the attention of the Founder of the System, and is in fact evident from Kārikā 3 which nobody can dare pronounce as interpolation. And what to do with definite statements about the *Kaivalya* so pointedly made in Kārikās 17, 19 and 21?

[1] J. N. Mukerji : Sāṁkhya or the Theory of Reality, Calcutta, 1930,

Are these also interpolations? I cannot accept that "Kaivalya" means here "individualising causality" (see *op. cit.*, p. 49, Note). How does it differ from "Bhoktṛtva" and what about "Mādhyastha"? The explanation on page 61 is anything but convincing. The line "*Sākṣī cetā kevalo nirguṇaś ca*" (Śv. Up. vi 11) from an Upanishad, which is usually taken to be the original source of the Sāṁkhya, would vehementally protest against the kind of interpretation that Prof. Mukerji gives to these terms.[1]

5. That the Sāṁkhya Philosophy had an original idealistic bias which peeps through its Classical cloak of Realistic Dualism also becomes evident if we consider the allied question as to whether there was any recognition of the Supreme Lord in the System from the very beginning or whether the acceptance of God was later made as a mere concession to human weakness. Kapila was a fearless thinker and there is something of the heroic in making him deny God and the authority of the Vedas. Compare the kindred case of Kaṇāda the Founder of the Vaieśṣika System. But all the usual texts which are put forth as the original sources for the Sāṁkhya (e.g. Kaṭha and Śvetāśvatara Upaniṣhads and portions of the Mahābhārata) are unanimous in accepting the Supreme Lord. Are all these texts perversions of the original atheistic Sāṁkhya, as has been sometimes maintained? The question cannot be fully gone into in this place[2]. Suffice it here to say that if the Puruṣas are to be many and if there is to be a distinct evolution of the Prakṛti for each Puruṣa—and both these are accepted doctrines of the Sāṁkhya at all periods—one has to combine with these two doctrines a belief in Godhead which alone can account for the commonness and uniformity of our sense-experience. This has been admirably illustrated in the Philosophy of Berkeley. Later on, when the Maulika-Sāṁkhya view of a multitude of Pradhānas was given up and by the

[1] It is also news to be told that the Sāmkhya Philosophy of the Gitā preaches Karmayoga (p. 89). A statement like this is enough to make Sankara seek reincarnation! Compare "*Jnānayogena Sāmkhyānām Karmayogena Yoginām*".

[2] See History of Indian Philosophy, Vol II, The Creative Period, Pages 412—427.

substitution of Tanmātras for Veśeṣas or Viṣayas an attempt was made to conceive of the cosmogenesis as a physical fact and not a psychological phenomenon, God came to be viewed as a supernumerary entity and was dropped outright, the sister School of the Yoga having retained him more for practical reasons than as a philosophical necessity. Aśvaghoṣa at any rate, in the account that he gives in the *Buddhacarita* of the philosophical views of Arāḍa Kalāma, the Sāṁkhya preceptor of Gautama Buddha, tells us that this Teacher believed in a Supreme Self with whom the liberated souls become one (*op. cit.* xii. 63-65). And we have no reasons to suppose that Aśvaghoṣa was interested in making a wilful perversion of the original Sāṁkhya teaching. Thus the original theism of the System would seem to confirm the view as to its original idealistic trend. Idealism in fact was very much in the air in the Upaniṣadic circle where the Sāṁkhya Philosophy was conceived and nurtured and we have every reason to expect that it would show the influence of the dominant ideas of the period.

The problem proposed for solution in this paper does not accordingly admit of a simple categorical answer. We could however, in the light of what has been said hitherto, state that the Sāṁkhya exhibits an incipient idealistic bend, which the System has been all along endeavouring to overcome with varying measure of success. The Vedānta-sūtras proclaim themselves against the Sāṁkhya as Realism and Dualism; but Vijnānabhikṣu is not without some justification for holding that what the Vedāntists attack is a man of straw and that the original and true Sāṁkhya can very well be reconciled with the Vedānta Philosophy as he conceives it, the way to such a reconciliation being already indicated by Lord Śrikṛṣṇa in the *Bhagavadgītā*.

POONA

S. K. BELVALKAR

HAR BILAS SARDA, M.L.A.

THE RISHIS OF INDIA

I feel honoured by the opportunity given to me by my respected friend, Dewan Bahadur Har Bilas Sarda, M.L.A., to pay my humble tribute of worship to the memory of the life and achievements of Swami Dayanand, at once one of the makers of modern India and one of India's last Ṛishis. I, however, feel myself oppressed by an overwhelming sense of my incompetence to make a memorial contribution worthy of the high subject proposed for me. Taking advantage of the wide latitude given to me in the choice of a topic for this memorable occasion in celebration of the Semi-centenary of Ṛishi Dayanand, I choose to write a few lines embodying some general observations on the particular type of thought and culture for which Indian Ṛishis, the real makers of Bhāratavarsha, have stood through the Ages. And yet even this particular theme which suggests itself to me as an appropriate one for publication in the Dayanand Commemoration Volume, hardly lends itself to a general, and, much less, to a brief and casual treatment such as I have been proposing. What I am, therefore, going to say on the vast and profound subject must not be understood or expected to represent any sustained discourse with any organic unity or following any well-thought-out design, but rather some observations made at random.

The thought and culture of the Ṛishis are best found in their characteristic features in their highest and normal form and strength, in that part of Vedic literature which goes by the name of the Upanishads and Āraṇyakas. It is, therefore, to these works that we must turn to understand the essentials of Hindu culture and civilization. Though these are supremely philosophical and profoundly metaphysical documents, they cannot escape from the geographical and social back-ground and environment with which they are inextricably bound up, and inevitably betray the secular life of the times in which they were produced. The historians can thus wring out of these philosophical and religious books ample material for constructing an account of the civilization of the age which is unique in the whole course of Indian History for the height of its intellectual and spiritual achievements.

Some of the more important Upanishads like the Bṛihadāraṇyaka and Chhāndogya purport to record the proceedings and transactions of learned Assemblies or philosophical Congresses which were convened by the kings of the times to pay their homage to learning. King Janaka of Videha was the most distinguished of such kings who summoned to his court all the learned men of the Kuru-Pāñchāla country (roughly the country from Delhi to Lucknow) to meet in a conference for purposes of debate and discussions between the exponents of different philosophical systems and schools, so that the merits of each might be thrashed and brought out. Such a conference lasted for days together, and the successful disputant, who could maintain his own philosophical position against all attacks and silence all criticism by his answers, not only won for himself the first position among the philosophers of the times but won for his system and theories also a similar position of acknowledged pre-eminence and popularity. At the conference under Janaka (which, by the way, was perhaps our earliest literary conference) the position of primacy among the philosophers was won by Ṛishi Yājñavalkya not merely by his superior intellectual ability and powers of debate, but also the superiority of the philosophy he was standing for, the superior soundness and comprehensiveness of his doctrines, the adequacy of his system which could give satisfactory explanations of the many perplexing and profound problems of life and death, soul and immortality which were put to him by the exponents of the other philosophies and systems in their search for their correct solutions. In fact, these problems, as Prof. Deussen has justly remarked, have defied solution to this day and Yājñavalkya's answers to them mark him out as one of the greatest philosophers. The royal recognition individual *sādhanā*. This is how we see him in public places, and assemblies at the courts of kings, vigorously participating in debates, only that the saving knowledge which was his individual possession might be known to all, and not for any selfish desire for name, or fame, or wealth which was so liberally bestowed on him. Thus when his social service was accomplished, and his philosophy was established, he did not tarry a day longer in the world, but quietly returned to the obscurity of the forest whence he came, to investigate further, in solitary contemplation, the unknown and the unknowable. On the eve of this renunciation, he called to his side his two wives to announce his intention and divide his property which was not quite inconsiderable in value, considering the royal bounties bestowed on him for his learning. Poor Kātyāyanī, the good house-wife, meekly submitted to her lord's proposal, but Maitreyī was a woman of far different stuff. Before accepting the position proposed by her husband, she put him the preliminary question whether by her earthly possession, by her husband's lavish gifts, she would attain what was her heart's desire, *viz.*, immortality. Equally prompt and precise was her husband's reply: not by earthly possession could she win the heaven of immortality, but only the pleasure which these could buy. Maitreyī's reply was not less spirited: "Give me only that by which I can be immortal, and not the thing which could attach me the more to the life mortal." Thus Maitreyī received from her husband the supreme gift of the highest knowledge and became a Brahmavādinī. The Upanishads thus demonstrate the learning and the freedom of their mutual intellectual and spiritual intercourse to their mutual benefit. Let us re-capture in this modern age something of this liberty of learning and this elevated conception of the mission of the woman in national life.

While the Upanishads tell us of the intellectual life of the times that centred round the courts of kings that were its best patrons, it must be understood that they themselves owe their origin not to the busy haunts of men, but to the solitude of the forest where alone they could be developed unhindered by the distractions of social life. The case of Yājñavalkya taking recourse to the woods to develop further his philosophy is an illustration to the point. The very title of the class of works called Āraṇyakas tells us how some of the highest Indian wisdom is embodied in the books of the woods. The schools of higher learning in India were always the hermitages of the forest whence flowed the knowledge that has built India. As the poet, Sir Rabindranath Tagore, has somewhere stated, the civilization of India has flowed from her forests and has not been the work of her cities. Her Vedic culture and civilization were due to her Ṛishis and to their plain living and high thinking in their solitary rural retreats and sylvan hermitages or Āśramas. Her Buddhist culture, too, originated in the woods of Gayā, in the deer forest of Sāranātha, and in the groves in the outskirts of cities like Rājagṛiha, Kapilavastu, and Śrāvastī where the Buddha poured out his teachings before his devout Saṅghas or congregations. Later on, these teachings attracted to the Buddha as his devout disciples even the crowned monarchs and the merchant princes, like King Bimbīsāra of Magadha, King Prasenajit of Kosala, or the commercial magnate Anāthapiṇḍika. The culture that flowed from her forest ultimately inundated the whole of India.

These sylvan schools, which had thus developed the entire thought and culture of India, were like natural formations gathering round the nucleus of a great personality and were not artificially constituted like a commercial concern of a joint-stock enterprise such as modern schools very often are. The basis of such schools was the personal relationship between the teacher and the taught who were naturally drawn to him by the magnetic force of his character as much as his learning. Such a teacher was a maker of men. Our modern schools are not like these vital associations, for their basis is the cash-nexus and they are governed by artificial and mechanical rules. But life and growth cannot be trusted to such artificial constitution. No wonder that our modern schools so largely fail of their purpose. Even our so-called national schools fare no better. Most of them are only national in name with the perhaps possible exceptions of Śāntiniketana and the Gurukula which are trying to be national also in their actual working. Enough study is not yet made of our truly national ideals and practices in education. The early history of Indian education is yet to be written. As has been already indicated above, our national system of education is to be understood in its best and normal form in the Upanishads which constitute its richest results and the most complete justification. That profound philosophical literature, which is universally admitted to register the high-water-mark of human speculation, was after all but the product of those small schools, Āśramas or hermitages, silently fulfilling their purpose in the solitude of the forests like the great and beneficent agencies of Nature, like the Sun and stars, "their glorious tasks in silence perfecting" (Matthew Arnold). Systems of education must be judged by their results. The schools that could bring forth such literary creations as the Upanishads and could produce the minds that conceived them stand in no need of defence or vindication. They also set before themselves the highest conceivable ideals in education. The subject they taught was nothing short of the highest knowledge, Brahmavidyā, the knowledge of the Ātmān or the Absolute—when that knowledge was won, it included all, or the intermediate and secondary grades of knowledge.

Thus has ancient Indian culture been the product of unique schools and systems of education. Besides producing the richest record in the world's literature, they produced quite a bountiful crop of great men, most of whom attained to the pinnacle of perfection in their own spheres. Leaving aside the hoary Vedic Ṛishis of antiquity like Vasishṭha and Viśvāmitra, where may we find the equals of Vālmīki and Vyāsa, Kālidāsa and Māgha in poetry, Pāṇini, Kātyāyana and Patañjali in grammar; Kapila and Kaṇāda, Gautama and Jaimini, Patañjali and Vyāsa in philosophy; Chāṇakya and Chandragupta, Aśoka and Harsha as empire-builders and in state-craft, or lastly Mahāvīra and the Buddha, Śaṅkara and Rāmānuja in spirituality and saintliness? The race of her great men was not extinct so long as India had been able to preserve her indigenous scheme of life and education against alien influences. Even mediaeval India, which was so largely left to herself and to her own self-governing institutions in matters of her learning, culture and social and religious life, had carried forward unbroken the record of great men, represented by such universally adored names as those of Chaitanya, Rāmadāsa, Kabīra, Guru Nānaka or Tukārāma. India has been expressing her soul through these great men that have appeared in all ages of her history, so long as she has been able to retain in its integrity the external apparatus or machinery for the organization of her social and cultural life which alone can make such great men possible. The external organization of her life has evolved only in response to the inner needs of her soul. Her self-expression had determined its own means and modes. The spirit must choose its own embodiment.

It is to the unique credit of India and her culture that one of her later-day Ṛishis, Swami Dayanand, was able to achieve his fullest self-expression by dint of sheer soul-force, for which India has stood through the ages, the compelling force of character which prevailed against and completely subdued the gathering forces of an alien environment and domination, of an ill-assimilated materialism and modernity, to which India would have completely succumbed under British rule, but for the timely appearance of such a saviour as Dayanand.

LUCKNOW RADHAKUMUD MUKERJI

SWAMI DAYANAND SARASWATI—SOCIAL REFORMER

I claim no special knowledge of any particular reform due to Swami Dayanand Saraswati in the religious thought or social sanctions of modern Hinduism; but I have this advantage that within seven years of the death of the Swami in Ajmer, I went to live and work in that city, and my stay there of more than thirty years brought me many opportunities of personal contact with institutions established by his followers to carry on reforms inspired by the founder of the Arya Samaj. Due to this circumstance no doubt, the courtesy has been extended to me of an invitation, which I gladly accept, to contribute a paper to this Commemoration Volume.

However high the name of Swami Dayanand stands as a student and teacher of religion, it is as one of India's greatest benefactors as a social reformer that he will go down in history. He did not set out to found a religion, but to rescue his people from what he seems to have regarded as the dead hand of the popular Hinduism that prevailed around him and of which the ministers were of the same priestly caste to which he himself belonged. He was convinced that at the foundations of that religion were vital truths whose living force had thrown up, again and again during the centuries, searchers, interpreters and exponents of its scriptures, yet the net result, as he saw it in his day, was that the ministration of religion had become a closer privileged profession than ever, but religion had not been brought into touch with the practical needs of the life of his people. The most forceful currents of the thoughts of these researchers had run into deep channels of abstruse intellectual speculation from which only the erudite few could derive any good. The hard metaphysics of the eighth century Śaṅkara had, indeed, been much softened by the more practical Rāmānuja of the early twelfth century. Rāmānuja and his school did the greatest service in diverting thought from the seductive philosophy of *māyā* to personal devotion, and the like, but it had not been adequately effective.

Dayanand was well versed in the lore of these sages of antiquity and he held them in the highest esteem, but he was a child of a different age and he recognised that it had other calls. He recognised that personal devotion and piety were no longer enough, but that by way of service to humanity was true devotion rendered to the deity. His countrymen and co-religionists were adrift, and nothing short of extensive reclamation by means of drastic social reforms would arouse them to a sense of their plight and save them from further degeneration. With a Prophet's insight he saw that "where there is no vision the people perish," and he set himself primarily to inspire his people with a vision of the manhood to which it was possible for them to rise, and of the reality of the impediments that hindered them. There must be escape from the formalities and conventions of so-called orthodoxy and from the superstition of unintelligent anthropomorphism, which image-worship generally is. But first there must be a return to the fountain-head of revealed knowledge and religion, to the Vedas, unobscured by the profuse mass of literature that had been built upon them—and a return to the only deity who is worthy of devotion namely, the God of the Vedas who is therein referred to in these words: "He who is our father and the progenitor of all things, who rewards every man according to his deserts, who knows all the heavenly bodies and habitable globes... who is one without a second, in whom all things are comprehended—Him let all strive to understand by means of friendly discussions."—Yajur., VII. 27.

Such was the tenor of Dayanand's thought and teaching in consonance with which an extensive programme of daring reforms was promptly undertaken and has since been pursued by devoted men and women of his following.

was given to Yājñavalkya in King Janaka's gift to him of a thousand cows with their horns hung with strings of gold-pieces, but greater than that royal recognition was the recognition given by the country to Yājñavalkya as the father of Hindu Philosophy. Yājñavalkya first laid with a scientific precision and logical rigour the foundations on which the later Hindu systems of philosophy have been built up. The entire stream of Hindu philosophical speculation may, indeed, be traced to the Upanishads as its source, and in the Upanishads the outstanding philosophical figure is that of Yājñavalkya.

It will thus be evident that literary conferences were first conceived of in ancient India as suitable agencies for the spread of learning by means of the public debates they organised for the truths to be thrashed out. This is the way of the British Association and all such learned conferences to this day. Secondly, the Upanishads point to the enthusiastic homage, and the lavish patronage, extended by royalty to learning in those ancient days. They tell also of the type of royalty of those days as illustrated in kings like Janaka of Videha, Aśvapati Kaikeya, Ajātaśatru of Kāśī or Pravāhaṇa Jaivali, whose passionate love and cultivation of learning and the highest knowledge made them easily the intellectual leaders of their peoples, besides being their political leaders. King Janaka figures in the Upanishads as one of the leading philosophers who once even imparted instruction to Yājñavalkya in certain abstract doctrines he had made his own, though in his turn he was later on taught by his whilom pupil. The court of Kāśī under her learned king Ajātaśatru attracted to itself a concourse of scholars of the times, the proudest of whom, Dṛipta Bālāki Gārgya, who challenged the intellectuals of several provinces, had his pride of learning humbled by the King himself; similarly, Pravāhaṇa Jaivali, the king of the Pāñchālas, enlisted himself as a regular student of the Academy of Philosophers, called in the Upanishads, the Parishad, whose sittings he daily attended from his palace. Later on, he appears in the Upanishads as an original thinker noted for his mastery of certain special doctrines of Philosophy.

The Upanishads also tell us in connection with the Philosophical conference at the court of Janaka, how one of the philosophers who had actively participated in the debates and discussions in public was a learned lady of the name of Gārgī Vāchaknavī who sought to test the philosophical attainments of Yājñavalkaya by putting to him the straight question whether he could say that he had perceived the Brahman or the Absolute, as he could perceive a cow or a horse. The conception of philosophy or religion in India has always been that it should be lived and realised and should not merely be studied and learnt. It is to be understood that Gārgī was only the representative of a class of learned ladies in the time of the Upanishads, who could vie with men in their mastery of the highest knowledge and prove the equality of the sexes in respect of intellectual attainment. If the Upanishads lay down the national standard in matters of our culture and civilization, it is to be hoped, we shall work up to that standard as regards the education of our women whom we have permitted to lag so far behind men as regards intellectual pursuits and participation in public life.

In addition to Gārgī, honourable mention is also made in the Upanishads of another learned lady called Maitreyī, the worthy consort of the Ṛishi Yājñavalkya who had another wife, Kātyāyanī by name, of the ordinary humdrum pattern. The fame that was achieved by Yājñavalkya as the first philosopher of his time did not operate on him as the last infirmity of noble mind. The fame did not prove to be a fetter to bind him to the life of the world where alone it had its significance. The quest of the ideal which was never to be satisfied drove Yājñavalkya in his hoary old age, once more, to retire to the solitude of the forest where he had achieved his first enlightenment. Then the natural desire came up in him to invite others, if possible, to a share in that enlightenment, and preach the truth he had attained by his

To make the sacred Vedas an open book to all classes and all nations and, in India at least, to make them available, in the spoken language of the people is a bold invasion of the exclusive rights of the most ancient and powerful priesthood in the world. To admit into the family of the "twice-born and regenerate" those of the depressed and "un-regenerate" masses, who are regarded as outside the pale by reason of their *Karma* is venturesome defiance of a settled social order. Yet it only gives an extended significance to the truth:

"Help thou thy brother's boat across
And lo! thine own hath reached the shore".

To throw open all the benefits of an education inspired with Vedic Hindu culture is on the one hand opposed to long established traditions of the country, and on the other to the settled policy of the power that formulated the scheme for the education of India a century ago. To further the emancipation of women; to make Hinduism a proselytising religion—all these are startling innovations. Yet they are daringly included in the Arya Samaj programme of national reform.

How they are operating in wider fields, others will tell. My first-hand acquaintance is confined to a small province. There, most striking it was to see how prince and peasant alike reacted to the new movement, despite the suspicion and disapproval with which it was viewed in its early days by those in authority. Institution after institution sprang up for education, social relief and uplift and for propaganda under the leadership and guidance of many devoted voluntary workers whose energy seemed to grow with the passing years. The enthusiasm and tact of these won even the goodwill of an influential Railway Company, not alone to the extent of obtaining financial aid, but also facilities for the admission of youths educated in the Dayanand High School to the railway workshops for technical training.

Along-side with all this no observer could fail to note how the sense of public responsibility to organise with judgment and ability grew in the leaders with the work, and how the work prospered on all sides. It is a fascinating retrospect.

The spot where the remains of Dayanand were cremated in October, 1883, lies at the foot of the hill called Taragarh after the historical fort that stands on it. From the heights of this hill one obtains a perfect bird's eye view of the city of Ajmer which nestles in the valley below and which is "one of the most notable towns in India owing to its religious importance". Not only is Pushkar near Ajmer, "the King of all sacred places of the Hindus, but in Ajmer is situated the Dargah of Khwaja Muinuddin Chishti, the greatest and most renowned of all Muhammadan saints in India".[1] Looking down on this remarkable city one cannot but be struck with evidence of a great work being carried on there by the representatives and agents of many religious denominations, both Eastern and Western. You see the handsome temple of the ancient Hindu sect of the Jains, and are reminded of educational and other work being carried on by the Jains. There is the great mosque and Muslim school of Persian and Arabic study, and charitable institutions that cluster in and about the Dargah of the Khwaja. A cathedral and churches of four Christian denominations raise their spires. All these denominations, by their European or American agents, are engaged in educational, medical, evangelistic and other social work of the high order for which they are justly well-known everywhere in the world. Hindus, Sikhs, Parsis and others are all in evidence. In the midst of all this there stand out the many buildings belonging to the Arya Samaj—Lecture Hall and Boys' High School, Boarding House, Orphanage, Industrial Workshop, several Girls' Schools, and by no means the least important, the well-equipped Vedic Press, (first established at Allahabad in 1875 by Swami Dayanand himself and in 1890 removed to Ajmer) which prints and publishes the works of the founder and other literature of the Samaj.

As one reflects on the work that has been carried on by the

[1] *Ajmer : Historical and Descriptive*, by Har Bilas Sarda, F.R.S.L., p. 20.

VEDIC YANTRALAYA, AJMER.

Arya Samaj on the scale that these indicate, one must admit that it does not suffer by comparison with that carried on by any of the other bodies—and this, in spite of great financial disparity. Yet money is not everything. Against this handicap weigh the spirit, for example, of a Hindu lady, who on being widowed gave her all, not excluding her personal services, to establish a girls' school and to make this Gulabdevi Pathashala of hers an inspiration for the education of girls on lines that had been advocated by Dayanand.

If this be an example of what is being achieved by the followers of Dayanand in so many larger and more populous centres in a country whose population makes up a fifth of the human race, and in places beyond its borders, then Swami Dayanand's place as a Prophet and great reformer of men has indeed been established.

The Arya Samaj movement came to life at a time when the prevailing atmosphere of the land was not likely to allow it to grow unchallenged. Political thoughts were growing up that were later on to disturb a settled civilised Government under which India had for a century enjoyed peace and had progressed some way towards unity. The generally well-informed agents of proselytising religions, Christianity and Islām, seeing only the inferior sides of popular Hinduism, were not averse to aggressive evangelising. The monopoly of the hereditary Hindu priesthood to regulate every detail of the life of their people was beginning once again to be questioned. It was only natural then for the responsible representatives of all these and similar interests to sit up and take note of the new movement with no sympathetic regard, and it drew on itself suspicion from several directions. Happily the sanity of the leaders has not only allayed most of these suspicions but has turned minds, once unfriendly, to study and to understand each other's point of view as never before. If the habit of mutual dispassionate toleration should become more generally established, expelling the quite unnecessary hostility that still to a great extent unfortunately estranges the principal peoples of India from each other, who can calculate the blessings that would accrue to this great land? Perhaps the proverbially traditional toleration of Hinduism will yet attune itself to the needs of the age and help to win this future achievement.

ADDISCOMBE, SURREY,
ENGLAND

E. F. HARRIS

DAYANAND, MY GURU

I am proud of being a disciple of Maharshi Swami Dayanand. I have made a thorough study of his life. I have seen his birth-place and tried to understand the atmosphere in which he was born and brought up. I have been to almost all the places connected with his life and seen some of his contemporaries who gave me interesting details about his personality. I have seen the place that was the scene of the great and well-known debate at Benares, where the ignorant people failing to understand his noble and inspiring message, threw dirt and stones at him. He lived the high ideals of the Vedas and strongly felt that there could be no real happiness and peace without following them. The brightest features of the Ṛishi's life were celibacy and penance. His was a disciplined mind. Dangers, nay even insults, could not disturb him. His face was always calm, serene and bright. He was fearless, kind and tolerant. He spoke with a frankness that startled even the worst of his enemies. The beauty of his work lies in the fact that it was all selfless. He lived and died for us. The more I know him and understand him, the more I revere and love him.

MOGA, PUNJAB

MATHRADAS

SWAMI DAYANAND—AN APPRECIATION

WHEN in the middle of the last century, western science, religion and philosophy dawned upon the Indian mind, men of strong intellect, dis-satisfied with the present state of Hindus, awoke and began to preach reform. Among such religious reformers, Swami Dayanand was the most notable and the most effective preacher. He impressed upon the Hindu mind, the dogma of *one formless God* and one book of revelation, the Veda, and thus purified Hinduism of all the dust and rust that had gathered about it during many thousand years. The Vedic Saṁhitās are no doubt revered by all Hindus as their book of revelation, prayer and philosophy. But very few actually use them and understand or make any sense out of them. And so much of commentary and supplement, as well as legend, true or concocted, has gathered about them that they lie deep below buried under this heap of overgrowth. Swami Dayanand had the courage and the tenacity to unearth the Vedas and teach their meaning to devout followers. The Arya Samajists to-day are the real respecters of the Vedic Saṁhitās and, curiously enough, have that strong reverence for and faith in them which exists among the Muslims for their book of revelation, namely the Qurān. The Arya Samaj is a living force, chiefly in the Punjab, and like the living force of Muhammadanism, the living force of Arya Samaj must be attributed to the unique personal power of the founder as well as to its high teaching.

There are some subjects on which a Hindu may differ from Swami Dayanand, but there can be no question that he is the most effective modern reformer of Hinduism and that the Arya Samaj founded by him has done great good to Hinduism, especially in respect of the position of women, of Śūdras and even of the untouchables by throwing the Vedas open to them. Swami

Dayanand had naturally to fight with Sanātanī Pandits in many places and on many topics, especially on the interpretation of Vedic texts for which the Pandits relied mainly on Sāyaṇa's *Bhāshya*, supported by Yâska. Swamiji, therefore, undertook the work of interpreting Vedic Saṁhitās and succeeded in completing this task before he laid down his life.

Swami Dayanand's tall and impressive figure, his deep learning and ready wit and his *Brahmacharya* and unblemished asceticism were a great asset to him in disputation as well as in preaching. To-day the Arya Samaj founded by him has a large following in India, especially in the Punjab, where indeed it is needed for combating the growing influence of Muhammadanism. Swami Dayanand did not, however, attack Islâm but simply worked for the cause of pure Vedic Religion.

Mr. Phadke of Panwel, Thana district, who has written a history of all the religious reformers of modern India, has written a life of Swami Dayanand from which I may take the following chronology of Swami Dayanand's life for the curious reader. The Swamiji was born in 1824. In his 18th year, like Ramdas, he left his home, and in 1848 he became a Sannyasi. He saw the annexation of the Punjab in 1849 and the sepoy rebellion in 1857. He began his life of a religious preacher in 1864 at the age of 40 and in 1869 he had a disputation with orthodox Pandits at Benares. In 1875 was founded the first Arya Samaj in Bombay and in 1877 in Lahore. In 1883 he laid down his life, having achieved the work he had set before himself. Swamiji was a disciple of Swami Virjanand and left a worthy disciple in Swami Shraddhanand.

POONA

C. V. VAIDYA

THE SPIRIT OF SERVICE

THERE can be no greater tribute to the memory of Swami Dayanand Saraswati than an appreciation of the spirit of service which he has evoked in the followers of his faith. It is easy enough to profess belief in a body of theological doctrine; it is easier still to conform to details of ritual and ceremony; it is easiest to congratulate oneself on being among the spiritually elect and look down with contempt on those who may belong to other religions. But one of the true tests of religion is perhaps man's capacity to worship God's creatures and render some service to humanity of which he forms an integral part.

It was a very cold afternoon in December last, when as a member of the Punjab University Inquiry Committee, I found myself with my colleagues visiting the city of Ferozepur in the Punjab, to look up the local college and other educational institutions. As we finished our work and were in a hurry to motor back to Lahore, a band of earnest workers who were running a Hindu orphanage in the Cantonment came and requested us to pay a visit to the institution before we resumed our journey. It was with some reluctance that we accepted the invitation in view of the lateness of the hour, but when we actually went there we discovered, to our pleasant surprise, an institution the like of which one cannot see in many parts of India. A large number of orphans, girls as well as boys, rescued from starvation and death, were being sheltered, fed, clothed and looked after by an earnest group of workers, depending almost entirely on the generosity of the public and content not to look for any reward, except their own satisfaction in having done a good deed, by bettering the condition of a small corner of the world. As the shades of the evening twilight gathered round us, we looked at the cheerful faces of the children who crowded to have a glimpse of the visitors. It was clear they were being dealt with under kindly protection and were being transformed into persons capable of earning an honest livelihood. In the case of girls, they were being encouraged to settle down into respectable marriages or become nurses or teachers. There was an element of parental care for the well-being of the children displayed by the workers of the orphanage who were all devoted members of the Arya Samaj at Ferozepur. It was night-fall when we actually left for Lahore, but as we motored back in the darkness, our minds were full of deep appreciation of the noble work the results of which we had witnessed at the institution.

The scene is now in an extensive grove outside the city of Jullundur where the members of the Arya Samaj run a residential school for girls, the Kanyā Mahāvidyālaya, well-known all over Northern India for the last some decades. In various corners under the spreading trees, there were bands of happy girls dressed in the uniform of the institution, either busy at their lessons, or enjoying themselves in play with music and games. The institution seemed to be a part of the garden, buildings being reduced to a minimum and the classes held right in the open air. One was reminded of the French expression for a 'truant'—it is one "who studies in the woods". It is apparently possible at the Kanyā Mahāvidyālaya, Jullundur, to play a truant in this sense of the word, without any neglect of studies at the same time! It was a pleasure to see the hostel for the girls, there being an atmosphere of elegance and tidiness which was furnishing excellent training for those who, let us hope, will later be in charge of happy homes of their own. If I may be pardoned a personal reminiscence, I may mention that on seeing a printed appeal in the papers asking for help to girls undergoing instruction at this institution, I had sent some little money year after year, at one time, for the education of a girl whose name I remembered and about whom I made inquiries. It was a delight to be told that she had completed her studies and had married and settled down happily in life. I have never seen her, but I cherish this memory with genuine satisfaction.

Visiting the same city a few weeks later, I had the pleasure of presiding over the anniversary of the D. A. V. College there which within the last few years has developed into a Degree College containing about seven hundred students, all due almost entirely to the efforts of a single devoted worker of the Arya Samaj, Pandit Mehr Chand. Here is the example of a single individual, himself an honorary worker, who has laboured hard for years seeking the support of the public far and near, for the founding of an institution which might bring the blessings of higher education to a city which had a number of high schools but no college. Situated on extensive grounds of its own on the Grand Trunk Road before we enter the city, it arrests the attention of every visitor and can be seen with its numerous buildings, hostels and play-grounds, a busy centre of humming activity during the working hours of the day. To see the hundreds of students walking or cycling into the college in the morning, or scattering after the day's work and running to their homes in the afternoon is a privilege of which the builders of the institution can certainly be proud.

These three do not exhaust the educational institutions visited by me during last winter in the Punjab, testifying in an eloquent manner, to the great inspiration for service furnished by the founder of the Arya Samaj. It was my privilege to see numerous other colleges run by the members of the same society; the great D.A.V. College in Lahore, one of the largest educational institutions in India with an excellent Oriental Library under its auspices; the Dayanand Anglo-Vedic Intermediate Colleges at Moga, Hoshiarpur and Rawalpindi, not to speak of many high schools, all of which are inspired by the same desire to spread learning and to provide education, very often even to those who cannot afford it.

But I cannot refrain from making reference to another institution, not connected officially with the Arya Samaj, but run under its auspices, the League of Women at Lyallpur, at the last anniversary of which I had the pleasure of assisting, by distributing the prizes and speaking on the necessity of economic independence for women. A modest and unostentatious worker in this city of the Punjab, assisted by an equally earnest and devoted wife, has built up an institution for educating grown-up women, (married, unmarried or widowed) into the pursuit of some useful vocation in life, to enable them to earn their own livelihood, or supplement the meagre incomes of their families. Tailoring, embroidery, weaving and a number of other occupations are taught to women in their leisure hours and as many as four hundred have been brought under the influence of this institution. It is futile to talk of equality between man and woman, so long as woman has got to depend on her husband in an abject manner for food, clothing, shelter and other prime necessities of life. It is, however, in no spirit of feminist revolt that the workers in Lyallpur have attempted to tackle this problem, but out of a sincere desire to help the women to learn some useful occupation, so that they may not have to drift helplessly in the world in the event of misfortune, depending very often on the grudging good offices of some distant relations. There was an interesting exhibition of the work done by the women at the institution which demonstrated amply that it was not a mere show-place to impress the visitor, but a real school for the learning of practical work which may stand them in good stead in later life.

There are other institutions run by the Arya Samaj elsewhere in India, particularly in the United Provinces of Agra and Oudh, where I spent sixteen years of my active life and where I had seen the same spirit of service animating workers for the advancement of humanity, in more than one town. But I have perhaps said enough to indicate that the inspiration of Swami Dayanand Saraswati embodies one of the essential aspects of religion.

Auguste Comte had no hesitation in preaching that service of man was service of God and so long as members of the Arya Samaj can furnish such striking examples of the spirit of helpfulness in the interests of humanity, they may walk with their heads high among the religious faiths of the world and stand even as examples worthy of emulation by others.

I have often wondered what record many of us who believe in a future life will have, if on the Day of Judgment in the other world, we are called upon to state how we employed ourselves during our sojourn on earth. A large number of us can perhaps only say that we looked after the welfare of our wives and children; earned money in doing, may be, some honest work and advanced the interests of those near and dear to us. Proud however must be those who will have on the occasion, a more unselfish record to show to their credit, persons who have worked for the welfare of others and brought the benefits of happiness to beings whose lot has been cast amidst adverse circumstances in the world. In many places where the Arya Samaj flourishes, there are people who could render a very good account of themselves, if the time came for such a statement of their record of service.

AJMER

P. SESHADRI

SWAMI DAYANAND SARASWATI AND THE PUNJAB

I have been asked by that great champion of all good causes, Dewan Bahadur Har Bilas Sarda, to write something in appreciation of the great work of Dayanand Saraswati on the occasion of the fiftieth anniversary of his death, for publication in this Commemoration Volume. I find it rather difficult to say any thing on that subject, because I know I can never do justice to it. Moreover, I feel it impertinence on my part to try to say anything in appreciation of his work. I can only pay my humble and respectful homage to the work of that great Prince amongst men, who, though a *Sannyāsī* possessing no worldly wealth, ruled and still so many years after his death rules the hearts of innumerable men and women. He left this world, before I was born, but even then the atmosphere was so surcharged with his spirit that in my younger days I almost felt it, and that in spite of the fact that I belong to a family of Sanatanī Brahmins, who do not follow his particular cult. The influence of his teachings and his great personality was so wide-spread and deep that it left no one unaffected. And so in my childhood, I heard many stories of what a great man he was, how powerful, how learned, how strong and how magnetic in his personality. I was thrilled to hear of how he woke up the sleeping Hindus, how he took them out of the depths of their superstitions, how he stirred up their imagination and how he engendered in them the spirit of service and love of motherland. Thousands opposed him, but tens of thousands rallied to his banner wherever he went, till at last a spirited army of his followers was created who revolutionized the entire Hindu society, particularly in the Punjab. There was no aspect of life which was left out. Religion, the social system, customs and practices, education, sanitation, health, food, all came within the perview of his zealous followers. I have had the good fortune of coming into personal contact with some of the best products of his teaching. The fire that burnt in the hearts of Lala Lajpat Rai, Swami Shraddhanand, Mahātmā Hansraj and others, was lit up by Swami Dayanand. In his name they incessantly worked for the country and lifted the Punjab to the position in which it is to be found to-day. There is a distinct difference between the Punjab and other provinces, and that difference is brought about by the sustained work of his followers. There is less orthodoxy, less untouchability, less rigidity of caste here, no purdah system, greater freedom among women and on the whole, a much more reformed social life than in other provinces. The courage and stamina, which is a general characteristic of the Punjabi women, is the direct result of their Master's teachings. In short, his healthy influence has permeated the life-blood of the whole of the Punjab. In history he will be known not only as a religious Reformer, but as one of the fathers of the great Indian renaissance and the Founder of the modern Punjab.

LAHORE — RAMESHWARI NEHRU

——:o:——

I am very glad to hear that the fiftieth anniversary of the passing away of the great Swami Dayanand Saraswati will be celebrated in a fitting manner. Needless to say, the movement is really a praiseworthy one. The great services rendered to India by Swami Dayanand Saraswati, not only as a spiritual leader but also as a Social Reformer and scholar, are acknowledged by all and his name will ever be remembered with veneration. To him is due, in a great measure, the renaissance of Indian culture which we witness to-day and he was certainly one of the greatest men produced by India during the last century.

COLOMBO, CEYLON — S. PARANAVITANA

TRIBUTE

TO Swami Dayanand we owe the broadening of life in social and religious spheres, which we have witnessed since he began his mission. It was he who had the courage to proclaim the ancient truth, and free Hindu society from debilitating influences, which were undermining its strength. It was he again who realized that any people to be able to keep abreast of the times must not always remain on the defensive, but be ready to assimilate those who were ready to seek shelter under its wing. There is much work that remains to be done, but the road has been opened; and it is hoped that in the new times Hindu society will rise from the cremation ground of old superstitions, rituals and formalities into a self-confident, faithful and united Nation.

AIRA HOLME, SIMLA EAST — JOGENDRA SINGH

———:o:———

MAHARSHI Dayanand was one of the greatest Reformers of India. India was beset with many enemies, internal as well as external, when he was born. He was the first to see the evils of the caste system, and he tried to abolish it. He was the first Indian to pronounce women as equal to men and try to place them on the higher planes of life. In his mind there was no distinction of sex, caste or creed. He considered all Hindus to be one and indivisible. It is the duty of all Hindus to raise a fitting memorial to the man who did so much for the race, and taught them the first lesson of self-respect.

Maharshi Dayanand was great as a man, greater as an Indian, and one of the greatest as a Reformer.

BOMBAY — LILA MUNSHI

SWAMI DAYANAND—THE INDIAN LUTHER

THE fiftieth anniversary of the death of Swami Dayanand is an appropriate occasion for casting our eyes backwards on the career of this remarkable leader of men, exploring the inhospitable regions wherein the rill took its rise—how it subsequently gathered volume and ran into spate, inundating both the banks it ran through, levelling landmarks of hoary sanctity and throwing up fresh soil on the weathered and heavily drained surface of moribund Hinduism: the ameliorative zeal of Lord Bentinck had not till then touched the encrustation of stifling custom. The *pushṭi mārga* eroticism of Mahārāja-dom was not less devastating in its demoralization than the papacy of which Alexander VI. was a type, and Leo X. a hero. The pompous perversity of petty princelings was equally soul-constricting, whether in the Kathiawar of those days, or Germany of the period of reformation. The light of western learning was falling with the same piercing thoroughness in India as the eclairecissement which was the result of the opening up of the sources of Greek and Latin culture in Western Europe. Karsandas Mulji had crossed the black waters and dabbled in the new knowledge, more enticing because it was forbidden on account of its proselytising tendencies. Some of his writings remind one of Erasmus' famous dictum, "God hates a well-fed *corpulent* devoutness"—a sentence so appropriate to the Vallabhāchārya *sampradāya* of those days, so degenerated from the pristine purity of its pious founder.

His life-history is soon told. Dayanand fled away from a house where a middle class well-fed bourgeois life of a *Gṛihastha* awaited him. His secret departure had all the elements in it of the grand renunciation of Śākyamuni. He became the *chelā* of a *Sannyāsī* Vedāntist of the banks of the Narbadā and studied the Vedas and Vedāngas, so that none of the life-giving elements of

Hinduism might remain foreign to him. He set about to bring out a translation of the Vedas, much as Luther did of the Bible, and it can be said that he was the originator of the theological Hindi, puissantly polemic in its terseness and cumulative force as Luther of the racy German language—so very different from the turgid Latin of the middle ages— with its direct appeal and racy of the soil. Dayanand created the legend, the Aryan-voluble in the Hindi tongue: the *khaḍī bolī* which all can understand and none can claim as the exclusive possession of a section. He wanted to give an intelligible "*kitāb*"— book— to the Hindu, as the Muslim had the Quran and the Protestant Christian the Bible.

The German Reformation was born out of the bitter agonies of an ardent soul seeking after truth "Ich Kann nicht anders, gott helfe mir amen". "I cannot do anything but right; may God help me". Dayanand stood on the word of the comprehensive Vedas— that trans-Paurāṇic ocean of learning and his *Satyārtha-Prakāsh* was designed to be the spiritual companion of the Aryan as the Bible was of the German folk. Luther sang, "Eine feste Burg is unser Gott." Dayanand moored his boat to the keel of the Vedic vessel. Everything which now is, is implicit in the Vedas— a volume for all times.

Dayanand, however, had his difficulties. He realized that unlike the Christians and Muslims, the esoteric Hinduism of the Āchārya of his age had kept the mass of the Hindus uninitiated into the inwardness of the *arcana*. They were left unattended in the unsheltered portico of the temple of God. His face was obscured by the veil cast by centuries old ritualism, by the slavish observance of which alone He could be approached. The few elect cared more for the journey of the soul *Brahmaward* than for the spiritual salvage of the drowning Hindū-jāti. It was his ardent wish to erect an altar of God in every Aryan household. He wanted to make the world 'Aryan', a touch-stone, a *pārasa-maṇi* that ennobled to whomsoever it was applied and made him feel a few inches taller in his spiritual stature—just as a neophyte to Islām or Christianity feels— when he realizes that like Peter the fisherman or Amru the obscure, he can on accepting Christianity be the keeper of keys to heaven, and on conversion to Islām become the conqueror of the much-covetted Egypt. He maintained that every Aryan carried the hall-mark of equality on his forehead. As the Buddhist had proclaimed that he who had uttered the triple formula of the *Triratna*, was a brother, as the Vaishṇavas had attempted the projection of brotherhood on the scaffolding of Bhaktahood, so Dayanand felt that the magic word, Arya, would secure manumission from the disability of ages and like the Sikhs (*Śishya*) the initiated would find in the Arya Samaj temple, a haven of equality and fraternity.

The Arya Samaj bade fair to inaugurate a new era of unification and greatness for the Hindu world. In the Punjab where caste had been weak, where priesthood had taken its complexion from Sikh puritanism, the Samaj wielded a powerful influence. In Rajputana, it took root under the aegis of Maharana Sajjan Singh—a veritable Elector of Saxony, the protector of Luther. In the United Provinces, it marshalled under its banner the more militant Vaiśya who had inherited the traditions of Hemu; but when it came to Bengal or returned to the home-land Gujarat, it dashed itself against an impregnable rock. Bengal seeks everything in the frame work of poetry. No religion can take hold there which has not a halo of romantic feeling about it. *Satya* must come to it more like Goethe's "dichtung und wahrheit". Gujarat, the land of Burke's much-derided calculators and economists, with their catholicity of interests and level-headed outlook was—priest and caste-ridden. Renan in his fascinating autobiography quotes Descartes as saying that nowhere was he so well off in the matter of pursuit of his profession as Philosopher (carrying his "cogito ergo sum" to its logical extreme) as in Amsterdam, because "everyone was engaged in trade and there no one paid any heed to him". Renan airily concluded therefrom that where trade predominates there is an air of comfortable vulgarity and no one would send a Bruno to the stake. He was mistaken. If Dayanand had visited Gujarat in those days and challenged a battle as Hemāchārya did in the days of Kumārapāla, he would have had to drink hemlock sooner than Socrates in the Athens of Cleon. Should he like Luther have allied himself with Princes and set up an authoritarian creed, he would then have had, according to some, his Aśoka and his Constantine. Should he have compromised with icon-worship duly prevalent in Gujarat. The Jesuits would have proselytised China, had Gregory VII agreed to the acceptance of ancestor-worship as part of the Christian creed. But he refused to compromise with what he considered to be an error of faith. Similarly Dayanand stuck out and his tide of *Digvijaya* had to recede.

This uncompromising attitude, according to many was, his Paradise Lost. Reading India's history and the true position of Dayanand as one of the Āchāryas who wanted to take us back to the fountain source instead of starting a new religion— the "Paradise Lost" however was in disguise "Paradise Regained". Had Arya Samaj crystallized in the eighties of the nineteenth century it would have lost its elan vital, and ceased to grow. It is difficult to watch a torso and project conjectures as to what the completed work would have been like. Would it have compromised with Brahmanic Hinduism and accepted the Varṇa system as based on birth? Would it have gone the full length and admitted everyone to a plane of marital equality? It began well with commensality in messing. Possibly the towers of Varṇa by birth and not by *karma*, would have fallen at the breath of Dayanand at his nativity.

It is difficult, however, to contemplate the devitalizing consequences of the catastrophe— his untimely death. The reforming wave of the movement has advanced to its full height and its force is spent. It is now receding. A new wave is now in formation. Will it stop in its progress and make common cause with latitudinarianism or will it succeed in reaching the top and washing away, as Buddhism did, the last landmarks, which, according to some, prevent Brahmanic Hinduism from fitting into the procrustean bed of democracy; or will it appear as Hinduism transfigured with its emblem of the contemplation of *Ekamevādvitīyam*—its strong faith in *karma* and perfectability by individual effort—its insistence on a daily routine of the *Pañcha Mahā Yajñas* being performed in their modern setting and with their true inwardness attuned to modern aspirations? Professor Whitehead defines religion as what a man does with his solitude—the Arya Samaj has leavened the mass. It has given a definite orientation to the thoughts that occupy the Aryan in his solitude. That alone will strengthen and cement the matrix in which the Hindu is cast. This has nothing to do with his advancement on the mundane plane of politics. It is only concerned with character-building and it is with the present generation of Arya Samajists to take it to its full logical height and make Aryan faith a vitalizing force once again, so that when a person slips up one would be justified in uttering the words addressed by Kṛishna to dejected Arjuna—this is अनार्यजुष्टमस्वर्ग्यम् act, leave it off. In that case its uncompromising iconoclasm and insistence on human dignity, though it forfeited the partisanship of wordly rich Gujarat, has not been a mistake; and even if a mistake at that time one is tempted to say, *felix culpa*. Fortunate was that mistake. It has left Arya Samaj with the element of growth still left in it. There is, however, one danger ahead. The will o' the wisp of politics is likely to lead one astray. Political considerations are visibly cutting across the plane of natural evolution of soul-moulding forces. Luther succumbed to politics and switched his star on to the car of the Princes of Germany. This gave rise to the Erastian type of Protestantism (cejus regio ejus religeo) and religion instead of being the cement of union became the seed-bed of disunion, and the Thirty Years War followed as a result.

Is there hope of the promethean fire being kept burning to revivify Hinduism or will the siren-call of latitudinarianism point the way to compromise for purely political ends and cut the career of the reformer short? Then the Brahmanic Hinduism will still remain in need of another Dayanand to appear betimes to save the youth leaving traditional moorings and getting wrecked on the reefs of anarchic irreligion. The present Āchāryas of the movement alone can say what will be the next scene on which the curtain will rise— will it still be the stern puritanic soul-uplifting, all-uniting creed or will it be the comfortable self-satisfied exclusive creed of the class so aptly characterised by Peacock as "epicêre", when describing the predominant type of the age of Napolean III.

SRINAGAR, KASHMIR — VINAYAK N. MEHTA

IN the land of the five rivers, on the banks of which the Vedic hymns were first sung, however, the virile teachings of Swami Dayanand took deep root, and thanks to the inspiring example of the Swami, the Arya Samaj is to-day bearing abundant fruit and flower. One may not accept every word of those teachings and yet the fact must be admitted even by those who are not Arya Samajists that the Swami has made a very much needed contribution to the cause of progress by reviving the purer and more original doctrines of the Vedic Ṛishis. The stagnation in which Hinduism was rotting when Swami Dayanand inaugurated the Samaj was arrested by his great efforts and a spirit of change for the better was infused in the slumbering conscience of the Hindu community in Hindustan. May that spirit gather more and more strength in the years to come!

BELGAUM — A. B. LATHE

THE LAW OF CHANGE

CHANGE is the Law of Life; the universe, as a whole, has to renew itself constantly by this eternal principle. Every people has to adapt itself to the law of innovation and a nation that has not realised this fact, would degenerate, step by step, and finally would be cut off from the colossal column of that universal caravan which is always marching forward with Eternity.

Any river, any plain, any mountain, any tree, any man or nation is conducted to the new domain of existence, by the law of innovation and the love of change continuously changing its situation, its existence and renewing its manners of life.

Our beloved Orient, unfortunately during the last two centuries has been afflicted by spiritual, as well as material coagulation, which evil affliction has been and is yet, as I think, the main cause of the great calamities, which are still oppressing the East. This, I would call those calamities the penalty of nature upon those who have not obeyed the nature's laws. And so, in fact, every Oriental nation will, unless it changes its conduct and directs itself to the way of innovation, undergo such punishment.

As a matter of fact, the real pioneers of the East are those, whose lives were or are yet devoted to the creation of a social renaissance. Although to-day, in view of the present situation of the East, we are glad to show a sufficient number of the innovators whose works and reforms have restored to the Oriental nations the suffocated faculty of innovation; yet, we can never forget to call those few personages of the past the first pioneers, who were endowed with the necessary qualities of reformers and who lived and died for that sublime purpose.

Among those pioneers, I should name your deceased Swami

Dayanand Saraswati, whose valuable services in the cause of Hindu religion and uplift of his nation in the moral and social domains are too great to be fully described in such a short article. What he has achieved by denouncing the system of hereditary castes, as I would believe now, would, some day in the future, be confirmed as a high road to the unity and the progress of India. The institution of the Arya Samaj, of which he has laid the foundations on the ground of the Indian Renaissance, is and would, always, be looked at, as an argument to establish the self-consciousness of India and its intrinsic inclination to national emancipation. His commentary on the Vedas is a unique work by which he has illustrated once more the value of the great scriptures of ancient India, from which the well-known sages of India have been radiating their wisdom in all directions for the welfare and advancement of humanity. Thus, I feel it a duty of every Oriental like myself to appreciate what Maharshi Dayanand Saraswati has achieved, as the great work in the cause of India's national unity.

In conclusion, I avail myself of this opportunity to congratulate the Indian people for their remembrance and commemoration of their great personages, in the past.

TEHERAN, PERSIA — RAHIMZADAH SAFAVI

I have observed, during my travels in India, the effects of Swami Dayanand Saraswati's influence in earnest efforts to vitalise life in India with the Vedic ideal, which for thirty years has been a fundamental influence in my own life and in that of Mrs. Cousins; and for this much-needed service to India and the world, I offer our joint homage to his memory.

KANGRA VALLEY — JAMES H. COUSINS

To

MOTHER INDIA

We live where mountains crown your brow,
  Beside the Northern gate;
With brawny arms and limbs, we love
  And guard your high estate.

Where rice-fields smile towards the East
  We teem, a densely throng;
We seek to serve you with our feast
  Of varied art and song.

We toil beside your Western sea
  And garner wealth for you,
Bringing the magic argosy
  Across the distant blue.

Temple and tower have we wrought
  Toward the Southern shore;
The great God's glories have we sought,
  Through all the days of yore.

Whether we come from far or near,
  From North or South, or West
Or East, we are your children dear:
  O Mother, we are blest!

P. SESHADRI

SWAMI DAYANAND SARASWATI

IN the mind of occidentals, it is only polytheism and pantheism which are generally associated with Hinduism. But the mediæval reforming sects of Nânakpanthīs, Kabīrpanthīs, Dādūpanthīs, etc., show that the belief in and spiritual worship of One Personal God is not foreign to the genius of Hinduism. In modern times Ram Mohan Roy was the first Indian reformer to demonstrate that fact. But critics may say that, as he possessed a scholarly knowledge of Judaism, Christianity and Islām, in addition to that of the Brahma Sūtras and the Upanishads, he may have got his monotheistic ideas from non-Indian faiths. It is not necessary here to examine and refute this objection. But even such a specious objection cannot be brought forward in the case of the monotheistic doctrines promulgated by Swami Dayanand Saraswati.

When the period of his self-education and of intellectual growth was over, he began to preach his religious and social doctrines. According to his interpretation of the Vedas, polytheism, idolatry, and caste restrictions were un-Vedic, and he felt called upon to restore what he believed to be the pure monotheistic Vedic religion of the Aryans.

A few years ago when I visited Ajmer, the high priest of the temple of Brahmā at Pushkar showed me a stick which, he said, belonged to Dayanand Saraswati when he resided there temporarily before his promulgation of his Vedic doctrines. It reminded me of the Swami's religious and social militancy. He was fond of disputations, and liked to defeat his orthodox Hindu, Muslim and Christian opponents with the logical weapons he wielded. The big public disputation which he had with three hundred prominent Hindu divines at Benares was a very remarkable one. In the words of Lala Lajpat Rai, this event marked "the effective beginning of Dayanand's mission for a reformed Hindu Church."

In 1875 in Bombay he formally started the Arya Samaj. It was also in the same city that he published the *Satyārth Prakāsh*, containing an authoritative exposition of his doctrine, which underwent a final revision at Lahore in 1877.

The Swami wanted to realise the ideal of unifying India nationally, socially and religiously. To make Indians one nation, he thought it was necessary to free it from foreign rule. In order to make the people of India socially one, he wanted to eliminate the differences of caste and class. To make India religiously one, he desired to substitute his Vedic religion for all other religions prevalent in India. These three aims of Swami Dayanand have borne some fruit. For some time, from the nineties of the last century onwards, those of the Swami's followers who were connected with the D. A. V. College movement became the foremost agency for fostering a sturdy and independent Nationalism in the Punjab, the foremost political and social worker and sufferer of the group being Lala Lajpat Rai. Mrs. Besant ascribes "the undermining of the belief in the Superiority of the White Races to the spreading of the Arya Samaj and the Theosophical Society." In the domain of social reform the Arya Samaj has rendered signal service. By the uplift of the out-castes this religious body has acted as a true social deliverer. It has promoted inter-caste marriages and the marriages of widows and practically raised the age of marriage among its followers. Its educational and famine relief and orphan-saving enterprises have been remarkable. Perhaps the purely religious propaganda of Dayanand Saraswati has slipped a little to the background. But it cannot be denied that the Arya Samaj has done something to popularize monotheistic ideas among the masses of the people.

A foreign observer has summed up, "the Arya Samaj as a religious force working for social reform, which remains a great and powerful factor to this day in the national life of India, and one seriously to be reckoned with in its future".

CALCUTTA RAMANAND CHATTERJI

DAYANAND'S LEGACY TO THE PUNJAB

I

IN the middle of the last century, when the Punjab passed into British hands, society in the "Province of the Five Waters" was like unto a stagnant pool in the jungle. Inlets and outlets were choked up with muck. Over the bosom of the water was spread a thick layer of dirty green scum.

This layer was of a peculiar texture. A pebble pitched at it would pierce it; but as soon as it fell to the bottom, the wind would bind the bit that had been torn with the jagged edges and presently hardly a crack would remain to indicate that any violence had been attempted.

The beings dwelling under this green covering had become so used to the darkness that light let through any chinks that were made in it hurt their eyes. They therefore made haste to repair any damage that any one might do to the sheet shielding them from sunlight, rain and wind.

Britons discovered this phenomenon soon after they annexed the Punjab in 1849. Teachers in schools and colleges and missioners cast pebbles into this social pool. Some merely glanced off the surface. Others penetrated the covering, but caused small disturbance.

For every inch of space that these stones pierced—pierced, for the most part, unavailingly—a hundred yards of the pool flaunted its thick, scurvy sheet of green. It seemed to mock at the European and American preceptors. They might pride themselves upon the knowledge they had accumulated: but at the moment at least they were powerless to lift or to destroy the heavy blanket under which the Punjabis lived and moved.

II

Some six decades ago a monk charged with energy and determination emanating from a chaste life devoted to study and

SWAMI DAYANAND SARASWATI

contemplation, the dirty, thick coat of green scum settled upon the surface of the social pool in the Punjab. The sight disgusted him.

With all the might he possessed he began making holes in it. Like the hosts that Rama had carried into Lanka over the wondrous bridge built by Nila, the accomplished descendant of Visvakarmā, he hurled boulders and gigantic trees into it. They created tremendous gashes in it, irregular in shape and varying in size.

The beings who dwelt beneath it were dazzled by the glare of light that the Swami Dayanand Saraswati—as the monk was called—suddenly let in upon them. The stones he cast hurt them. They cursed him—heaped vile abuse upon him—called him a madman—mischief-maker. They tried to patch the rents he had made in their protective covering; but before they could do so he threw heavier and heavier missiles and the holes kept increasing in number and size.

Opposition and abuse served only to stiffen his resolve. He denounced the shibboleths and practices of the day as unworthy of the descendants of the Aryans of old. He deplored the fact that the noble spirit infused by the *rishis* of the Vedic period had disappeared. Even the shell that was being cherished was not the genuine article. It was a base imitation, manufactured during the dark ages through which Hinduism had passed. It was rotting and emitted nauseating odours.

His strength lay in his deep knowledge of Sanskrit literature and the courage and dialectical skill with which he made devastating use of that knowledge. Men who sought to controvert his statements lacked his erudition, or ready tongue, certainly his aggressiveness. The wordy duels in which he engaged with them left them disabled. The cry of "*dharma* in danger" that had been raised effectually against the alien missioners was of little avail, for Dayanand took his stand on the Vedic rock. Beliefs were uprooted. Men and women who had clung to them sought the Swami for spiritual succour.

They found that he was not merely a destroyer. He was a builder as well. He had a complete, carefully worked out scheme of life to offer them to take the place of that which he had demolished. He was, in reality, a Re-creator. He showed the people who flocked to him the way to rekindle the fire that had all but gone out. In the glow and warmth of that fire society could live and function vigorously.

III

The gods and goddesses were very much in evidence in the Punjab in those days. The lime-washed *śikhars* (spires), often the handiwork of men who had more faith than artistic sense, pierced the sky at many points.

Prayers began while the bath was being taken and, in the case of persons deemed religious, took up the best part of the forenoon. As the dark goblin of night swallowed the aging day, seemingly at a single gulp, the ringing of temple bells, the blowing of conches, the blare of double-curved copper horns and the clash of cymbals, proclaimed the hour when the devotional attitude must be assumed once again, whatever the mood of the moment.

Not always did the gods use the potency with which they were credited to keep the worshippers' feet firmly planted in the straight and narrow path of rectitude. It was nothing uncommon to meet a person of whom my mother used to say:—

"On his lips he has Hari's name,
With his hand he shears others of their substance."

IV

Life in the Punjab at that time was modelled upon a pattern which originally must have been designed for making a strait-jacket. Every line—every seam—every stich—was marked out. No deviation was permitted—not so much as by a hair's breadth.

In reality only the outer covering mattered. All was well so long as the upper robe was of the right hue and cut—so long as it was broidered in the approved fashion—and fell down in the folds ordained by immutable convention.

Beneath the clock the under-garments might be ragged and dirty. They might even be malodorous : for the pockets of the top-coat were ever filled with frankinscense and myrrh, which completely neutralized the smells beneath.

Any man who possessed the courage and dexterity to do so divested himself on occasion of his outer garments of convention and sat in negligé, finding distraction and recreation in the company of his boon companions. So long as he was discreet, he could do so with impunity.

But the outer and inner garments weighed heavily upon the soul. Not infrequently they destroyed it.

V

Some 400 years earlier, Guru Nanak had gone about the Punjab seeking to turn the people from stocks and stones towards the living, loving God; teaching men and women the futility of depending upon ceremonial observances to achieve salvation, and exhorting them to conquer lust and avarice and to lead lives of usefulness to the race. His nine successors had carried on a similar crusade.

The spirit that the Gurus had infused into the Sikhs (disciples) had worked wonders. Persons who had lived in craven fear had been turned into heroes. They resisted tyranny, even when enforced with the rack and pinion; and in the end broke it.

With the acquisition of power came however exhaustion and corruption. After the fall of the Sikh kingdom, the followers of the Gurus had, with a few honourable exceptions, gone back to the observances and practices from which their forefathers had been weaned.

VI

Hardly had Mulshanker—as Dayanand was known in his pre-monkhood days—entered his teens when he became conscious of the wrongheadedness of orthodox Hindu ways in Western India, where he had been born in a devout Brahmin home. The first ray of light pierced his mental vision on the Mahâshivarâtri night—the night sacred, above all nights and days, to Śhiva, originally the destructive element in the *Trimurti* (Hindu Triad), gradually elevated, at least in the sight of his worshippers, as the "god of gods" (Mahādeva).

When the whole family was roused to the highest religious ecstasy, the fourteen-years-old boy suddenly scandalized his father by asking him if the almighty God really resided in the phallus (*lingam*) they were worshipping. Stern was the reproof that the young doubter received; but it failed to put out the light he had seen.

That light kept on growing brighter. It forced him, as he attained his majority in 1845, out of his parental home. He wandered from place to place in pursuit of truth and knowledge, which for millenniums had rung with the echoes of Krishna's words and deeds. At Muttra, he met the Swami Virjananda—a modern *rishi* who had perceived that degenracy had crept into Hindu society during the post-Mahabhāratic war period and that society could be purged only if the Vedic institutions could be revived. Illumination (*bodhi*), in its full effulgence, burst upon him there some time between the years 1860 and 1863.

Filled with this philosophy of uplift, Dayanand toured about India, holding converse with priests of the prevailing faith and leaders of new thought and expounding to them the wisdom he had garnered and the scheme of life he had evolved. With the downrightness that springs from deep, single-minded conviction, he condemned image-worship.

No missioner—Mussalman or Christian—had ever been more uncompromising in his denunciation. But unlike non-Hindu preachers, he drew his inspiration from the Veda, which he proclaimed, was the repository of revealed knowledge, containing the seeds of even the experimental sciences. It spoke of the One existent by diverse names—now as Indra, again as Yama, and still again as Agni. But it recognized only one God—the Eternal, Formless Lord of all.

Religion that did not express itself in life, he taught, was not worth the name. A rational being must not act without determining that his action would be morally right.

Nor would he permit men to live for themselves. They must think of their fellow-men—their conduct towards others must be not merely just but also kind and loving—and must promote the public good.

VII

The crusade against image-worship exposed the Swami Dayanand to the wrath of the priestcraft. He might or might not have offended their susceptibilities: that depended entirely upon the nature of their interest in ritualism—whether it was sincere or merely financial. But his teachings vitally effected their purse.

The priests may not have been able to counter his arguments: but their armoury contained a much more powerful weapon. The way society was then organized in the Punjab made it a tool in the hands of the priestcraft and that tool was mercilessly used.

People lived in "joint families." Men and women related in various degrees were congregated under one roof.

The home, in fact, was a caravanserai in which the dwellers were ushered in by the midwife. The quest for lucre might take them away from it for a time. Normally however they stayed there until they were borne out over Yama's shoulders to the land of eternal bliss.

Supposedly the eldest male member in the household constituted the supreme authority over it. Power was, however often exercised by the eldest woman member—usually the grand-mother (sometimes the great-grand-mother). She was the chancellor of the exchequer and consequently the arbiter of the family's fate. Her touch was balm to the wounded soul—or was as hard as steel. It depended largely upon a person's age and sex and the state of the *materfamilias*' liver and nerves.

Infants were petted and spoiled in the "joint family." Youths had not a care in the world: but they were held in a vice expected to be tongue-tied. The older folks domineered over them, but as a rule, were proof neither against cajolery nor the tyranny of tears.

The discipline applied to women was far stricter than that

to which men had to submit. The home to them was a crucible in which the dross was constantly being purged from their nature.

Drones and workers found food, shelter and raiment within the "joint family." The do-nothings frequently had a little more of love, at least from the women's apartments, than the bread-winners.

Earnings were put into the common pool. Allowances were doled out to adults and adolescents. In that respect there was little difference between the grown-ups and the growing ones.

In crises, the "joint family" was a rock that the wildest storm could not shake. But existence led in the lee of a rock stunted growth. It seriously limited the scope for action and set a frontier for the development of individuality. It killed the sense of responsibility and initiative even before that sense was born.

VIII

The new arrivals in the caravanserai, as likely as not, were the products of immature bodies and still more immature brains. They arrived in this world, it was said, to amuse their grand-parents or their great-grand-parents and were commonly spoken of as "little dolls."

Marriage was regarded as a sacrament. That sacrament was thrust upon tiny tots, much as christening in Europe is.

Just as the European infant does not comprehend the language that is being used in pledging his allegiance to a God whom he has not chosen for himself, so, in the Punjab of that day no girl could grasp the significance of the words that tied her to a boy—tied her for the whole of her life and (it was said) beyond this life.

Though wedlock was considered a sacred institution, opportunity for leading the conjugal life in an open, honest, loving fashion was denied the couple. The only way in which it could be led in a purdah-ridden "joint family" made it appear something that must be kept hidden in a dark recess.

IX

The social code differed with the sexes. If a wife died, the husband married again, usually in hot haste. If she were childless for a time, she might have to put up with a rival—or rivals—with whom she would be expected to live like a "sister," no matter how wide the breach between them might be. If, on the contrary, her husband died she would be compelled to remain a widow for the rest of her life—childless though she be, or even a virgin.

These and other inequalities were no doubt originally ordained by man in the name of the gods. But in the days of which I write, women exerted greater pressure than men did in enforcing the injunctions. Shut in as they were from the outside world, they seemed to take great delight in insisting upon strict conformity with the social canons.

The purpose behind these efforts (more often than not hidden from them) was to prevent men from straying away from the rock of the home. The loose end of the rope that women held taut got twisted round and round their feet. They undoubtedly were the greater sufferers, since they lacked even the short tether they gave to men.

X

The Swami had felt, in his boyhood, the grip of the brahmin family in which he had been born. The pressure had grown intolerable by the time he reached his twenty-first year.

Home had provided little scope for the exercise of freedom of conscience. As he grew out of boyhood, so grew his relatives' insistence that an end be put to his celibacy. Fortunately for him and even more so for the *Samaj* (society) that he was later to inaugurate, his determination to prosecute studies unhampered by the marital tie proved stronger.

A time came when he could no longer bear the constant nagging and bickering. He left home. He shaved his head and donned the *gerua* robe. With the long staff and begger's bowl of the religious mendicant, he set out on that search for God that never ended so long as air went into his lungs and was exhaled from them.

His studies, particularly at Muttra, had shown him the unsoundness of the social policy pursued by the Hindus of his day. Men and women, he realized, had been created to be free beings. Unless they had individual liberty, they could not grow and attain to the highest stature.

The yoking together of mere infants by the bonds of matrimony ran counter to the practices that obtained during the era of Hinduism's glory. It sapped the vitality that should go into the gathering of intellectual and spiritual equipment with which to face the world. It injured the individual and—society. The weaklings that often resulted from child-unions became a charge upon others. The shadow of their misery projected far beyond themselves.

Nor could he find any sanction for the status that, in his day, was assigned to woman. In India's Golden Age the woman—not the girl—exercised the privilege of choosing the mate with whom she was to spend her life, adding to the material and spiritual wealth of the community; and making some contribution, however humble, to the prosperity of posterity through assiduously cultivating the flower of her womb.

He abhorred the enforcement of widowhood, though woman herself exerted much of the pressure. He did not find any Vedic sanction for the institution.

Like weeds that sprout and grow under tangled greenery and push out their heads and throw up their runners until they, that do not sustain life, kill the cereals and vegetables that nourish the body, these and other senseless social customs had originated and developed during the long, dark night through which Hinduism had passed. They must be uprooted, cost what that uprooting may.

XI

After he had left his *Guru* at Muttra, Dayanand concentrated his time and energy upon purifying and regenerating Hindu society. He insisted that every individual should have freedom of thought and action both within and without the home

He prescribed—as the *rishis* of old had done—brahmacharya for boys and girls—brahmacharya until they had attained maturity of body and mind.

Brahmacharya was to be devoted entirely to the service of Sarasvati. The knowledge acquired during this period was to be utilized not merely for personal benefit and the promotion of the welfare of kinsmen, but for the advancement of the community as a whole.

Few teachers have laid greater emphasis upon a person's obligation to work for the betterment of mankind than did Swami Dayanand. During the period extending from the twenty-fifth to the fiftieth year, when, in conformity with the Vedic canons, a man could assume the role of householder, he was charged not to forget his fellow-beings. After he had passed the meridian of life, he might devote his time to travel, observation, study and contemplation.

XII

Dayanand sought to reintegrate the Hindus, by taking away from the caste system the rigidity that it had acquired during the Dark Ages. He did not wish caste to be determined by the accident of birth, as had become the custom, but declared that, as in the Golden Age, a man should be classed according to his *guna* (qualities), *karma* (deeds) and *subhawa* (disposition). A person born as a *chandala* should, he proclaimed, be able to become a brahmin if he had the brahmin's nature and capacity and conducted himself as one. Instances of such elevation were not unknown when Hinduism was a living and growing religion.

The Swami Dayanand frowned also upon the practice of Hindus living within a series of ramparts pierced with gates that permitted egress but not ingress. The men and women born within these fortifications who succumbing to temptation, passed out, were not permitted to return. Outsiders, in no circumstance, could smuggle themselves in, much less boldly enter.

These ramparts, too, the Swami declared, had been thrown up during the Dark Ages. In the days of Hinduism's splendour, not merely individuals but large aggregations of them had been welcomed. The process of Hinduization was so rapid and so thorough that within a generation or two the progeny of the converts, or at any rate their progeny, could not be distinguished from the main body of Hindus.

XIII

Upon the wings of my memory float wisps of recollections of my boyhood days. The Swami had already passed beyond mortal ken, but the contentions that he had roused echoed and re-echoed in the Punjab. They seemed, in fact, to gain in volume and intensity with the passage of time.

The men and women who cherished beliefs he had assailed, whose observances he had denounced, could not bear to hear his name mentioned. The better to resist the activities of the workers inspired by him, they had gathered under the banner of the *Sanatan Dharma* (old religion), as they called it.

The Swami had however stolen a march over them. He had gone past the mediæval era, when the *Puranas*, held sacred by the Sanatanists, were composed, back to the rosy dawn of Hinduism, when the earliest Vedic hymns issued from the lips of the sages like a spring welling from the mountain side.

How well I recall the petty tyrannies to which men who had flocked to Dayanand's standard while he was alive or shortly after his death, were subjected. Their parents-in-law refused to permit their wives to live with them. Their brothers and sisters and cousins regarded them as strangers. Their caste-people would have nothing to do with them. *Hukka pani band* (literally, "no smoking, no giving of water") was the slogan of the hour.

The non-Hindus abiding in the Punjab were, if possible, even more hostile than the Sanatanists. The Muslims, almost entirely composed of ex-Hindus and their descendants, could not be expected to welcome Dayanand's move to re-Hinduize converts to Islam and even the progeny of such converts. Nor could the Christian missionaries do so.

The Swami's resolve to take rigidity out of Hinduism and particularly to uplift the lower orders of the community, menaced all proselytizing activities in the Punjab. It threatened to cut off the golden current from which the baptismal font had been fed.

XIV

There were political complications too. Dayanand had sought to create men who would not cheerfully submit to the role of intellectual or political subjugation that Indians of that era were expected to play. Most of them were content to abide in the valley into which they had slid down the slippery ladder of subservience.

Since the days of Macaulay—and even before—Englishmen had talked as if India had been a Sahara from which it was hopeless to derive any nourishment for the mind. The Swami had challenged such dicta and had proved that men who thus libelled our forbears were ignorant and prejudiced. By so doing he had strengthened the forces that were working to liberate the Indian intellect from the enslaving influences of the Occident.

The followers of Dayanand appeared to officials who had become used to the servile ways of self seeking Indians "uppity"—to use an expressive term coined in the Southern States of the American Union to characterize Negro-Americans who, utilizing the opportunities created for them by the successful issue of the Civil War, comported themselves as free men. The independent attitude assumed by the Arya Samajists, their insistence upon reviving the old culture and upon setting up institutions where boys and girls could acquire education free, as far as possible, of official control, and participation in movements calculated to raise Indians—politically and otherwise—to their fullest stature, rendered them suspect in the eyes of the Indian Civil Service men, then preponderatingly non-Indian, who dominated the Punjab where, at the time, there was hardly any public opinion to be reckoned with.

XV

Dayanand's followers were able to weather these storms

because in an incredibly short time, their roots had gone deep into the Indian soil. Social and political tempests thrashed their branches about but failed to uproot them. The strain evolved by the Swami was indeed hardy. It could withstand the frosts of neglect and the worst contumely and perversity, without showing any injury. He had imparted to it something of the tenacity of purpose and aggressive moral courage that had distinguished him from the general run of his contemporaries.

His followers possessed in great abundance the spirit of self-reliance and self-help. They also were capable of making great sacrifices.

In some ways most important of all, they had learnt to realize the value of organization. Dayanand had not left to chance the propagation of the revived faith: but had established societies for the purpose wherever he had gone; and tried to link one with the other.

This was a wonderful legacy. It has not only enabled the Arya Samajists, as his followers are proud to call themselves, to regenerate themselves and through regeneration to perform educational, social and political work of which any section of the community may justly be proud, but has also acted as a leaven in other sections. Who shall indeed say just how much of the progressive movements in the Punjab, where for some inscrutable reason the Arya Samaj has thriven more than in other parts of India, owe to this legacy?

Dayanand must certainly be accorded a high place among the makers of modern India.

MUSSOORIE — ST. NIHAL SINGH

SPIRITUAL PURITY, THE BASIS OF MATERIAL PROSPERITY

(Vaidika Dharma, the Source of Samsarika Abhyudaya)

धर्मादर्थश्च कामश्च स किमर्थं न सेव्यते । (M.-Bh.)

The Title of This Paper

WHEN I was asked by Śrī Har Bilas Sarda, the widely respected author of *Hindu Superiority* and of the Sarda Bill to raise the Age of Marriage, to make a contribution to this Commemoration Volume for the Ardha Shatābdī celebrations of Swami Dayanand's Life and Work, I pondered long as to what the title should be of my mite.

"The Revival of the pure Vaidika Dharma"? This was the great Swami's heart's wish and his life's work. The noble words, "Vaidika Dharma", etymologically, in their full significance, mean all the best that the modern words 'Scientific Religion' can convey. But they would not appeal to the several large communities which do not call themselves Hindu, but which also inhabit India (and are therefore rightly called *Hindi*, in the near West, i.e., Persia, Arabia, Turkey, Egypt), and whose welfare also the great Reformer must have had at heart. Also, most of our Pandits too would not recognise 'Vaidika Dharma' at all, if it appeared before them in the garb of 'Scientific Religion'.

"*Varṇāsrama* Dharma"? This is the *practical result* of the application of the *theoretical*, philosophical and psychological *principles* of 'Scientific Religion' to human affairs. This Varṇa Dharma, 'the Scheme of the *Rights and Duties* of the several *classes* which make up Society'; this Social Organisation, or Organisation of the whole Human Race; and this Āshrama Dharma, this orderly, systematic, laying out of the *Rights and Duties* of the several *stages* of each Individual life; this Individual Discipline and Organisation;—this Dual

Code of Life, this interweaving of Socialism and Individualism, is the very Flower-and-Fruit of the great tree of which Veda, 'Knowledge', *all* True Science, is the Root. The re-growing of such Flower-and-Fruit, by bathing and re-vivifying the almost dried-up Root with the waters of fresh interpretation, was clearly the object of the Swami's labours. Yet these fine words, *Varṇa* and *Āshrama*, having lost their real primal significance through the eroding and corroding action of Time, Mahā-Kāla, were liable to the same objections as Vaidika Dharma.

Names, titles, are all-important. Ill-chosen ones may repel readers from the best matter. Well-chosen ones may attract to the poorest stuff. A rose, under another name, may smell less sweet; may not be smelt at all. We have therefore to choose a title which might appeal to all sorts and conditions of men. 'Material Prosperity' appeals to the vast majority of mankind, patently; 'Spiritual Purity' to the remaining few, and, with limits and reservations, to a good many among the others. The two together—embrace all mankind. "Spiritual Purity, the Basis of Material Prosperity" (and not merely of non-material prosperity, *dharma* which would be *ihārtha* as well as *amutrārtha*)—would probably lure the tough-minded as well as the tender-minded readers, the modern go-aheads as well as the ancient sleepy-heads, the wideawake economicians, politicians, and downright physicians as well as the dreaming metaphysicians, the clever up-to-date scientific experts, as well as the old-fashioned pandits, mullas, and padris.

So this was the title decided on.

Religion and Civilisation

Every fresh proclamation by a great soul, (1) of the One Eternal Essential Religion of the Oneness of God, the Supreme All-pervading Principle of Life, the Universal Father, (2) of the consequent Brotherhood of Man, and (3) of the resultant natural Duty of whole-hearted Love and Service of God by Love and

Service of Fellowmen, as the indispensable condition of all peace, prosperity, progress and happiness—every such reproclamation has been followed by a fresh civilisation in human history.

5,000 to 600 B. C., and 600 B. C. to 700 A. D. Vaidika Upanishad Period; Bauddha Period

This Essential Spiritual Religion, embodied in the Upanishads and the Gītā, formed the basis of the ancient Indian civilisation from about 5,000 B.C. to about 600 B.C. Then it decayed. Tirthaṅkara Pārshva-nātha, about 850 B.C., and again Tirthaṅkara Mahāvīra Jina, about 600 B.C., endeavoured to put new life into it. But chiefly the Buddha, contemporary with Mahāvīra of India, Laotse and Confucius of China, and Pythagoras of Greece, proclaimed it in a new form, here, some 2,500 years ago, revived the decaying civilisation, and gave it a new lease of life.

This re-stored intellectual and emotional energy of the people indirectly helped the growth of the magnificent Empire of Chandragupta and his teacher and prime minister, Chāṇakya-Kauṭalya, (contemporary with Alexander and his teacher Aristotle, and almost so with the emperor Shi-hwang-ti and the philosopher Mencius of China), and directly developed the yet more magnificent, and, what is far more, in all history matchlessly *beneficent*, empire of Chandragupta's grandson Aśoka '*Priya-darśī*', the 'Tender-eyed', the 'Lover of Mankind'. Its vitality lasted for about 1,200 years. Then, having exhausted its missionary fervour, its preaching and teaching ardour, its literary activity, its colonising enterprise, it began to fail. Yet it lingered on for another 400 years or so, here and there, in this country.

During this period, the *Vishv-ātmā*, the *Ruh-i-Kul*, the Oversoul, sent two other great teachers; the Messiah, to the Hebrew race, nearly 2,000 years ago, "not to destroy but to fulfil" the Old Testament by the New; and the Prophet, to the allied Arab race, some 1,400 years ago, to give to it the same Eternal Word of God in the language of the Quran.

"Innahū la fī zubūr-il-awwalīn...Le kullé qaumin hād..."(Q) (This that I am now uttering unto you is to be found in ancients' sayings too; for prophets have been sent to every race).

These two forms of Religion, the Christian and the Islamic, were also predestined to come to India, and to make their contribution to the new civilisation which is to grow up, under the guidance of Providence.

Buddhism declined, together with its corresponding magnificent civilisation, i.e., its special language and literature, its architectural and other arts, its forms of worship, its social manners and conventions, etc., because, it would seem, of the loss of 'virtue', and the gradual growth of indolence, love of ease, luxury, avarice, vice, sin, *tāntrika* practices of 'black magic', hypocrisy, and crimes and, finally, political 'intrigues', in the great *vihāras*, the monastery-universities; and because of the fostering of excessive Buddha-idol-worship, and literalism and formalism outside the *vihāras*—in consequence of all which the priests lost the trust of the people.

Then Śaṅkar-āchārya taught the Eternal Spiritual Religion afresh in the sixth century A.D. (or seventh, or even eighth, according to some scholars). Owing, however, to various social causes and reactions, and to the activities of some of his immediate predecessors, Kumārila and his followers, who had tried hard to revive the ritualistic side of the Vedic religion, in opposition to Buddhism, certain hardenings of internal divisions and differences of caste, sub-caste, etc., were left behind, in place of living elasticity and power of transformation and assimilation. Such rigidity may perhaps have had some use in that time of active antagonisms, for marking off Buddhists from Brahmanists, or as a safeguard against looseness in sex-relations, or as a help in reducing vocational misfit or excessive competition; but afterwards, running to irrational excess, it became a source of great weakness and degeneration. The essentials of Buddhist culture and its main forms of life-expression were gradually re-absorbed in the new revival of Vedic religion (not without the accompaniment of conflict and some bloodshed) and merged and disappeared therein, after the recognition of the Buddha as a great spiritual *avatāra*, and of his teaching as identical in essence with Śaṅkar-ācharyā's.

Having, during many centuries, spread, like the banyan tree, long branches over, and dropped strong ærial roots and planted them firmly in Ceylon, Tibet, China, Japan, Burma, Siam, and the adjoining countries and Islands, (and perhaps wafted a few missionaries, like leaves, to far-off Mexico and Peru also, across the Ocean, as some researchers and enthusiasts are beginning to think, guessing that Yucatan is Yoga-sthāna, and Guatemala is Gautam-ālaya)—having done this, Buddhism dried up in the original root and trunk, whereby Greater India lost its great adjective.

Harshavardhana, emperor of North India, with his capitals at Sthānéśvara (Thaneshwar) near Delhi and at Kānyakubja (Kanauj) was contemporary with the Prophet Muhammad, and nearly so with the Persian King Nausherwān the Just, for having been born within whose reign the Prophet congratulated himself. He seems to have made some effort to reconcile Brahmanism and Buddhism, and gave generous hospitality to the famous Chinese Buddhist traveller and scholar, Hiouen Tsiang (or Yuan Chwang), about the middle of the seventh century A.D.; but his effort was not successful.

700 A.D. To 1,600 A.D.

Śaṅkarāchārya; advent of Islām and Christianity; Sants and Auliyās

Just about this time, i.e., the middle of the seventh century, A.D., Islam came to the shores of Malabar, and then, a little later, in the last years of that century, to those of Sindh. To the Malabar coast, Arabs had been coming for long, in pre-Islamic times, for trade purposes. And in these southernmost parts of India, Islam spread slowly and quietly, by peaceful attraction, without any political pressure, down to the end of the thirteenth century A.D., when southern India was invaded by Alauddin's general, Malik Kafur.

In northern India, too, down to the end of the tenth century, i.e. the beginning of the raids of Mahmud of Ghazni, there was very little fighting between the followers of the two religions as such, except perhaps in Sindh. We may also note that Mahmud Ghaznavī was almost an Indian. The countries now called Afghanistan and Baluchistan were parts of India in his day, and their population, and also of great parts of Turkestan, was wholly Hindu or Buddhist, shortly before his time, and largely so in his day. His raids too were, in motive, probably very much like the *dig-vijaya*, *ashva-medha*, and *rāja-sūya* raids of Hindu kings. From the eleventh to the sixteenth century, the new religion and the old competed with one another, for the favour of the Indian people, somewhat more strenuously. Yet, it seems, they did so without any clear collective consciousness, on either side, that it was a struggle between the religions as such. The battles were principally motived by the ordinary ambitions of warrior-chiefs for political supremacy, martial glory, extension of territory, etc. 'Clerical' writers, contemporaneous or subsequent, of chronicles, poems and histories have coloured their accounts more or less thickly with the *odium theologicum*, and given a fanatical and very unwholesome 'religious' complexion to the incidents. If Indian History, in all these centuries, is carefully scrutinized, it will be found that there have been as many battles between Hindu king and Hindu king, and between Mussalman king and Mussalman king, as between Hindu king and Mussalman king; and also that, in very many of these battles, Hindu as well as Mussalman soldiers and captains have been present on both sides. Mahmud Ghaznavī himself had Hindu soldiers in his armies, and one of his great generals was a Hindu named Tilak. No doubt there was a great deal of savage slaughter of human beings, and barbarous vandalism in the utterly unnecessary destruction of the finest buildings, religious and secular, and, of course, no end of plunder and rapine; but that was common to all wars all over the world in those 'medieval' centuries, the general horror being relieved by generous acts of personal chivalry, here and there. We may also note that the religio-political wars and persecutions in other parts of Asia and throughout Europe, in all that period, were far more bitter and murderous, far more sharply defined as between Christian and Moor or Pagan, or Crusade against Saracen, or Inquisitional torturing of heretics, or war between Roman Catholic and Protestant, etc.

The incoming religion was an openly proselytising creed. The indigenous religion had thrown away and lost the vital power of assimilation, very clearly embodied in the Vedic injunction,

कृण्वन्तो विश्वमार्यम् ।

"*Aryanise*, civilise, the world". The noble significance of the word 'Arya', from 'ṛi,' to go, indicated by its etymology, may be expounded thus,

निवारणार्थं आर्त्तानां भर्तुं योग्यो भवेत्तु यः ।
अर्य्यते सततं चार्त्तैः स आर्य इति कथ्यते ॥

"He who is worthy to be approached for help in trouble, and to whom people in distress run for relief therefrom—he is Arya". The self-denying, other-helping, philanthropic person is the true Arya.

This assimilatively civilising, reforming, refining power, inherent in the very nature of Essential Religion, as a message for all from, and a call of all to, the God within and without—this power, the indigenous religion had formerly possessed and exercised fully and freely. Thereby, in pre-Buddhistic and Buddhistic times, it had, by ceremonies like the *vrātya-stoma*, accommodated and incorporated all sorts of 'nomad' groups, tribes, communities, scattered all over India, or coming from outside, into its own *śālīna*, 'settled' industrial–economical–political–religious organisation—of *chātur-varṇya*, four temperamental-vocational classes, which are 'the four inevitable natural estates of every civilised (or even semi-civilised, or even un-civilised) realm', and which are only systematised and regularised in and by Varṇāśrama Dharma with clear partitioning and balancing of rights and corresponding duties between the four. Not only had it lost this power of inclusion and assimilation; it had begun to exclude, to positively drive out; it was ossifying into innumerable mutually 'touch-me-not' castes and sub-castes.

Only when Hindus at large realise that 'Hinduism' has developed prolific germs of fissiparous degeneracy within itself, whereby it has literally driven away millions, generation after generation, from its own fold into the folds of other religions—only then can the further rapid decay of Vaidika Dharma be stayed; only then will it revive and purify itself, as Swami Dayanand desired, and will help to purify other religions also, by force of active example, from that excessive literalism, formalism, insistence on non-Essentials and neglect of Essentials, which is the main cause of all religious conflicts; only then will it draw the world's attention to those Spiritual Essentials which are common to *all* religions, and the insistence on which alone can promote good will and righteousness, and *therefore* peace and material prosperity throughout the human world.

It is well known that followers often try to outrun their leaders, and ruin their work by excess of zeal. History tells us that the Prophet Muhammad desired K͟hālid to bring to him a certain Arab chief, for persuasion into the fold of 'Islām', which word also has a noble significance, viz., "Love of God and submission to His will, whence inner and outer *salm*, *śhānti*, peace'. K͟hālid was unfortunately short of temper, long of sword, strong of arm. He was fashioned for the work, not of teacher and preacher, but of soldier. The Arab chief demurred to his peremptory summons. Instead of bringing him whole, body and soul, K͟hālid brought his head, separated from both, to the Prophet. Muhammad expiated the great sin by much fast, vigil, and prayer to God for forgiveness. So the Vedic scriptures, while enjoining cleanliness of body and purity of mind, as do all scriptures of all religions, nowhere give countenance to the self-righteous exclusiveness and hypocritical 'don't-touch-ism' which are the most outstanding features of Hinduism to-day.

It cannot be re-iterated too often that while Hinduism may have lost some adherents because of other reasons, it has lost a vastly greater number by perfectly voluntary conversion, out of spontaneous choice, as a means of quick and easy escape from the tyrannies of the caste-system, into the more sympathetic and solidarian brother-hood of, and lesser inequality of status in, the new religion. That in 1,200 years, from 700 A. D. to the present times, the Muslim population has grown from nil to about 25 p.c. and only 25 p.c. and the Hindu shrunk from about 100 p.c. to about 65 p.c., and only 65 p.c. (the remaining 10 p.c. being covered by other religions, Christian, Parsi, etc.)—this fact is mathematical proof, on the one hand, that the Hindu 'majority' as such has never thought of oppressing any other religious 'minority' as such, but has, instead, fostered many such minorities and helped them to grow in its midst; and, on the other hand it is proof that Islam has not spread by the sword, but by its 'attractiveness' for the so-called 'lower castes' of the Hindus, and by the 'repulsiveness' of Hinduism for those 'lower castes'—'repulsiveness' proved by the very adjective 'lower', *nīcha-jāti.*

Yet sufficient core of virtue was left in the older religion to enable it, not only to avoid complete extinction, but to touch and stimulate a responsive chord in the being of the younger. Many good and great teachers, *sūfis* and *auliyās*, *ahl-i-dil*, 'men of heart', as distinguished from *ahl-i-daul*, 'men of worldly goods and worldly mind', gradually arose in India within the pale of Islām, or came from outside, to teach to the people, as far as possible, in the new language of the times, in popular form, the *ilm-i-sīnā*, 'the doctrine of the heart', *Tasawwuf*, that is to say, the eternal Ātma-vidyā, Upanishad, Parā-vidyā, Guhya-vidyā, Rahasya-vidyā, as distinguished from the *ilm-i-safinā*, 'the doctrine of the page', aparā-vidyā; the 'spirit' as distinguished from the 'letter', the substance from the form, the core from the surface, the *jñāna-kāṇḍa* from the *karma-kāṇḍa*, the *haqīqat* from the *shariyat*.

On the other side, within the pale of Hinduism, appeared from time to time, good and great teachers, earnest men, devotees of God, *bhaktas* and *jñānīs*, *sadhus* and *sants*, saints and sages, individuals belonging to the same 'spiritual race' as the *sūfis* and *auliyās*, who also taught the same eternal truths in popular language and endeavoured to tone down the differences of the surface between creed and creed and caste and caste. Vedānta and Yoga of the one side, *Tasawwuf* and *Suluk* of the other, began to recognise fraternal resemblance in each other's faces. In the last quarter of the sixteenth century, the Emperor Akbar, like Emperor Harshavardhana, made a brave effort at reconciliation, an effort to complete, with the help of political influence, the spiritual work of the hermits, *durweshas* and *sannyāsis*, *faqīrs* and *mahātmās*, *ākhunds* and *swamis*.

But the time was not yet ripe. More heating and melting of the metals, in the fire of unhappy contests, was needed before they would weld into a sound and useful alloy. Similar, nay, much hotter, fires of wars due to fanatical frenzy were being used by Providence in the West, simultaneously, to stimulate, on the one hand, 'collective consciousness', 'common sentiment', on the plane of *mind*, in respect of deliberately-held *principles* of life-conduct, (as distinguished from merely physiological 'herd-ing' or even racial or national 'horde-ing', on the plane of the *body*), and, on the other hand, to make human beings realise the *reductio ad absurdum* of bigotry in religion; then to usher in the Age of Science; to lead that age, by excess of reaction, to the contrary extreme of frantic sensuality and irreligion and fanaticism in science, whence world-wars and world-bankruptcies; and then, let us hope and pray, to bring round again, on a much higher level, in the cyclic *chakra* of *saṁsāra*, the world-process, the Age of Religious Science or Scientific Religion, when the Human Race as a whole will see that Spirit and Matter, Soul and Body, Religion and Science, are interdependent, are aspects of the same one Truth.

The Gradual Fusion of Hindu and Islamic Cultures

In the centuries after the tenth, Islamic religion and also political rule slowly advanced, and 'Hinduism'—no longer true Vaidika Dharma—receded, socially and also politically, largely because of the same spirit of 'separation', and 'each for himself', and consequent weakening, internal and external. Yet the natural and inevitable result of all these historical processes was that Hindus and Mussalmans were constantly influencing each other, affecting and changing each other's ways of life, as neighbours, in times of peace, and even in war, for both Hindu and Muslim soldiers were often to be found on each side. All this tended necessarily towards an amalgamation of cultures. Even so, to-day, we see assimilation of European ways of thinking and living, by well-to-do Hindus and Mussalmans both, going on in the larger towns, and serving as a means of closer approximation between these two. The difference is that this new assimilation is one-sided, not reciprocated by the western resident, because he is politically dominant over both Hindu and Mussalman in a manner in which these two never have been over one another, and because he lives apart, is not a neighbour, is not a child of the soil (as every Indian Mussalman is now, being a descendant of Hindu ancestors), does not adopt India as his motherland, and does not make it his home permanently.

The amalgamation of the two cultures progressed slowly, because the outer forms of the two religions were different (though scarcely more so than those of the several sects of Hinduism or even those of Islām). But it progressed steadily because of constant neighbourhood and the interweaving of manifold social relations, and because, after all, the inner truths of both were the same.

They accepted ideas and practices from one another in philosophy, science (medicine, astronomy, etc.), fine arts

(architecture, music, painting, calligraphy, illustration and illumination of manuscripts, weaving and embroidering and dyeing of fine cloths, shawls, blankets, carpets of cotton, silk, wool, and gold and silver thread, jewellery, perfumery, etc.), and crafts (metal-working, utensil-fashioning, weapon-making, etc.). The ways of living (housing, clothing, dietary, etc.) approximated more and more. Both joined in each other's festivals freely. Hindu and Muslim kings wore the same type of dress, at least for formal occasions. Many of the most favourite flowers and confections of India to-day have Persian-Arabic names ; *halwā, barfi, murabbā, sharbat, gul-āb, gul-i-daudi, gul-i-shabbu, itr*, etc., have become household words in Hindu homes; so *dal, chapātī, roṭī, pūrī, kachaurī, tarkārī, phal, sāg, achār, pān, belā, chamelī* etc., in Mussalman homes. The names of the cloths, clothes, utensils, and articles of furniture, used by Hindus and Mussalmans alike, are an inseparable mixture of Sanskrit and Arabic-Persian words. It must also not be forgotten that if Muslims are meat-eaters, so are the vast majority of Hindus, the only difference being that the one avoid one animal, as too beneficent to humanity to be killed, and the other another as too unclean to be eaten. The scriptures of both equally forbid spirituous liquors.

As Hindus have added to their pantheon and their scheme of worship, all sorts of Muslim *takiyās, dargāhs, maqbarās, faqīrs, auliyās*, so would the Muslim masses have probably taken to *mandiras, tīrthas, sādhus, yogīs*, etc., also, if only Hindu priests had been less narrow-sighted and exclusive, and more large-hearted and liberal-minded. As it is, millions of Muslims offer milk and eatables on the altars of *Sītalā*, the goddess of small-pox, in villages, and, less 'happily', Shia Mussalmans have learnt to imitate the 'dont-touch-ism' of the Hindu.

Notwithstanding the exclusiveness of the Hindu, neo-Muslims often kept up relations with their old Brahmin priests. Learned men, poets, physicians, and astrologers of the other community were almost always attached to the courts and houses of royal and other powerful families of each community. In legal matters also, there was approximation. The Khojas of the south follow Hindu law. The Muslim Taluqdars of Oudh, like their Hindu confréres, observe the law of primogeniture, though it is not in accord with Fiqah. Muslims in the U. P. and the Punjab seldom give the daughter's share to her, though Fiqah requires it.

Such approximation was natural and inevitable, when the vast majority of the Muslim population was recruited from the ranks of the Hindus, and could not give up lifelong habits at once or altogether. Indeed, if the custodians of the Vaidika Dharma had retained the needed qualities of head and heart, they would have easily retained all this population in the old religion, and, more, would probably have been able to absorb the new-comers into it. As it was, the comparatively very few Mussalmans who came from other countries, when they settled here permanently, were compelled by the social and climatic conditions of the country to adopt many of its habits. Converted Hindu women, married into Muslim households, retained many of their religious and semi-religious customs and practices, and considerably modified Muslim home-life. If Hindu chiefs, in those early days, could have had the necessary length and breadth of vision, and could have, not only given daughters to, but taken daughters from friendly Muslim chiefs—as Pauraṇika Kshattriyas married women of the *deva, daitya, rākshasa, yaksha, gandharva, nāga,* and other races, as Chandragupta married a Greek princess—the fusion of the two cultures and religions would have been completed long ago.

The tale of the political and other alliances and friendly social relations; of chivalrous mutual loyalties to the extreme end, as in the case of king Hammīra of Ranthambhor and his Muslim refugee against Sultan Alauddin; of religious reformers in both communities with common aims of rapprochement, and of their partial success and partial failure, because of the action of priestcraft and kingcraft on the inherent weaknesses of human nature—this tale might be prolonged indefinitely.

Errors, evil ideas and evil practices have a tremendous power of persistence. The curse of caste-exclusiveness has crept into even the Muslim and the Christian populations of India, here and there, though, of course, in a milder form 'Milkī' Muslims try to marry with only 'Milkī' Muslims, and 'Khatik' Muslims with only 'Khatik' Muslims, e.g. in the U.P., and, in Goa, *Brahmin Khristis* (Christians) with *Brahman Khristis* and *Kshattriya Khristis* with *Kshattriya Khristis*, and so on. That a pernicious idea or practice, patently evil and irrational, may yet keep a whole vast and even intelligent, educated, civilised, nation in its vampire grip, for centuries after centuries, is illustrated by the fearful custom of the cramping, torturing, and disfiguring of women's feet in China—which was abolished only recently, after the great revolution there, in 1912. The case of the mutually 'untouchable,' rigidly hereditary castes and sub-castes of India is similar.

God, presumably, wants the world-drama to be prolonged indefinitely, and a drama is not possible without the *māyā* of both good and evil, true and false, love and hate, alliance and conflict, laughter and tears. Therefore the fusion is being delayed.

Almost the most important consequence, and the clearest proof, of the amalgamation, is the steady growth and development of the Hindustānī language, the destined Lingua Indica, in its two forms, Hindī and Urdū. But even here, Providence, for further testing, strengthening and educating of the people, has introduced antagonisms. The Upanishad tells how,

यद्देवा अकुर्वंस्तद् दैत्या अभिद्रुत्य पाप्मना अविध्यन् ।

"What the gods tried to do, of and for good, their step-brothers, the Titans, ran after and stained with sin and evil." The Purāṇic conception of the divine saint Nārada fomenting quarrels between kings by exciting their pride; the Hebrew conception of the Archangel Azaziel commanded by God to become Satan and tempt human beings for their testing and ultimate salvation through suffering—all expound the same eternally-repeated phenomenon. 'Religional' and 'political' mis-leaders and wire-pullers are always staining unselfish work with selfishness, always thwarting the efforts of the good leaders to guide mankind in the right direction. God would not be known if he were not contrasted with Satan. As the Persians say,

> "Subūt-i-shay ba zidd-i-shay."
> "All things are proven by their opposites".
>
> नूनगुणस्वपक्षो हि पूर्वपक्षैः प्रकाश्यते ।
> अस्तित्वमपि पक्षस्य प्रतिपक्षमपेक्षते ॥

Since 1,600 A. D.: The Larger Synthesis

A larger and fuller synthesis was needed than even the mysticism of the saints and the idealism of Akbar had contemplated, and than was possible in their day—a synthesis based on a more varied and more extensive experience, by the whole of India, and of more religions than two, and to be achieved with the help of the rationalising, reconciling, wedding power of widespread *science* and *philosophy*.

Accordingly, a third great religion and its corresponding civilisation, with potency of extraordinary material power, was brought upon the scene by Providence. Portuguese, Dutch, French, and English exponents of Christianity ('stained' with excessive avarice, as Islām is with violent excitability, and Hinduism with superstitious and hypocritical self-righteousness), came to India, and gave new turns and forms to the growth of the new culture. The emotional, as well as intellectual, political, economic, and scientific education of the people, for their ultimate solidarisation, through experience of new ways, new ideas, new conveniences, and the far too heavy price that has to be paid for them in the shape of new miseries, was intensively and extensively stimulated.

The convulsive and greatly belated effort made by India

in 1857, to recover her political footing, rapidly slipping away, or, rather, already slipped away, from beneath her, failed—because she had not yet learnt the lesson that Providence wished her to learn. She had yet to pass through more sad experience of 'separatism' and its consequences, in all the main concerns of life—religion, as the root and trunk, and domesticity, social relations, education, recreation, economics, politics, as the shoots and branches thereof. She had yet to realise—as indeed have all the mutually antagonistic nations of East and West alike, and as those of the West are trying to, slowly, through the new ideas and new methods of the League of Nations—that we are all parts of One Great Whole, all members and limbs of the same One Organism, like head, arms, trunk, and legs,

Bani-Ādam āzā-i-yak-dīgarand,

मुखबाहूरुपादवत्,

and that rational consultation, conference, co-operation, accommodation, are far more beneficial to all concerned, in the long run, than passional militancy, rivalry, sabre-rattling, aggressive self-assertion, and other-exclusion.

After 1857, the soul of Muslim religion and culture concentrated itself in one person largely for a new effort of self-rejuvenation. A great leader arose among the Mussalmans—Sir Sayad Ahmad Khan. He felt that if Islām was to be preserved from decay in India, some departure had to be made from the traditions of religious as well as political orthodoxy. He saw the necessity of taking the younger generation in hand. His great educational work, with its consequences, some foreseen, and others unforeseen, because of complications with new religio-political movements, is well-known.

Swami Dayanand Saraswati

By some deep disposition of the same all-pervading Oversoul, of which smaller credal, racial, national group-souls may be regarded as limbs and organs, the soul of Vaidika culture and

SWAMI DAYANAND SARASWATI

religion awoke almost simultaneously to a keen sense of the great weaknesses that had come upon it and were eating at its heart like cankers; and it also felt premonitions of the Materialism that was advancing from the west, in the wake of the foreign political domination, to despiritualise and demoralise India, by hypnotising it with the glamour of machine-power, and making its mind a mere machine for copying the outer mischievous ways of western civilisation, without their counterbalancing virtues.

The soul of Vaidika Dharma, in its urge of self-preservation by self-renewal, concentrated itself also in one individual largely for a time. A great leader arose among the Hindus also, simultaneously. Swami Dayanand Saraswati, after deep heart-searchings, wanderings in forests and in mountains, and inner conversion of soul from formalism to essential philosophical and spiritual religion, felt it his mission to purify Vaidika Dharma from the manifold evils that had crept into the practice of it and corrupted it very largely from a blessing into a curse. He felt inspired to endeavour to re-Aryanise, re-civilise, India, along lines that would restore the best of the old, and make possible the selection of the good and avoidance of the bad in the new. He retired from the world, became a 'sannyāsi'—a true 'missionary of God', vowed to poverty, devoid of worldly riches and desires, so that spiritual riches might flow in, in ample measure, in their place—and began the work of his mission, by public preaching, in Agra, in 1863. "Back to the Vedas; worship the One God within and without all; organise yourselves, organise your society, by the true *Varṇa* and *Āśrama Dharma*, of *karmaṇā varṇah*, 'four natural vocational classes according to temperament', and 'division of the individual life into the four natural stages', regularly"—this was his cry, as against *multitudinous*, time-wasting, intellect-stunting, superstition-fostering, separatism-nourishing *worship* of idols, animals, plants; and against rigidly hereditary and mutually 'touch-me-not-caste.'

Swami Dayanand began his public teaching in Agra, in 1863, as said above; and the Arya Samaj was founded, in Bombay, in 1875. Sir Sayad Ahmad's first school was started in Moradabad in 1861; and in 1875 was started his school at Aligarh which, two years later, became the M.A.O. College. Swami Dayanand wrote rationalist commentaries on the Vedas, with extraordinary learning. So did Sir Sayad Ahmad on the Quran. Both were *anathema* to the orthodox Pandits and Maulvis respectively. From 1863 to 1883, Swami Dayanand wandered incessantly, all over the Upper and larger half of India, like the Buddha, preaching, and holding disputations with the orthodox pandits, in town after town, and arousing keen interest and controversy among the Hindu public. The movement took strongest root in the Punjab and Western U. P., but its influence spread all over India, and helped to energise many other movements in which the reviving life of the Indian people is trying to find expression. After the Swami's passing away, as the best memorial to him, a D. A. V. School was founded at Lahore in 1886. It developed into a College in 1888. Its name is significant of its purpose, like that of the M. A. O. College of Aligarh, and, to-day, it is one of the most distinguished educational institutions of the land.

Swami Dayanand may certainly be said to be the first pioneer and principal author of the latest Hindu revival, as Sir Sayad Ahmad Khan of the Muslim. Justice M. G. Ranade, himself "a man truly great, judged by no matter what standard,"—this is the generous verdict of an Englishman, Kincaid, in *A History of the Maratha Empire*, I, 271,—wrote of the Swami, after his death:—

> "Religious fervour,... a daring and adventurous spirit born of a confidence that a higher power than man's protected him and his work, the magnetism of superior genius... a rare insight into the needs of the times and a steadfastness of purpose which no adverse turn of fortune could conquer, a readiness and resourcefulness rarely

met with,...true patriotism which was far in advance of the times, and a sense of justice tempered with mercy—these were the sources of strength which enabled him to organise a great movement like the Arya Samaj".

The Growth of Collective Consciousness

Many other movements and forces are very interesting and important to consider, for historical as well as practical purposes, in connection with the religious and moral growth of mankind, e.g., the Wahābi movement of Arabia, the Doukhobortski of Russia, the Babis and Bahāis of Persia, the Spiritists of U.S.A., the Theosophical Society (which has branches in all the continents, including some fifty civilised countries of the Earth), and, with special reference to the Hindu and Muslim revivals of India, the Brahmo Samaj, the Qādiānis, the Deobandi Anjuman-i-Islāmia, the Poona Śarva-janika Sabhā, the Fergusson College, the Gaṇapati festivals and Śivājī celebrations, the Nāgarī Prachāriṇī Sabhā of Benares, Swami Vivekānanda's mission and Ramakṛishna Homes of Service, the Shibli Dār-ul-ulum, and finally the Hindu Sabhās and Muslim Leagues. But they cannot be dealt with here at length, though they have all helped, directly or indirectly, the two revivals, the growth of the two collective communal consciousnesses, the two distinct common sentiments. The two have, very unfortunately, been separate and separatist, under the pressure of internal and external circumstances and crafty and sinister influences acting on human weaknesses.

The general idea of socio-religious reform may be said to be common to the Arya Samaj and Sir Sayad Ahmad's school of thinkers. At one time, the latter were dubbed as Néchāria (naturists) by orthodox Maulvis, some of whom have been heard to say jocularly to friendly orthodox Hindus: "Your Arya Samajis are our Wahābis". The Arya Samaj is as iconoclastic and unitarian in theory, as Islām. Yet because the one believed exclusively in the sacredness of the Sanskrit language and the word of the Veda, and the other in that of the Arabic language and the word of the Quran, and the one thought that one set of forms was the only correct way of worshipping God, and the other that another ritual was the only such, and neither cared to look beneath the words and the rites and note that the same ideas and heart-feelings and aspirations underlay both the different ways and terms, the preachers of each began to use very harsh language against the other, Khudā was overpowered by Khudī, Brahma was defeated by Māyā and the two sets of reformers clashed violently, and hindered the general progress instead of advancing it.

As a thoughtful writer of the Qādiāni sect says: "Custom, convention, book-worship, letter-worship, mullā-worship, pīr-worship, these, in short, were so many fetters on the Mussalman's soul, keeping it in a state of perpetual slavery. Death and decay was consequently the order of Muslim society".[1]

It will be readily observed that the words of the quotation describe Hindu society equally well and exactly, if we only substitute Pandit, Purohit, Guru, for Mullā and Pīr, and add tomb-worship in the one case and idol-worship in the other. It is also a noteworthy coincidence that Ghulam Ahmad of Qadian began his reforming work shortly after Swami Dayanand and Sir Sayad Ahmad began theirs. The motive idea of all was the same socio-religious reform. Yet because of the defects permeating the mental and moral atmosphere of the country, mentioned before, they, any more than the Wahābis or Ahl-i-Hadis, have not progressed as they should and would have, if they could have joined hands, on the common platform of science and reason and the new Lingua Indica, for the general welfare of the Indian people instead of any particular section, as the Japanese, Shintoists, Buddhists, Confucians, and Christians, or the Egyptian Mussalmans and Christians (Copts) have done for the welfare of their respective countries.

[1] Muhammad Yakub Khan, *Mirza Ghulam Ahmad, the Man.*

The Hindustānī language, splendid achievement and proof patent of the amalgamation, in one most important respect, of the Hindu and Muslim cultures, with its two forms, Hindi and Urdu, has done very great work in newly unifying India, by spreading a common medium of exchange of thought all over India. It has travelled into all corners of the country. Hindus by the million have studied Urdu; by the lakh, Persian; by the thousand, Arabic; and Mussalmans by the lakh, Hindi; and by the score, Sanskrit. If Mussalmans have studied Sanskrit little, the reason largely is that Pandits would not teach them. Scores of Mussalman poets have written splendid Hindi poems, some being classics of the highest order; and hundreds of Hindus have written admirable classic Urdu poetry as well as prose. Partly out of aversion to intellectual exertion, and partly out of mere communalist *zid*, Hindus and Muslims have, for sometime now, been jibbing, the one against so-called 'high Urdu', the other against 'high Hindi'. No doubt, some writers, in each, affect an unnecessarily stilted style; still, the knowledge of a few hundred extra words, Arabic-Persian for the one, and Sanskrit for the other, is eminently desirable. As the famous German thinker, poet, and statesman, Goethe, has said, "no one knows his own mother-tongue properly, unless he knows some foreign language also." The one way to get behind the sound to the sense, to distinguish between the word and the thought, to overcome letter-worship, to transcend not only idolatry but Vedolatry, Quranolatry, Biblolatry, is resolutely and with unbaffled intelligence, to recognise the same thought, the same friendly familiar face, behind many masks of many languages. The *Yoga-sūtra* points to the need for such discipline of the soul:

शब्दार्थज्ञानविकल्पैः संकीर्णा सवितर्का ।

Educational Institutions and the Collective Consciousness

Two other educational institutions, besides the D. A. V. College, which have directly helped in the Hindu Revival, may be referred to here. The Gurukula of Kangri was founded in 1902, by Swami Shraddhananda (then known as Mahatma Munshiram), a heroic figure, in life and in death, and worthy successor of Swami Dayanand. This institution is a direct product of the Arya Samaj. The other is the Benares Hindu University. It began as the Central Hindu College, founded in 1898, by Dr. Annie Besant, to whom also India owes especial gratitude. The original idea of Dr. Annie Besant and her Indian and European colleagues was to start a Theosophical College, where the common essentials of all the living religions would be taught side by side and consistently with other subjects, especially scientific. But the idea was not found workable. The more limited and feasible one was decided on, of an institution where endeavour should be made to rationalise and liberalise Hinduism by teaching modern subjects as well as the essential principles of Sanātana Ārya Mānava Vaidika Dharma (the same as those of the other living religions also, with the one exception of the systematisation of Varṇa and Āśrama), and thereby to solidarise the heterogeneous mass of Hindus, crumbling into thousands of fragments under the delusion of rigidly hereditary castes and sub-castes and mutually exclusive sects and sub-sects. The C. H. College grew into the Benares Hindu University in 1916, through the self-sacrificing and unremitting labours of Pandit Madan Mohan Malaviya. The M. A. O. College also became the Aligarh Muslim University in 1917.

A New Departure Needed

Such institutions have undoubtedly done great good work in their day, and helped to unify and strengthen their respective communities splendidly. But now they are over-shooting the mark, and stimulating, not healthy emulation, but harmful rivalry and antagonism.

It is high time that they should drop their 'denominational' and 'communal' names and character, and become simply and purely 'religious' and 'scientific, rational, and national', in the best sense of the several words. 'Good customs, by excess, do grow corrupt; then the old order should yield place to new, that God fulfil himself in other ways'.

If this is not done, the fissiparous tendency will increase, and instead of progress there will be terrible regress. Already we have not only Hindu and Muslim Universities and many Hindu and Muslim schools and boarding houses, but also a Kayastha Pāthaśālā, a Bhumihār College, a Kshattriya College, a Khālsā College, a Shiā College, many Arya Samaj Colleges and Schools, many Sanātana Dharma Colleges and Schools, many Christian Colleges and Schools, Agrawāl Schools, Khattri-Sārasvata Schools, Anglo-Bengali Schools, Chaube Hostels, Rajput Hostels, Kshattriya Hostels, Vaiśya Hostels, Marathi and Punjabi and Bengali Hostels, and so on. So, beginning with a general Social Conference, intended to reform, re-organise, and unify all Indian society and social life, we are now having scores upon scores of Conferences of the most miserable little sub-castes, even the names of which one had not come across before, unless one had occasion to wade through a Census Report. So, in matters civic and politic, each wretched little group, consisting of one petty sub-sect, however small in numbers, calling itself a 'minority', wants to have its own representative in every elective body of nominal or actual Swarāj, local or general self-government. So, trade-unions and services-associations and professional-associations are multiplying, each to promote the interest of *its own* members *against* all others—and this is happening not only in the East, but in the West, whence indeed the East has caught the new social diseases and their quack remedies. So, it appears, in the West, in pursuance of the principle of 'self-determination'—the same thing as Swarāj or self-government, but coined by President Wilson for just a change, as the other was getting hackneyed and monotonous,—many more new little States have, and are trying to, come into being, as based upon separate linguistic or racial or sub-racial groups. So, in India, new little Provinces, with 'separate' administrations, are forming.

What is this acute 'separatism' due to?— a separatism, the *reductio ad absurdum* of which is that every individual should 'self-determine' himself away and apart from every other self-determining individual.

It is due to the forgetting of the real nature of that *Swa* which, when rightly known, is the quintessence, the source, the ever-upwelling fount, of all genuine Religion, all Spiritual Purity, all unselfish trust and co-operation, whence all Material Prosperity; and, when wrongly misconceived, is the cause of all Spiritual Impurity and selfishness, whence perpetual *internecine* dissensions and consequent material misery. We have forgotten that '*Swa*' means the higher, unifying, all-including, un-selfish Universal Self; and have come to believe that it means only the lower, smaller, false, separative, self-ish self.

Circumstances made the separate development of the two communal common sentiments, Hindu and Muslim, inevitable, and even desirable, for the purpose of solidarising countless fragments into at least two strong groups, though the serious error of not keeping in the fore-front, as guiding Pillar of Light, the Ideal of the Higher Unifying Self, is frustrating even that purpose.

The Way of It

The time has come when a further and more difficult, but absolutely necessary, synthesis is needed, viz., the solidarising of the two sentiments and groups into one sentiment, Humanist Patriotism, and one group, the Indian Nation, or, better, the Indian *People*—for the word People has softer, more humane, more inclusive, and less aggressive and exclusive, associations than the word Nation.

This is possible only by a systematic study of (1) The *Essential Unity of All Religions*,[1] in all educational institutions,

[1] If detailed exposition be desired, the present writer's book, so-named (published by the Theosophical Publishing House, Adyar, Madras) may be referred to.

and (2) of the ancient *Science of Social Organisation*,[1] the true Varṇāśrama Dharma, in comparison with the many modern schemes of socialism and types of states and forms of government, to see whether (3) *Ancient Solutions of Modern Problems*,[1] which problems are harassing all nations and not only the Indian, are or are not practicable.

So long as there were some three hundred quarreling Daimyos (Rajas, Maharajas, Nawabs) in Japan, with a nominal Emperor Mikado) and a real Shogun (Prime Minister)—so long it was in imminent danger of being swamped beneath the flood of advancing western civilisation. But innate tremendous reserves of virtue and strength transformed the pygmy, by the miraculous power of the utter self-sacrifice and renunciation of the Daimyos, in two short weeks of June 1869, into a giant ready to face the world. Japan was inspired by, and aglow in every tissue with the Higher Self, even though she may not have clearly recognised—perhaps does not yet clearly recognise—that Higher Self, in consequence of which non-recognition, she is in danger of internal troubles.

If India is to recover her soul, if the work of the great Swami is not to go in vain, if the innermost and best hopes and wishes of all genuine reformers are to be fulfilled, if Material Prosperity is to come back to India, she must clearly understand the meaning of Spiritual Purity, must understand the nature of the true Spirit, the Higher Self, irrespective of, nay, as above and apart from, all particular languages and words and books (whether Veda, or Qurān, or Bible, or Avestā, or Grantha, or Tripiṭaka, or Agama), and must learn to recognise the Goodness and Wisdom, which are that Higher Self's primary manifestation in the human world behind any and every credal mask and label, wherever such Goodness and Wisdom may be found.

The Charter Oath of Japan (1868) says:—

"Knowledge shall be sought throughout the world to greatly

[1] If detailed exposition be desired, the present writer's book, so-named (published by the Theosophical Publishing House, Adyar, Madras) may be referred to.

rear the foundation of the Empire". Ancient *Manu*, the foundation of Vaidika Dharma as primal Digest of the Veda, enjoined the same, long ago:

स्त्रियो रत्नान्यथो विद्या धर्मः शौचं सुभाषितम् ।
विविधानि च शिल्पानि समादेयानि सर्वतः ॥

"Good brides, valuable sciences and arts, useful laws, sound ways of hygiene and sanitation, excellent sayings, wise maxims, and gems and jewels of all kinds—shall be gathered from everywhere". (The indication of inter-marriage, under proper conditions, may be noted incidentally).

Genuine Religious Reform consists, not in blind self-assertion and other-rejection, but in re-interpretation of the old, in conformity with changing times and circumstances and newly discovered facts; in rejection of whatever of our own 'old' has become unsuitable, in acceptance of whatever of any other's 'new' is shown by attested reason to be useful, and in grafting of it on to the good in our 'old'. This is what Swami Dayanand seems to have essayed in his new *Veda-Bhashya*:

पुराणमित्येव न साधु सर्वं
न चापि काव्यं नवमित्यवद्यम् ।
सन्तः परीक्ष्यान्यतरद्भजन्ते
मूढः परप्रत्ययनेयबुद्धिः ॥

Follow, not the Letter, but the Spirit

When men grow too much attached to forms and words, and begin to neglect the Spirit, then that Spirit, as Providence, arranges to get the forms and the languages broken up and replaced by others, whether the forms and words be religious (Veda, Qurān, Bible; Mandir, Masjid, Church; Svastika, Crescent, Cross; Image, Maqbarā, Eikon; etc.) or political (monarchy, oligarchy, republic, autocracy, aristocracy, democracy, nationalism, patriotism, glory, 'my country, right or wrong' etc.). The ultimate purpose of religious conflicts and political wars seems to be to lift Mankind from narrow-minded 'nationalism' and 'religiosity' to Philanthropic

Internationalism and Humanism.

Attachment to mere words and catchwords is such a great hindrance to the progress of the soul, that all scriptures warn us against it.

> Gar ze sirre mārifat āgah shawī,
> Lafz bi-guzārī, sue māni ravī.
> ग्रन्थानभ्यस्य मेधावी ज्ञानविज्ञानतत्परः ।
> पलालमिव धान्यार्थी त्यजेच्छास्त्राण्यशेषतः ॥

" Beware of the letter which killeth, and follow the Spirit which giveth life".

We must all learn to see the common 'meaning' behind the various 'words' of the various scriptures. We should dwell on the good points of others, the bad of ourselves. We should help others to find out the bad in themselves, by pointing out the bad in ourselves; by setting a good example. This is what the Swami endeavoured to do, when he pleaded against the corruptions that had crept so abundantly into Hinduism. Not by picking holes in other religions, and opposing and rejecting them, but by dwelling on their good points and combining and assimilating them with those of our own; not by emphasizing differences, but by insisting on agreements, may followers of the various creeds be reconciled. If we want peace and unity between the followers, we must first emphasise the essential unity between the religions. If we go on saying that the religions differ but that the followers should unite, we shall never succeed in uniting them.

In Japan—whose conditions, a hundred years ago, were, in many respects, similar to those of India, except that she was an island, and had a much smaller and more compact population—" Formalistic Confucius was welcomed, apparently without any friction (the indigenous religion being Shintoism). Democratic Mencius and other high apostles of classic note followed. Buddha together with his grumbling disciples, was received—it is true with some grumbling at first—and taken close to the bosom.

Mystic Laotse and his inscrutable adherents were not repulsed. The egoist Yang and the cosmopolite Mih were read and tolerated. The great reconciler was the saintly statesman, Prince Regent Shotoku, to whom the country owes much for its elevation from the status of semi-barbarism to that of culture, himself a devout Buddhist, an ardent patriot, and a thorough Chinese scholar. He announced the following principle:— "Shinto is the source and root of the Way, and, shot up with the sky and the earth, teaches man the primal Way; Classicism (Confucianism) is the branch and foliage of the Way, and bursting forth with man, it teaches him the middle Way; Buddhism is the flower and fruit of the Way, and appearing after man's mental power matured, teaches him the final Way. Hence, to love one in preference to another only shows man's selfish passion'........"[1] Christianity, at first repelled, because of political reasons, had hands extended and arms opened to her, so soon as those reasons vanished. "The introduction of another foreign system of faith will add a new cubit to the stature of the nation's mind, without depriving its predecessors of their authority. Indeed, each new religion enlightened the old".[1] And spiritual things and material things cannot be separated. Some western writers have "treated liberty entirely apart from religion; but historians will scarcely be able to sever the two. Without the right conception of personality, liberty is mere license. We talk of equality; but is the idea of equality possible without that of the Brotherhood of Man, which is a corollary drawn from the belief of the Fatherhood of One God? We talk of woman's rights and female suffrage; but can we have a just conception of sex equality without grasping the higher synthesis of personal equality of all individuals? We talk of social justice, of amelioration and relief; but is it possible to comprehend their real import, without first accepting the spiritual relation of man to man in the scheme of the universe?"[1]

[1] Dr. Inazo Nitobe, *Japan*, pp. 61, 365-370 (Modern World Series).

These are quotations from a Japanese writer. It is very re-assuring to find the ideas one holds valuable, regarded as such by another mind also—a mind of very high quality, too—and expressed by it in other words. The testimony of a son of marvellous Japan, who is not only a thoughtful and brilliant writer, but a 'practical' man of affairs, having worked for seven years in the International Secretariate of the League of Nations at Geneva, to the connection between Religion, on the one hand, and Civics-Politics-Economics, on the other, or, in the words of our title, between Spiritual Purity and Material Prosperity, is very valuable. We of India have to achieve similar purity by genuine Religious Reform, in the spirit of acceptance of the thoroughly tested Good, wherever it may be found, and the rejection of the Bad, however dear it may have become to us—always under the guidance of the One Supreme Spirit, Param-ātmā, the One God within and without all, the Universal Self, the Cause of all Synthesis, and of Co-operation in all Good Works.

The Spiritual League of All Religions as Complement of the League of All Nations

A great step is taken in the march of civilisation when men agree to have their disputes decided by a disinterested, impartial, philanthropic, rational third man as 'arbitrator', instead of settling them by duelling and the fighting of retainers. (The modern 'law-court' is very different from the 'philanthropic arbitrator', by the way. It only repeats the physical duelling and hired sword-play in terms of intellectual duelling and hired tongue-play, and is more ruinous to the parties concerned, perhaps, than the older way. It illustrates the psychic law of 'Titans' 'staining with sin' the work of the gods). A very great step, the penultimate step, in civilisation will be taken when the nations all agree to decide their disputes, not by war, but through Tribunals composed of the most venerated 'Ṛishis' of all the nations. In the ancient days of India, it seems, such

Ṛishis used to act as travelling Inspectors of States and Kings, besides having permanent locations in several famous Āśramas, to which kings and ministers used to go for instructions The Human Oversoul seems to be making a great effort to induce mankind to take this step towards the Great Synthesis, the larger concept of Human Brotherhood, on the Material, i. e., political and economical side, by means of the League of Nations, started in 1920, and located at Geneva, after the lesson of the need for it had been driven home by the awful devastation of life, labour, resources, during the World-War. The League has its travelling and inspecting Commissioners also. But the work of this penultimate step will not be really and sincerely done, will not be completed, until the ultimate step is taken, of evolving a Spiritual League of All Religions, which is the indispensable complement to the Material League of Nations. The Theosophical Society, which was born in the U S. A. in the same year that saw the birth of the Arya Samaj in India, viz., 1875, had in it, perhaps still has, the seed of such a Spiritual League in it. The U. S. A. made a great effort to vivify the seed, with its Parliament of Religions, in 1893. It is making yet another and apparently much greater effort, with the World Fellowship of Faiths, to be held also at Chicago this year, 1933.

Conclusion

The Arya Samaj can make a very valuable contribution to this work of placing the Keystone on the Arch of Civilisation, and fulfilling the purpose of great Reformers like Swami Dayanand, by interpreting afresh the Varṇāśrama Mānava Dharma in the light of the Upanishads, the Jñāna-kāṇda, the Ved-ānta, the Crown of the Veda; for this Vedānta teaches of the One Life and Consciousness which runs through and upholds all the Universe, which is the Principle of Unity amidst Multiplicity, which is the source of the Righteousness, on the achievement of which, all things else add themselves, and the realisation of which in and through Varṇāśrama Mānava Arya Vaidika Sanātana Dharma is the essence of the Spiritual Purity whereon only is based lasting Material Prosperity.

॥ ॐ ॥

आत्मा एव अधस्ताद्, आत्मा उपरिष्टाद्, आत्मा पुरस्ताद्, आत्मा पश्चाद्, आत्मा दक्षिणतः, आत्मा उत्तरतः, आत्मा एव इदं सर्वं, इति। स वा एष एवं पश्यन्, एवं मन्वानः, एवं विजानन्, आत्मरतिः, आत्मक्रीडः, आत्ममिथुनः, आत्मानन्दः, स स्वराट् भवति, तस्य सर्वेषु लोकेषु कामचारो भवति। अथ ये अन्यथा इतो विदुः, अन्यराजानः ते क्षय्यलोकाः भवन्ति, तेषां सर्वेषु लोकेषु अकामचारो भवति। ······ एतद् एव अहं मनुष्याय हिततमं मन्ये यन् मां विजानीयात्।······ सः अन्वेष्टव्यः सः विजिज्ञासितव्यः।······ स आत्मा स विज्ञेयः।······ स स्वराड् भवति य एवं वेद। (उपनिषदः)

ॐ सर्वस्तरतु दुर्गाणि सर्वो भद्राणि पश्यतु।
सर्वः सद्बुद्धिमाप्नोतु सर्वः सर्वत्र नन्दतु॥ ॐ

BENARES

BHAGAVAN DAS

SWAMI DAYANAND

I wish to mention this, that Ṛishi Dayanand's contribution to the cause of the regeneration of Hindu Society is so great, that he may be regarded as one of the greatest Hindus of the nineteenth century. His doctrines in the field of the social uplift of so-called depressed classes of India will in future be more and more appreciated by the Hindu Society. In this connection, one cannot but think of the services rendered by late Lala Lajpat Rai, Swami Shraddhanand, and the leaders of the Arya Samaj movement and the Gurukula. The work of the Arya Samaj in spreading education among the women of India is the best example of what Swami Dayanand wished to do to save the Hindu Society from degeneration. May I say that your (Har Bilas Sarda's) noble efforts to check child-marriage and to spread education among the women of India is also a living monument to Ṛishi Dayanand's influence?

Lastly, I wish to say that a nation or society cannot live, unless it becomes conscious of its mission in relation to the progress of humanity. Swami Dayanand, through his teachings, succeeded in infusing a new spirit into Hindu Society. The Arya Samaj has done a very great service to the rejuvenation of Hindu Society, and it is imperative that it should adjust its activities as well as its social outlook in accordance with the latest demand of *Time* and the social needs of the Hindus. It must be prepared to assimilate all that is best in the West and inculcate it among the Hindus. Deterioration of Hindu Society began with its isolation; it aided in strengthening encrusted superstitions. Let us hope that the followers of Ṛishi Dayanand will work with a world-vision for the regeneration of the Hindu Society and Humanity.

MUNICH, GERMANY — TARAKNATH DAS

SWAMI DAYANAND SARASWATI

INDIA is a land of infinite diversity and yet some of the earliest researches into human Unity have been conducted on the Indian soil. The earliest documentary evidence of this pursuit of unity in diversity is to be found in the Vedas, the most ancient literary document of the Indo-European family. The Vedas pre-suppose the existence of the Pre-Aryans, no longer a mere historical hypothesis, but visualized clearly to-day through the marvellous archæological finds of the Indus Valley civilization. It was the genius of the Vedic Aryans to have assimilated the Non-Aryan elements into a supreme Aryan synthesis in the Vedic Age. Amidst the bewildering multiplicity of *varnas*, the Vedic Aryans ever remembered and adored the *Supreme Being* above all *varnas.* That was the key-note of the success of the Vedic experiment; and the foundation of all that is enduringly Indian was laid in the Vedic age partially reflected in the grand literary wreckage of our Vedic literature. Age after age new thinkers, new jurists, new sociologists have attempted to build ever so many new systems; but their principles of co-ordination or conflict pointed ever towards the Vedas with the phenomenal tenacity of a deathless historical memory.

The limpid current of Unity came to be choked so often under the historical *débris* of diversity, but our great spiritual Teachers and Leaders have ever attempted to rekindle our ancestral memory of Unity through millenniums. Swami Dayanand Saraswati was such a leader and while we offer our respectful homage to his sacred memory on the fiftieth anniversary of his death, we only pay our tribute to the eternal principle of Unity pervading Hindu thought and civilization.

By tragic contradiction, alas, Hinduism came to be synonymous with divisions and discriminations of the worst type ! And it was in that age of degradation of our national history that there appeared a few individuals whom our so called "educated" India ignored for years and yet who are coming into their own by their inalienable birthright to immortality. The 19th century history of India opened with the prophetic career of a Brahmin of Bengal, Ram Mohan Roy (1772-1833), the founder of the *Brahmo Samaj*, who fought single-handed to re-establish Unity, (the basic truth of the Vedanta) in the relation between man and man. A Brahmin boy of Kathiawar was born in a town in the Morvi State to grow into Dayanand Saraswati (1824-1883), the founder of the *Arya Samaj*. The fiftieth anniversary of the death of Dayanand synchronizes with the centenary of the death of Ram Mohan Roy; and we cannot help reflecting, what would have been the character of the world-opinion about India, if there were no Ram Mohan Roy and no Dayanand Saraswati to redeem the gloom of our disgrace and degradation in relegating to the rank of the "depressed classes", forty to fifty millions of our own people, inhabiting the same country, sharing the same joys and sorrows! Whatever opinion posterity may have about the equipment of Dayanand to explain and interpret the Vedas, it cannot help benefiting by the intuitive urge in the great Reformer to purge Hindu society of the *caste-system* and to give the Hindus a new lease of life through equalisation of status and unity of purpose. Fifty years after the death of Swami Dayanand, another great leader from Kathiawar, Mahatma Gandhi has to stake his very life for the vindication of the same principle with reference to the same depressed classes. Thus Ram Mohan and Dayanand are still alive. Our homage to those Great Unifiers of our history and gratitude to them for their inestimable contributions to the cure of our diseased society and the uplift of our degraded people!

CALCUTTA UNIVERSITY

KALIDAS NAG

RAM GOPAL

DAYANAND—THE MAN AND HIS MISSION

Personal

DAYANAND lay on his sick-bed, which in a few days proved to be his death-bed, in a room of the Bhinai House at Ajmer in the month of October 1883. As a boy of twenty years, and one deeply imbued with the ideals and teachings of the Arya Samaj, I went several times to that house and enquired of others after his health. He was my ideal Ṛishi in those youthful days, and I looked upon him almost as a god. The enquiries, daily made about his condition, gave one little hope for his recovery, but, as the saying goes, "while there is life, there is hope," though ever so little. This hope was at last extinguished on the evening of the 30th October 1883, when, with the setting of the Sun in the heavens, the Sun of Sanskrit learning and social and religious reform also set. I was then present in the adjoining room together with my school friends, Messrs. Har Bilas Sarda and Ram Bilas Sarda, and the sad news filled our youthful anxious hearts with sorrow and our eyes with tears. Next day, his bier was prepared and his dead body conveyed to the crematorium, followed by a huge procession consisting of his numerous admirers and sympathizers. There he was cremated and his ashes collected in a casket and brought over.

Swami Dayanand visited Ajmer several times on his lecturing tour during the six or seven years prior to his death. The fame of his lectures and of his exposition of the Vedas and Śāstras spread all over the city. I was then an inmate of the Boarding House of the Government College, Ajmer. The Superintendent, Master Jamna Das, was as eager as were most of the boys to go and hear him. Before I saw him and heard his first lecture, my youthful imagination had pictured Swamiji as one of the old Ṛishis,— slender, tall, with a copious tuft of hair on his head, and a long flowing beard, as represented by the current pictures of the ancient Yogīs. But when I went and saw him for the first time in flesh and blood, to my amazement I found him a great and striking figure,—clean-shaved on head and face, bare-bodied with only a *laṅgoṭī* on, nearly six feet tall, strong, muscular, well-knit, and of ample proportions— a figure almost Herculean in its build and strength, and splendid enough to excite the envy of any professional athlete or *pahalwān* (wrestler). There was yet another surprise in store for me when I heard his lecture. I thought that his discourse would be couched in the old orthodox style— as archaic, flat and dull, dry and jerky, as that of the ordinary *kathās* by the priests of Jainism or Brahmanism which I had occasionally heard before. But Dayanand's discourse was quite different, both in matter and manner, being full of the current topics of social and religious abuses and their reform, and illuminated by flashes of wit and humour and interesting anecdotes to illustrate his points. Two or three of these have still stuck in my memory:—

(1) गबरगंड राजा, टके सेर भाजी टके सेर खाजा—

In the reign of the haughty but foolish and muddle-headed kings, vegetables and greens were sold at the same rate as sweetmeats. Everything was at a dead uniform level.

(2) गबरगंड राजाओं का न्याय देखो—

"Look at the justice administered by such royal dunderheads." A complaint was brought to a *Gabargaṇḍa* Rājā by the owner of a wall which through excessive rain had fallen down, while a goat was passing by and was killed by the fall. Each party charged the other with mischief and destruction. The Rājā decided that each party was to blame. The wall-owner was sentenced to pay the price of the goat, while the goat-owner was to pay the price of the wall. Such was the equal justice of Gabargaṇḍa Rājās in their kingdoms.

(3) चढ़ो बेटा सूली पर, स्वर्ग का दरवाज़ा खुला है—

BHINAI HOUSE, AJMER,
where Swami Dayanand Saraswati breathed his last.

"Get up on the scaffold, my son; the gate of Heaven is open to you." In time of danger, the cowardly priests used to hide behind and place their followers in front of the firing line with all sorts of inducements.

So far as my brief, boyish, personal observation went, I never saw him in a hurry, impatient, angry, upset, or in a haughty mood. He was always calm-tempered and unruffled, but ever active and determined. In his talk and discourse, I noticed a peculiar charm, a soft smile playing about his lips. His face seemed to me to be the index of a mighty force, a tremendous energy, a determination and courage to conquer all obstacles and accomplish his task. So great was my youthful fascination and admiration for Swamiji that I used to go to his place of residence, sit down and watch elderly people talking to him and asking questions on various topics. Once my father took me along with him to Swamiji and introduced me to him. I was then a lad of about seventeen. Swamiji spoke a few kind words of encouragement to me advising me to be always active as a *Vidyārthī* (student) in learning *Vidyā* and in improving myself. The kind look, tone, and speech of the great man so indelibly impressed themselves on my mind that they have remained fresh and full of life to this day. I treasure that incident as one of the most inspiring memories of my boyish days. He was my first Inspirer, my first Torch-bearer. Since then, I have tried to drink deep at the fountain of Learning and have kept my mind open to the reception of truths discovered by the truth-seekers and truth-propagators of the world.

General

A Great and Good Man—Dayanand was a great and good man, a great reformer, a grand personality. But to call a man great and good, we must know some of the elements that constitute greatness and goodness:—

(a) The mental attitude and effort to search for truth, to cultivate the passion for truth, to follow the light of truth wheresoever it may lead its votary,— this is one element;

(*b*) Simplicity, sincerity, veracity in thought, speech and deed, is another;

(*c*) Courage, fearlessness, self-sacrifice, valiant determination to express and propound the truth that is in one, is yet another;

(*d*) A large heart full of sympathy, benevolence, charity for weak, erring and suffering humanity, coupled with intelligent study and endeavour to relieve and reform such humanity, is the fourth element.

Can there be a nobler, a grander sight in this world than to see a well-equipped, resolute man, a hero, a great thinker, constantly striving with heart and brain to break the bars and barriers, the chains and fetters of the human mind, and working for the uplift, emancipation and well-being of the millions of his fellow-beings sunk in ill-health, ignorance, apathy, slavery and poverty? Dayanand possessed these elements of goodness and greatness in a large measure. He had his own vision of reform and reconstruction of Hindu Society and he laboured hard to fulfil that vision. Other thinkers and workers, prophets and pioneers, in India and other parts of the earth, have their visions and ideals of a renovated society, and they are busy with their plans and endeavours to realize them. All honour to each and every one of that noble band!

His Passion for Truth—In his Autobiography, Dayanand says:—" The purpose of my life is the pursuit of Truth in thought, speech and deed." Truth was indeed the dominant passion of his life. He began, as most of us did, at that time, as an orthodox Hindu. But in the light of his ever-expanding study, knowledge, and experience, he changed his earlier beliefs. Starting as a devotee of the cult of Śiva, he became a Vedāntist, and at last, a worshipper of the One God who (in the Vedas) was expressed and characterized under many and diverse names. Rejecting the pious literature of later times, the medley of *Purāṇas* and the books of the *Mahābhārata* which the orthodox priests and pandits exalted as sacred scriptures, he came to place his entire faith and reliance on the Vedas. But he laid particular emphasis on the common root and meaning of the word *Veda* and *Vidyā*, that is, knowledge or science. Thus the one fundamental article of his creed was Truth as discovered by knowledge or science. He believed that "the four Vedas were the books of True Knowledge". There was however no limitation, no finality to Truth and he laid no such limit or boundary to its search and discovery. After giving his conception of God and His Attributes, in the first two principles of the Arya Samaj that he established, he laid clear and unqualified emphasis on our duty to accept Truth and renounce Untruth whenever discovered. This is embodied in the Fourth Principle as follows:—

> "We should always be ready to accept Truth and to renounce Untruth."

It is worthy of note that he did not in any manner qualify and narrow the principle of Truth, or our duty to accept Truth by any such words "as discovered by me, or as enunciated by the Vedas only". He meant that we are to look for, investigate, discover and accept truth from every source, in every department of human endeavour and activity. One of the highest and noblest, maxims of Hinduism is—सत्यं परमो धर्मः

> "The highest religion is the religion of Truth."
>
> "The greatest reverence is the reverence of Truth."

Let us, therefore reverence and follow truth with an open mind and heart. *This is clearly the one lesson, the one inspiration, to be drawn from the life and teachings of Dayanand.* Most healthy minds, if left in a free and fertilizing environment, go on growing and changing their beliefs,— religious, political, social or economic, in the course of their development and in the light of their larger experience and knowledge. There is a positive danger in remaining for ever static or stationary all our life. The clothes of our body have to be changed with its growth, as well as those of the mind with its development. I remember how, now that I am old, in my 70th year, I have dropped many of my beliefs of childhood, boyhood and manhood. I have passed by and left behind many a sign-post, many a mile-post—each of which I had once thought as the last post or goal—in my pilgrimage to the shrine of Truth. I look back upon those early childish beliefs with a smile now; but they appeared so real, so truthful, then. How I once believed thoroughly—with the thoroughness of ignorance—in fantastic myths and legends, in magic and witchcraft, in the marvels and miracles said to have been performed by holy men or by gods and demons, and in all the extraordinary stories of ghosts and demons, witches and wizards, told me by elderly folks. These were soon dispelled and shattered by the wholesome teaching of the Arya Samaj. New beliefs and convictions have since come to me and I am still on the road to Truth. The process of change and development, begun by Dayanand, has been carried on by other thinkers, philosophers and scientists. It has continued so far, and I hope and wish that it will continue to the last.

Static vs. Dynamic Forces—In a well-ordered, educated and disciplined society, there should be a just balance, a happy equilibrium, between the static and dynamic social forces. But there are times in human history when, through diverse unfavourable conditions, that balance is disturbed and static forces come to predominate over the dynamic. Such was the case with India for over ten centuries. But with the advent of the British rule, there came more settled and favourable conditions of life and progress. One of the indirect, undesigned results of English education and foreign culture was perceptible in the stirrings of a new life, new thoughts and ideas, an awakening to the religious, moral, political and social evils and abuses in our midst. Several great leaders and reformers arose in the land clamouring and agitating for the removal of such wrongs and abuses and founding several organizations to carry out the needed reforms,—the

Brahmo Samaj, the Theosophical Society, the Prârthanâ Samaj and others. But the most powerful and extensive of all reform movements was the Arya Samaj founded by Dayanand who gave it a deep, democratic basis by insisting on the oneness of God, our common humanity and on our common well-being or prosperity.

His Ideals—Dayanand voiced the ideals of Human Solidarity, of Progressive Humanity, more than any other man of his time in India. This is conclusively borne out by the Ten Principles of the Arya Samaj. Excluding the first Two, which are in the nature of a personal confession of faith in God and His Attributes, we come to the Third which enjoins the Aryas (gentlemen or civilized persons) to study the Vedas and Sciences. With a liberal interpretation of these terms, Aryas and Vedas, there will be no dispute about the excellence of the principles. But all the other seven Principles are wide enough, vital and beneficent enough to apply to all mankind. They are ethical injunctions, commandments, or duties, to which no possible objection could be taken by any individual, or group of individuals —nation, society, social group or organization of any size or kind, scientific, ethical, religious, political, or sociological. I have looked far and wide for similar principles or provisions, for similar articles of creed, in any other religious organization—Christian, Muslim, Buddhist, Hindu or Zoarastrian—but I have not found them, or anything like them, in any of those great Faiths. There is not a trace of narrow-minded dogmatism, infallibility, intolerance or exclusiveness as is seen in other religions, excepting only Buddhism. They are characterized by utmost catholicity, liberalism, and liberty, allowing full and free scope for the exercise of our individuality and of our freedom to think, act, choose, and behave as moral beings, with a disposition—

> "To be ever ready to accept Truth and reject Falsehood;" *(4th Principle)*
>
> "To be actuated by Love, Righteousness, and Justice,

in our dealings with others;" (*7th Principle*)

"To dispel *Avidyā* (ignorance) and diffuse or promote *Vidyā* (knowledge or Science);" (*8th Principle*)

"Not to be content with promoting one's own happiness or well-being but to consider one's welfare only in the welfare of all;" (*9th Principle*)

"To have due regard to one's own individual freedom and development with the ultimate object of promoting general weal; or, in other words, subordinating, disciplining and developing self so as to promote social welfare." (*10th Principle*).

Thus the claim is well-founded that Dayanand *voiced* the highest ideals of the human race, the ideals of man's moral conduct and progress, both individual and collective.

As a Religious Reformer—Every sane and thinking patriot of India was filled with pain, resentment and disgust with the priestly class for having cramped, dwarfed and enervated Hindu society by its numerous harmful ordinances, evil practices, and immoral sanctions in the name of religion. Dayanand also lamented these wrongs and showed his intense dislike of their ill-effects. Of the many telling phrases and expressions he coined and put in circulation to mark his condemnation of them, there are two that have stood out in my memory ever since I heard them uttered from his lips—(1) पोपलीला (Popish play, fraud or deception) and (2) पुजारियों और पंडों का पाखंड (priestly pomp and imposture). *He knew the dangers of Fanaticism, Intolerance and Bigotry of a narrow, religious mind.* He must have had an idea of the tragic history of the struggle for freedom of thought which, checked and thwarted, has brought untold mischief and ruin to mankind, but which, encouraged and fostered, has led to progress, social health and civilization. We see how, in Europe, the frightful incubus of the Roman Catholic religion threw back and strangled for nearly a thousand years the civilization bequeathed by Greece and Rome. That religion was not content with spiritual power only, but aimed at and grasped the civil power of the State also. And, becoming powerful, it throttled all progress of thought, all civilization, by founding the Inquisition. By establishing its Inquisitorial Courts in various countries of Europe, but principally in Spain, France and Italy, it aimed at crushing out all independence and originality of thought that seemed to differ in the slightest degree from its irrational beliefs, submissive habits and narrow outlooks on life and nature. Every student of history is familiar with its repressions, punishments, tortures and atrocities. Every school boy knows how it imprisoned the great philosopher Bruno and the scientist Galileo. Bruno was kept in prison for eight years, coerced and tortured to recant and, failing to recant, was sentenced to be burnt alive and executed in Rome; while Galileo, though seventy years old, was imprisoned and tortured for discovering and asserting the truth that the earth moved round the sun, and, on recanting, was let off. Dogmatic Religion thus blocked the way to intellectual progress for a thousand years in Europe. But when startling discoveries and inventions were made, such as the discovery of America, the invention of the art of printing, Writers, Thinkers and Reformers arose and challenged the right and authority of the Romish Church. Martin Luther, the greatest and boldest of the Protestant Reformers of the sixteenth century, was one of the heroic band. It was then that the European Renaissance began. The dynamic forces, so long pent up, were now liberated and led to the revival of arts and letters, science and philosophy, inspite of the ever relentless and unceasing hostility and opposition of Religion. History shows the eternal warfare between science and religion. To avert this danger of hostility and warfare, to prevent the poisonous falsities and fallacies of Dogma and Superstition from taking root in society and government, Dayanand made ample safeguards by laying the utmost emphasis on these fundamentals :—

I. "The search, discovery and acceptance of truth

wherever found, and by whomsoever found, and by whatsoever means found;"

II. "The motive force of all our actions should be Love, Righteousness and Justice in our dealings with others;"

III. "That our true well-being and happiness should lie only in the well-being and happiness of all our fellow-beings."

As a Social Reformer—He denounced the superstitions, harmful and misleading beliefs, customs and practices of Hindu society. I remember him thundering against the demoralizing effects of child-marriage, the extravagance of marriage expenses, the insanity of post-mortem feasts, Purdah system, denial of female education, idolatry, superstition, caste, untouchability, and all the cramping customs, laws, usages, and beliefs, which have made Hindu life one life-long repression, a galling yoke, a slavery of the most unmanly, soul-oppressing type. Take only one evil, for instance, the horrible caste-system, and look at its blighting effects on life and intellect. It has made all the members of caste utterly helpless puppets, like so many sheep blindly following the example of the flock, with its thousand interdicts about food and drink, about sanctity and pollution, about social intermingling, and social intercourse. A member of one caste, however friendly, must not eat or drink with one of another caste on pain of excommunication. He or she must not cross the seas; must not eat interdicted food or drink: a girl must not marry late; one may not marry outside the caste. It has taken away one's individual choice or liberty of action in all the important events of one's life. It has cut up and divided society into numerous water-tight compartments, into so many reserved, isolated and exclusive groups. As another Indian Reformer (K. C. Sen) reminds us,—

"Look at yourselves enchained in customs, deprived of freedom, your better senses and better feelings smothered under the crushing weight of customs !......

> "Say from your own experience whether you are not hemmed in on all sides by a system of things which you cannot but hate and abhor; whether the spiritual government, under which you live, is not despotism of the most galling and revolting type, oppressive to the body, injurious to the mind, and deadly to the soul ?
>
> "Are you not yoked to some horrid customs (practices and beliefs) of which you feel ashamed and which, to say the least, are a scandal to reason ?"

Dayanand opened the eyes of his countrymen to most of these evils. He worked for the emancipation of Hindu society all his life, by pen and tongue, by debate and discussion. With this laudable object, he wrote his great book *Satyārtha Prakāsh* (The Light of Truth). Such end and object of human effort has been expressed by another scholar, thinker and patriot, Mahadev Govind Ranade, in these words :—

> "To renovate, to purify, and also to perfect the whole man by liberating his intellect, elevating his standard of duty, and developing to the full all his powers...... With a liberated manhood, with buoyant hope, with a faith that never shirks duty, with a sense of justice that deals fairly by all, with unclouded intellect and powers fully cultivated, and, lastly, with a love that overleaps all bounds, renovated India will take her proper rank among the nations of the world."

Conclusion—In this short paper, I have spoken of the man simply as Dayanand without prefixing or affixing any high-sounding embellishments. Nonetheless, I reverence him as a great soul, a great emancipator of the race according to his light. Adjectives and epithets mostly hide the true man and cover him with a false glamour. Kings and priests, temporal and spiritual despots flourish in a submissive society and demand such titles. They love florid, fulsome praise and flattery as the very breath of their nostrils. They are the great sinners in encouraging the spirit of slave-mentality. In oriental despotisms, how often do we not see or read of servants, slaves or followers running into hysterics in praising their masters, superiors or high-placed persons, using hyperbolic language, piling up extravagant epithets and honours on the objects of their praise? Each petty Rājā, Chief, or Landlord loves to be called by his subjects and followers,—Lord, Lord of the Earth, Source and Centre of all Power and Prosperity, etc. Every member of the self-styled sacred or privileged class, such as an ordinary Brahmin, a priest in yellow robe, a Sādhu smeared with ashes, no matter how ignorant and worthless he may be, expects to be, and is usually accosted and reverenced as Mahārāja (a great person), *Swami*, Master, Father, or by other highsounding titles. The West has largely dropped this bad habit. But the East with its conservative traditions still holds on to it. A sane and sturdy manhood ought to rebel and set its face against this kind of unjustified, senseless worship and exaltation. In speaking of the subject of this character sketch as only Dayanand, we place him in the *Valhalla* of immortals,— Rāma, Kṛishṇa, Arjuna, Vālmīki, Patañjali, and a host of other great souls, ancient and modern. The manhood and individuality of each stands in full light and lustre by its own worth.

BANGALORE

RAMGOPAL

SWAMI DAYANAND, ONE OF THE GREATEST SONS OF INDIA

A great friend has asked me to jot down what I know of the Greatest Indian who has adorned the nineteenth century. He is known throughout the world and hardly needs any introduction. I have had the pleasure and good fortune of listening to his learned sermons. His disciples are now celebrating his fiftieth anniversary at Ajmer.

Swami Dayanand was a true Maharshi. He revived the Vedic religion and showed that it fitted in with the lofty ideals of human fraternity. Monotheism and fellow-feeling were the soul of his creed. To idolatry and the caste-system he was bitterly opposed. Peace and sympathy were his watch-words, and social uplift his goal. Formation of high character and admission of the fair sex as equal partners were his dear aims. He placed education in the forefront, and to impart useful knowledge and to inculcate principles of true religion he founded many a 'Gurukul'. Child-marriage he condemned as vigorously as he supported widow-remarriage and thus he wanted to root out the two corroding cancers of Hindu Society. So dear was the sense of pure justice to him that in his theology he has propounded the constitutional character of the Almighty Himself.

He was a commanding personality, a Sanskrit scholar of the first order, a great philosopher, a true patriot, an ardent social reformer, a conscientious searcher after truth, a rousing preacher and an embodiment of all that is virtuous. The earnestness, the energy and the enthusiasm with which he ceaselessly carried on his noble mission throughout his life has earned him an undying name.

It is no wonder if he is not viewed with a kindly eye by members of other religions. After all his creed is recognised, and that very reasonably, to be a dangerous rival. Here admission is unrestricted and tenets convincing and unassailable. I am glad to say that the Samaj is gradually and steadily adding to its fold. It would amuse some people to know that I have come across one or two distinguished personages who appeared to be lulled into the belief that the Arya Samaj is dead. I had the pleasure of discussing the question with them heart to heart—with what results, I need not say. Personally, I see a great future for the Samaj, if the preachers devote themselves mainly to the religious side and avoid the pitfalls of politics.

UDAIPUR — SUKHDEV PRASAD

I join in paying my tribute to the memory and work of Swami Dayanand Saraswati.

INDORE — G. D. MADGAVKAR

I appreciate the very great work, social and educational, which the Arya Samaj and its workers are doing throughout North India and some times even in certain places in the South. I wish your endeavour every success.

WALTAIR, MADRAS — RADHA KRISHNAN

SWAMI DAYANAND—SOME FEATURES OF HIS CHARACTER

SWAMI DAYANAND was unquestionably the initiator of the movement for the rejuvenation of India. He was, as he said in one of his discourses, about fifty years ahead of his times. Almost all the potent ideas that are now producing a kind of spiritual convulsion in the land, we owe to him. In the seventies and early eighties of the last century, he worked for Swadeshi, removal of Untouchability, a common language, emancipation of women and Swarājya. Unfortunately the period of his active ministry was very brief. It may be considered to have begun with the establishment of the Arya Samaj in 1875 and came to an abrupt end in 1883. What are eight or ten years for missionary work to be done in a vast country like India, a country steeped in ignorance and superstition ? And yet the transformation that Swami Dayanand succeeded in effecting in Indian character and out-look in these few years was truly amazing. His work has been carried on by the Arya Samaj. This work has been rather slow: it has, however, been steady and solid, and the Arya Samaj is to-day probably the best organised and most virile organization in the country, engaged in social and religious reform. The personality of Swami Dayanand has left a deep impress on the Arya Samaj, and is a very important factor in determining the out-look of the individual Arya Samajist. Swami Dayanand passed away fifty years ago, but he is a more potent force to-day than he was when he was alive. 'Was alive' did I say? He *is* alive to-day and *will* be alive so long as his influence persists. Swami Dayanand's life was eventful. A study of his life and achievement is very edifying ; but equally edifying is the study of the spirit that was behind the work that could catch the eye. Can we have a peep at the inner workings of the mighty spirit that was in him? Let us attempt.

What strikes me most in Swami Dayanand's character is his great love of Truth. He was all his life a seeker after Truth. This love was awakened in him when he was a mere boy and by a very common-place incident. Genius has been described as one-tenth inspiration and nine-tenths perspiration. Without worrying about the proportion of the two elements, we must, I think, accept inspiration as a necessary ingredient in genius. And this inspiration is often nothing more or less than seeing the significance of facts that awaken no curiosity in others. Countless men before Newton had seen apples fall to the ground, but had not been led to think of the Law of Universal Gravitation. To read the Law in the fall of an apple required the genius of a Newton. Similarly, countless boys and adults in India had seen a mouse behaving unceremoniously to an image of a so-called god or goddess, but the sight had left them unaffected. This was not so in the case of Swami Dayanand. He saw the sight and became inquisitive. Can this image which cannot defend itself against a mere mouse deserve our homage? Can it do us any good? And harm? This question made him restless. 'I must find an answer to this', said he.

He was guided in finding a solution to his problem by his great teacher, Swami Virjanand. Swami Dayanand came to the conclusion that man's spirit should bend in worship to God and to Him alone. Spirit is greater than matter. Swami Virjanand was a strong Monotheist, a believer in the Vedas. He wanted to preach the truth as he saw it, but suffered from a great handicap. He was blind. In Swami Dayanand, he found a disciple to his taste. When the period of instruction was over, Swami Virjanand enjoined upon Swami Dayanand the duty of preaching Vedic Dharma. Swami Dayanand accepted the behest of the Master and resolved to dedicate himself to the task. He was already a seeker after Truth; his *guru* now turned him into a missionary.

Swami Dayanand was a fearless propagandist. He was very rugged, and never minced matters. He was merciless in his denunciation of vice and superstition in all their forms. But his bosom was full of the milk of human kindness. By shifting emphasis from birth to worth as determined by qualifications, function and disposition, he placed the body politic on a truly democratic basis.

Swami Dayanand was a man of boundless energy. The source of this energy was his absolute faith in God. He felt that whatever he was doing was God's work and he was a mere instrument for doing it. And when the end came, he surrendered himself to God in a spirit of perfect resignation. His last audible words on the death-bed were—"Wonderful are Thy ways, O Lord! Thy will be done!"

I can just make a reference to his enthusiasm for ideals, his keen critical power, his knowledge of classical Sanskrit Literature, and his firm grasp of realties. Swami Dayanand was a great soul; a Scholar, a Saint and a Hero—all combined in one person.

He was a great son of India, one of the greatest that India has produced; and nobly and well did he serve the Motherland. Let each one of us draw what spiritual sustenance one can from meditation on his life and character on the occasion of the *Nirvāṇa* Semi-Centenary.

D. A. V. College,
Cawnpore

DIWAN CHAND

I have great respect for all I know of Dayanand Saraswati and I wish all success to the Commemoration Volume.

Hampstead

HENRY W. NEVINSON

THE ARYA SAMAJ

WHEN about the beginning of the nineteenth century, the British Government was firmly established over the whole of this country, it ushered in an era of peace and tranquillity, causing the renaissance of modern India. There was freedom of thought, freedom of speech, and freedom of action. The attention of the people, especially of the Hindus, was directed towards an impartial consideration of the environment in which they were then placed,—religious, social and intellectual. Hinduism was then a farrago of faiths, ranging from the atheistic Advaitism of Shankarāchārya to the gross and merciless rites of the *Tantrists*. The only feeble bond that held them together was the common belief in the Veda as Divine Revelation. On the other side, Hinduism was surrounded by two religions—the most robust and aggressive of the period—which were drawing away a large number of Hindus into their folds. While the lower classes were generally converted to the Muslim faith, the higher educated people embraced Christianity. There was again a scientific environment which was the sole creation of the British Government in India by the construction of the steam engines, railways, telegraphs and so forth. The intellectual thought of Europe, such as was manifested in the inventions of modern science, enthralled the mind of Young India. The serious attention of the learned or educated Hindus was thus directed to a critical study of the environment in which they were placed, and the problem that confronted them most was how to bring about a synthesis of the old and the new, a fusion of the East and the West and thus regenerate India not only intellectually but also socially, ethically and religiously. Many reformers arose, such as Ram Mohan Roy, Devendra Nath Tagore and Keshab Chandra Sen in Bengal who founded and spread the Brahmo Samaj, and

Mahadeva Govinda Ranade and others who started the Prārthanā Samaj in Bombay. While this social upheaval was astir, there was a young Brahmin called Mul Shankar from Kathiawar, who, at the age of fourteen, saw mice running over and defiling an image of Siva and whose mind therefore recoiled from idol-worship. What with bereavements and what with the dread of matrimonial entanglement, he ran away from his home and spent about eighteen years of his life in quest of truth. It was this young Sādhu from Kathiawar who afterwards called himself Swami Dayanand and founded the Arya Samaj in 1875 in Bombay when he was fifty-one years old. Although this Arya Samaj was first inaugurated in Bombay, it was not till it was established in the Punjab that it began to show its real vigour and activity.

We thus see that there were three movements of reform which marked the Renaissance of modern India, namely, the Brahmo Samaj of Bengal, the Prārthanā Samaj of Bombay and the Arya Samaj of the Punjab. If we make an impartial survey of their achievements, it cannot be gainsaid that the Arya Samaj at present stands the first and foremost of these movements. Not only has it the largest followers but it has permeated the lower strata of the Hindu Society. On the one hand, it has well-nigh stopped the conversion of the Hindus to Muhammadanism and Christianity. On the other, it has reclaimed many people who were originally Hindus, but had been converted to the Muslim or Christian faith. And the question arises why is such a phenomenon scarcely noticeable in the history of the Brahmo or the Prārthanā Samaj. How could such a marvellous result be attained by the Arya Samaj alone? In fact, such a question cannot but obtrude itself on the mind of a historian. Religion has been aptly compared to a piece of land, for the good crops from which not only the nature of the soil but also the farmer is responsible. The phenomenal activity displayed by the Arya Samaj must therefore be the result of the mentality and character, not only of the people of the Punjab and the United Provinces where the movement is strongest, but also of the founder of the Samaj who prepared the seed of faith and ploughed and sowed in into the moral soil of a Province. Here we are concerned only with the second aspect of the question. And it cannot be denied that Swami Dayanand was endowed with an imagination of a high order which exhibited itself not only in the nature of his doctrine but also the manner in which he preached it. The first point that we have to note in this connection is the name which he gave to his movement, namely, Arya Samaj as contrasted with Brahmo or Prārthanā Samaj. It is scarcely necessary to add that of those three, Arya Samaj is by far the best name that could be invented. It cannot but appeal to the imagination of a Hindu. All the sacred scriptures of India whether of the Brahmins, Buddhists or Jains make mention of that word. Whether we hear of a chosen race or of a noble doctrine, the word 'Ārya' is dinned into our ears. What is called Hinduism has been designated as Ārya-dharma. And the Hindus have all along been styled Aryas, not only in writings but also in inscriptions. Arya is thus the most beautiful word to conjure with. And we cannot but admire the inspired mood which prompted Swamiji to christen his movement, Arya Samaj.

The second point that we have to notice in regard to the mentality of the founder of the Arya Samaj is the third item that he has inserted in the Decalogue of the official creed. It runs thus: "The Vedas are the books of true knowledge, and it is the paramount duty of every Arya to read or hear them read, to teach and preach them to others". If we compare the creed of the Arya Samaj with that of the Brahmo or the Prārthanā Samaj, we find that there is absolutely no difference in regard to its articles of belief except in regard to just this item No. 3. Whether we consider the attributes of God or the ethical precepts recommended for practice, we find there is a perfect identity between the three Samajes. It is only the attitude towards the Vedas that differentiates the Arya from the other two Samajes. The founder of the Arya Samaj, we are told, made overtures to the leaders of both the Prārthanā and the Brahmo Samaj to effect an organic union. No such union was effected even temporarily, though for some time there was something like a partnership between the Arya Samaj and the Theosophical Society. Fortunately, there was no such permanent fusion anywhere. Otherwise, the Arya Samaj would not have been able to achieve what it has done. Whether we take the Brahmo or the Prārthanā Samaj, it is essentially based on eclecticism. Neither the Brahmo nor the Prārthanā Samaj looked upon Veda as Divine Revelation, and it selects whatever is good and solid in every religion. Such an eclectic religion is no doubt the grandest thing to contemplate and follow, but just because it is eclectic, it can appeal to the intelligent few only. That is no doubt one great reason why Brahmo or Prārthanā Samaj has not attracted many people to its ranks. The members of these two Samajes have cut themselves adrift from the Hindu society. You may have the finest head with the finest brain in it, but if it is not placed on a human body, it cannot possibly function. You may similarly have the finest possible eclecticism, but if it has no organic union with any society, with any traditions, manners and customs, it will be confined to a microscopic minority and will soon evaporate.

The Arya Samaj, on the other hand, looks upon the Vedas as "the books of true knowledge". This cannot but appeal to the imagination of the Hindus. Hinduism may be a congeries of sects, having hardly any other thing in common, but this they do possess in common, namely, their unshakable faith in the Vedas as Divine Revelation. When Swami Dayanand, therefore, laid stress on this aspect of the Vedas, it might have shocked the critical faculty of the scholar, but it enabled him to gain a number of followers from amongst the Hindus. Is there any Hindu who ventures to cast any kind of slur on the Vedas? If he does, he forthwith ceases to be a Hindu. When the Divine Revelation of the Vedas is once admitted, then any reformer like the Swamiji can proceed with his work of the regeneration of India. Do the people worship idols? Is there any sanction for it in the Vedas? Surely, he who has read the Vedas knows full well that no such sanction is forthcoming from these scriptures. So Swamiji could effectively wage internecine warfare with the idolatrous practices of his time. Or take the caste-system. The classes like the Brahmin, Kshattriya, Vaiśya and Sudra have no doubt been mentioned in the Vedas. But do the Vedas uphold any such caste-system as is at present prevalent in India—a caste-system which prohibits interdining and intermarriage. Most certainly not. This explains the marvellous results achieved by the Arya Samaj in the Hindu community. The latter regard the Vedas as Divine Revelation; and taking its stand upon them, the Samaj points out that all the evil practices that have crept into Hindu Society, not only have no sanction from the Vedas, but are opposed to the spirit of those scriptures. This is, indeed, a most wonderful method of reforming modern India, the credit for which goes solely to the founder of the Arya Samaj. May he inspire his followers to complete the noble work begun by him!

CALCUTTA — D. R. BHANDARKAR

I wish every success to your celebration of the Semi-Centenary of the great figure which India has produced.

TOKYO, JAPAN — (BARON) H. E. HAYASHI

SWAMI DAYANAND AS AN EDUCATIONIST

SWAMI DAYANAND was great — great in many ways. He was a born leader—a giant among men. In the words of Madame Blavatsky, "India never saw a more learned Sanskrit scholar, a deeper metaphysician, a more wonderful denunciator of any evil than Dayanand, since the time of Śaṅkarāchārya". A seer, saint, and scholar, he was not merely a Yogī, but a man of action; it is this feature of his character which appeals to me most.

And this hero of action, fought and worked in many fields. Like many other great men, he was reviled, stoned, persecuted — even poisoned to death. He saw far ahead of his time; his vision of the future was clear; his diagnosis of the ills from which the Hindu body-politic suffered was perfect. We realise now that the remedies he prescribed are the only ones needed to purge the society of its evils and cure it and make it healthy and strong.

His services to the Hindu nation are writ large in the pages of history, his services to humanity, the world will recognise one day and then assign to Swami Dayanand the place among world-teachers which he deserves and which properly belongs to him. But whether that day comes in our life-time or not, this much has been clearly demonstrated in the brief space of 50 years that Swami Dayanand came not a day too soon to save the Hindus and free a caste-ridden, priest-ridden people. He showed us the right way to get rid of our weakness, to grow powerful, and to fulfil the great mission entrusted to us by God. He roused a lethargic people, he infused new life into dead bones, and to-day the Arya Samaj is a monument of his labours, a living proof of our growing strength, the envy of the world and the hope of our people.

In this article, I do not propose to speak of Ṛishi Dayanand as an emancipator of women, as an apostle of Swadeshi or as an ardent patriot. I shall confine myself to Swami Dayanand as an educationist.

Now, what were the principles which he believed to be of fundamental importance in the matter of the education of our boys and girls?

In the first place, he believed that a true and sound system of education should have for its goal, the religious and moral welfare of the young. Consequently, according to him, religious and moral training was the foundation on which the educational edifice ought to be built; he had no sympathy for a system of education which neglected the most essential and enduring part of man and which divorced religion from morality. Character-building, of which we hear so much in these days, occupied a prominent place in his scheme of education, but he held that true character-building was not possible unless boys were taught their duty to God and Man.

Secondly, Swami Dayanand preached that a long course of 18 years' hard study—say from 7 to 25—demanded a store of energy and vitality in the young which it was impossible for them to possess without enforcing on them a life of celibacy and insistence on chastity and Brahmacharya. This Brahmacharya was the glory of the Hindu system of education; the stress laid on it by Swami Dayanand is unique and unparalleled in the history of any other country and nation. We hear so much of sex-education at the present moment; the superiority of the ancient Aryan system of education lay in this that the ancient Guru imparted the instruction not in theory, but so supervised the diet and regulated the habits of his wards that they grew up to be strong, stout, sturdy Brahmachārīs; the environment itself favoured the cultivation of this virtue. Is anything like this possible in our large cities with all the allurements of the cinema and the theatre, with all the temptations of enjoyment and indulgence before our young men?

Tapasyā, not indulgence; service, not enjoyment; simplicity, not luxury; sacrifice, not selfishness; *Dharma*, not godlessness; duty, not pleasure, we find as the ideals of students of those days. The world is crying for a system of education which will once again assign to personal purity the place which it had in our system of education. I could give extracts from writers who deplore the present sad state of affairs, but space will not permit me to do so. Co-education is simply slavish imitation of the West.

Thirdly, practical personal Hygiene was an essential part of Swami Dayanand's scheme of education. I know that Physiology and Hygiene are taught in our Schools. I know also that boys can name the bones of the human skeleton, identify a plague flea under a microscope and so on and so forth. But this is not the type of Hygiene teaching which boys need to-day; the boys were made to put into practice the rules of Hygiene *then*, they cram the rules of Hygiene *now*.

Let us have a look at the daily routine of a boy of those days. He used to rise early in the morning an hour and a half before sunrise, he went out into the open, green fields, he saw the golden, gorgeous sunrise, he cleaned his teeth daily with a fresh tender twig; took a daily bath; he said his prayer and practised Prāṇāyâma (deep correct breathing) which promoted long, healthy life. It is now being recognised by Western writers that the Hindus could control their Energy and store up their Energy, and refine their Energy, largely by their power of controlling their breath or Prāṇāyāma (vide, *Healthy Breathing* by Eustance Milies, M. A., Assistant Master at Rugby and Amateur Champion of the World Racquets and Tennis). This was one of the reasons why students in ancient times were generally free from anger, resentment, and worry.

Fourthly, Swami Dayanand's system of education lays stress on the intimacy of relationship between the teacher and the pupil; the relationship is one of father and son. The boy was to all intents and purposes a member of the teacher's family. When the boy goes for admission to a school, the teacher, as the

Scriptures tell us, holds him as dear and near as the mother a child in the womb. The teacher's duty is to bestow all the loving care of a mother: Where else can we find the conception of teacher's duty so beautifully expressed? We generally complain of the low level of intellectual development reached by our students; what else can we expect when a wide gulf separates the student from the teacher? We know that the secret of success of a Cambridge and Oxford man is the personal touch between the tutor and the ward.

And, fifthly, Swami Dayanand laid emphasis on Hindi being made the medium of instruction. He abandoned Gujarāti in favour of Arya Bhāshā. He felt, as most educationists have begun to feel to-day, that foreign language as a medium of instruction was a handicap, a dead weight, which retarded the growth of the Indian boy's mind. He was not a conservative in any sense of the term; he favoured Indians going abroad in quest of knowledge; crossing the seas had no terror for him. He said that knowledge should be gathered from all corner and sources. But with all this he felt that a sound system of education was one which made a student feel proud of his language, his country, proud of his nation's past, proud of her glory. This, according to him, could never be achieved if Hindi and Sanskrit were relegated to the back-ground.

And, lastly, in Swami Dayanand's system of education, the rich and the poor, the high and the low, the prince and the peasant, the high caste and the low caste, the Brahmin and the Harijan all read together, eat together, live the same life, undergo the same discipline. The state provides free and universal education not merely upto the Primary stage, but for all the 18 years upto the highest stage; in exceptional cases even upto the age of 36 or 48; the state is to provide for the education of the citizen; in vain shall we look elsewhere for a grander conception of the duty of the State in the promotion of education: Swami Dayanand's system was, in the truest sense of the term, a democratic one. All were equals in the eye of the teacher. There were no grades of tuition fees. Kṛishṇa and Sudāmā were class-fellows. And the result of this system of education was this that when princes left their Guru's Aśramas, they were manly—men of character, fit to rule the State; the lowest had opportunities to rise to the highest scale in society. Separate Chief's colleges have no place in Swami Dayanand's scheme of education.

There is a good deal more in Swami Dayanand's writings which deserves the careful thought of educationists. Government and people have begun to realise that the schools and colleges should be sufficiently away from large cities, far from the haunts of men. I hope the day is not far off when the value of open air schools also will be generally acknowledged.

Educational institutions in ancient India had an environment which promoted serious thinking and a spirit of enquiry and research. Boys were then in direct communion with nature, they were free from the cares and anxieties of home; such single-minded devotion to studies extorted the admiration of the world. The Guru used to give the following advice as his student was about to part from him. "Tell the truth, and never neglect your studies, follow Dharma and never neglect your studies, and so on." One realises the value which the teachers of the past attached to studies. 'Never neglect your studies' is the burthen of the song, it is the theme of the convocation address of those days.

These were the views of Ṛishi Dayanand on education; he lived up to these teachings and taught by example, not merely by precept. Religion was the breath of his life. Brahmachaṛya was the glory of his life, he had a burning love for Sanskrit and Hindi; his devotion to his teacher was without a parallel. What is more touching than the last scene when he takes leave of Swami Virjanand? His teacher, we know, though the ablest of men, was not a man of sweet temper; Dayanand had many proofs of it during his stay with the Guru. But he loved him with a love all his own. The man who had lived on parched gram and read in the flickering light of small earthen lamps, which Hindu women leave at temple gates and wells, had nothing to offer to his Guru as Dakshiṇā. And yet no pupil may see his Guru empty-handed. He took a few pieces of cloves and presented them to the teacher and then bowed his head in reverence. Ah! the humble offering was more precious to the Guru than diamonds and jewels and precious stones could ever be. But that was not the Dakshiṇā acceptable to him. A true disciple lives to fulfil the mission of his master; and the disciple said, "Pray, let me know your commands." And the teacher asked for his life as an offering at the altar of the motherland. And did Dayanand hesitate? His faith, his affection, his patriotism were all known to the Guru, and so when the Guru implored him to go abroad and spread the Vedic truths which he had been taught, Dayanand gave his word of honour to carry out the behest. With the torch of the Vedas in his hand, how he showed us the way is a matter of history. He toured over the length and breadth of India, as few had done before; he toiled and toiled, wrote and wrote, spoke and spoke, he slept sleepless nights feeling for the woes of our motherland and then people saw that he was no ordinary mortal, no agent of the Christian Missionaries, but India's Saviour. The Semi-Centenary Celebrations of the Maharshi will show to the world the hold he has over the people's mind and imagination; the ever-increasing number of his followers, their ever-increasing activities, their spirit of service and sacrifice, all infused into them by the Great Ṛishi fill us with new hopes, new aspirations, with nobler resolves and we feel with a conviction never felt before that the day is drawing near when the Vedic truths in their pristine purity will be the Universal creed of mankind—let us all work for that day, for this is the one way in which we can pay off but little of the Maharshi's supreme debt.

LAHORE

RAM RATTAN

DAYANAND: AN APPRECIATION

IT is a popular superstition, perhaps with some basis of fact, that faith and religious vision do not go hand in hand with scholarship. The glimpse of the unseen, of the light that never was on sea or land, is not usually accessible to the scholar over-burdened with the learning and intellectual acquisitions of the ages. Some would go further and assert that such a store-house of knowledge is inimical to any kind of originality in emotion or thought. Yet there are exceptional individuals who illustrate how scholarship, instead of damping inspiration, can so control it that it may be of the greatest use to average humanity.

No student of Dayanand's life can fail to be struck by this wonderful combination of original vision and painfully acquired learning. The story of those three years of his life at Muttra from 1860 to 1863 appears as nothing less than romantic: here is one who had been leading the life of an ascetic for nearly fifteen years and who even before that had given evidence of his unique spiritual gifts. He had already passed through various stages of belief more as a result of intuition than of study or anything else, but was apparently dissatisfied with what he had gained and practised. Now in years of maturity he came across the Indian prototype of Browning's Grammarian and proved to be such a patient disciple as even the enthusiasm of the classical Renaissance did not produce. Three hard years of intense discipline and concentrated study made him a master of Pāṇini's Grammar and Pātañjali's commentary, and what was more important, they trained him for the great task of expounding the Vedas and made him conscious of his true mission of re-awakening the knowledge of the Śāstras in the ignorant and indifferent Hindus of his days.

This, after all, is his distinctive contribution as a Religious reformer of the nineteenth century that he asked every Hindu to learn the truth by turning to his own scriptures. Many erroneous beliefs were being cherished, many false doctrines were being preached, but to combat these mistakes and fallacies it was not necessary to turn to the West, to the teachings of Christian Theologians and Philosophers. One had simply to look back to the treasurers of his own land and to interpret the works of the ancient sages in the proper fashion to arrive at the essence of the truth. It has been pointed out that as a religious reformer Dayanand is parallel to Luther, that whereas Luther's cry was "Back to the Bible", Dayanand's was "Back to the Vedas". That he could raise this cry and emphasize it as other Hindu religious reformers could not, was due to his study of Sanskrit religious literature for years and a conscientious endeavour to gather the scriptural truths which had unfortunately been forgotten.

Thus Dayanand's position in the history of religion is parallel to that of Burke in Politics: reform is necessary, evils must be eradicated, but it is no root and branch policy that is advocated. Every effort at change is necessarily a leap in the dark, but we can make it much less risky than what it usually is by consulting the authority of the past and taking our stand on truths which have stood the test of ages. Moreover it is the past of our own land that has to be scrutinised, its intellectual and spiritual treasures carefully apprehended before we can mercilessly criticise the degeneracy of the Moderns. It is no universal religion that is preached by Dayanand; he does not attempt to harmonise the truths of the scriptures of various lands. He would most probably have agreed with the Persian Mystic who said: "He who disbelieves in all religions is a knave, but he who believes in all is a fool". The true religion of the Hindus is what he attempted to expound and illustrate with the help of prophetic vision and a scholar's equipment which some may criticise but none can help admiring.

LUCKNOW UNIVERSITY

N. K. SIDHANTA

Swami Shraddhanand

THE HIGHER PHASE OF ARYAN FAITH

I saw Swami Dayanand Saraswati at Arrah, in Bihar, when I was a little boy of twelve years. The Swami was staying in a garden-house belonging to the Mahārājā of Dumraon. I had heard of the Swami's arrival at the Government school and, impelled by boyish curiosity, asked one of our peons to accompany me to the garden. We got there just after sunset. The Swami had just finished his physical exercise. He was wearing only a loin-cloth and there were a pair of fairly large Indian clubs in front of him. He asked me and the peon a few questions, and then placed his hand on my head and blessed me. In the evening, he gave a lecture at our school. I just saw him coming dressed as he is represented in his likenesses and then ran home. We were not permitted to stay out after nightfall, and in any case, I could have understood nothing of the lecture.

During my lengthy stay at Lahore as Editor of the *Tribune* newspaper, I was in intimate touch with the Arya Samaj and the leaders of that movement in the Punjab. I knew Rai Bahadur Mulraj, who had personally known Swami Dayanand, Lala (now Mahatma) Hansraj, the Honorary Principal of the Dayanand Anglo-Vedic College, Lala Lalchand, the President of the College Committee, and Lala Lajpat Rai, Honorary Secretary of the Committee. I also knew Lala Munshi Ram of Jullundur, afterwards well-known as Swami Shraddhanand. Dr. Jaisingh was the moving spirit of the Shuddhi movement and converts from all religions were freely admitted to the Arya Samaj. The *Satyārtha Prakāsh* written by Swami Dayanand and his teachings were the basic principles of the religion of the Arya Samaj. The Vedas were accepted as revealed and the foundations of the true faith. The Purāṇas and the worship of idols were rejected. The distinctions of caste were not recognised. All the members of the Arya Samaj had an equal status; there was no ascendancy of Brahmins. Every one had the right to perform the *Havana* rite. No one was denied the right to study the Vedas. There were no privileges for the twice-born. Vedic *mantras* were chanted by students and members of the Samaj. Swami Dayanand was a reformer in the widest sense of the word. He stood for the dissemination of the Vedic religion among all classes of the people in India. Women were to have equal opportunities with men in intellectual and moral uplift. The whole world was welcome to study and absorb the teaching of the Vedas. So far as the Arya Samaj was concerned, untouchability did not exist. Just as Rāmachandra, the *avatāra* and Kshattriya prince and king, embraced the Chāṇḍāla Guha as his friend and had no objection to partake of the food offered by the king of the untouchables, so is the Arya Samaj ready at all times to admit the untouchables into its fold.

The activities of the Arya Samaj have been as varied as they have proved successful. There are Gurukulas, colleges, schools for boys as well as girls, orphanages and widows' homes. Propaganda work is done by a large number of preachers. The Arya Samaj has provided numerous examples of splendid self-sacrifice and complete devotion. The great thing to remember is that the ancient Aryans and the Ṛishis never pursued aggressive methods. The light of knowledge was available for all who sought it; there was no compulsion of any kind, no polemics, no heated argument.

In those ancient times all conditions were favourable to the cultivation of the intellect and the spirit. The Aryan colonists and settlers lived in the shadow of the eternal Himalayas. That in itself was a never-failing source of inspiration. On the banks of the Sarasvatī, which has now disappeared, the Ṛishis lifted up their voices and chanted the lofty hymns of the Sāmaveda. No surroundings could be more peaceful or more solemn. All around was the silence of vast primal forests. The soil was virgin and yielded an abundant harvest with very little effort. Life was simple; there was no crowding, no hustling. There was large leisure and all the external and internal conditions of life were conducive to thought. At the back-ground of the landscape towered the mighty mountains, the abode of silence and the eternal snows. This was the homeland of a gifted race, the far-famed Āryāvarta whose traditions have come down the ages. Other branches of the Aryan race, in other parts of the world, became great and famous, and they fill a large space in history, but not one of them could rival the Aryans of India in the achievement of the spirit. No other race has produced such great thinkers or so large a number of holy men. The *tapasyā* of the Ṛishis was unknown out of India. Such prolonged, profound meditation has never been practised in any other country. Almost with the breath of life came the light of an exalted faith. The incense of the Homa-fire filled the nostrils of the young and the old, the chant of the Vedic hymn filled the ears of the hearers. In the *tapovanas*, the Ṛishis taught their disciples, the Brahmachārīs who studied the Vedas and the Vedāṅgas. Young damsels, the daughters of such Ṛishis as were married, went about their work, watering the plants and feeding the tame antelopes. Kings came in humble guise and sat at the feet of the masters to learn of their wisdom. It was a wonderful period in the history of the human race.

The Aryans were a race of manly men and womanly women. Among the men were to be found mighty warriors, profound thinkers, men of unequalled wisdom; among the women were maids of surpassing loveliness, matrons as wise as the wisest men. Renunciation was practised as a supreme attainment. Apart from the scriptures, other great books taught the impermanence of worldly ambitions and the fleeting character of worldly and material possessions. In the Rāmāyaṇa, Rāma, the great and godly king, laid down his kingdom and entered the waters of the Sarayū river to be absorbed into the effulgence of the Lord Vishṇu. In the Mahābhārata, the five Pāṇḍava brothers and their consort Draupadī, after winning back their kingdom by the prolonged and devastating Kurukshetra war, renounced it and went up the Himālayas. One after another, they perished and King Yudhishṭhira alone survived to enter heaven in the living body. In all paths of life, the supremacy of the spirit was proclaimed and the temptations and ties of life were considered of no account. The siren-voice of the world and the lure of enjoyment appealed in vain to men and women. In the flesh they were mortal like all other created beings, but they were always sustained by the consciousness of the immortality of the soul, and they spurned the sordid attachments and ambitions that usually make up life. Their spirits reached out beyond the illusions of *māyā* and were borne aloft on the wings of realisation and meditation. Other peoples in other lands have declared themselves the chosen people of God, with or without justification. The ancient Aryans of India made no such claim, but they were beyond question the elect of the human race.

The revelation in the Vedas is mainly concerned with the elemental forces of nature. The lofty hymns move to a stately measure and the sonorous chant of the *mantras* fills the hearer with awe and reverence. But the quest of what lies behind the manifested phenomena of nature never relaxed until the truth was revealed and the sages realised the all-pervading immanence of a single Energy, the Creator—out of which all things proceed. Hence the fulfilment of the Vedas in the Vedānta, containing Brahmavidyā or the Jñānakāṇḍa. In the concluding portion of the Ṛigveda is to be found one of the loftiest hymns in the whole range of scriptural literature pertaining to the mystery of creation. It is the 129th Ṛik in the tenth *Maṇḍala*. It is overpowering in its solemnity, majestic in its movement. It is the hymn beginning न असद् आसीद् नो सद् आसीत्. A translation of the *mantra* is appended:—

"There was neither Existence nor Non-Existence;
The Kingdom of Air, nor the Sky beyond.
What was there to contain, to cover in—

Were there but vast unfathomed depths of Water?
There was no Death there, nor Immortality;
No Sun was there, dividing Day from Night;
Then there was only *That* resting within *Itself*;
Apart from *It* there was not anything.
At first within the Darkness veiled in Darkness,
Chaos unknowable, the All lay hid:
When sudden from the formless Void emerging,
By the great power of Heat was born that Germ.
Thereafter came Desire, the primal root of Mind;
Being from non-Being proceeded—this our Ṛishis know:
What was the Cause—above, below?
What vital force impell'd this parting here?
Who knows whence this was born, or how it came?
The gods themselves are later than this time:
He only, the Creator, truly knoweth this;
And even He, perhaps, may know it not."

What fathomless depth of thought underlies these sublime lines? There is the conception of a time before creation and then follow the self-questioning of the seeker after the truth, the course of an earnest but hesitant mind, an overwhelming consciousness of the mystery of creation, the dawning knowledge of a supreme Creator mingled with an uncertainty about the fullness of his knowledge, for the last words of the hymn are स अंग वेद यदि वा न वेद. Where are we to look for such loftiness of thought, such nobility of expression?

In the Upanishads, which form the complementary portion of the Vedas, the concept of the deity is definite and clear. Two of the oldest Upanishads, the Īśāvāsya and the Bṛihadāraṇyaka, form part of the White Yajurveda. The Īśāvāsya is part of the Mantra portion of the Veda itself, the Bṛihadāraṇyaka is the Brāhmaṇa portion of the Veda.[1] Several *mantras* in the two Upanishads

[1] According to Swami Dayanand Saraswati, *Brāhmaṇas* do not form part of the Vedas. *Editor.*

are common. The Upanishads are a marvel of concentrated thought and expression, and their terseness makes them exceedingly difficult of comprehension. The contrast between the brevity of expression in the Upanishads and the diffuseness of the Purāṇas is both suggestive and instructive. Extraordinary application and concentration of mind are essential to the understanding of the Upanishads, while he who runs may read and understand the Purāṇas with their inexhaustible record of miraculous happenings. That explains why the students of the Upanishads are so few whereas the Purāṇas appeal to the many. To the vast majority of Hindus—the Vedas and the Upanishads are merely a name, but even the ignorant classes have traditional knowledge of the Purāṇas, which have become a sort of folklore.

The predominating note in all the Upanishads is the exaltation of the Brahma, the supreme diety, who is designated by various names. He is not to be confused with the other Devas like Indra, Agni, Vāyu,[1] for he is without a second—एकमेवाद्वितीयम्. The God of the Upanishads is conceived very differently from the God of the Old Testament. The Semitic or the Jewish conception of God stands on a lower plane than that of the Aryans. The Upanishads are penetrated, through and through, by a solemn comprehension of the all-prevading majesty of God. In the Bṛihadāraṇyaka Upanishad is to be found that wonderful prayer which is unrivalled in any other language असतो मा सद्गमय, तमसो मा ज्योतिर्गमय, मृत्योर्मा अमृतं गमय etc. Freely translated, the prayer reads thus:—From untruth lead me unto the truth, from darkness lead me unto the Light, from death lead me unto immortality. O Revealed, reveal thou in myself; O Terrible, turn thy beneficent aspect towards me and save me for all time.

Answers to other important questions are to be found in the Upanishads. In the fourth *prapāṭhaka* of the fourth part of the Chhāndogya Upanishads is related a striking story which shows

[1] Swami Dayanand Saraswati held *Agni*, *Vāyu* occurring in the Vedas to be names of God. *Editor.*

that neither the sacred thread nor family heredity was essential to prove that a man was a Brahmin. A widow named Javālā had an only son, Satyakāma. The boy wanted to become a disciple of the Ṛishi Gautama and asked his mother to tell him the *Gotra* of his family so that he might inform the Ṛishi. Javālā said she did not know his gotra as she was always busy in attending to the guests who came to the house and she never remembered to ask her husband his *gotra*. She was married when young and became a mother, and shortly afterwards a widow. "All that I know is that my name is Javālā and your name is Satyakāma. When the Āchārya asks you, tell him you are Satyakāma, the son of Javālā." Questioned by Gautama about his *gotra*, Satyakāma faithfully repeated what his mother had told him, whereupon the Ṛishi said that no one except a Brahmin could tell the truth as Satyakāma had told it and he was satisfied that the boy was a Brahmin. The Ṛishi invested Satyakāma with the sacred thread and accepted him as a disciple. Jāvāla Satyakāma afterwards became a great Ṛishi and the Jāvāla Upanishad is named after him. The distinctive characteristic of a Brahmin was that he never deviated from the truth.

Again, the Advaita doctrine, so subtly and exhaustively propounded by the great Śaṅkarāchārya in his commentaries on the Upanishads, is mainly intended to convey a profound lesson in humility. When man realises that he has no separate existence apart from the All-Soul which embraces all being, he can have no cause and no justification for an independent self-consciousness or any sense of superiority. This is clearly and conclusively demonstrated in the story of Śvetaketu in the Chhāndogya Upanishad. Uddālaka Āruṇi, a Ṛishi and the father of Śvetaketu, sent his son to the family *Guru* for study when the boy was twelve years of age. For twelve years, the lad stayed with the Guru and studied the four Vedas. At the age of twenty-four he returned to his father full of the arrogance and pride of learning. His father noted this and considered it essential that his son should be meek and humble. He asked Śvetaketu whether along with the scriptures, his Guru had taught him the knowledge of self, without which all learning was in vain. Uddālaka himself was a profoundly learned and very wise man, and had expected that the Guru would impart this knowledge to his disciple. Śvetaketu was puzzled by the question asked by his father and replied that he had received no such teaching and had no knowledge of self. Thereupon Uddālaka proceeded to instruct his son and by nine different lines of reasoning convinced him that the whole universe possessed a single soul, the सत्, and all souls were identified with it. At the conclusion of every argument, Uddālaka impressed on his son the fact that there is only one Existence and he told his son, 'Thou art That'—तत्त्वमसि. Śvetaketu became humble when he acquired his knowledge.

Apart from the Advaita doctrine, which roughly resembles the monism of pantheism, the Dualism or द्वैतवाद of the Upanishads is obvious as expounded in the commentaries of Madhvāchārya and other commentators. There is a clear distinction between Brahma and Jīva, the Creator and the created. The invocation in the Īśāvāsya Upanishad in the sixteenth *mantra* is a prayer of the Jīva to Brahma. In the Kena Upanishad there is a beautiful parable proving the supremacy of Brahma over the other gods. Agni, Vāyu and Indra considered themselves the greatest among the gods and they thought there was no other divinity more powerful then themselves. To disabuse them of this conceit Brahma appeared before them in the form of a Yaksha. He placed a straw before Agni and challenged him to burn it. Agni failed to do so and the Yaksha next laid the straw before Vāyu and asked him to lift it. Vāyu found himself powerless to do so and when Indra approached the Yaksha, he vanished. Thus the Gods realised that Brahma was the supreme deity.

The Vedas and the Upanishads inculcate pure Monotheism, and this is the basis of the teachings of Swami Dayanand and the foundation upon which the Arya Samaj rests. The Arya Samaj movement has taken a firm hold in the country and there are branches of it outside India. It is the largest reform movement in the country and a good deal of mission work is being done in connection with it. Important educational and social work is being actively carried on by the Arya Samaj. Neither caste nor untouchability is recognised. The ideal of the Arya Samaj is the ancient Aryan ideal, the *yuga* of the Vedas and Vedānta. The God of the Arya Samaj is the God of the Vedas and the Upanishads. The proposal of fittingly commemorating the Dayanand Nirvāṇa Ardha Shatābdī, that is the half a century that has passed since the great reformer and teacher left the world, will commend itself to every patriotic Indian who loves his country and his people, and all India will join in wishing the Arya Samaj continued success and prosperity.

BANDRA, BOMBAY — NAGENDRANATH GUPTA

I am a sincere admirer of the great man, whom I remember to have seen and heard nearly sixty years ago in this city: and I fully appreciate the work he has done as a Social Reformer and scholar. I am only sorry that age and health should come in the way of any active expression of sympathy with his work.

POONA — **MAHADEVA B. CHAUBAL**

UTILITARIANISM IN HINDU SOCIAL PHILOSOPHY

Based on Śukranīti

(a) The Logic of *Loka-hita* (Utilitarianism).

POLITICAL philosophy is, as the very title implies, a branch of philosophy. It may not, indeed, have to discuss the theory of perception or the nature of reality with which the philosophies technically so-called have to deal. But both in category as well as in substance, the intercourse between political philosophy and these other philosophies is intimate.

How do the Śukra authors stand in relation to the philosophical systems of their days? A question like this may not be inappropriate to ask, while examining the economic categories and doctrines of Śukranīti. The problem is to ascertain the real value of the materialism such as was propagated by the Śukra authors in the light of the prevailing bodies of knowledge in other fields.

We are aware that the world in which the authors were discussing their special problems, namely, those bearing on *Saptāṅga*, was a richly diversified one in point of the number of *Vidyās*. Their name is legion, so to say, the authors have informed us (IV, iii, line 45); and more precisely, we are told, there are thirty-two primary branches of learning (IV, iii, lines 51-128).

So far as the so-called philosophies (*darśanas*) are concerned, the Śukra authors know them to be perhaps more than six. It is clear, at any rate, that the conventional six are quite well-known to them. But it is interesting to note that the six have not been mentioned by them "as a group" (IV, iii, 55-56).

This is a curious item and, incidentally, may possess some value in the question of chronology. The relevant passages in the Śukranīti cannot, certainly be as old as the times when the philosophies were not yet known to be six. These must have to be accorded a date posterior, say, to Haribhadra's *Ṣhaḍḍarśana-Samuchchayasūtra.*

But how far posterior? The fact that the authors do not call the philosophies six in number in the same breath as they describe the *vidyās* as thirty-two, seems to point to a period in which the figure 6 as indicating the number of philosophical systems had lost its special significance. Can we then take it that the intellectual atmosphere is oriented to the conditions which gave rise to Mādhavāchārya's Sarvadarśana–saṅgraha (1331)? But of this more, later (sub-section *d*).

The impact of all these sciences, and especially of the six philosophies on Śukranīti, may be postulated as a matter of course. That the authors were working *en rapport* with the professors of other academies, is evident from the chapters on minerals, plants, animals, architecture, sculpture, painting etc. These chapters may, indeed, be regarded as almost wholesale incorporations from specialised treatises on the subject dealt with.

But in regard to some of the philosophies, at any rate, the impact seems to be not so much one of assimilation as of antipathy and repulsion. The authors are quite explicit on the question of their intellectual credo. They are thoroughly convinced that their own science (*Nitiśāstra*) is more important than every other science (I, lines 20-24). For, what food is in the physical organism of an individual, that the *Nitiśāstra* is in the body politic.

The authors do not certainly disparage all the sciences outside of their own field by name. They have singled out only four, namely, grammar, logic, Mimāṁsā and Vedānta (I, lines 14-20). We are told, for instance, that one can master a language even without studying grammar. In the same manner, treatises on logic may be dispensed with by persons who are bent on the pursuit of truth. Similarly, one does not have to memorize Jaimini's lectures in order to master the rituals necessary in Vedic performances. Nor is it an absolute necessity to study the

Vedāntic disquisitions in order to be convinced of the frailties and littlenesses of the "world and the flesh".

The comparative insignificance of these four *vidyās* is further exhibited from another angle of vision. Nor is every human being on earth, we are to understand, likely to be in need of these sciences. And as these sciences have no utility outside of their circumscribed horizons, they can be useful to a very limited number of persons, to the "specialists". But what can the teeming millions do with these specialized branches of knowledge—the men and women of the work-a-day world who have to pursue their commonplace round of duties?

The position of Śukra authors has been most categorically declared at the very commencement of their work. "Other sciences", say they, "are but *kriyaikadeśabodhi*, i. e. have, for their subject matter, certain limited interests of mankind". "These must certainly yield the palm to *Nītiśāstra* which does not deal with *ekadeśa* (one aspect or domain) of human affairs (*kriyā*), but is, on the contrary *sarvopajīvaka* i. e. helpful to all, aye, an instrument in, or, so to say, a pivot of, the social order. Verily, Kauṭilya (Book I, ch. II) had caught the right Śukra tradition, when he stated that there is but one *vidyā* on earth, namely, political science, in the estimation of Śukra and his scholars".

Such being the value of their science in their own eyes, the materialism that the Śukra authors preach is self-conscious and aggressive. The doses are quite strong and are not diluted with solutions of *non-nīti* thought.

They have not cared to indicate by bibliographical references the kind of philosophical symposium they used to enjoy. But the manner in which they have analysed the economic foundations of the *Saptāṅga* does not fail to betray the company they kept. From top to bottom, they are interested in the investigation of the utilities and the ways and means of human welfare.

Their sole gospel is furnished by social service, *lokahita* (I, lines 4-5), or utilitarianism.

(*b*) The Realism of Sachchakas

To use another modern term, it is not in the "idealistic" strands of thought that the Śukra authors are interested. The philosophies of Berkeley and Hume which seek to eliminate the external world and posit the exclusive existence of the mind, converting the universe into nothing but a system of mental states, would have left no impress upon the brains of the writers of Śukranīti. And, of course, they would have nothing to do with the Hegelian "absolute" soul as the entity, should it have been adumbrated in their *goshṭhī* (club) or *parishat* (academy) by certain professors of "the other sciences".

On the contrary, should it have been necessary for them to declare their philosophical or metaphysical article of faith they would have sought their natural allies among one of other systems of "realism". The distinction between idealism and realism is an eternal item in human thought. The philosophical *milieu* of the Śukra authors was fully aware of it. And it was up to them to choose which system to follow.

It is not necessary to read literally the ideas of "modern" idealism (Hegelian and Anglo-Hegelian) or "neo-idealism" (Crocean) and the realism and pragmatism of American professors, or the neo-realism of Bertrand Russell's *Analysis of Mind* in the metaphysical controversies of ancient and mediæval India. But that the world was a pluralistic one and that the scholars as well as laymen had to decide for themselves, consciously or unconsciously, between one or other ism, is evident on all hands.

In what academies or *Kutūhalaśālās* (halls for curio-seekers, knowledge-hunters or truth-investigators) the Śukra economists sought affiliations in order to equip themselves with an adequate *Weltanschanung* (world view) it is not difficult to discover. One interesting story, coming as it does, from Buddhist tradition, may serve as a specimen for the point in question.

Śākya the Buddha is said to have been abroad lecturing on the impermanence and unsubstantiality of body, sensation, perception and so forth. This sort of idealistic annihilation of the world of external objects was not to go unchallenged from the side of those who believed that body, sensation, etc., were not items to be trifled with. Śākya, therefore, had to encounter opposition of various shades from the "stormers and stressers" of his times.

The *Chulasachchaka Sutta or Majjhima Nikāya* narrates how one of the great high-brows of the day, Sachchaka Nighantaputta, invites Śākya to an open debate. (1) Sachchaka's thesis was quite a chip of naturalism. He propounded the supreme value of the Mother Earth in the world of nature as well as in the world of man.

"Whatsoever seeds and plants grow and expand and come to maturity", thus argued Sachchaka, "do so all in dependence upon the earth, and, firm based upon the earth, and thus come to maturity". It is this solid earth of mud and stones that furnishes equally the basis of all human endeavours. Sachchaka went on in his argument, vehemently emphasising the point that "whatever deeds that require strength are all done in dependence upon the earth, and firm-based upon the earth and that these deeds cannot be done in any other way."

The analogy of the earth was then exploited by Sachchaka in order to substantiate his thesis of the dignity of body, the dignity of sensation etc. What the earth is to plants and human beings, said he, that the body is to the individual. "By body is this individual man, and firm-based upon body does he bring forth deeds good or evil". The argument is carried forward in regard to sensation, perception etc.

Sachchaka is evidently an uncompromising champion of the doctrine of the physical basis of life. And, yet, one will have to admit that this exaltation of the body, sensation etc., this

(1) Bhikku Silachara's *First Fifty Discourses*, Vol. II pp. 84-88 in Nalinaksha Dutt's *Early History of the Spread of Buddhism* (London 1925), pp. 60-63.

See also Mahati-sutta, and Bri-jala-sutta, etc. in Rhys-Davids' *Dialogues of Buddha* for some of the other Vitaṇḍās (discussions) bearing on realism.

glorification, in one word, of materialism, does not rise to the pitch such as is embodied in the dogma of "economic determinism" or "materialistic interpretation of history", strictly so called, with which Marxianism is identified. For, Sachchaka's world-view, materialistic as it is, does not assert that life, mind, culture or law, religion, philosophy, science and fine arts are but the reflexes of the physical foundations. The casual relation is wanting in Sachchaka's philosophy, but it is this casual concatenation that furnishes the key-note to "modern" materialism.

The controversy between Śâkya and Sachchaka is but typical of the philosophical conflicts (*Vitaṇḍâs*) in old Hindu thought. And Śukra's materialism, as manifest in the analysis of the territory and finance, two of the seven limbs of the state, is ideologically in tune with the ideas of Sachchaka. To the authors of the Śukranīti, the external world is not to be explained away as but a unit of mental states. The physical objects are, in their estimation, solid pragmatic realities.

The story of Śâkya *vs.* Sachchaka has incidentally brought out another feature of intellectual polarity which will help to throw fresh light on the materialism of the Śukra philosophers. The dialectic of the one is the exact opposite of that of the other. And we are reminded at once of one of Marx's statements in the *Kritik der Politischen Oekonomie.* "With Hegel", says he, "the mind or the absolute (the world-reason) is the creator of the real. With me is the process quite otherwise. I consider the ideal to be nothing else but the material established in the human brain".

The logic of modern materialism is thus a direct antithesis to Hegelianism, i.e., idealism par excellence. It is only reasonable to find that in its philosophical affiliations, the materialism of Śukranīti was oriented to a mentality or mentalities the furthest removed from the Śâkyan.

(c) The Sāṅkhya Basis of Secular Studies

Sachchaka, as contemporary of Śâkya, the Buddha, is certainly too "old" for Śukranīti in the form in which we have it to-day. But the anti-Hegelian spirit, to employ a modern term with a retrospective effect, such as Sachchaka's story reveals, has always been a living force in the Indian philosophical work. And the Śukra authors, no matter to how many successive ages the cycle may belong, have always had the opportunities to fraternize with the Sachchakas of their days and exploit their findings in the interest of their own investigations.

Take, for instance, the six philosophies of the "older tradition". These in their developed form are certainly younger than the thoughts recorded in the Dialogues of the Buddha. Now, if the very environment in which Śākya, the Buddha, preached, could not fail to furnish a philosophical stimulus to the economic realism of the Śukra authors, they would have found an equally congenial atmosphere in the *vitaṇḍā* or discussions of the *darśana* academies.

At first sight it might appear, indeed, that these "six systems" on account of their pre-occupation with "salvation" would repel the Śukra economist. But this can, at least, be only a superficial view. For, at least, three of them, namely, the *Sāṅkhya*, the Vaiśeshika and the Nyāya deal more with the facts and phenomena of physics or natural philosophy rather than with the mental and moral philosophy proper. Thus they happen to furnish just the scientific foundations of materialism such as an economic system demands for its theoretical groundwork.[1]

No system of thought could be more serviceable to an economist than, for instance, the *Sāṅkhya*, which constitutes the very anti-thesis of Vedāntic mysticism. By establishing a rigid dualism it effectively segregates the spiritual from the material. And its "material" alone is powerful enough to be the cause of everything that happens in the non-spiritual world.

The matter of *Sāṅkhya* is not only real, it is eternal and indestructible at the same time. And the material world

[1] The physico-chemical and mechanical theories of the "philosophical schools", have been analyzed at length in Brojendranath Seal's *Positive Sciences of the Ancient Hindus* (London 1915). See also Sarkar's *Hindu Achievements in Exact Science* (New York, 1918).

self-evolving as it is, does not need the postulate of a God or a divine machinery.[1]

The very possibilities of a secular science, material or moral, are then to be sought in the *Sāṅkhya* philosophy, harnessed, as it is, with its purely naturalistic rationalism. Nor is this realistic agnosticism the exclusive characteristic of the *Sāṅkhyans*. However much the professors of the *Vaiśeshika-Nyāya* systems might differ from the *Śāṅkhyans* in the theories concerning the constitution of matter, the method of approach to the problems of the universe was identical. Even *buddhi* (intelligence) is grouped by the *Nyāya* philosophers in the same category as earth, water, air and other material substances.

As long as the *Sāṅkhya*, the *Nyāya* and the *Vaiśeshika* were there, the Hindū students of mental, moral and social phenomena never had to feel that their feet were off the ground. The idealism of the Vedānta such as is in its extreme form might interfere with an objective investigation of the pluralities of the universe on the alleged ground that the many do not exist or that the only reality is the Brahma, mind, soul or whatever else it may mean, could be always challenged or rectified with the weapons forged in the other schools.

(*d*) Orientations to Nāstika-Matam

The Śukra materialists, then, were not alone in the field. They had but to draw upon the experience of other intellectuals who were oriented to the world in their own way. Their colleagues in different branches of materialism were many, and *Nītiśastra* could flow on smoothly along the well-established currents of thought.

It seems that during the more recent phases of its development, the Śukranīti cycle was being enriched with the findings of a new school of philosophical materialists. This school has been

[1] Garbe's *Sāṅkhya Philosophy, eine Darstellung des indischen Rationalismus* (Leipzig, 1894), pp. 130, 137, 207, 232, 237, 238.
Cf A.M. Pizzagalli's *Cārvāka Nāstika e Lokāyatika* (Pisa, 1907), pp. 74-77.

described by the Śukra authors as *Nāstika-matam* or system of the Nāstikas (IV, iii, lines 108-109). In their estimation the Nāstikas are important enough to be described as representing one of the thirty-two branches of learning.

Now, whom do the *Śukra* authors call Nâstika ? Three characteristics are described by them as marking this system. First, we are told, that "reason" is the chief feature in the Nāstika theory. In the second place, the Nāstikas are said to explain the origin of all things by reference to "nature". And thirdly, they do not believe in the existence of the Vedas. They are thus sceptics, but not necessarily atheists.

Whatever be the characteristics of Nāstika philosophy, it is evident that the Śukra authors consider it to be quite a "respectable" system of thought. They enumerate it in the same dispassionate colourless, scientific manner as they enumerate the Vedas, Upavedas Darśanas etc. And here, *en passant*, we touch another aspect of the chronological problems.

The word Nāstika has been traced by Pizzagalli in his brochure, *Cārvāka Nāstika Lokāyatika*, as far back as the *Maitrāyaṇīya* Upanishad (3, 5), one of the latest Upanishads. It occurs several times in the Mahābhārata (XII, 181.1-6; XII, 322-16, XII, 121-38). Manu also knows the term (II,10-11. III 150, IV, 163; XI, 66-67).

But in none of these instances does the word describe the representative of a "system" of thought. It conveys simply the derogatory sense of a general character. By using Nāstika, the writers want us to understand a negator, one not abiding by the Vedas and Smṛitis etc., or perhaps, very often, an "ill-mannered" "uncultivated" boor, even a vicious sinner and so forth. Down to Manu, nobody could think of mentioning a *matam* (body of knowledge, doctrine, or system of thought) as being the handiwork of a school of Nāstika, not to speak of listing it in a schedule of the science along with the conventional *matas* of historic tradition.[1]

[1] Pizzagalli pp. 24, 28, 32. According to this Italian scholar, *artha* and *niti* literature embodies the most genuine expression of Hindu materialism.

The Śukra authors, however, are bold enough to do so. Shall we say that this boldness is but an expression of their "liberalism"? Is it that they are tolerant or catholic enough, being students of materialism, to invite the "reason-worshipping" philosophers into the fold of the established convention? Or shall we say that this boldness points to the lateness or "modernism" of the passage in which the expression occurs? Perhaps we may take it in both ways. The Śukra authors or, at any rate, those of their cycle, responsible for the incorporation of the list of the thirty-two *vidyās*, are at once liberal and modern.

We know as a positive fact that it is in Mādhava's "compendium of all the philosophies", known as the *Sarva-darśana-saṅgraha* (1331 A.C.) that the Nāstika philosophy is, for the first time, presented as a *mata*, a system of thought. It is described as *Bṛihaspatimata*, also as *lokāyatika*. The Chārvākas, who are generally known to be professors of Nāstika doctrines, have derived their inspiration, according to the tradition recorded by Mādhava, from *Bṛihaspati*, the *purohita* (priest) of Vedic gods. And this *Bṛihaspati*, we are assured further, is none other than the traditional father of *Nītiśāstra* and *Arthaśāstra*.

Mādhava, as the follower of Śankarāchārya, is, of course, a Vedāntist, i.e. the furthest removed from the disciples of *Bṛihaspati*. But he is objective enough to give the Devil his due, and include the system of the Chārvākas in his examination of the "sixteen systems" prevailing in his time. Indeed, he accords this system the very place of honour in his book, although, no doubt, as Pizzagalli points out, for dialectical reasons. Mādhava's mission is to establish the supremacy of Vedānta. And in order to do this, he has to proceed in a climbing series—demolishing the systems one by one at each step. Naturally the least Vedāntic or rather the most anti-Vedāntic system conceivable is the *Bṛihaspatian* philosophy, the *Nāstika-matam*. So Mādhava's book has to commence with his very antithesis, namely, *Bṛihaspati*.

The Śukra authors, however, have no special axe to grind,

so far as this *matam* is concerned. They can afford to be genuinely objective and mention it as a fact of the philosophical universe. It is then very probable, chronologically speaking, that *Sarva-darśanasaṅgraha* is responsible for the place of Nāstika theory in the Śukran list or that both belong to the same intellectual complex.

Śukra's description of the Nāstikas agrees in "general features" with that given by Mādhava. The Chārvākas, says this Vedāntist author, are used to denying *pāralaukikam artham* (other-worldly interests). According to them, everything exists through its own *svabhāva* (nature). Their logic recognises no *anumāna* (inference), but is based solely on *pratyaksha* (observation or perception). They believe that the soul is indentical with the body. The pursuit of pleasure is the sole teaching of their ethics. And so on.[1]

The definition of *Nāstika-matam* in *Śukranīti* is not, as a matter of course, as elaborate as in *Sarva-darśana-saṅgraha*. But it is precise enough to lead one to believe that this compendium of the sixteen system was not unknown to the Śukra authors. To this extent, perhaps, an aspect of the chronological question may be taken to be solved.

But, for the present, we are interested in the philosophical orientations of the Śukra economists. The account rendered of the Chārvākas by Mādhava possesses, as one can notice, certain characteristics which would appeal very powerfully to the mentality of the Śukra philosophers. Whether the Śukra authors be prepared to deny the existence of the Vedas or not, there is no doubt that the "rationalism" and *svabhāva* theory (naturalism) of the Chārvākas would fit in quite well with their general trend of thought. The logical and psychological affiliations of Śukranīti with *Nāstika-matam* may be considered to have been intimate.

Then there is an historical affinity as well. Mādhava says, as we have seen above, that the founder of *Nastika-matam* is

[1] Cowell's *Sarva Darśana-Sangraha* (London, 1894); Muir's article on Indian materialists in the *Journal of the Royal Asiatic Society* (1862); Hopkins's *Great Epic of India* (New York), Pizzagalli, pp. 52-53, 56.

identical with the founder of *Nītiśāstra* and *Arthaśāstra*. That common founder is known, indeed, to be *Bṛihaspati*, who as priest of the gods, is bound to be the sworn enemy of Śukra, the preceptor of the *asuras* (demons). It is not quite clear, therefore, how the name of *Bṛihaspati* would have sounded in the ears of the professors of the Śukra cycle. But, perhaps, by the fourteenth century, the old feuds between the Vedic gods and demons, Bṛihaspati and Śukra, had retired into the limbo of oblivion. And the *Sukra* investigators of *artha* and *nīti* would have found no difficulty in accosting as comrades and holding *tête-ā-têtes* with their colleagues of the Bṛihaspati cycle in one and the same *goshṭhī* or *parishad*.

It is not necessary to identify the Śukra professors of economics, politics and allied sciences with the Sachchakas of the Buddhist tradition, or with the *Nyāya-Vaiśeshika-Sāṅkhyans* or, finally, with the *Nāstika-Chārvāka-Lokāyatikas*. Only one point has been sought to be established. It is that the anti-Vedāntic, anti-Hegelian, anti-idealistic trends of thought were varied enough all through the ages to furnish the positive foundations of which a materialistic scheme of *loka-hita* (Utilitarianism) can be built up.

CALCUTTA — BENOY KUMAR SARKAR

—:o:—

I appreciate the greatness of the work performed by Swami Dayanand Saraswati.

LONDON, W. C. I. — L. D. BARNETT

SWAMI DAYANAND SARASWATI AND INDO-ARYAN CULTURE

SWAMI DAYANAND SARASWATI was a great reformer of the nineteenth century. He was an Indian first and an Indian last. To him everything sublime was traceable to the Vedas, the fountain-head of knowledge, be it moral, political, natural, or of any other kind. He was deeply convinced of the infallibility of the Vedas and was of the opinion that in them every scientific truth was to be found, though *bīja-rūpeṇa*. It was owing to this conviction that in his commentaries, he interpreted the Vedic hymns in a way which was different from that followed by his predecessors and which he considered to be the right one. His endeavour to trace the laws of gravitation, telegraphy, the secret of locomotion, etc., to those revealed books was a result of his courage of conviction. He was not the only person of this age to have such ideas, for similar notions are to be found in that wonderful book, namely, *Secret Doctrine*, which only gifted persons could write. To find out the formula of the composition of water, which is technically expressed by H_2O, from the ***Rik Mitram huve putadaksham varuṇa cha risadasam*** is the outcome of such convictions. That great teacher of humanity has stated his views in the chapter named *Svamantavyāmantavya-prakāśh*, which he has appended to the *Satyārtha Prakāśh*, one of his chief books. He firmly believed that the four Vedas—the *Saṁhitā* only—were the Revealed books, meant for the welfare of the whole world. He held this view on the authority of the Vedas themselves.

The verse :—यथेमां वाचं कल्याणी मा वदानि जनेभ्यः ।

ब्रह्मराजन्याभ्याꣳ शूद्राय चार्याय च स्वाय चारणाय,

the great Swami asserted, clearly says that '*this*' '*vāch*' i. e., the Veda was meant for every human being, be he a Brahmin, a Śūdra or even a Chāṇḍāla. Furthermore, to him the

Gāyatrīmantra was meant for all mankind, including women, who, he held, were equally entitled to become *brahmachāriṇis* and to read and even teach the Vedas. His views about this question are pertinently put in the 'smṛiti' (tradition)—

पुराकल्पे तु नारीणां व्रतबन्धनमिष्यते ।
अध्यापनञ्च वेदानां सावित्रीवाचनन्तथा ॥

A reformer of such ideas could not but be a staunch supporter of female-education and Swami Dayanand's advocacy of the cause is well-known. He was totally against child marriage, which, on the authority of the Ṛigveda, he held to be un-Aryan.

The principle of transmigration of souls, he said, was applicable to all mankind and final emancipation was to be won through good *karma* and the grace of God. He was a believer in the principle of the four *varnas*, namely, Brahmin, Kshattriya, Vaiśya and Śūdra, which, like the Ṛishis of yore, he held, depended on the personal acts of an individual and *not* on the birth of anybody. There was no other caste system for him. Further, his conviction was that every individual, be he an Indian or a resident of foreign lands, was eligible for the performance of '*Yajñas*', provided the individual was of good character and behaviour. The high class '*Vipras*' who carried the Indo-Aryan culture to distant lands like Java, Sumatra or Borneo, professed the same doctrine by performing these rites in those lands, as is evidenced by the epigraphs which have been found engraved on the sacrificial pillars still standing in those countries. He believed that *Brahma* (God), *Jīva* (Soul) and *Prakriti* (Matter) are indestructible, endless and beginningless, and that the true Aryans who dwelt in Āryāvarta never worshipped the Omnipresent and Omnipotent Father of the Universe through *idols* of any kind. For him, and rightly, there was no *dharma* higher than Truth and no sin more heinous than falsehood :

न हि सत्यात्परो धर्मो नानृतात्पातकं परम् ।

The quintessence of Indo-Aryan culture in the eyes of the great Swami Dayanand Saraswati was :—

निन्दन्तु नीतिनिपुणाः यदि वा स्तुवन्तु
लक्ष्मीः समाविशतु गच्छतु वा यथेष्टम् ।
अद्यैव वा मरणमस्तु युगान्तरे वा
न्याय्यात्पथः प्रविचलन्ति पदं न धीराः ॥

"Whether he is upbraided or praised, whether prosperity comes or goes at will, whether he dies or lives, a true Ārya never deviates from the path of righteousness;" and this he preached and inculcated throughout his life. It was for this very principle that he sacrificed his noble life. Verily, the definition of Deva he has put down himself, is applicable to him. These fundamentals of Indo-Aryan culture were inculcated by every Āchārya of this land, and he preached them wherever he went. The Swami might well be taken as one of the *Kāraka Koti yogins* who came to India to preach the Vedic Dharma and thereby remove social evils from his *mātṛibhūmi*. An embodiment of *Brahmacharya* and an undaunted preacher of Dharma, Swami Dayanand Saraswati was throughout his career an excellent illustration of the true Aryan culture.

OOTACAMAND — HIRANANDA ŚASTRI

———:o:———

I wish the Dayanand Nirvāṇa Ardha Shatābdī that is to be celebrated in October next, every success. Swami Dayanand's work as a social reformer cannot fail to evoke the admiration of all who have the good of the Hindu community at heart. He was probably the first to realise, among other things, the injustice of treating a very considerable part of the population of India as untouchables and consequently advocated the removal of such restrictions. For that alone, the Hindus owe him a deep debt of gratitude.

INDORE — S. M. BAPNA

SWAMI DAYANAND AND HINDU SOCIAL RE-VALUATION

DAYANAND SARASWATI is the last Hindu social epoch-maker in the true line of the Buddha and Śankara. And the surprising fact is that the type should have recurred at a time when the Hindu tradition of true Hindu times seems to have become dead and obsolete. The time when the Swami arose was one of the stage of the supremacy of a Personal God, a concept purely Semitic, fully established by the neo-Vaiśnavism of the Muhammadan period and lately confirmed by Christianity. That at that time a man of the type of Śankarāchārya should arise, when Sanskrit culture had practically fully and long ceased to be the vehicle of Hindu life, when the Vedanta had become a belief of the past, that a Brahmin Sannyasi should arise to demonstrate once more that the theory of the Vedantic God alone could be true, that a personal God is an impossibility— to rationalise the theory of God and to find a large, wide-spread acceptance in the Hindu mass—in a mass which had fallen a prey to the superstitious conditions of medieval Christianity was indeed a *miracle.* To see a tall, lustresome figure, from whose lips flowed torrential Sanskrit, launched on a theological *dig-vijaya* in an India under a Christian Power of unthinkable political strength, was to cause disbelief in that received notion that a cultural revival of a masculine type, and specially, the enthronement of a rationalism virile enough not to admit an arbitrary rule of a personal Deity over man, was not possible in a subject society, a society subject to an alien civilization. The rise of a Dayanand in the nineteenth century is a phenomenon which baffles the historian. But there are such life-germs in the civilization of the Hindus which evidently make it indestructible and which are beyond the ken of that empiricist observer called the historian.

The present reformed and rejuvenated Hinduism is solely

a gift of Dayanand Saraswati. Dayanand had the humanity of the Buddha, but he combined with it the preservative complex of Śankara. The Buddha denounced the whole social structure as based on false notions of birth and caste inequality and preached a revolution. Dayanand emphasized, on the other hand, the traditional conservative regard for the Vedas and Vedic culture, but he did not have the limitation of Śankara and rose above it and pronounced that the theory of caste was false, un-Vedic and un-Hindu. Such a thing which was a negation of the laws of Manu and a contradiction of the accepted view of the *Purushasukta*, would not have been accepted by Hindu Society, unless it came from such a national type as Swami Dayanand who spoke Sanskrit with the ease of the Ṛishis, who had the selflessness of Narada and Durvasas, who could consume the cause of injustice with the fire of his speech like the Buddha, and who could be irresistible in polemics like Śankara. He proved a super-man. He overpowered the mystic professional Guru; the sectarian; the upholder of *avatars*; the worshipper of gods and stones, places and pilgrimages; the miracle-worker; etc., etc. He installed the man in the street into his true position in society, he put him in direct worship of one God, like Muhammad. And his god was the Hindu rationalistic God to whom man never becomes a helpless slave. The Sannyasi Dayanand gave freedom to the soul of the Hindu, as Luther did unto the European. And he forged that freedom from inside, that is from Hindu literature itself.

He did something still greater which his predecessors from the Buddha to Ram Mohan Roy had failed to achieve. He established the falsity of caste from the orthodox national standpoint and made the Hindus disbelieve that theory as Hindus. True Vedic Hinduism, he gave the message, is equality by birth. You become an Arya, that is that noble race of Hindus, by your deeds, not by brith. He opened up the Vedic civilization even to the non-Hindu, to the foreigner and gave him a chance to avail himself of that supreme Dharma.

The social revolution of Swamiji has come to be accepted within fifty years of the ascetic's death. He shook the conscience of the Hindu—the real Hindu—making the masses who could only read and understand the language in which Swamiji left his permanent literary discourses. He wisely, like the Buddha, composed in the most popular vernacular, Hindi—the present-day imperial Magadhi. I have witnessed the working effect of the words left by the Swamiji. People who opposed them most (and I have been mostly associated with them) began to believe in an aspect of the Swamiji's theory to-day, in another aspect tomorrow without realising that they were becoming Dayanand's followers. To-day when a Vaisya, an ex-barrister, has risen to the height of saints, his social programme which is merely a repetition of the Shuddhi programme of the great Swamīji, his fellow-Gujarati, has become acceptable, only because the Rishi-like Dayanand had made it possible through the Śastras and the Veda, by dint of his prophetic exposition after the Hindu fashion. Saints cannot change Hindu society, they cannot give new values; it is the Brahmin and the Sannyasi who alone will bring forth a new order. It is the aristocrat, who destroyed aristocratic privilege in France, that can destroy and re-build. It is the Brahmin—the true aristocrat of Hindu society—who has always led and given new values and hence new life to Hindu society.

Dayanand was not only the greatest Indian of the nineteenth century, Dayanand does not only continue the dynasty of Visvamitra, Narada and Śankara; he has a *high place amongst the modern liberators of mankind.* In the nineteenth century there was nowhere else such a powerful teacher of monotheism, such a preacher of the unity of man such a successful crusader against capitalism in spirituality. Above all, to us Indians, he is proof that the race is alive and can re-adjust its social values.

I, as a common citizen, as a recorder of facts, and as a non-Arya-Samajist most respectfully bow to the memory of that great spiritual and social reformer, the Hindu *zeit-geist.*

PATNA K. P. JAYASWAL

SWAMI DAYANAND SARASWATI

FIFTY years have passed since Swami Dayanand Saraswati left the scene of his activity, and every European who has tried to follow the development in India in the last decennium will easily understand why his compatriots want to give expression to that gratitude towards him. The ideals which he wanted to see realised in India are such as must necessarily appeal to the Western world.

The ancient Aryan civilization of India came to Europe as a revelation, and was often considered as the common inheritance of the whole Indo-European race, which the European nations must study, in order to understand their own past, and, through this past, their present individuality and their future. And it was realised, sometimes with enthusiasm, that the first known beginning was not barbarism, but a society when lofty ideas were conceived and a rich and energetic life was led.

We do not any more think that we are descended from the Vedic Aryans, but we are still apt to feel a certain pride in the achievements of our old Indian cousins. And we understand how the Vedas are regarded in India, now after it has been realized that they are due to the direct ancestors of the Indians of to-day and that their ideals can, moreover, become the foundation upon which India's future can be based. This conviction is apt to strengthen that national self-respect without which no people can hold its own. And when it is gradually spreading in India to-day, that is largely due to Swami Dayanand Saraswati.

Century after century, the Vedas had been handed down from teacher to pupil, but more as a sacred tradition than as a living force. Their ideals could no more be realized in a vigorous and energetic life, and the Upanishads, which had never quite lost their hold on the Indian mind, could show the way towards

ANASAGAR LAKE, AJMER.

emancipation from mundane life, but not to self-assertion in the modern world.

The Swami never got tired of preaching that, in reality, Vedic religion is apt to satisfy the cravings of modern man and to give him strength in the struggle of every day's life, and that the ancient Vedic civilization can be revived and lead to a national renaissance. It is not separated from the ideas of the modern world by an unbridgeable chasm. It can well be reconciled with them, and can even lead to a clearer understanding of modern problems. The schools and colleges bearing his name have never been content to repeat ancient formulas. They have filled them with new life and trained their *alumni* to become intelligent and fully efficient members of modern society.

There is still another feature in the Swami's work which strongly appeals to European minds: the stress he laid on the uplift of the depressed classes. Also here he showed himself as a nationalist with lofty ideals and high aims.

He did so much for his country, and outside of India sympathy will be felt with his compatriots when they come together in order to celebrate the Semi-Centenary of his demise.

OSLO, NORWAY — STEN KONOW

WE have to acknowledge his (Dayanand Saraswati's) great merit in having given a strong impulse to Vedic studies in India, and having shown that idolatry has not the sanction of the Vedas. If the founder of the Arya Samaj had done nothing else, but rouse his followers to a vigorous fight against the folly and dangers of the modern caste-system, he would deserve to be honoured as one of the great leaders of men in modern India.

PRAGUE II, OPATOVICKA 8,
CZECHOSLOVAKIA — M. WINTERNITZ

SWAMI DAYANAND

I have always looked upon Swami Dayanand Saraswati as one of the greatest men of India and the greatest of his type since the time of Śaṅkarāchārya. He was physically, intellectually and morally a giant and a man who represented the best type of Vedic Aryans. Though entirely innocent of English and so-called modern culture, he had a wonderful grasp of the realities of life. He was a revivalist and can be justly described as the author of the Aryan renaissance of the latter part of the nineteenth century. His life and work can be discussed in their various aspects, but there are three features which strike me as most prominent among them.

As a religious teacher, the first and foremost thing that characterises his work is the simplification of the Hindu religion and Hindu scriptures. As a deep scholar of the Vedas, he had realized that Hinduism as practised in modern times was anything but the religion taught by the Vedas and other books based on the Vedas. The Vedas had been buried under a heap of books which in the popular mind had taken the place of the scriptures. He removed this heap, layer by layer, and laid bare the real scriptures of the Hindus, the four *Saṁhitās*. He emphasized that the Vedas alone were the infallible repositories of religious teaching, and other books deserved respect in the same measure only as they approximated to the teaching of the Saṁhitās. This was a great achievement in itself, as it removed the great confusion that was prevailing in the minds of the Hindus at the time of his advent, when almost everything written in Sanskrit was supposed to be sacred and given the position of a scripture. The Brāhmaṇas, the Upanishads, the Darśanas, the Smṛitis and the Purāṇas were assigned their proper place, but only subsidiary and subservient to the Saṁhitās. With the simplification and the classification of the scriptures, he also strove to simplify the doctrine and belief of the Hindus. Anything that was inconsistent with the teachings of the Vedas was not worthy of belief or practice. From this resulted the re-assertion of the purest form of Monotheism and the rejection of belief in gods, goddesses, incarnations, *Śrāddha* ceremonies and the practice of idol-worship and pilgrimages to sacred places as a means to salvation.

The second great feature of Swami Dayanand's mission was an attempt at the consolidation of the amorphous mass of the Hindus. This he tried to accomplish by giving them a common belief in one deity, in one scripture and a common mode of worship. He had realized that the mode of worship followed by the Hindus was too individualistic; thousands of Hindus visiting the same temple, worshipping the same idol one after the other without any communion of worship did not make for a united community. He established the Arya Samaj to provide a common place of worship where those who believed with him could sit together and carry on congregational worship, and it is certainly inspiring to find some times thousands of Aryas sitting in one hall reciting the same prayers in chorus and singing the same hymns. He also realised that caste-distinction was a hindrance in the way of Hindu consolidation and he preached that caste was not to be determined by birth but by qualifications, character and occupation. The doors of the Arya Samaj were thrown open by him to the Brahmin and the Pariah alike and it is refreshing to find that in Arya temples the Śāstrīs and the shoe-makers are seated side by side reciting the same Vedic texts and sacred hymns every Sunday. As another step in this direction, Swami Dayanand preached that the Vedic religion was a universal religion and was open to members of all nations irrespective of their caste, creed or colour. Born Mussalmans and Christians have been taken into the fold of the Arya Samaj and I know of one instance where a born Sayad is actually officiating as priest to a whole Arya congregation.

The third feature of Swami Dayanand's work that strongly appeals to me is, so to say, the rejuvenation of the Hindu mind. The Hindus had fallen into an abyss of pessimism, despondency and self-depreciation. Swami Dayanand rescued them from this and inspired them with a sense of pride for their past glory and an ardent hope and optimism for the future. The result is that whereas the ordinary Hindu suffers from a spirit of defeatism and depression, Swami Dayanand's followers are often full of ardour and enthusiasm which non-Hindus have sometimes described as fanaticism. The Arya Samajists are, as a rule, ambitious and entertain high aspirations for the future. They believe that their country was great in the past and will once more become great. They believe that their religion is the best in the world and would one day be recognized as such by followers of all religions. Unlike the ordinary Hindus, an Arya Samajist is always anxious to convert others to his own faith and in his religious attitude shows a catholicity and liberality hardly conceivable in an ordinary Hindu. He does not think that his religion is like a weak thread liable to be snapped under the least strain of contact with non-Hindus, but looks upon it as a strong and unbreakable cable which would bear any kind of strain in the clash of creeds.

The impetus given by Swami Dayanand still continues, and it is really remarkable that all the present day activities of Swadeshi and the crusade against untouchability, caste etc., were all anticipated by Swami Dayanand Saraswati. His inspiration has led to the establishment of a large number of educational institutions, orphanages, widows' homes and various organizations for the uplift of the depressed classes. I am personally convinced that only the Arya Samaj can provide a really efficacious solution of the difficulties of caste and the amelioration of the depressed classes, and the stronger it grows the stronger will be the Hindu community.

SIMLA — GOKAL CHAND NARANG

VRĀTYASTOMA

(Readmission into Hinduism of the Depressed and the Fallen classes)

VRĀTYA is one of the most interesting words in the history of ancient Indian Society. The accepted meaning of this word is "fallen from *vrata*," that is, degraded on account of neglecting the duties of one's *varṇa*. Vrātya popularly denotes a person who neglects sacraments; in short, neglect of Vedic Saṁskāras accounted for one being a Vrātya. Thus, a Brahmin not invested with the sacred thread up to the sixteenth, a Kshattriya up to the twenty-second, and a Vaiśya up to the twenty-fourth year is a Vrātya. According to the *Manusaṁhitā*, "the most prominent and, chronologically, the earliest among the metrical law-books in India," the Vrātyas were those who neglected the primary duty of the Aryan society, *viz.*, Sāvitrī or uttering the sacred formula of Gāyatrī. It may be stated in this connection that *Patitasāvitrīka* is a term synonymous with Vrātya in Sanskrit lexicons. The *Manūsaṁhitā* also refers to Vrātya Brahmins, Vrātya Kshattriyas and Vrātya Vaiśyas, and points out various denominations of their respective children from Vrātya women.[1] Yājñavalkya in his *Smṛiti* lays down the 16th, the 22nd and the 24th year as the highest limit for the *Upanayana* ceremony of the Brahmins, Kshattriyas and Vaiśyas respectively and that those who become *Sāvitrīpatitas*

[1] द्विजातयः सवर्णासु जनयन्त्यव्रतांस्तु यान् ।
तान्सावित्रीपरिभ्रष्टान् व्रात्यानिति विनिर्दिशेत् ॥ २० ॥
व्रात्यात्तु जायते विप्रात्पापात्मा भूर्जकण्टकः ।
आवन्त्यवाटधानौ च पुष्पधः शैख एव च ॥ २१ ॥
झल्लो मल्लश्च राजन्याद् व्रात्यान्निच्छिविरेव च ।
नटश्च करणश्चैव खसो द्रविड एव च ॥ २२ ॥
वैश्यात्तु जायते व्रात्यात्सुधन्वाचार्य एव च ।
कारुषश्च विजन्मा च मैत्रः सात्वत एव च ॥ २३ ॥ *Tenth Chapter.*

on crossing their limit become outcastes of all religions, and have no right to sacrament without Vrātyastoma sacrifice.[1]

Classical Sanskrit literature throws but little light upon Vrātya and the strong hold which this important word has exercised on the minds of the Aryan people throughout the ages.[2] We have, therefore, to go to the Vedic literature for this. The word 'Vrāta' is used in several passages of the Ṛigveda[3] and later works to denote 'troop' or an indefinitely large number. One passage of the Ṛigveda refers to the troops of the Maruts by three different terms—*Vrāta*, *Śardha* and *Gaṇa*. From Ṛigvedic references we conclude that Vrāta referred to the hordes of people outside, and even hostile to, the Ṛishi society or Brāhmanic circle. In Vrāta we have a correct and grammatical derivation of Vrātya — व्राते समवेता व्रात्याः [4]. The Seventeenth chapter of the *Pañchaviṁśa* (or *Tāṇḍya*) *Brāhmaṇa* of the Sāmaveda contains much information about the Vrātyas and deals with the Vrātyastoma or the purificatory rite for their assimilation in the Brahmanic fold. The following lines contain relevant extracts from the 17th chapter[5]:—

[1] आषोडशाद्द्वाविंशाच्चतुर्विंशाच्च वत्सरात् ।
ब्रह्मक्षत्रविशां काल औपनायनिकः परः ॥ ३७ ॥
अत ऊर्ध्वं पतन्त्येते सर्वधर्मबहिष्कृताः ।
सावित्रीपतिता व्रात्या व्रात्यस्तोमादृते क्रतोः ॥ ३८ ॥ *First Chapter.*

[2] Vrātya is still used in Marāthi in the sense of a vagabond. We come across a very good instance of a Vrātya Kshattriya in the history of the Marāthās. A few centuries before Sivāji, only two *Varnas* — Brahmins and Non-Brahmins (or Sudras) — were recognised in the Deccan. When Sivāji established a small but independent principality, he desired to have his coronation celebrated according to the *Veda-vidhi* in order to claim equality of political status with other kings. But there was one hindrance to the realisation of his ideal. According to the ancient Hindu scriptures, only a Kshattriya could be crowned a king. To the Brahmins, Sivāji was a Marāthā, hence a Sūdra. They were, therefore, not prepared to consecrate a Sūdra as a king Sivāji then got a genealogical table prepared and tracing the origin of the Bhonsla family from the Sisodias of Mewar, it was pointed out that by neglecting Kshattriya customs the Bhonalas had become Vrātyas. Thereafter Visvesvara Bhatta (nicknamed Gāgā Bhatta), a very learned Pandit of Benares and the greatest Sanskrit theologian and controversialist of the day, was invited to express his opinion. Visvesvara Bhatta declared that Sivāji's coronation ceremony could be performed just in accordance with the Vedas, after he was purified (he being a Vrātya Kshattriya) according to the Sāstric injunctions. Then Sivāji was annointed King after his undergoing purificatory rites .

[3] I, 163,8 ; III, 26, 2 ; V. 53, 11.

[4] Dacca University Bulletin, No. VI, p. 4.

[5] *Tandya Mahabrahmana*, Vol. II., pp. 350-66 (Edited by Anandachandra Vedāntavāgisa in *Bibliotheca Indica*, Calcutta, 1874).

In the first section, we are told—"when the Devas (gods) retired to Heaven, their followers who wandered on earth as Vrâtyas (or lived in temporary settlements), became dejected and came to the spot from which the gods went to Heaven. But they did not know the necessary prayer-chant and the metre by which they could be re-united with the Devas. The gods sympathising with their unfortunate brethren directed the Maruts to teach them the necessary prayer-chants with the metre. Thereupon, the Maruts gave them sixteen prayer-chants (*Shoḍashastoma*) in the *Anushṭubh* metre, by means of which they were re-united with their gods.

"The *Hīna* (or depressed) Vrâtyas get degenerate and wander about as Vrâtyas (or live in temporary habitations), neither practise *Brahmacharya*, nor can till land nor carry on trade. This prayer (known as Shoḍasha) has the power to elevate them. In this, the priest recites the prayer-chant (Sâman) called *Dyautāna*. It is named after *Dyutāna*, the chief house-holder (Gṛihapati) of the depressed gods. He (Dyutāna) belonged to the fallen Marudgaṇas. With his fallen brethren he performed the sacrifice, chanted this hymn and became prosperous.

"Those Vrâtyas are called *Garagir* (swallowers of poison or speakers of poisonous words), who eat food fit to be eaten by the Brahmins, who regard cultured speech as hard to pronounce, who inflict capital punishment on those who do not deserve death and who, though not initiated, speak the language of the initiated. This prayer called Shoḍasha is powerful enough to destroy sins."

After this brief introduction of the Vrâtyas and the merits of the prayer-chants necessary for their purification, the Brâhmaṇa contains the following remarks:—

> "The Vrâtya house-holder (Gṛihapati), who wishes to perform this sacrifice should wear a turban (*ushṇīsha*), carry a whip (*pratoda*) and a kind of small bow (*jyāhroḍa*), ride a rough chariot (*vipatha*) covered with planks, put on a black garment (*krishṇaśam vāsaḥ*) and two skins, black and white, and wear also

a silver ornament. The others, subordinate to the leader (gṛihapati) have garments with fringes of red, skins folded double and sandals or shoes. The Vrātyas hand over their goods (shown above) to whomsoever.[1] Thirty-three Vrātyas come with their chief house-holder to participate in the sacrifice and only thirty-three attain elevation and prosperity."

The second section (Kāṇḍa) of the seventeenth chapter deals with the purification of those who were accused and condemned (*nindita*) for some sin and hence outcasted. The *nindita* Vrātyas were admitted by means of the Shaṭshoḍashī hymn.

The third section is devoted to another kind of Vrātyastoma (dvishoḍashī), intended for the purification and re-admission of those Vrātyas who were called Kanishṭhas (Juniors), that is those who had been regarded as outcastes at a comparatively young age by reason of their living among outcastes. The fourth section describes another variety of Vrātyastoma suitable for re-admission of those who called themselves Jyeshṭhas (Seniors) and, being impotent (Śamanīchāmeḍhra) had gone to live with the outcastes. Kushītaka (a sage), son of Samaśravas, was the first householder among such Vrātyas to perform this sacrifice.

The prayer and rite, described above, is also met with in the sixth section of the eighth chapter of the *Lāṭyāyana Śrauta Sūtra*[2] of the Sāmaveda. From it we learn that the Vrātyas wishing to perform this sacrifice should select as their *gṛihapati* the most learned or the purest in descent or the richest among them and they should partake of the sacrificial food after their chief. It also informs us that at least thirty-three Vrātyas were required for performing the sacrifice. The Sūtra contains

[1] The Brāhmaṇa is not clear on this point, but according to Sāyana, the commentator, it refers to the unpurified Vrātyas or the Brahmins of the Magadhadesa.

[2] The *Srauta Sutra of Latyayana* with the commentary of Agnisvami (Edited by Anandachandra Vednātavāgisa in Bibliotheca Indica, Calcutta, 1870), pp. 576-85.

frequent references to the *Pañchaviṁśa Brāhmaṇa* and says in conclusion that the performance of the Vrātyastoma sacrifice secures for the Vrātyas the rights and privileges of the first three regenerate classes, the *Dvija Varṇas*, i.e. they may learn the Vedas, perform sacrifices and make presents to the Brahmins. The Brahmins too may impart Vedic knowledge to them, receive presents at their hands and even dine with them.

The summary of the portions of the *Pañchaviṁśa Brāhmaṇa* and the *Lāṭyāyana Śrauta Sūtra* in the foregoing lines is not likely to be perfectly intelligible without some observations thereon. From the above account it would be clear that Vrātya means one who has fallen or degraded, in short, one having gone outside the pale of Vedic Brāhmanism. Vrātyastoma is, therefore, a prayer (or a prayer-chant) to be chanted in the *Anushṭubh* metre for the regeneration of the fallen.

There were four varieties of Vrātyastoma intended for the four classes of Vrātyas. The ceremony for the purification and regeneration of the Vrātyas was in one particular at variance with other great Vedic ceremonies. Whereas in other ceremonies, one sacrificer and his wife in the sacrificial hall were required, here we come across thousands of sacrificers. One of them, the richest, the wisest and the most powerful, acted as *gṛihapati* or the Patriarch and others merely followed him. Thus the ceremony in question seems to be a convenient device by which thousands of Vrātyas were admitted to the Brāhmanic society. Frequent occurrence of such ceremonies led to the admission of innumerable hordes of nomadic Aryans into settled life. When admitted into Brāhmanism, the purified Vrātyas had to leave their possessions of Vrātya life to those who still lived as Vrātyas or to the Brahmins of Magadha who were often looked down upon by members of the Ṛishi society.

The first kind of Vrātyas appear not only as identical with nomadic Aryan hordes, but also somewhat antagonistic to the Aryan population of settled areas, viz., the Ṛishis or Brahmins.

To point out the difference, the Ṛishis used gold ornaments, while the Vrâtyas had silver ones; the Ṛishis had chariots, the Vrātyas carts only. In Ṛishis' chariots the planks were nailed, while the Vrātyas had their planks tied with strings. The Brahmins' head-dress was tied round their heads, while the Vrātyas wore it slantingly. The Brahmins had reins to restrain their horses, but the Vrātyas had sticks with leather thongs. The Ṛishis used two garments to cover the upper and lower halves, while the Vrātyas had only one tied to their loins by two strings. The Brahmin's clothes lacked in borders, but the Vrâtya had black borders. The Ṛishi possessed bows, bow-strings and arrows, but the Vrātya's bow had no string.

Mr. Rajaram Ramkrishna Bhagvat holds[1] that the first class of Vrātyas mentioned in the *Pañchaviṁśa Brāhmaṇa* was divided into two categories—(*a*) the depressed (*hīna*) who were non-Aryans and (*b*) degraded Aryans (*garagir*), the first being a case of conversion *en masse*, pure and simple, and the second that of re-admission. This, however, is a mere guess. There seems to have been only one class and the non-Aryan origin of the Vrātyas is not probable, for it is clearly stated that they spoke the language of the initiated. They were thus apparently Aryans. The statement of the *Pañchaviṁśa Brāhmaṇa*, that they find cultured speech difficult to pronounce, leads us to conclude that their speech was akin to some form of Prākrit. Arhants (saints) and Yaudhas (warriors) of the Vrātyas mentioned in the Sūtras correspond to the Brahmins and the Kshattriyas. Other particulars also confirm the view that the Vrātyas were not outside the pale of Aryan culture. Absence of agriculture or commerce in Vrātyas testifies to the nomadic life of the people. But the fact that they could be re-admitted to the Brāhmanic society by performing the prescribed ritual, shows that they were not Non-Aryans.

Those for whom the second kind of Vrātyastoma was

[1] Journal of the Bombay Branch of the Royal Asiatic Society, Vol. XIX., p. 359.

intended appear to be persons who might have fled from the Aryan folds to avoid justice and after passing some years in banishment among alien people, might have longed to come back to their kith and kin. Vrātyas requiring purification or re-admission in accordance with the third kind of Vrātyastoma were probably Aryans denationalised by living for a number of years among the depressed races. The fourth kind of Vrātyastoma was necessitated on the return of a member of the Aryan stock from amidst the depressed classes in old age. This was a case of re-admission and not conversion.

On their admission to the Brāhmanic fold, Vrātyas were permitted to attain equal status. No racial distinctions were observed and Brahmins and consecrated Vrātyas used to partake of food cooked by each other. The study and teaching of Vedas, performance of sacrifices for themselves and others, in all these Vrātyas were treated as equals of Brahmins. Not only this, but the revelation of Ṛiks and Sāmans, as also attainment of supreme proficiency, is noticeable in purified Vrātyas one of whom, Kaushītaki, had the privilege of having his name associated with a collection of Brāhmaṇas of the Ṛigveda. It is also interesting to note that the process of purification, which is fully treated of besides *Pañchaviṁśa Brāhmaṇa* in the *Lāṭyāyana* and *Drāhyāyana Sūtras* of the Sāmaveda and *Kātyāyana Śrauta Sūtra*[1] of the White Yujurveda had its beginning long before the composition of the *Pañchaviṁśa Brāhmaṇa.* Dyautāna-Sāman, which plays an important part in the Vrātyastoma, was revealed to a Ṛishi named Dyutāna who was a Gṛihapati of the Vrātyas before purification—a fact which goes to prove the revelation of Sāmans to a purified Vrātya.

For a proper understanding of the reasons which led our Aryan ancestors to institute a convenient *modus operandi* for the assimilation of the Vrātyas, we must go back to a period of

[1] *Kātyāyana Srauta Sūtram* with the commentary of Mahāmahopādhyāya Sri Karkāchārya (Edited by Madan Mohan Pāthak Vyākaraṇāchārya in the Chowkhamba Sanskrit Series, Benares, 1908), pp. 839-92.

remote antiquity when Vedic Dharma prevailed in a major part of Northern India. In ancient society, Brahmins were looked upon with utmost veneration on account of their high intellectual and moral attainments. The Ṛishi Society of old was almost identical with the Brāhmanic circle. By reason of emanation of the highest ideas of Vedic culture from the Brahmins, Vedic religion became synonymous with Brāhmanism. A few centuries preceding the Christian era mark the period of the fullest development of the Brāhmanic ritual. The cult of sacrifice was the predominant note of the period. In the sixth century B.C. two great names in the religious history of India loom large before our eyes—Gautama Buddha and Tīrthaṅkara Mahāvīra. Both these celebrities made earnest efforts for the spread of Buddhism and Jainism in Northern India. Magadhadeśa (Bihar) was the cradle of these religious systems, and from there they spread to different parts of India. Unparalleled development of the sacrificial cult in Brāhmanism gave rise to excess of animal slaughter and the preponderance of *Hiṁsā* through the length and breadth of India. The birth and growth of the religion of Buddha and Mahāvīra, both of which were based on the solid foundation of the principle of *Ahiṁsā*, really constituted the expansion of a hostile movement which meant a sense of relief to the disgusted votaries of the then Brāhmanism who gave a hearty welcome to the new faiths and embraced them in thousands and thousands. As soon as the Brahmins found that a fairly large section of the population in every province had joined the Buddhists and Jains, they dubbed these heterodox elements as *Vṛishalas*, an epithet which denotes a killer or destroyer of Dharma. It is interesting to note in this connexion that Vrātya and Vṛishala became almost identical in connotation. In complete agreement with the spirit of the times, we find in the *Manusaṁhitā* a statement about certain Kshattriyas, which says— "Gradually through the loss of sacred ceremonies (i.e. Vedic ritual) and by not seeing Brahmins (viz. on severing their contact with

Brahmins) the following families of Kshattriyas have reached the condition of Vṛishalas among men; Puṇḍrakas, Oḍras, Draviḍas, Kāmbojas, Yavanas (Greeks), Śakas (Indo-Scythians), Pāradas, Pahlavas (Persians), Chīnas (Chinese), Kirātas, Daradas and Khaśas.[1] This statement only shows that the Kshattriya tribes described above had been reduced to the condition of outcastes (those outside the pale of Vedic religion) in the opinion of the Brahmins, because the former severed their Brāhmanic contact, meaning thereby that they accepted an alien faith—Buddhism or Jainism.

An anecdote from the *Vishṇu Purāṇa*[2] furnishes interesting information on this point. We are told that Prince Bāhu, son of Vṛika of the Ikshvāku family was vanquished by the tribes of Haihayas and Tālajaṅghas and his country was over-run by them. In consequence of this he fled into the forests with his wives and died in the neighbourhood of the residence of the sage Aurva. Aurva prevented Bāhu's queen from mounting his funeral pyre, because in his opinion a valiant prince, a monarch of many realms, an offerer of many sacrifices, a universal monarch was in her womb. In obedience to the sage's advice she gave up her intention. The sage then conducted her to his abode where after some time she gave birth to a very splendid boy who was named Sagara. The holy sage invested Sagara with the sacred thread, instructed him in the Vedas and taught him the use of arms. When the boy was capable of reflection, one day he asked his mother the reason of their dwelling in the hermitage. His mother, in reply, related to him all that had happened. Upon hearing that, Sagara was highly incensed and

[1] शनकैस्तु क्रियालोपादिमाः क्षत्रियजातयः ।
वृषलत्वं गता लोके ब्राह्मणादर्शनेन च ॥ ४३ ॥
पौण्ड्रकाश्चौड्रद्रविडाः काम्बोजा यवनाः शकाः ।
पारदाः पह्लवाश्चीनाः किराता दरदाः खशाः ॥ ४४ ॥ *Tenth Chapter.*

[2] Book IV, Chapter III. Wilson's Translation, Vol. III., pp. 289-95.

vowed to recover his patrimonial kingdom and exterminate the Haihayas and Tālajaṅghas, by whom it had been over-run. Accordingly he put almost all the Haihayas to death, and would have, also, destroyed the Śakas, the Yavanas, Kāmbojas, Pāradas and Pahlavas, but they applied to Vasishṭha, the family-priest of Sagara, for protection. Vasishṭha regarding them as annihilated (or powerless), though living, thus said to Sagara: "Enough, enough, my son! Pursue no further these objects of your wrath. In order to fulfil your vow, I have separated them from affinity to the regenerate tribes, and from the duties of their castes." Complying with the injunctions of his spiritual guide, Sagara contented himself with imposing upon the vanquished nations peculiar distinguishing marks. He made the Yavanas shave their heads, the Śakas to shave half of their heads; the Pāradas wore their hair long and the Pahlavas let their beard grow in obedience to their commands. He deprived these as well as other Kshattriya races, of the established usages of oblations to fire and the study of the Vedas. Thus separated from religious rites, and abandoned by the Brahmins, these different tribes became Mlechchhas (i.e. Vṛishalas). After recovering his kingdom, Sagara reigned over the seven-zoned earth with undisputed dominion.

This Paurāṇic statement establishes beyond doubt that the above-mentioned Kshattriya races were members of the Brāhmanic fold, but on their embracing an alien religion they came to be looked upon as Mlechchhas or Vṛishalas by the Brahmins. Membership of the religions of Buddha and Mahāvīra by Brahmins, Kshattriyas and Vaiśyas not only resulted in their being dubbed Vṛishalas, but the authors of later Smṛitis went to the length of laying down the necessity of purification in case of those votaries of Brāhmanism who visited Aṅga, Baṅga, Kaliṅga, Saurāshṭra (Kathiawar) and Magadha except on pilgrimage.[1]

[1] अंगवंगकलिंगेषु सौराष्ट्रमगधेषु च । तीर्थयात्रां विना गच्छन् पुनः संस्कारमर्हति ॥
This verse is quoted in *Tattvabodhini*, commentary on Bhattoji's *Siddhantakaumudi* in connection with the Vārtika on Pāṇini's III. 2.115.

Needless to say that these provinces were strongholds of Buddhists and Jains. This injunction of the Smṛitis was, therefore, purposely laid down to stop all contact of the followers of Brāhmanism with the people of alien faiths.

Vrātyastoma sacrifice, as described above, was greatly instrumental in securing the absorption of the degraded and the depressed Aryan folk of nomadic habits into the settled life of the Ṛishi society. We should also take note of the fact that the same ceremony rendered invaluable help in re-admitting *en masse* those converts to Buddhism and Jainism—the so-called Vṛishalas—in the pale of Brāhmanic Hinduism. This process of "admitting among themselves a vast concourse of men belonging to the same race, but addicted to nomadic habits" or converted to alien faiths, speaks volumes in favour of Vedic Aryans' foresight in devising ways and means to integrate the various component parts of the Aryan Society into one organised whole and to maintain the numerical strength of the nation, in those days of hoary antiquity known to us as the Vedic period of Indian history. It is the wonderful elasticity in the Aryan system of faith that enabled the Aryan settlers in India entirely to incorporate all heterogeneous elements in the population into a common system of religious faith and social life.

In the last quarter of the nineteenth century, Maharshi Dayanand Saraswati stressed the revival of the ancient Vrâtya-stoma under the guise of Shuddhi, a term so easily intelligible to a man in the street. Shuddhi movement will ever remain as an eternal monument of Swami Dayanand's foresight and his invaluable services to the Hindus as a great social reformer. It has gone a great way towards the regeneration, and re-admission into the Vedic Dharma, of thousands and thousands of such Hindus, whose ancestors under the stress of circumstances in centuries gone by, had to take shelter under the banners of Islām and Christianity. The Shuddhi movement could not make much progress during the life-time of Swamiji; but thanks to the unflinching zeal and ceaseless activity of Swami Shraddhanand and other worthies of the Arya Samaj, Hindu society has succeeded in reclaiming in recent years thousands of Hindu converts from alien faiths.

I close in the hope that this paper on Vrātyastoma, in which lay the germ of the modern Shuddhi movement, which was so dear to Swamiji's heart, will serve as my humble contribution of homage to the memory of the great Ṛishi, the great social reformer, the great teacher and the fighter of organised evil in the pages of the Dayanand Commemoration Volume.

AJMER — RAMESHVAR G. OJHA

—:o:—

DURING my visit to India in 1931, I became acquainted with the extensive educational work of the Arya Samaj, especially as represented in its system of Gurukulas. These schools are undertaking an important function in retaining the interest of Indian youth in the ancient literature and traditions of India, and in uniting with this interest an appreciation of contemporary civilization. This work, which owes its inception to Swami Dayanand Saraswati, promises to be of substantial aid in this difficult period of transition. It is one of the privileges as well as of the necessities of an ancient civilization to conserve and re-interpret the treasures of the past while living in the present, and co-operating with all the agencies which tend to create the future.

CAMBRIDGE, MASSACHUSETTS — W. ERNEST HOCKING

MAHARSHI DAYANAND SARASWATI ON UNTOUCHABILITY

MAHARSHI Dayanand like all other Vedic Ṛishis of ancient India has proved on irrefutable grounds that the Vedas alone are the paramount Religious code of all the members of the Arya Samaj. He always uses the word *Satya-Vidyā* (True Knowledge) or *Satya-Śāstra* (Books of Scientific and Rational Truths) for the Vedas. The whole Sanskrit literature with one voice declares the Vedas to be the *Param Śāstram* (Principal Books of Scientific and Rational Truths). In Apte's English-Sanskrit Dictionary we find twofold meanings of the word *Śāstram* which corroborates the position that Vedas being Śāstra cannot be the books of Human History: Śāstra—(*a*) Any department of knowledge (*b*) Science.

Now in order to prove that Ṛishi Dayanand was against untouchability we shall quote Vedic Texts from his epoch-making *Veda-Bhāshya* or the commentary on the Vedas. His commentary is based chiefly on Vedic *Nighaṇṭu* and the *Nirukta* of Yâska, the acknowledged Rational commentator of the Vedic words.

Ṛigveda on the Problem

The last three *Mantras* of the Ṛigveda are known as bearing on the constitution of Samaj or Universal Society. Their subject matter or "*Devatā*" as given in the Veda is the "*Saṁjñānam*" or wisdom. Any '*Manushya*', i.e. a man or woman of this planet, is ordained to fulfil the commands therein.

The first *Mantra* begins thus:—

संगच्छध्वं संवदध्वं सं वो मनांसि जानताम् ।
देवा भागं यथा पूर्वे संजानाना उपासते ॥

(ऋ० मं० १०, सू० १९१, मं० २)

संगच्छध्वं (associate ye all in public meetings).

संवदध्वं (have ye all free discussion).

सं वो मनांसि जानताम् (acquire ye all through wisdom).

देवा भागं यथा पूर्वे संजानाना उपासते (Follow the foot-steps of your learned elders who have shown by their example devotion to Duty or *Dharma*).

This *Mantra* clearly removes the ban of *Aspṛiśyatā* (untouchability). It gives even the untouchables the right of becoming members of a progressive society and also gives them the right of free discussion.

Śrī Swami Dayanand, Śrī Devendranath Tagore and Śrī Bal Gangadhar Tilak have all translated this and the other two *Mantras* of this *Sūkta* and there is no contradiction as to their interpretations of these *Mantras*. This translation is based on all these three renowned Sanskrit Scholars of India.

The second *Mantra* is:—

समानो मंत्रः समितिः समानी समानं मनः सह चित्तमेषाम् ।
समानं मंत्रमभिमंत्रये वः समानेन वो हविषा जुहोमि ॥

(ऋक् मं० १०, सू० १९१, मं० ३)

समानो मंत्रः (Do ye all the study of Vedas).

समितिः समानी (Have ye all free and equal right in the membership of the legislative body).

समानं मनः सह चित्तमेषाम् (have ye all free voice in the framing of the resolutions in it).

समानं मंत्रमभिमंत्रये वः (Do ye practice co-operation thoroughly).

समानेन वो हविषा जुहोमि (The Almighty ordains that all men should follow His commands and have all dealings in Truth and Justice).

The third *Mantra* runs thus:—

समानी व आकूतिः समाना हृदयानि वः ।
समानमस्तु वो मनो यथा वः सुसहासति ॥

(ऋक् मंडल १०, सू० १९१, मं० ४)

समानी व आकूतिः (Let all your actions be according to the dictates of Duty).

समाना हृदयानि वः (Don't injure the feelings of others).

समानमस्तु वो मनः (Consider thoroughly before taking any step).

यथा वः सुसहासति (Help and give aid to each other).

The 18th *Mantra* of the 36th chapter of Yajurveda is as follows:—

दृते दृꣳह मा मित्रस्य मा चक्षुषा सर्वाणि भूतानि
समीक्षन्ताम्। मित्रस्याहं चक्षुषा सर्वाणि
भूतानि समीक्षे। मित्रस्य चक्षुषा समीक्षामहे ॥ (यजु० अ० ३६, मं० १८)

It means:—O God! thou art the remover of all troubles. I take a vow that all men behave unto me like a friend and I shall behave unto all men like a friend; and we all mutually behave like friends.

This *Mantra* inculcates the principle of Universal love and removes the ban of untouchability from mankind.

The following is another *Mantra* from the 30th chapter of the *Yajurveda, Mantra* 5

ब्रह्मणे ब्राह्मणं क्षत्राय राजन्यं मरुद्भ्यो वैश्यं तपसे शूद्रं
तमसे तस्करं नारकाय वीरहणं पाप्मने...॥ (यजु० अ० ३०, मं० ५)

which says:—God has given these things for the diffusion of knowledge of Vedas and God. Those men are Brahmins or scholars of the Vedas who have attained communion with God. *Rājanya* are those men who care to protect the country and its Government, i. e. the head of the Government. For the rearing of cattle, merchants and traders are Vaiśyas. For performing duties, the form of service or penance, are the Śūdras—the men who can serve faithfully.

Śūdras not looked down upon in Vedic Times

From this *Mantra* we conclude that in Vedic times Śūdras were not looked down upon. Their profession and work is styled as penance in the *Veda-Mantra*. Hence there can be no question of their being untouchables. All Sanskrit scholars admit that according to the most ancient lexicon, NIRUKTA, all the words of the Vedas are 'YAUGIC' which means that they are derivatives and this *Mantra* supports the contention of Nirukta inasmuch as it never thinks any man born of Brahmin parents as a Brahmin, but to him who can become a scholar of the Vedas and who can commune with the Almighty. Similarly for Kshattriya, Vaiśya and Śūdra.

Corroboration from the Gītā

The following verse from the *Gītā* corroborates the above quoted Vedic principle that the four *Varṇas* are based according to their attainments:—

चातुर्वर्ण्यं मया सृष्टं गुणकर्मविभागशः । (गीता, अ० ४)

Śyt. Bal Gangadhar Tilak in his learned preface to the *Gītā* while interpreting this verse has made it quite clear that in Vedic times the constitution of the four *Varṇas* was a sort of division of labour.

यथेमां वाचं कल्याणीमावदानि अनेभ्यः ।
ब्रह्मराजन्याभ्याꣳ शूद्राय चार्य्याय च स्वाय चारखाय ।
प्रियो देवानां दक्षिणायै दातुरिह भूयासमयं मे कामः
समृध्यतामुपमादो नमतु ॥ (यजु० अ० २६, मं० २)

In the above *Mantra*, God ordains—"as I reveal the Vedas unto you, similarly you must teach and preach the Vedas to all Human beings".

The God says:—

यथेमां like me वाचं this Veda कल्याणीम् beneficial आवदानि teach and preach अनेभ्यः for all human beings ब्रह्मराजन्याभ्याम् for Brahmins and Kshattriyas शूद्राय for Śūdras च and अर्याय merchants and tradesmen च and स्वाय your individual self च and अरखाय cobbler प्रियः dear देवानां of learned men दक्षिणायै for fees and donations इह in this world भूयासम् I become and अयम् this मे mine कामः desire समृध्यताम् may be fulfilled thoroughly उपमा to me अदः that satisfaction नमतु may I gain.

This *Mantra* of the *Yajurveda*, 26-2, contains the word '*Araṇāya*' which means 'a cobbler', but nowhere in the *Mantra* do we find any sign as to the untouchability of a cobbler. On the other hand, this *Mantra* clearly lays stress on the following words '*Janebhyaḥ*' which means 'for all human beings'. Further we find that this *Mantra* is very explicit about giving Vedic education from a Brahmin down to a cobbler.

Some fifty years ago this *Mantra* was translated by Maharshi Swami Dayanand Saraswati, and for a decade it was a point of controversy between the Sanātanist orthodox school of Pandits and the Arya Samajist Pandits. But a well-known Sanskrit scholar of Bengal, Pt. Satyavrata Sāmaśramī, who is neither a member nor a supporter of the Arya Samaj and who is well-known for his Sanskrit research work to the Government of India, has in his latest book *Aitareya Ālochanā* not only given a similar translation and exposition of this epoch-making *Mantra* but has in plain words, by giving reference of Swami Dayanand Saraswati and the translation which the great Ṛishi Dayanand made fifty years ago, corroborated every word of the same. He like Ṛishi Dayanand says that from the Brahmin down to the cobbler, every human being is entitled to the study of the Vedas.

The sixth *Mantra* of the 40th chapter of the *Yajurveda* is

यस्तु सर्वाणि भूतान्यात्मन्नेवानुपश्यति । सर्वभूतेषु चात्मानं ततो न विचिकित्सति ॥

यस्तु that man सर्वाणि all भूतानि beings एव certainly अनुपश्यति realises after obtaining knowledge आत्मन् एव supported by God सर्वभूतेषु all human beings ततः after न not विचिकित्सति despises any human being. This *Mantra* of the Yajurveda is also found in the *Iśopanishad*. Where in the place of *Vichikitsati* only the word *Vijugupsate* is given, and its translation by all Sanskrit scholars of the world is the same as that which is given above, i. e. 'a theist cannot despise any human being in the universe'. An American poet says 'Let no man call God his father, who does not call man his brother'.

In the *Atharvaveda*, *Kāṇḍa* XIX, *Sūkta* XV, *Mantra* VI:—

अभयं मित्रादभयममित्रादभयं ज्ञातादभयं पुरो यः ।
अभयं नक्तमभयं दिवा नः सर्वा आशा मम मित्रं भवन्तु ॥

we find the words, *Sarvā Āśā Mama Mitram Bhavantu'* which means that all human beings in all the countries of the world should behave unto me like a friend.

Some say that Śūdras and women are not allowed to utter the following Gâyatrī *Mantra*:—

ओ३म् भूर्भुवः स्वः । तत्सवितुर्वरेण्यं भर्गो देवस्य धीमहि । धियो यो नः प्रचोदयात् ॥यजु०अ०३६,मं०३॥

The last words in the *Mantra* say 'May God inspire the intellects of us all with His divine light.' Hence this prayer freely gives the right to Śūdras and women alike for recitations. Again some say that women and Śūdras are not entitled to utter the most sacred monosyllable '*Om*'. The following *Mantra* of the *Yajurveda* chapter XL, No. XV clearly lays down that every human being whether male or female or a saint or a cobbler has the right to recite the sacred '*Om*'.

ओ३म् क्रतो स्मर क्लिबे स्मर कृतꣳ स्मर ॥ (यजु०अ०४०, मं०१५)

O ! (क्रतो *Krato*) doer of deeds you should think that; *Om Smara* (you must recite and meditate).

समानि प्रपा सह वोऽन्नभागः समाने योक्त्रे सह वो युनज्मि ।
सम्यञ्चोऽग्निं सपर्यतारा नाभिमिवाभितः ॥ १६ ॥

O men ! remember that you are equal *Samāni Prapā*) you should have wells, water works and baths in common (*Saha*) yours (*Anna Bhāgaḥ*) you should prepare your food conjointly and sit for dinner together (*Saha*) yours (*Samāne Yoktre Saha*) there should be no reservation in your travelling carriages and cars and other means of conveyance (*Yunajmi*) the God ordains that you should remain united like (*Ārāḥ*) the spokes of a wheel (*Abhitaḥ*) in the navel (*Nābhimiva*) at the time of performing the '*Yajña*' of fire (*Agnim*) conjointly (*Samyañchaḥ*) mutually do good to each other.

This *Mantra* clearly gives permission even to sit at '*Homāgni*' and also to have common wells etc., as mentioned above. Hence we can say boldly that there is no touch of untouchability in the Vedas which are regarded by Hindūs and Aryas as their Sacred Books.

Inter-caste Marriage in Ancient Times

The seer (Ṛishi) of the third *Maṇḍala* of Ṛigveda was Vishvāmitra Ṛishi, who was well-known and was a Kshattriya by birth. The *Svayaṁvara* of Draupadī is a proof of inter-caste marriages. Arjuna who performed the *Matsyavedha* had come to the *Svayaṁvara* in disguise of a Brahmin. Draupadī was the daughter of a Kshattriya.

The seer (Ṛishi) of the seventh *Maṇḍala* of Ṛigveda was Vashishṭha who, according to the *Mahābhārata*, was the son of a prostitute.

Vyāsa, the author of the *Mahābhārata* was a son of a Śūdrā *Matsyagandhā*. Parāśara was also a Śūdra born.

In the *Bhavishya Purāṇa*, *Pratisarga Pūrva*, *Khaṇḍa* IV, chapter XXI it is written that by the order of *Devī* Sarasvatī Kaṇva Ṛishi converted 1,000 *Mlechchhas* from Egypt and 2,000 were made *Vaishṇavas*. Further it is said that those who were converted returned to Egypt being educated and were known as Brahmins with *Śikhā* and *Sūtra*.

The late Dr. Pandya of the Training College for Men, in his famous book, "*Education in the Baroda State*" has stated that beginning from the early Vedic times to the advent of Megasthenes there was no sign of untouchability in India.

Right of Salvation

Even Professor Maxmüller and all other historians admit that there was no idol worship in Vedic times, hence the question of entry into temples by untouchables cannot arise.

The following Vedic *Mantra* from the well-known *Purusha Sūkta* clearly gives personal right to an individual for knowing God and the last words of the *Mantra* say that for salvation there is no other path but the knowledge of God.

वेदाहमेतं पुरुषं महान्तमादित्यवर्णं तमसः परस्तात् ।
तमेव विदित्वाति मृत्युमेति नान्यः पन्था विद्यतेऽयनाय ॥ १८ ॥

वेद I know अहम् myself एतम् aforesaid पुरुषम् omnipresent God महान्तम् omnipotent आदित्यवर्णम् divine light तमसः परस्तात् far from ignorance तमेव to him alone विदित्वा having known मृत्युम् to death and trouble अति एति crosses अन्यः another पन्थाः path अयनाय for goal of salvation न विद्यते there exists none.

Common Crematory for All

In the *Atharvaveda*, chapter XIX, we find that for a village it is ordered that the dead body of a village man should be taken in a bullock cart to the common cremation ground for burning. It shows that in Vedic times the dead bodies of even cobblers were burnt in the same crematory where Brahmins burnt their dead bodies.

Though now-a-days Hindu untouchables bury their dead bodies, the following Vedic text clearly gives them the right of burning their dead bodies :—

भस्मान्तꣳ शरीरम् ॥ य० अ० ४० । १५ ॥

This means that every human body must be burnt to ashes.

No Sweepers in Vedic Times

From the Vedic times down to the advent of the Muhammadan invasion, there was no such man as *Bhaṅgī* or *Mehtar* for removing night-soil either in Hindu Indian villages, or countries like modern Japan and China.

This clearly solves the problem of untouchability as it proves that there was no untouchability in the Vedic times.

BARODA

ATMARAM

ŚRĪ SWAMI DAYANAND SARASWATI ON UNTOUCHABILITY AND UPLIFT OF DEPRESSED CLASSES

SO far as my study of Śrī Swami Dayanand Saraswati's sacred works, teachings, lectures, debates etc., guides me, Swamiji has nowhere specially dealt with the subject of untouchability and uplift of the depressed classes, but from his views expressed on other subjects such as *Varṇāśrama Dharma* and on the interpretation of the Vedas, Śāstras, Upanishads, Bhagavadgītā, Manusmṛiti etc., my impression is that he was deadly against any differential or preferential treatment being given owing to the birth of any person in a high or low *varṇa* or in a high or low caste or profession. According to him the *Varṇa-vyavasthā* rested on *guṇa*, *karma* and *svabhāva* (quality, action and temperament) and not on birth. According to him it was due to good or bad *saṁskāras*, associations, training, character etc., that the *varṇa* of every individual was determined. Cleanliness, truth, sacrifices, knowledge of God, study of Vedas and other good qualities and habits enable a person who is born in a Śūdra family to enter a higher *varṇa*. Similarly the converse of this is that uncleanliness, untruth, ignorance of God and Vedas and other bad qualities and habits degrade one from Brahmiṇ *varṇa* to a Śūdra. There is in Vedas and old Scriptures no such thing as untouchability due to birth. Uncleanliness makes every person untouchable, whether born in a Brahmin, Kshattriya or Vaiśya family, while cleanliness makes every person born in a Śūdra family touchable. An untouchable becomes touchable as soon as he cleans himself by washing his body, clothes etc. Similarly a touchable loses his touchability as soon as he allows his body or clothes to be unclean. According to Swamiji it is cleanliness which removes untouchability. As a matter of fact, a Brahmin so long as he is unclean is untouchable and a sweeper so long as he is clean is touchable. Cleanliness and touchability are co-relative terms as cause and effect of the same conditions. There is no untouchability inherent in the bodies of persons so long as they are clean. All the four *varṇas* being based on *guṇa*, *karma* and *svabhāva* are different parts of the one and the same Hindu polity including depressed classes and are absolutely necessary for the whole machinery of civilised life of the Hindu nation. *Varṇas* based on *guṇa*, *karma*, and *svabhāva* are to be found in all other civilised nations in one or other form. What we call a Brahmin is the Missionary class in England; what we call a Kshattriya is the Military class in England, what we call a Vaiśya is the Trader class in England, and what we call a Śūdra is the Labour class in England. According to Swamiji out of the four brothers born of the same parents one can be a Brahmin, the other a Kshattriya, the third a Vaiśya and the fourth a Śūdra according to his own individual profession and qualifications, just as in England one brother may choose for himself a missionary line, the other a military, the third trade and the fourth a labour line according to his own qualifications, merits and acquirements by his free choice, inclination and taste. The present condition of Hindu society which forces a Brahmin's son to remain a Brahmin whether he has got the qualities of a Brahmin on not and to force a sweeper's son to remain a sweeper, even though he has got all the qualities of a Brahmin and is not suitable for sweeper's work, is against the Vedas as interpreted by Swamiji. The present state of Hindu society basing *Varṇa-Vyavasthā* on birth and not on merits is of recent date due to ignorance of Vedas, and forcibly presses circular parts of its machinery through square holes and square parts of the machinery through circular holes; and the result is that the whole machinery of the present Hindu society has become disorganised and useless, and cannot be organised and made to work out its high ideals, social, religious and political, unless and until the untouchability due to birth is abolished root and branch, and depressed classes are given full rights of social, religious and political equality with caste Hindus. The following are quotations from Vedas, Śāstras Upanishads, Bhagavadgitā and Manusmriti etc., to which Swamiji has referred in his writings and as to the correctness of which no Hindu has upto this time raised any question or doubt.

१. "अथा ते अन्तमानां विद्याम सुमतीनाम् । मा नो अति ख्य आगहि" ॥ (ऋक् १।१।८)

२. "चातुर्वर्ण्यं मया सृष्टं गुणकर्मविभागशः" ॥ (गीता ४ । १३)

३. "जन्मना जायते शूद्रः संस्काराद्द्विज उच्यते" ॥ (मनुस्मृति)

४. "न विशेषोऽस्ति वर्णानां सर्वं ब्राह्ममिदं जगत् ।
ब्रह्मणा पूर्वसृष्टं हि कर्मभिर्वर्णतां गतम्" ॥ (महाभारत, शान्ति पर्व, अ० ८८)

५. "अद्भिर्गात्राणि शुध्यन्ति मनः सत्येन शुध्यति ।
विद्यातपोभ्यां भूतात्मा बुद्धिर्ज्ञानेन शुध्यति" ॥ (पंचमहायज्ञविधि)

६. "विद्याविनयसम्पन्ने ब्राह्मणे गवि हस्तिनि ।
शुनि चैव श्वपाके च पण्डिताः समदर्शिनः" ॥ (गीता ५ । १८)

७. "यस्तु सर्वाणि भूतान्यात्मन्नेवानुपश्यति ।
सर्वभूतेषु चात्मानं ततो न विचिकित्सति" ॥ (यजु० अ० ४०, मं० ६)

८. "आर्यः यः स्वमिव परमपि पश्यति" ॥

The life-long sacrifices of Mahatma Gandhi in and out of British India to abolish untouchability and hatred between man and man, and specially the last twenty-one days' hard fast-ordeal challenging death, which has been successfully accomplished on the 29th May, 1933 by the Almighty God sparing Mahatmaji's life to uproot untouchability and hatred between man and man not only from Hindus, but also from all other societies in the world wherever this evil exists is quite in accord with the teachings of Śrī Swami Dayanand Saraswati. They are bound to have good effect on the few Paurāṇic Hindus who still persist in treating certain castes as untouchable, depriving them of their rights of drawing water from public wells, educating their children in public schools and their entry in Hindu temples of worship along with the caste Hindus.

LAHORE — BAKSHI SOHANLAL

DAYANAND AND UNTOUCHABILITY

SWAMI DAYANAND was responsible for a great revolution in Hindu religion. I would, however, confine my remarks to a phase of his activities on which although there was great opposition then, yet to-day all parties among Hindus seem to be united. I refer to the position of the so-called untouchables.

For the present day people, it is difficult to visualise the great gulf that existed between the caste Hindus and the Harijans during the period when Swamiji raised his voice to prove from Śāstras that there was no such thing as Varṇa by birth. He recognised no authority which gave inferior position to the Harijans by reason of birth.

It was this inspiration, which gave strength to the late Swami Shraddhanand and others to organise the Dalitoddhār and Achhūt-Sudhār movements. Men like our philanthropist Mr. G. D. Birla are all working under the inspiration as converts to Swamiji's cult. Thus, the spade work was done and the ground prepared by the disciples of Swami Dayanand. On this the foundation of the present movement for the uplift of the Harijans is being laid. The solid work done by the disciples of Swami Dayanand under the spell of his miraculous inspiration, is bearing fruit, and the credit for this work must go to Swamiji.

Future generations will realise the worth of his foresight and keen observation. He was not an idealist, but a practical Reformer. How people would have worshipped him if he were alive to-day can better be imagined than described.

ROHTAK LALCHAND

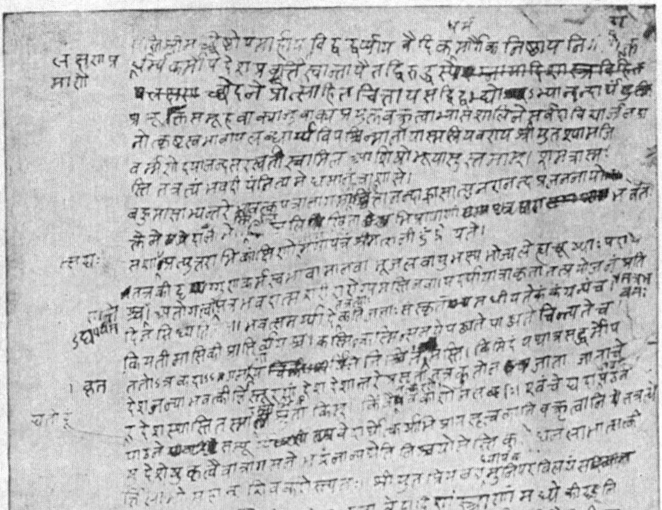

Facsimile of a letter, Meerut dated the 13th of July 1880 A. D., written by Swami Dayanand Saraswati in his own handwriting to Shyamji Krishna Varma at Oxford.

DAYANAND SARASWATI—A TRIBUTE

I had the good fortune to see the great Śrī Swami Dayanand Saraswati in his life-time at Bombay. I attended his lectures and discussed their contents in private conversations with him on numerous occasions. His photographs and pictures that I see everywhere do justice to his physical features, but cannot reproduce the light that shone bright in his eyes, nor can they convey any idea of the charm of his voice and the influence of his personality which pervaded all his movements and captivated everybody who came into contact with him. He addressed large audiences sitting on his elevated seat which in public meetings used to be a chair and in private conversations, his favourite small mat.

He was a very great Sanskrit scholar with a speciality in Grammar, and his mind was amply stored with knowledge of physical and other sciences studied both in the ancient and modern way. So his illustrations taken from his practically inexhaustible source and skilfully directed to impress his hearers were very effective. His eloquence was of the old Áchārya-style, and his delivery-style and the method were so taking that thousands were held spell-bound, and very favourably disposed towards his doctrines.

In this world a thing generally does not go on smoothly. A hitch starts up somewhere, and gradually gathers strength to stop, or at least to clog, the growth of a new propaganda. In his case the obstacle assumed the form of dissent from his interpretation of the Vedic texts relied on by him. The controversies that arose like all things of the kind have a beginning but no end. They are rife still and one cannot easily imagine the moment when they would cease. He founded the Arya Samaj.

My object in writing to-day is to honour the memory of the great founder of the Arya Samaj and I render my homage with great humility and most sincere reverence.

AMRAOTI — G. S. KHAPARDE

THE PASSING OF FOREIGN MISSIONS

WHEN Swami Dayanand Saraswati began his labours in India, as a religious and social reformer, he met with bitter opposition from the organised Christian missionary propaganda. The Christian missionaries, almost unchecked and unresisted at that time, threatened the very existence of Hindu life and openly avowed their determination to destroy the Hindu religion. Some of the Christian zealots even predicted the utter collapse of Hinduism at no distant date. But Swami Dayanand Saraswati met the challenge of the Christian propagandists and envisaged a brighter future for the Sanātana Dharma. His work has borne abundant fruit. Now at the Semi-Centenary of the demise of the Swamiji, one sees the twilight of Christianity and its emissaries engaged in death-bed repentence.

I discreetly refrain from saying anything about Roman Catholic Christianity. Catholicism or Romanism, all Protestant Christians aver, is unethical, unspiritual, anti-God, and socially and politically retrogressive. How progressive the Roman Catholic church is may be judged from the fact that until 1829, every book which said that the world was round was put on the *Index Expurgatorius* !

In general, there are two types of Protestantism: popular Protestantism and intellectual Protestantism. The recent American names for them are Fundamentalist and Modernist. Fundamentalist Protestantism is as authoritative as the Roman Catholic church. Basing its authority on a book, the Bible it accepts every word and syllable, every comma and semicolon in the Holy Writ as revealed by the Almighty himself. They regard this tome as the source-book of Geology, Zoology, Astronomy, Anthropology, Physics, Chemistry and Biology. Needless to say that the whole evidence of modern science is against such puerile belief. Fundamentalist

SHYAMJI KRISHNA VARMA

Protestantism is rapidly waning before the advance of education.

Modernist Protestantism accepts the Bible, as it accepts any other writing, on its intrinsic merits alone. It rejects much of the Old Testament as belonging to the category of myths and legends. Its advanced scholars doubt the authenticity of any of the four *Gospels* and even question if Jesus was a historic figure.

The one striking feature of current Christianity is its innumerable divisions and sub-divisions. There are in this country one hundred and sixty-seven varieties of Christian religion, and at least forty more not listed. Some of the churches are more interested in ducking—otherwise baptizing—than in social justice. Americans have such sects as the Six Principle Baptists, the Two-Seed-in-the-Spirit Predestinarians, the Duck River Baptists, the Pilgrim Holiness Brethren. There are two sects of *Brethren, Conservative* and *Progressive*, split on the question of whether a man's coat shall have one button or two, the two-buttoners being *Progressive*. The funny part of it all is that each church of each sect claims to own the only true faith. The Christ of one warring church denies the Christ of the other, and they are all cutting each other's throats in the effort to make one *proselyte*.

Realizing the approaching collapse of the missionary movement, a Protestant Foreign Mission Commission of investigators was sent from America to India, China and Japan a year ago, and it has just submitted its report analyzing missionary problems in the Orient. This report is embodied in a fat volume, entitled *Re-Thinking Missions*. It is full of the inevitable Christian bias; but the book on the whole is revealing. It admits that the majority of the missionaries are "of limited outlook and capacity." They have narrow proselytizing aims and are too much occupied with Biblical mythology. They are plumb ignorant. The Commission declares, however, that the work of the Christian mission must needs go on. It insists that "there is not alone room for change, there is necessity for change". There should be radical alteration in the salesmanship of Christian salvation.

What shall these changes be ? What will be the new formula which will make the pill more appetizing ?

The members of the Commission have been forced to recognize grudgingly that certain principles within the religions of the East are sound. Having been persuaded to abandon somewhat the religion of fear for a religion of beneficence, the Commissioners feel that there is less urge to threaten the Hindu, the Muhammadan, or the Confucian with hell-fire and more urge to direct him to "a better way of living". The hell-howling old mossbacks are no longer needed. Moreover, the Eastern people will no longer tolerate the Western assumption of superiority in race and in religion. The Western brand of culture will not sell now in the East, as it once did. The Great War, it admits, has torn the veil from the eyes of the Orient: the shameless barbarity and the horrible immorality of the War have thoroughly exposed the fallacies in Western culture generally, and Western religion specifically. The Commission, therefore, holds that the only forms of missionary endeavour which will be useful to-day to secure converts are the hospitals, schools, agricultural stations and the recreational establishments. These should be the instruments of aggressive evangelization. Through these institutions, the Westerner is urged to lead the East to the baptismal font. In short, if the opportunity to proselytize is not to be scuttled when the Orient is still apparently appreciative of some of the Occidental institutions, the missionary must give up his arbitrary doctrines and a *holier-than-thou* attitude. More than that, he must use ruse and catch his prospects unaware. Will he succeed better ?

Christian missions have been in existence in Asia for many, many years. Even the Protestant foreign missionary enterprise in the Orient is almost two centuries old. Christianity has been established on the Malabar coast in India for a longer time than in the British Isles. Yet there is to-day not one in a 100 of the people of India who has been converted to Protestant Christianity, and not one in 1,000 of the Chinese. As for Japan, where there is complete national independence, Christianity is a dead issue.

Religion is not the passion of life, not a supreme source of living either in America or in Europe: religion is only a minor interest. Mahatma Gandhi said a few years ago that no matter what the Westerners say, their real God is money. Mahatmaji has come nearer telling the truth on the subject, than any other man that I can think of now.

As one on the sidelines, I find that modern Americans regard their religion as an extra baggage of outworn theology and superstition, and are reluctant to carry the load much farther. I also see that missionary administrators are meeting with rapidly decreasing enthusiasm in the United States: they find fewer money givers to missions and still fewer men willing to be recruited for foreign mission field. The current is running strongly, not only against the church, but against the foreign mission. What does this portend? The question at once arises that if Christianity is discredited and dying and is about to be discarded in Christian America, why all such fuss about spreading Christian propaganda in non-Christian Asia? Why all this uproar about "saving" the tinted peoples of "the dark places of the earth"?

After all, this business of sending emissaries to foreign lands as evangelisers is very costly. The Protestant churches of the United States alone spend for foreign mission, 40 million dollars annually. (A dollar, in normal times, is worth about three rupees).

Just how many American missionaries are operating in India and how many dollars they are spending, I am unable to say at present. But I do know that as China offers the greatest Oriental market for American goods, the American artists in evangelism are spending more dollars to convert and baptize the Chinese "heathen" than any other people in the East. The flag follows the missionary. There are no less than 120 varieties of American Protestant sects represented in the Republic of China. Altogether they have spent, so far, the stupendous sum of half a billion dollars on that nation.

There were in China a few years ago about 8,000 Protestant missionaries in 700 cities; to-day there are about 5,000 in 400 cities. A short while ago the Roman Catholics had 4,000 missionaries in China; now they have been reduced by two or three hundred.

Then, too, converting the Chinese seems an expensive business. Dr. Clarence E. Miller, Treasurer of the Lutheran Church in the United States, reported recently that the cost of proselytizing the Chinese was 1,300 rupees a head. On the basis of Dr. Miller's calculations, it would take 175 billion dollars to make China safe for Jesus.

The ecclesiastical go-getter has always been an integral part of the imperialistic advance of the West. The evangelists are patriots first, and everything else in lesser measure. As an instance of the inter-relation of the Western church with the Western state, one recalls the speech which President McKinley made to the delegation of Methodist bishops who called at the White House to congratulate him on his decision to annex the Philippines at the turn of the century. President McKinley assured the bishops that his decision to annex came "through direct leading from God, after continued nights of prayer, and was inspired by a desire to Christianize the Philippines as our brothers for whom Christ died." It was a call from Jehova that the Filipinos, who had already been converted to Catholicism by the Spaniards, should now be "Christianized" by the American missionaries and be made American subjects! The church-press gave this pure and uncontaminated bunk of Mr. McKinley a wide circulation and it was generally accepted, among the church-going members of the United States, as one more evidence that the war with Spain had been ordained by God.

The Christian missionary movement was part of the larger expansive movement of the West in the nineteenth century.

Expansion, as a recent writer in *Harper's Monthly Magazine* points out, was made possible by the power derived from newly invented machine; but its success in the non-industrial East bred a conviction of divinely ordained superiority. That conviction was a delusion, an egregious absurdity. The Westerners, however, comforted themselves with thinking that right and truth were with them alone, and God was their right hand. They come out to the Orient, politically to conquer; economically, to exploit; and in religion to convert—all three being phases of the same phenomenon: domination of the East by the West.

Not long ago the Rt. Rev. Lord Bishop of London was on a *junket* to America. With his right hand on an American flag and his left hand clutching a British flag, he exhorted in a public meeting: "Keep alive the spirit of brotherly love in both our nations. Remember, divided England and America fall. United, we can rule the world." The follower of the humble Nazarene, preaching a cult of brotherhood, wants to rule the world.

Even to-day the missionaries in India are allied with the powers that be. They accept financial favours from the Government of India for the maintenance of many of their institutions, and thus obligate themselves in advance to support the British position. Few indeed are the missionaries who realize that they are compromising their moral standing. Apparently they are incapable of moral and ethical insights.

The missionary has always been a tool of imperialism and economic exploitation. He tries to pass the running wolves of imperialism for the brother-lambs of the "natives". His servility to the big magnates of capital and finance is only equalled by the pastors of church who once justified slavery by Bible texts and drew their incomes from the servitude of Negro bondmen.

The authors of *Re-Thinking Missions* are conspicuously silent regarding the tragic, evil effects of imperialism, particularly in the Orient, and the responsibility which morally rests upon missions and missionaries for the abolition of this anti-Christ philosophy of life.

Do they realize that men cannot be made whole or saved apart from the political or economic system in which they live? How can they ignore the wicked mental and spiritual effects upon a people who live under a foreign imperialistic bondage?

As a matter of fact, our authors have joyously surrendered themselves to a hackneyed slogan of imperial psychology in saying, "It is not the business of the mission to meddle in politics, least of all in the politics of a foreign country in which it is a guest." How can the missionaries in countries like India, Ceylon and Burma be the guests of the government? The government is just as alien as are the missionaries themselves. It has been rightly suggested by some of the American publicists that missionaries in subjected nations of the Orient are no more the guests of a ruling government than they are of the great historic Hindu, Buddhist or Muslim religious communities. The fact that the holy men of the Christian mission try to keep company with imperialism and with moral integrity at the same time is evidence of their ignorant naivete, to say the least.

Indeed, some of the strange thoughts and ideas of this latest report of missionary activities are of a kind to worry a Socrates, and I am not one. But its fallacies partly account for the futility, weakness and frustration of much of the Christian mission work in India.

IOWA, U. S. A. SUDHINDRA BOSE

SWAMI DAYANAND SARASWATI

SWAMI DAYANAND SARASWATI

ON

HARMONY BETWEEN THE VEDAS AND SCIENCE

SWAMI DAYANAND maintained that the Vedas contain the germs of all knowledge, and that their teachings are in perfect harmony with Science. It is hardly surprising that this has been looked upon as a very extravagant and unreasonable claim by Western people and by many others who have received Western education. For a conflict between Science and Religion was a special feature of European History for several centuries.

In Western Europe, Science was first cultivated by the Arabs and Saracens who translated many Greek works, started colleges, developed arithmetic, algebra, and trignometry, and laid the foundations of astronomy, chemistry, and physics. But scholars of science soon came into conflict with the Christian Church which smelt serious danger to its established dogmas from the researches of Science. The inquisition was regularly instituted in the 13th century by the Roman Church to try and punish heretics. It became more rigorous in the 15th century. Torquemada, who was Inquisitor-General for eighteen years, burnt 10,220 persons at stake, 6,860 in effigy, and otherwise punished 97,321 men. To name a few eminent scientists who were victims of the wrath of the Church, Galileo was prosecuted for believing in the Copernican theory that the earth moves round the Sun, and not the Sun round the earth. Under the menace of torture he confessed, but recanted, and was thrown in prison. Bruno was burnt for teaching the plurality of worlds. It was after the Reformation that the persecution of science and scientists practically ceased.

Muhammadanism was also not very tolerant to the spread of knowledge and science. The *dictum* of Caliph Omar or his general Amru under which he ordered the destruction of the great Library of Alexandria in the 7th century is well-known: "If a book teaches what is contained in the *Qurān*, it is useless; if it teaches what is against the *Qurān*, it is heretic and should be destroyed."

Persecution of science or scientists is altogether unknown in the history of Vedic religion. The reason is not far to seek. The very word "Veda" means knowledge, being derived from *Vid*, to know, and is cognate with the English word *wit* (wisdom). It has thus the same signification as the word "Science" derived from Latin *scio*, to know. In ancient India all sciences were believed to be derived from and based on the Vedas. The most important branches of the Vedic literature were:—

(*i*) The four *Upavedas* (literally "subordinate Vedas") viz.—

(1) *Āyurveda* or the Science of life including the sciences of Medicine, Surgery, Hygiene, Chemistry, Physiology Anatomy, etc., (2) *Arthaveda* or the Science of Economics; (3) *Gandharvaveda* or the Science of Music including also Drama, Dancing and other æsthetic arts; and (4) *Dhanurveda* or the Science of War.

(*ii*) The six *Vedāngas* (lit. "limbs of the Veda") viz.—

(1) *Śikshā* or the science of phonetics and Orthoepy; (2) *Kalpa* including (*a*) *Dharma Sūtras* or the Principles of Law, (*b*) *Śrauta Sūtras* or the rules of Vedic rituals, (*c*) *Gṛihya Sūtras* or the rules of Domestic ceremonies, and *Śulva Sūtras* or the principles of Geometry; (3) *Vyākaraṇa* or Grammar; (4) *Nighaṇṭu* or Philology; (5) *Chhandas* or Prosody; and (6) *Jyotisha* or Astronomy.

(*iii*) The six *Upāngas* (lit. "subordinate limbs of the Veda") viz.—the *Darśanas* or the so called six schools of Philosophy including Logic, Metaphysics, Psychology, Ethics and also Physics.

The view that the Vedas contain the germs of all knowledge is found in the works of Sanskrit literature. Thus we read in *Śatapatha Brāhmaṇa*—

> स ऐक्षत प्रजापतिः "त्रय्यां वाव विद्यायां सर्वाणि भूतानि । हन्त
> त्रयीमेव विद्यामात्मानमभि संस्करवै इति—शत० १०।४।२।२१-२२ ॥

"The Lord of all creatures surveyed (the universe saying), "All beings are comprehended in the triple science (i.e. the Veda). Yes, this triple science alone, let me employ for the elevation of the soul."

Taittirīya Brāhmaṇa repeats the same thing :—

> अथ सर्वाणि भूतानि पर्यैक्षत् । स त्रय्यामेव विद्यायां सर्वाणि भूतान्यपश्यत् ।
> अत्र हि सर्वेषां छन्दसामात्मा सर्वेषां स्तोमानां सर्वेषां प्राणानां सर्वेषां देवानाम् ।
> एतद्वै अस्ति । एतद्ध्यमृतम् । यद् ह्यमृतं तद् ह्यस्ति एतद्ु तद् यन्मर्त्यम् ॥

"Then God surveyed all the created things. He saw all created things in triple science only. Here is the soul of all *Chhandas* or metres, all *stomas* or praises, all life and all knowledge. This alone is; this verily is immortality. What is immortality, that alone is. And this is what is for the mortals."

It may be explained that the Vedas are called "triple science" *trayīvidyā* because they deal with (1) *Jñāna*, knowledge (2) *Karma*, works and (3) *Bhakti* or *Upāsanā*, worship or prayer, corresponding to the three functions of the human mind viz., knowing, willing, and feeling. This is not inconsistent with the fourfold division of the Veda into the four Saṁhitās, viz., Ṛigveda, Yajurveda, Sāmaveda and Atharvaveda, wherein knowledge is sub-divided into *Jñāna* or general knowledge, and *Vijñāna* or special knowledge. The Ṛigveda (or the Veda of *Ṛichās*) deals chiefly with general knowledge; the Yajurveda (or the Veda of *yajña*) deals chiefly with *yajñas* or works; the Sāmaveda (or the Veda of *Sāmans*) deals chiefly with worship; and Atharvaveda (or the Veda of *Atharvans*) deals chiefly with special knowledge.

Swami Dayanand has not contented himself with merely asserting the old view. In his *Introduction to the Commentary on the Vedas* he has by way of illustration quoted profusely from the Vedas showing that their teachings are in complete accord with Science, and that many scientific truths which were not known in Europe before a century or two are clearly mentioned or hinted at in the Vedas. Within the limits of this short essay, it would be impossible to adduce any detailed instance. The curious reader is referred to the English translation of the book by Pt. Ghasiram, M.A., LL.B.

Only one instance may be given. The Vedic doctrine of cosmogony is not based on the theory of creation *ex nihilo* (i. e. creation of the universe out of nothing), which is taught by the three great Semitic religions (viz. Judaism, Christianity and Muhammadanism), and is so repugnant to Science. The Vedas teach that the world is evolved from primordial or pre-existing matter, *prakṛiti*. In his *Introduction to the Commentary on the Vedas*, Swami Dayanand has quoted the well-known *Nāsadīya Sūkta* (Ṛigveda, VIII, 7, 17) and the *Purusha Sūkta* (Yajurveda XXXI) on this subject. The following verse of the *Taittirīya Upanishad* succinctly states the theory of biological evolution as well as the evolution of a planet from a nebulous or even a still more rarified state of matter *viz. ākāśa* or ether :—

तस्माद्वा एतस्मादात्मन आकाशः संभूतः, आकाशाद्वायुः, वायोरग्निः, अग्नेरापः,
अद्भ्यः पृथिवी, पृथिव्या ओषधयः, ओषधिभ्योऽन्नम्, अन्नाद्रेतः, रेतसः पुरुषः ॥

"By Him, the all-pervading Spirit, was produced ether; from the etherial state came out the gaseous state, from the gaseous state the igneous state, from the igneous state the molten state, from the molten state the solid state; from the solid earth came out herbs; from herbs the food (or other vegetables); from food the seed of animal life; from the seed of animal life, man."

Let nobody suppose that Swami Dayanand Saraswati is alone in giving a rational or scientific interpretation of the Vedas. His interpretation is in consonance with the most ancient commentaries contained in the *Brāhmaṇas* and in Yāska's *Nirukta*. The *Sāṅkhya Darśana* lays down: बुद्धिपूर्वा वाक्यकृतिर्वेदे "The contents of the Veda are in conformity with Reason." It is the mediæval commentators, Sāyaṇa, Mahīdhara etc., who, following the degenerate theology of Paurāṇic times, have fastened on the Vedas the superstitious practices and unscientific beliefs of their own age. It was Swami Dayanand who by his correct interpretation restored the Vedic religion to its pristine purity, and showed that their teachings were in complete harmony with Science. And there is no reason why there should be any conflict between *true* Religion and *true* Science. For God is the source of both and both should be based on Reason, the divine faculty by which man is enabled to understand the *word* of God (i.e. the Vedas), as well as the *work* of God (i.e. nature).

TEHRI GANGAPRASAD

WHATEVER one may think of the correctness or otherwise of Swami Dayanand's interpretation of many Vedic passages, one cannot withhold one's admiration for a man whose work perhaps more than that of any other individual has helped to make India conscious of itself as a unity with some distinctive contribution to make to the culture of the world as a whole.

R. L. TURNER

HAVERBRACK,
BISHOP'S STORTFORD

1. यदा यदा हि धर्मस्य ग्लानिर्भवति भारत ।
अभ्युत्थानमधर्मस्य तदात्मानं सृजाम्यहम् ॥ ७ ॥
परित्राणाय साधूनां विनाशाय च दुष्कृताम् ।
धर्मसंस्थापनार्थाय संभवामि युगे युगे ॥ ८ ॥ (गीता, अध्याय ४)

2. Faizi's rendering in Persian:—

چو بنیاد دین سست گردد بسے — نمائم خودرا بشکل کسے
که حفظ ریاضت گزنیان کنم — مراعات عزت نشکبان کنم
بریزئیم خون ستم پیشگان — جهان را نمائم دار لامان

3. Rendering in Urdu in *Momokshoo Bhāshya* of Rai Chuttan Lal:

هراکرتی هے جب دهرم کی کمی — هوپاپون کی بیشی اے بهارت تبهی
عیان کرتا هون اپنی نج آتما — جرکهلاتا آوتار هے برملا
جرسادهو هین اُونکی مدد کیلئیے — جو هین دشتجن اُنکی رد کیلئیے
رهے دهرم قائم ادهرم هووے دور — میرا هوتا یگ یگ مین هے یئون ظهور

4. Dr. Besant's rendering in English:—

"Whenever there is decay of righteousness, O Bharat, and there is exaltation of unrighteousness, then I myself come forth," (7) For the protection of the good, for the destruction of evil-doers, for the sake of firmly establishing righteousness, I am born from age to age." (8)

The above quotation from the Gīta is generally regarded as an authority for the doctrine that God assumes human form to remove great calamities and cure ills that beset mankind from time to time. In other words, people from times immemorial have cherished belief in Avatars and Millineums. They believe that whenever sinfulness, wickedness and oppression take a predominant turn in this world, God manifests himself to readjust that which has been rendered chaotic. And one need not quarrel with this faith of the faithful. The quotation from Gīta calls attention to a universal phenomenon, true to all ages, countries and conditions. We find Mr. Herbert Spencer formulating this doctrine as a scientific fact. In his "First Principles" he says:—

(1) "In all cases, then, there is a progress toward equilibrium. The Universal co-existence of antagonistic forces which, as we before saw, necessitates the decomposition of every force into divergent forces, at the same time necessitates the ultimate establishment of a balance.

(2) "Equilibration: By this ultimate principle is provable the tendency of every organism, disordered by some unusual influence to return to a balanced state.

(3) "As in the individual organism so in the social organism, functional equilibrations generate structural equilibration".

It is exactly this balancing contrivance which great men bring about by their existence.

Again, it is common experience that through neglect of laws of health, the individual constitution goes on depositing foreign matter which when reaching a certain degree of accumulation, bursts forth into what the physician terms, disease Whether it takes the form of a boil, a billious attack or blood poisoning, it is always an effort on the part of the human system to purge itself of foreign matter and then to resume its normal course of life. Similarly the social organism, in its daily life, through corruptions, aggressions, oppressions and tyrannies of various kinds, finds itself diseased and prostrate like the sickman. Life, whether individual or aggregate, becomes a suffering, and humanity not only humbled and degraded, but almost dead and defunct. It is at such a crisis that an AVATAR appears to perform the task of establishing order and destroying oppression. To put it simply "it is when your facts and persons grow unreal and fantastic by too much falsehood that the great man runs for refuge to the world of ideas, and aims to recruit and replenish nature from that source". And such was the life of Swami Dayanand Saraswati. It is but natural to believe in great men; it is to them that the world owes from day to-day, from era to era and from age to age, the preservation, the progress and the uplift of humanity. Great men are not individuals but phenomena. They come, they see, they conquer. When Swami Dayanand first opened his eyes to the state of society in India, he saw how the *Aryan* race in its Eastern habitat had gravitated to a condition of decay and demoralisation, how it had lost its purity, prestige and glory. It filled his heart with sorrow. How he set before himself the task of regalvanising, how he devoted his life to the work of rescue and restoration need not be recounted here, for the life of Swami Dayanand is a mighty and manifest page of the modern history of India.

Swami Dayanand in his introduction to his great work the *Satyartha Prakash* (Light of Truth) thus formulates his ideal of life, "My chief aim in writing this book is to unfold Truth, which consists in expounding truth as truth and error as error. Our aim has been to further the advancement and good of mankind, and to help men in the ascertainment of Truth whereby they could embrace the truth and reject falsehood, because there is certainly no other way of elevating the human race." Let us borrow from Emerson;

"Nature seems to exist for the excellent The world is upheld by the veracity of goodmen; they make the earth wholesome, they who lived with them found life glad and nutritious, but I find him greater when he can abolish himself and all heroes by letting in the element of reason, irrespective of persons, this subtiliser and irresistible upward force, into our thought, destroying individualism; the power so great that the potentate is nothing. Then he is a monarch who gives a constitution to his people; a pontiff who preaches the equality of souls and releases his servants from their barbarous homages; an emperor who can spare his empire."

Swami Dayanand had undoubtedly transcended individual existence and when he ceased to help and guide us in the physical life he passed into an effect. He became the exponent of a vaster mind and will. His opaque self, by the miracle of his death, became transparent with the light of the First Cause.

AJMER

GAURI SHANKER G. VERMA

DAYANAND THE MYSTIC

THAT Rishi Dayanand was a great moralist is admitted by all; that he was an equally great mystic is known only to a few.

During his later life when he had assumed the role of a teacher, and had to do with common men and women, he very strongly emphasised human exertion. God, according to him, was just in his dispensation of rewards and punishments. Divine mercy was shown in the bestowal of common boons on all creatures, both human and sub-human. The Sun, the Earth, the stars, air and water and all other blessings that are shared by all living beings are a fruit of Divine Benevolence. For the particular good derived from them by each individual, his actions, past or present, are responsible. These common gifts are a creation of God's mercy —His favours, which being open to all, show no partiality.

Rishi Dayanand laid great stress on Divine Equity, as that was the great need of humanity at the time. Human effort stood at a great discount. Sweet lullabies of the mercy of God had for centuries been sung into the ears of devotees. Saint after saint had taught complete dependence on the favour of Heaven, which being absolutely free, was believed to know no law. Such teaching, while it discouraged action, gave latitude to the evil propensities of evil-doers. An autocratic God was to be guided in His dispensation of favours and penalties by His uncontrolled will. He might punish virtues and reward evils. What motive could such religious instruction have for doing good? While belief in justice makes for manliness, the concept of uncontrolled will, brooded over from day to-day, begets servility with all the vices that attend this cringing attitude of mind.

For the common man, belief in justice is thus a necessary article of faith. For him God is an unrelenting Judge. More charming, however, than this conception is the conception of a

Heavenly Father. *Pitrnām pitrtamah: Most fatherly of fathers. Ambitame: Of mothers most motherly.* How enrapturing are these epithets applied in the Veda to varied concepts of the Deity. In practice a father may—in fact he does—hold the scales of his kindness even among his sons. Their waywardnesses he punishes. Of their vices he tries to purge them. To the dutiful and loving son, however, he is an embodiment of justice as of love. The love of a father knows no bounds. Of a father, whose one great distinctive feature is His infinitude, the love and kindness are bound to be infinite. These can be properly experienced, however, by those of His children who have experienced His infinitude. Such sons of Man, or what is the same thing, of God are termed by the Veda *Amrtasya putrāh*, Sons of the Immortal. They have left evil behind. They are embodiments of active energy. Their life is a lesson in ceaseless activity. The pleasure of the Father in Heaven is to them the only prize, Prize Inestimable in terms of human good. Love of God is spontaneous. It is independent of its human recipient's merit. Even sorrows meted out by His hand are mercies in disguise. They are meant to chasten our spirit. Such is the feeling of the child-like devotee. While the calculating man of the world will invest in virtue in the hope of reward, the confident Heir of Heaven whom the Veda calls *Divah Sūnuh* will offer good as a sacrifice to the Beloved Father, whose fostering care it is impossible to recompense by any amount of filial virtue on the part of man.

One such *Divah Sunuh*, Heir of Heaven, was Ṛishi Dayanand. That he had an immediate experience of Love Infinite is referred to in an autobiographical note of his. He writes:—

"Then after a month I, in accordance with their instructions, went to the temple of Dudheswara Mahādeva near Ahmedabad, where they had promised to initiate me into the subtle mysteries of Yoga and the method of realising them. There they fulfilled their promise and sent me into ecstasies. By the kindness of these Mahātmās I gained a complete mastery of Yoga and its practice. I am highly grateful to them. They did me a great favour."

That besides the method of inference through logic there is a direct way of realisation of the soul is stated by him in a letter to Col. Olcott:—"Many Aryas did realise, *do realise*, and will realise the nature of the soul by a knowledge of the Veda and the Śastras and meditation in Samâdhi.

(*Letters and Advertisements of Ṛishi Dāyanand*, Part I, Prayer 57).

That there are living examples of such realisation among Aryas of to-day is also pointed out in the above extract. The Rishi's reference is unmistakably among others to his own self. Practice in the line of these experiences bestows on men certain spiritual powers which, to materialistic observers appear miracles. In a letter written from Meerut, Ṛishi Dayanand explains "what people call witch-craft" is "an achievement of (mental) science". (*Letters and Advertisements*, Part I, Prayer 20). To Madam Blavatsky he writes that he possesses spiritual powers and would teach the way of their achievement to those who wish to learn and practice them. To a public demonstration of them, however, he was strongly opposed. (*Letters and Advertisements*) Psychic science recognises to-day the power of man to see beyond the range of physical vision, and to divine future events, as if they were taking place just before the eyes of the observer. In Ṛishi Dayanand's life we find record of such happenings. At Monghyr, one Rajnath Sharma became a disciple of the Ṛishi. In the evening, as he was repairing to the Swami's residence he came across a snake. The first question of the Ṛishi, as the lad came before him, was as regards that incident. Another day, a servant brought fuel which he had received *gratis* from a dealer. Rajnath was ordered to reprimand him as he had *begged* for firewood. The Ṛishi had through some sort of clairvoyance divined his misconduct. The coming of Rajnath's father in search of his son was similarly intuitively perceived half an hour before the truant lad's parent actually came before the Ṛishi. At Lahore, the Sage advised a newly betrothed youngman to postpone his marriage till after he became thirty years old.

It was about that age that his death took place and the Seer's advice was, as it were, by a miracle, found to be opportune. (Pt. Lekh Ram's Biography of Ṛishi Dayanand).

At Udaipur the Ṛishi seated in *padmāsana* posture rose above the ground and made a circuit of the room in that unsupported condition. *Dayanand Prakash* by Swami Satyanand). While on his death-bed he appeared to P. Gurudatta M.A., in a vision in the course of which the latter saw two distinct images. One was the Ṛishi breathing his last. The other presented the Sage as a world-teacher delivering a sermon to hankering humanity. (*Gurudatta Lekhāvali*)—Modern psychology refers such incidents to the subconscious mind of the observer. In that case, too, these events are highly significant as illustrating the mental power of him who exerted such miraculous influence on his followers.

The existence of entities superior to matter and possessing powers greater than mechanical and chemical forces is amply evidenced by these *siddhis* which to the Yogi are at a certain stage a proof direct of the developing capacities of his soul. As soon, however, as he has attained to an intuitive vision of the Spirit Divine, these mental gifts are to him of no greater value than the material possessions and gains that he has already discarded. He now literally revels in his love of God. A few outpourings of Ṛishi Dayanand recorded in his *Aryābhivinaya—Book of Aryan Prayer* may form an index to the condition of his mind overwhelmed by the ecstasy of such absorbing love. He appears to have had a constant vision of Divine Presence, which he is anxious never to lose (Part I, Prayer 49). Through every pore of his being there pealed messages of Divine Immanence. Songs of Heaven reverberated around him, and these he implored the Celestial Singer to strike up in the chords of his heart (Part I, Prayer 52). The incessant sermon which the Divine Preceptor is every moment delivering in the heart of man is to the saint His vocal mouth facing all directions (Part I, Prayer 39). In the battles that humanity is waging against evil he invokes God to fight as a soldier on the side of the righteous (Part I, Prayers 24, 26). In Prayer 28, Part I, God appears to him to be perceptibly moved and in his kindness showering favours on His servants. Prayer 36 is an invocation for a complete ecstasy of spiritual emotion. In Prayer 37, the Lord is asked to make the human heart His abode and rejoice therein as does a house-holder in his own house.

The realisation of the devotee being personal, gives God the character of a similar person. The former imagines that the joy which he feels is not a simple one-sided gift on the part of the latter. The gift, on the contrary, appears to him mutual, so that the feast is partaken of by two, whereby the pleasure is redoubled. In Prayer I of Part II we meet with some such feeling on the part of Dayanand, who with God is a fellow-partaker of a delicious tryst.

In several of his prayers he begs for the gift of a world-empire for the Aryas, but in this he would make them but the servants of God's will which alone he would like them to execute through this sovereignty, so that the Aryan kingdom would in other words be the kingdom of God. (Part II, Prayer 1). The wish to be God's instrument finds expression again and again in these outbursts of passionate self-surrender. The determination of his destiny, he is most happy to leave to divine disposal. (Part II, Prayer 13). In prayer 15, he prays for the moral amelioration of the devotee " to God's mercy ". " For it is the moral rectitude of his children that reflects credit on the parent." " And again, " Be happy, Lord, in the happiness of us children." What a genuine note of *bhakti* is struck in the following lines:—

> "In thy generosity, Lord, shower on us all blessings. The capacity to win thy pleasure we totally lack. We ourselves cannot at all act in conformity with Thy wishes. But Thou, Lord, raisest the fallen and the lowly. Make us, then, in thy kindness happy ". (Part II, Prayer 38).

Dayanand had the true mettle of a saint in him. He was a man of supreme resignation. He had direct experience of the Spiritual Presence that nestled him in the lap of a loving mother. The divinity that is immanent in things was intuitively realised by him. This constituted his never-failing feast of supreme felicity. The oft-recurring privations and hardships that beset his earthly career drowned their murmur in that overflowing flood. The high moral ideals to which he stuck at his life's peril were just a part and parcel of the supernatural framework of that sublime spiritual order in which the universe is set, and which he, with the eyes of his spirit, every moment saw. He had sensed reality. According to Yāska's definition, a Ṛishi—Seer—is one who sees *dharma*. A Ṛishi—Seer—in the truest sense of the term was Swami Dayanand, the founder of the Arya Samāj.

A great peculiarity of Ṛishi Dayanand's mysticism is that he does not discard reason. His arguments form a happy synthesis with his mystic vision, so that those who are without this latter gift may gather solace from a belief grounded on reason alone, while those who *have* this grace may not, by over-immersion in that fount of bliss, be thrown off their balance as all-sided worshippers. Mahātma Munshi Ram (later Swami Shraddhanand,) when he was yet a boy reading at College, saw the Ṛishi and entered thrice into a discussion with him as regards the existence of God. Silenced in argument, he yet said he was not convinced. The Ṛishi repeated to him a verse of the Upanishad and said, "Conviction, my lad, will be brought to thee by God's grace. Wait for the hour when thou *shalt* be convinced." Aye: the hour came and he who later had the supreme luck to lay down his life at the altar of Ṛishi Dayanand, did, by a consecration of everything he possessed, signify his gratitude to the seed sown by the hopeful glance of his Guru which had, after a mysterious process of inner incubation, blossomed all of a sudden into a spring tide of grace. The vision of the Ṛishi was contagious, as all mystic vision is. The Arya Samaj owes a galaxy of redeemed and devoted *bhaktas* to simple contact of the Ṛishi.

GURUKULA, HARDWAR CHAMUPATI

SWAMI DAYANAND AS NATION-BUILDER

SWAMI DAYANAND was one of those great men to whom India owes a deep debt of gratitude. The educated Hindus of Northern India, with rare exceptions, are amongst his followers, admirers or sympathisers. By his revival movement, he built a *pucca* dam against conversions from Hinduism. By his deep learning, by his lofty moral character, and by his steadfast adherence to what he believed to be true, he succeeded in changing the entire outlook of the Hindu society of his times.

As a religious reformer, he waged a relentless war against idolatry, against priesthood and against every kind of sham and superstition, believed in, or practised by his countrymen. As a social reformer, he was a staunch advocate of *Brahmacharya* and of purity and restraint in married life. He spoke and wrote against child-marriage and succeeded in raising a spirit of revolt amongst the thoughtful Hindus, against the physical and moral evils ensuing from this pernicious custom. He drew the attention of Hindu society to the pitiable lot of child widows, and encouraged their re-marriage. To prevent Hindu helpless children from falling into the hands of non-Hindus, he advised and encouraged the opening of orphanages and *āsramas*. In fact, by his towering personality and by his incessant preaching, he created a deep stir amongst the Hindus of his times and roused them out of their age-old indifference, apathy and inertia.

Swami Dayanand was a staunch Swadeshi, and fully realised the economic dependence of Indians. By his example, by his writings, and by his lectures, he encouraged and preached the universal use of Indian-made articles.

Above all, Swami Dayanand was a true patriot and succeeded in creating a love of country among all those who came in contact with him. He did not directly concern himself with what is popularly known as politics. He did not want to deal with consequences or results. Like an expert and a far-sighted gardener, he busied himself in looking after the soil and its sowing. He thought it useless to criticize or quarrel with the grown-up tree or its product. He abstained from dealing with the top, but like a sage and a seer—as he was—he occupied himself with working at the root. He realized that all the political troubles were due to want of character amongst his countrymen. He rightly believed that if Indians became physically strong, religiously pure and socially simple, their political emancipation will follow. In his opinion, strong, honest, truthful men with character, could not remain political slaves for a long time. With this conviction in his mind, Swami Dayanand applied himself heart and soul to his religious and social work. He spent his life in strenuously and earnestly fighting against social evils and religious superstitions, and by successfully driving them out of Hindu society, he laid the foundations of a virile nationhood.

It is true that the Arya Samaj was not a political organization, nor did it, as such, take part in current politics. But every Arya Samajist was a heretic and an iconoclast. His opposition to Christian missionaries and their proselytising work, his uncompromising attitude towards corruption and official oppression made him conspicuous in every sphere of life. An Arya Samajist being a puritan in religion, an expert in debate, a defender of the weak and the oppressed, came into prominence wherever he was. Every follower of Swami Dayanand came to be known as a religious enthusiast, a genuine social worker and deep lover of his country.

Thus Swami Dayanand was not only a unique religious revivalist and a great social reformer, but was the foremost nation-builder of his time. All honour to him and to his sacred memory.

LAHORE DURGADAS

SWAMI DAYANAND

SWAMI DAYANAND is one of those spiritual giants of India to recall whose many achievements takes one's breath away. His mastery of the Vedas with the new light thrown on them would alone have marked him out as a man of the Epoch. But it is not as a Savant only he is regarded great, he holds his thrall over the hearts of thousands of his countrymen as a man of action and revivalist.

An untramelled Mind, an unclouded Intellect, a fearless Heart, these are the springs from which flowed the cataract of utterances that swept away superstition, ignorance and apathy from a country long held prisoner under them. He put Upper India back to Aryan culture and the people found back their soul.

Freedom of thought and action was his watchword! Equality of man he preached from the housetops. What he preached, his followers practised. The viper of untouchability was tackled and dealt a blow on the head in Arya Samaj circles half a century before the conception of a campaign against it in political spheres. A superman of superb Heart and Head and Body was this Swami, with a piece of loin cloth only as his sole worldly possession. He opened the portals of greater life to his countrymen by rewriting the History of Hindustan in letters of Martyrdom. Great alike in Life and in Death, we hail his memory with all reverence.

CALCUTTA — SAROLADEVI CHAUDHURI

DAYANAND IN 1933

THE ARYA SAMAJ was something of a novelty—a challenge especially to the ubiquitous missionary preaching the gospel of Jesus—only a generation ago. To-day it is only the advanced wing of resurgent Hinduism which, while looking back merely for purposes of a respectable and ancient source of theology, has its eyes riveted on the future, which wants to regain the glorious moments of its past, when everything useful, though alien, was annexed to the absorbent fabric of its social and religious organisation. It was this dynamic quality which Swami Dayanand wanted to recapture with a view to save the age-worn and disease-ridden body social of Hinduism from utter dissolution. Hinduism had ceased to look forward; it had even lost the feeling of its own impotence and come to look upon the shackles of its own creation as its principal sheet-anchor. It had lost itself in hair-splitting interpretations of ancient texts and rigid observance of meaningless ritual and customs. Hinduism was prostrate with the burden of the past. Dayanand came on the scene at a psychological moment. His creed was simple; it was meant to give something definite, concrete and tangible to the man in the street who was apt to lose himself in the maze of speculative Hinduism. Dayanand was no visionary. He was a practical idealist. He is to be counted among the ranks not of scholars like Śaṅkara or Rāmānuja, but among the galaxy of men of action like the great Guru Govind Singh. If the latter created an irresistible Khālsā out of the poor and downtrodden peasantry of the Punjab and the western districts of the United Provinces, it was the ambition of the Swami to refashion the entire Hindu society into a vital, well-knit brotherhood of men, bound by the ties of a simple but well-understood code of behaviour—the new Arya Samaj. He saw in the passivity of old Hinduism the beginning of death. He, therefore, was not content with the supercilious pride of the orthodox Brahmin that consideration of numbers was only the occupation of parvenu creeds, which foolishly look upon the swelling ranks of their adherents as the surest proof of their inherent superiority. He wanted his new Samaj to be open to all—especially those that had erred into other faiths as a result of circumstances. But the organisation of caste-groups was an impassable barrier to the progressive realisation of the dreams of this great nation-builder. Swami Dayanand condoned the existence of castes; the Samaj was therefore a superstructure that was reared on the ancient foundations of these exclusive, incoherent and often antagonistic social groups. The result was that the Samaj became merely a group of social reformers, who principally occupied themselves with objects rather mundane than spiritual. The principal planks on their platform were the emancipation and education of the depressed sections of Indian Society—women, especially widows, and the recently christened group of Harijans. Modern caste-organisation, however, can never effectively assimilate new accretions; for the new-comer could not generally be accomodated in any of these traditional and jealously exclusive groups especially in matters of marriage. The result was that the door that Dayanand had sought to open to the fold of renaissant Hinduism remained unfrequented. Caste as a unit of social organisation is rigid and unaccomodating when it comes to the fundamental problem of marriage, which alone means the real assimilation of the outsider in the body social. The Sikh Khālsā was otherwise constituted. It welcomed all who cared to come to the Gurudwara—the door of the Guru. Like Islām, it made no distinction between the old and the new. All were the chosen—the Khālsā with the result that a new community—brave, active and virile was born from what must have been at best an amorphous mass of poor and unpromising material. The Khālsā is therefore perhaps better suited to reclaim and to uplift the Harijans than Hinduism proper. But the fire of the great Guru seems to be burning low. The Samaj of Dayanand was different. It was primarily the movement of the educated middle-classes—the typical *bourgeois*. While the Samaj was young and new, it attracted attention by its aggressive tone towards all other creeds. But its principal emphasis was really on questions of social reform, rather than on matters purely religious. It was therefore but natural that the nascent fire of the Arya Samaj—the name itself is significant—should diminish in intensity with the course of time, for each of the principal reforms for which Dayanand Saraswati had to wage heroic battles of dialectical skill with the exponents of orthodox Hinduism, is now recognised merely as a matter of course—a question of common sense and expediency rather than of logical argument. The fire of social service is still there and the Arya Samaj has done wonders especially in the Punjab and in the United Provinces to arouse the inert mass of Hinduism into a brotherhood of real "*Aryas*". Dayanand was a fighter all his life—a fighter against ignorance, superstition and fraud and the Samaj that he has left, is by no means quiescent. But times have changed. There is no longer any need for that biting, mocking and crude dialectic which offended, and often hurt, the susceptibilities of those who did not fully share the theological dogmas of the Samaj. The Arya Samaj is now entering on the second chapter of its existence—the phase of deliberate and constructive reorganisation of the entire body of Hinduism. Its theology and its ritual are to an outsider matters comparatively unimportant. What matters is the spirit of sacrifice, of service which Dayanand personified in himself and which so many of his great followers and disciples have embodied in their lives. May that fire never die!

FATEHPUR

N. C. MEHTA

DAYANAND AND ARYA SAMAJ

DAYANAND! what a name to conjure with in the Hindu world of Upper India. Where would the Hindus in this part of the country—and as subsequent events have shown in other parts, too—have been but for the inoculations of self-confidence given by the said Swami. "Blessed are those who can cure us of our self-despisings" and so is Swamiji thrice blessed. For did he not correctly read the signs of the times in which he was born and rather than yield to fruitless introspection and cursing like Hamlet, the times in which he was born as out of joint, he, manfully, in the midst of prejudices and passions, stuck to his doctrines and sacrificed himself to give life to his faith in Hinduism and its eternal truths. Western education was silently but surely corroding into the Hindu religious mind, bereft as the former was of its religious aspect. Its virility and newness was flooding away the old and overgrown Hindu teachings. Men educated under the purely secular Western system found themselves adrift, till these castaways were naturally hauled over board by zealous votaries of other religions. Our stowaways had a welcome with others: this increased our disintegration. The sensitive Hindu community whose strength in old days lay in adaptability forgot the secret of its success and strength and permitted their dear kith and kin to bid good-bye to their ancestral faith: it even was helpless in the face of the activities of others and lacked both in a saving creed and an organisation. The advent of Swami Dayanand was absolutely timely: he it was who fulfilled this want and who burst asunder the all-pervading but emasculating effects of effete practices and founded the Arya Samaj. While showing the beauties of Hinduism, he demonstrated that there were weaknesses elsewhere also—weaknesses which, in theory and in practice, are bound to creep round all human doings in course of time and which are sure to cover the divine common truths underlying all religious creeds uniformly. At the same time he showed effectively that Hinduism need not tortoise-like withdraw in its shell when faced with danger: he even gave it pointed horns which could be used as defensive instruments to enable it to survive in the world if it chose to. To my mind, the greatest value of Swamiji's teachings lies in this.

We may differ with some of the methods adopted subsequently by some of his followers of the Arya Samaj. But on the whole the Arya Samaj has done such a lot of good work as a pioneer in the field of education and social reform, in the field of service and sacrifice for public weal that I, for one, have not the heart to throw stones at it for the annoying tactics which it may have adopted sometimes towards those who did not see eye to eye with it entirely. The Arya Samaj is now somewhat moribund: it is showing signs of exhaustion: it has allowed itself to be engulfed in stronger tides: it has perhaps outlived its usefulness. But the impetus given by the great Swami Dayanand can never die. His is now a popular spirit with the Hindus. His is the glory of having, in modern times, checked the dead rot among Hindus and given them a purpose in life to live for and work for in the midst of difficulties and discouragements.

NAINITAL

SITARAM

SWAMI DAYANAND SARASWATI

SPEAKING at one of the annual commemoration meetings at Bombay, Mr. Justice Ranade attempted, with characteristic thoughtfulness, an analysis of the elements of greatness in men, applied those tests to the career of Swami Dayanand Saraswati and reached the conclusion that the Swami fulfilled the conditions and was entitled to a place among the great men of India of the nineteenth century. Half a century after he passed away, Dayanand's name is still a venerated household word throughout Hindu India and his great work still flourishes, still draws devoted converts to its bosom. I here refer, as I need scarcely say, to the Arya Samaj, which can without exaggeration be said to have transformed the face of the Punjab and greatly influenced—for the better—other provinces of northern India. To a true Hindu it will ever be a matter for reverent gratitude that the Swami preached the cult of the Vedas as the revealed word of God, and that he brought back nationalism to its only true and enduring basis.

For the greatness of Swami Dayanand to be acknowledged and the work of the Arya Samaj to be admired, it is not necessary that a person should become devotee of the Swami or a member of the Samaj. The element of the hero-worshipper is so active in the typical Hindu that it is never superflous for him to be impressed with the profound observation of Lord Acton's, that 'absolute devotion to mortal man' ought not to exist. God the Creator, the Preserver and the Destroyer is the only Absolute in the universe, and 'absolute devotion' is exclusively His due; not even of the Higher Beings in the higher worlds, of varying status and authority and at different stages of a spiritual development. Much less can 'absolute devotion' be claimed by or given to men, be they ever so great. It is one of the misfortunes of this world, and perhaps of no country more than of India, that this truth is often overlooked and from time to time one or another great man is deified as it were. And it is one of the drawbacks of movements and organizations like the Brahmo and Arya Samajes, the Theosophical Society and the Radhaswami *Satsang*, that there is an element of narrowness in them and the founder or head of each of them is thought by their respective followers to be infallible. It is still more unfortunate that the evil has of late invaded the political field and because a man is a great soul, 'Mahatma', who has attained a loftier spiritual height than almost any of his contemporaries, it is mistakenly thought that he must necessarily be a perfect political leader. At one end educated Indians have developed an exaggerated habit of criticism to the detriment of effective team work, while at the other many of them have become almost pathetically uncritical of the doctrines and acts of one or another person to whom they give their homage. Both of these excesses have got to be corrected and it should be recognised that 'moderation is like a silken string that runs through all the virtues'.

To me it is enough to be thankful for that in her decadent days, after more than a thousand years of foreign invasions and political and priestly subjection, India has produced and continues to produce, such great men as Paramhansa Ramkrishna and Swami Vivekananda, Ram Mohan Roy and Dayanand Saraswati, Dadabhai Naroji and Mahadeo Govind Ranade, Keshav Chandra Sen and Ishwar Chandra Vidyasagar, Mohandas Gandhi and Rabindranath Tagore. Their countrymen adore them while living, and treasure their sacred memories when they have climbed to higher regions. They are of the nature of imperishable institutions more than of transitory beings, and live for ever as the inspirers of their smaller countrymen. Of this band of immortals is the great hero of this publication, and to him and his great and noble and enduring work I hereby pay my humble and reverent tribute of equal admiration and respect.

ALLAHABAD

C. Y. CHINTAMANI

INDIA'S CONTRIBUTION TO WORLD-CIVILIZATION

The Law of Reflection of Heat and Light

POPULARLY, burning glass is associated with the name of Archimedes (C. 287-212 B.C.) born at Syracuse, in Sicily.

There is a story that he hung up huge reflectors and focussing the rays of the sun on the sails of the Roman ships when they were within a bow-shot of the harbour walls, caused the whole fleet to be burnt. The story however seems to be a later invention. For it is mentioned neither by Polybius nor Livy, nor Plutarch. Archimedes was a man of science. Not only did he discover important laws and invent several useful things but he also wrote scientific treatises. His reputation was great and wide-spread. His contemporaries were very much impressed by his remarkable achievements, and all sorts of things came to be attributed to him. On the other hand, he knew the law of refraction of light—a remark from his lost work *Kato II TPIKA* being quoted by *Theon* of Alexandria—it may be safely assumed that he was familiar with the law of reflection of heat and light. He wrote a work entitled *EPI AI II OUAS* 'sphere-making', which has been lost. So after all he may have constructed some burning instrument, with which the story of the Roman fleet came to be associated.

In any case, it is certain that Archimedes is not the first to discover the law of reflection of heat and light or to construct a burning mirror. References to burning glass can be traced to a remoter antiquity in Greek Literature and the following passage from Aristophanes' '*The Clouds*' will be enough to support this statement.

Soc. —Capital! But I will again propose to you another clever question. If a suit of five talents should be entered against you, tell me how would you obliterate it?

Strep.—I have found a very clever method of getting rid of my suit.........

Soc. —Of what description ?

Strep.—Have you ever seen this stone in the chemist's shops, the beautiful and transparent one, from which they kindle fire ?

Soc. —Do you mean the burning glass ?

Strep.—I do. Come, what would you say, pray if I were to take this, when the clerk was entering the suit and were to stand at a distance, in the direction of the sun thus and melt out the letters of my suit ?

The Clouds was written C. 423 B. C. Aristophanes is assigned to C. 450-C. 385 B. C.

In India, however, the law of reflection of heat and light was discovered at a still earlier period and burning instruments were used for practical purposes. The Poetic and Creative age of the Vedic Saṁhitās was followed by the prosaic period of the Brāhmaṇas when the creative talent had practically exhausted itself and ritualistic practices were elaborated in an unprecedented manner. The performance of sacrifice was regarded as one of the most important, perhaps the most important function of life as even the gods were controlled by sacrifice, the right performance of which was therefore most desirable. It would be needless to point out that the minutest detail connected with sacrifice i. e., the altar, the brick, the stick, the grass etc., was regarded as sacred. The degree of sacredness of a particular object was in direct proportion to its distance from earth: that is to say, atmospheric objects were more sacred than terrestrial objects while celestial things were the most sacred. It was held that there were three kinds of fires or three different forms of fire. (*i*) Terrestrial (*ii*) Atmospheric i. e. lightning (*iii*) Celestial, i. e. the sun. Each latter was more sacred and therefore more efficacious than the former. The desire of the sacrificer was to sacrifice with celestial fire. The gods will be better pleased and he will win better reward. This necessity resulted in the discovery of the law of reflection of heat and light. The earliest reference to the production of fire direct from the sun-rays is found in Nirukta of Yāska. Oriental scholars differ with regard to the date of Yāska. However a general unanimity fixes his lower limit as not later than 500 B. C. But on internal evidence, Yāska can be proved to have flourished earlier. His upper limit is the period of the Āraṇyakas, several of which he quotes in the Nirukta. It is remarkable that he quotes a large number of passages (about 700) from the Ṛigveda, Sāmveda, Atharvaveda, Yajurveda, Brāhmaṇas and Āraṇyakas but not a single passage from any of the Upanishads. The word, Upanishad occurs in the Nirukta once only, not in the sense of a philosophical text but in the sense of esoterical doctrine. Again the esoterical doctrine is not in connection with metaphysics—the main theme of the Upanishads—but merely in connection with an interpretation of a Vedic stanza. It is clear therefore that Yāska is not familiar with the Upanishads. This means that he belongs to a pre-Upanishadic period. As the Buddha (6th century B.C.) studied the older Upanishads and adopted the doctrine of *Karma* and transmigration from them, it is obvious that the Upanishads must have been in existence at least a hundred years before him. The Upanishads cannot therefore be assigned to a period later than the 7th century B.C. And Yāska is earlier than the Upanishads and should therefore be assigned to about the 8th century B.C. I may add that I have taken the minimum and the lowest possible date.

Yāska is by no means the first discoverer of the law of reflection of Heat and Light. The law must have been discovered a long time before him for he belongs to a period when enthusiasm for sacerdotal ritualism (कर्मकाण्ड) was waning and the foundation of metaphysical speculation (ज्ञानकाण्ड) was being laid. Yāska has merely transmitted the process of the practical application of the law. He has described the method of producing fire from its atmospheric form i.e. lightning and also from its celestial form i.e. the sun. This knowledge was no doubt handed down from generation to generation by means of an oral tradition.

The passage from the Nirukta is the following:—

अयमेवाग्निर्वैश्वानर इति शाकपूणिः ।

विश्वानरावित्येते उत्तरे ज्योतिषी । वैश्वानरोऽयं यत्ताभ्यां जायते । कथं त्वयमेताभ्यां जायत इति । यत्र वैद्युतः शरणमभिहन्ति यावदनुपात्तो भवति मध्यमधर्मैव तावद् भवति । उदकेन्धनः शरीरोपशमनः । उपादीयमान एवायं सम्पद्यत उदकोपशमनः शरीरदीप्तिः ।

अथादित्यात् । उदीचि प्रथमसमावृत्त आदित्ये कंसं वा मणिं वा परिमृज्य प्रतिस्वरे यत्र शुष्कगोमयमसंस्पर्शयन् धारयति तत्प्रदीप्यते । सोऽयमेव सम्पद्यते । *Nirukta.*

I give below my English translation of the Sanskrit passage; "This very (i. e. terrestrial) fire is Vaiśvānara", says Śākapūni The upper two lights (i.e. atmospheric and celestial lights—lightning and the sun) are called Viśvānara. This (terrestrial) fire is called Vaiśvānara (lit. born of Viśvānara) because it is engendered from them (upper lights). But how is it engendered from them?

When lightning fire strikes a place of shelter (e.g. a tree), and as long as that object is not seized upon, it retains the characteristics of the atmospheric fire. But as soon as it is seized upon, this very (terrestrial) fire is produced which becomes extinguished in water and blazes in solid bodies.

Now the following is the process of its production from the sun. The sun having first revolved towards the northern hemisphere (i.e. after the vernal equinox) a *person* holds a polished (piece of) white copper or crystal focussing the sun-rays in a place where there is some dry cow-dung without touching it, it blazes forth and this very (terrestrial) fire is produced."

The method of producing fire direct from the rays of the sun as described in the Nirukta is quite clear and practical. Yāska has however taken the precaution to add that the process should be resorted to after the vernal equinox, i.e., the 23rd of March.

It may be objected that the method described in the Nirukta merely represents empirical knowledge acquired in course of time and does not indicate that the law of reflection of heat and light had been discovered. To this, my answer is the following. A reference to the passage from *The Clouds* of Aristophanes—quoted above—shows that the method of producing fire from the sun was empirical knowledge and we cannot be at all sure that the underlying law was understood, for no alternative to the use of crystal is proposed. But Yāska mentions several alternatives. The very fact that Yāska has proposed alternatives shows that he knew the law of Reflection. If alternatives had not been stated, then a knowledge of the law itself would have been doubtful although in that case, the credit of the first practical application of the law of Reflection would belong to India. But with several alternatives proposed to produce fire direct from the rays of the sun, the knowledge of the law itself can no longer be doubtful. I therefore claim that the law of Reflection of heat and light was first discovered in ancient India.

The ancient Chinese are not known to have possessed the knowledge of producing fire from the sun. Their ancient works like the Shuking, Semachêng, Lietse, Huai-man-tse etc., do not contain a single reference to the process. Even the burning glasses or crystals are not mentioned.

Among the Arabs, burning glasses were not known before the 12th century A.D. The earliest reference to the burning glass is found in a work on medicine. It is entitled *Jami Mufridatil Adwiyah wa Agziyah* by Ibn-al-Baytar Nabati Maliki Abu Muh'd Abdullah, a pupil of the famous botanist Abou'l Abbas. The former was born in 1197 A.D. in the native town of Malaga. Later, he migrated to Seville and in 1219 A. D. he set out on a voyage of exploration in the East. He was patronised by Najamuddin, the Sultan of Egypt. He travelled in Syria, Mesopotamia and penetrated as far as India. He wrote several works but his masterpiece is the Materia Medica, the *jami* etc. This was translated into French by Leclerk in 1887, from which work I quote the following passage:—

C'est une espéce de verre.........on le trouve dans la mer

indienne.........Frappé par le fer trempé, il donne d'abondantes étincelles. La premiere sorte n'est autre que le cristal. Sil'on expose cette pierre aux rayons du soliel, que l'on observe les rayons qu'elle émet, et que l'on soumette ã ces rayons un morcean de linge noir, il s'enflamme et se consume et si l'on veut, par ce moyen, obtenir du feu, on peut l'employer.[1]

I translate the French passage as follows :—

"It is a kind of glass.........one finds it in the Indian Ocean ....struck by light, it gives numerous sparks. The first kind is nothing but crystal. If one exposes it to the rays of the sun and observes the rays which it emits and if one puts a piece of black cotton to these rays, it will become enflamed and burn itself. If one wishes, one can employ this method to obtain fire."

Thus the history of burning glass and the discovery of the law of Reflection of Heat and Light can be traced to a remote antiquity. This incidentally shows us that an ever-growing desire on the part of the sacrificer to perform it in the best possible way in order to win the best reward was responsible for the discovery of this important law. It is interesting to note how the same motive repeats itself in Europe.

The Latin poet Orpheus has composed a poem in Latin entitled *Orphica*. Relevant verses of this poem, 170-184, are quoted here :— "The deity cannot resist the prayers of him who bearing in his hand a refulgent and transparent crystal, betakes himself into a temple; his wish will surely be granted. When crystal is placed on dry wood-shavings, while the sun-rays strike it, smoke will soon arise, then fire, and at last a bright flame, regarded as sacred fire. No sacrifice is more pleasing to gods than when offered by means of such fire." As Orpheus belongs to the second century A.D., the practice and the knowledge of the law were prevalent in India more than a 1,000 years earlier than the Latin poet.

LAHORE

LAKSHMAN SWAROOP

[1] See 2183. French Trans. by Leclarc, Paris 1877, Volume III, Page 342.

DAYANAND AND THE ARYA SAMAJ

I am not a member of the Arya Samaj. That makes it all the easier for me to pay my tribute to the remarkable personality of its founder and his great achievements. Swami Dayanand Saraswati was a Protestant, but he was also a Reformer. It is not necessary to agree with all his views or to subscribe to his interpretation of the scriptures in order to appreciate his valuable contribution to Hindu society in the nineteenth century. In so many phases of national life, his influence has been beneficial and great. Together with Raja Ram Mohan Roy, he has the distinction of modernising the ancient religion of Hinduism. In the Punjab and the United Provinces especially, it is difficult to exaggerate the extent and depth of the impression produced by his teachings. For myself, I have been struck more by the educational side of the activities of the Arya Samaj than its other sides. In the domain of education, the Samaj has been responsible for evoking the missionary spirit—the spirit of sacrifice and of service, of surrender to the greater good, which unfortunately had lain dormant in Hindu society for generations. In Northern India, there is hardly a town without a D. A. V. High School and many of the larger cities have also their D. A. V. Colleges. It has been my good fortune to visit some of these institutions. In all of them I have been impressed by the tremendous hold which the personality of Swami Dayanand has on all who are associated with them. Teachers and the ever-changing generation of students alike come under his spell and because of this, they ever afterwards have the rich experience of contact with a spirit that is mighty yet.

In the revival of enthusiasm for Sanskrit, the Arya Samaj has played a unique part. The onrush of Western thought and culture threatened for a time to sweep Indians off their feet and make them lose their intellectual balance. A generation ago Sanskrit Literature and Hindu Philosophy were looked down upon by the modern educated Indian as relics of the barbaric past. If there is to-day a feeling of reverence and an attitude of intellectual curiosity, much of the credit is due to the Arya Samaj.

I have not referred to the educational experiments of the Arya Samaj as evidenced by the various Gurukulas that it maintains both for boys and girls. My knowledge of them is limited and even more limited is my enthusiasm for experiments that seek to make us revert to the hoary past; but I have met a few persons educated at the Gurukula of Kangri and I am satisfied that in the case of a few individuals the system adopted there has worked satisfactorily. Whether it is suited to large numbers is a different question. What matters is that in an age of routine and convention, the Arya Samaj had the courage and the independence to strike out a line of its own. To that effort and that endeavour, recognition is due. Others, happily still with us, will be able to refer to Swami Dayanand on the basis of personal knowledge, but the younger generation that was not privileged to know him will decline to believe that even they can have greater admiration and respect for the great Reformer whom this volume seeks to commemorate.

ALLAHABAD

AMARNATHA JHA

Maharaja Pratap Singh

Mahadeva Govind Ranade

R. B. Lala Mulraj

Lala Saindas

Mohanlal Vishnulal Pandya

PRINCIPLES OF THE ARYA SAMAJ

AFTER winning the Premchand Roychand scholarship of the Calcutta University, I was staying in Murree at the beginning of the summer of 1877, with my brother the late Lala Shiv Dayal B.A., then Assistant Engineer, and preparing for the pleadership Examination. The late Rai Bahadur Doulat Ram, who was at that time Superintendent of the office of Postmaster General, Punjab, came to Murree from Lahore. He was full of enthusiastic admiration for Swami Dayanand Saraswati, who was then at Lahore. Swamiji's discourses had made a deep impression on his mind. I used to meet him almost every day. He was never tired of speaking about Swami Dayanand and his lectures. He gave me to read two or three issues of Swamiji's *Veda-Bhāshya-Bhūmikā*, which he had brought from Lahore. I was then about twenty-two years of age. I made up my mind to see Swamiji. I left the cool and bracing hills of Murree and came in the midst of the grilling and scorching summer to Lahore, to see and hear Swamiji. In those days there was Railway line from Lahore to Jhelum. I reached Lahore in the afternoon. I went the same evening to hear Swamiji who was then staying in Dr. Rahim Khan's Kothi which, was situated between Chhajju Bhagat's *samādhi*, and the dissection Hall of King Edward Medical College. There is a lawn now at the site. When the lecture was over, I was introduced to Swamiji. After this I used to see Swamiji almost every morning and hear his discourse every evening when he was at Lahore. Before coming to Lahore, Swamiji had founded the Arya Samaj at Bombay and framed the Niyama-Vyavasthā. When it was proposed to establish the Arya Samaj at Lahore, I was asked to take part in drafting the constitution of the Arya Samaj. With the help of the Arya Samaj Niyama Vyavasthā and under the guidance of Swamiji, the ten Niyamas containing the principles of the Arya Samaj and the forty

Upniyamas containing the constitution of the Arya Samaj were drafted. Some of the prominent members of the Brahmo Samaj, Lahore who had taken part in inviting Swamiji to Lahore desired Swamiji to exclude reference to the Veda from the principles. But Swamiji did not accept their suggestion. On this the members of the Brahmo Samaj ceased to contribute to the funds which were raised for defraying the expenses of Swamiji and his establishment. After the Niyamas and Upniyamas had been framed, the Arya Samaj was founded at Lahore in the summer of 1877. I was elected the first president of the Arya Samaj, Lahore.

After the organisation of the Arya Samaj at Lahore, Swami Dayanand Saraswati founded several Arya Samajes in different towns in the Punjab and elsewhere. The Niyamas and Upniyamas of all the Arya Samajes were the same as had been framed at Lahore. The Bombay Arya Samaj also adopted the same Niyamas and Upniyamas. When a person wishes to be enrolled as a member of the Arya Samaj he is required to sign an application which is as follows:—

> I, with pleasure, agree to act according to *Uddeśya* (as detailed in the Niyamas), please enrol my name in the Arya Samaj." (Footnote to Upniyama 3).

A person who agrees to act according to the Niyamas of the Arya Samaj is enrolled as a member of the Arya Samaj. He is not required to believe in the articles of faith as detailed in the *Mantavya* of Swami Dayanand Saraswati, or in the philosophical tenets, theories and doctrines propounded in his works. Nor is he asked to acknowledge the Bhāshya (Commentary) of Swami Dayanand on the Vedas as true and free from mistakes, or to accept him as an infallible guide. I may mention that in December 1883, when the first meeting of the Paropakāriṇī Sabhā was held at Ajmer, shortly after the death of Swami Dayanand Saraswati, it was suggested that a member of the Arya Samaj should acknowledge in writing that they believed in the *Mantavya* of Swami Dayanand Saraswati. On this, the late Lala Sain Das who was then President of the Arya Samaj Lahore, stated forcibly that he and the other members of the Arya Sȧmaj had great regard for the opinions of Swami Dayanand Saraswati, but they were bound to act according to the ten Niyamas only.

Those who want that it should be essential for a member of the Arya Samaj to believe in some articles of faith in addition to the ten Niyamas do not realise that they are narrowing the sphere of the Arya Samaj and turning it into a sect. The foundation on which the Arya Samaj was established by Swami Dayanand was very broad and ancient. It is very unfortunate that the object for which Swami Dayanand Saraswati founded the Arya Samaj is being forgotten and lost sight of. He wanted to revive the study of the Veda and of the works of Ṛishis and thereby to resuscitate the Hindus. He had no intention of founding a new religion or forming a new sect. As the members of the Arya Samaj have ignored the object of Swami Dayanand Saraswati, the Arya Samaj has been split up into two sections, and has not been able to extend its sphere of usefulness to the same extent as it would have otherwise done.

Swamiji's object in founding the Arya Samaj was to organise a society which would devote itself to bettering and raising the Hindu community. Swami Dayanand included in the ten Niyamas of the Arya Samaj all that is necessary for the making of a noble, virtuous and religious man. He required a member of the Arya Samaj to believe in one true, everlasting and unincarnate God. He required a member of the Arya Samaj to do *Swadhyaya* that is, enjoined on him to read the Veda and to hear it read and to recite the same to others. He made it an essential condition for entering the Arya Samaj that a man should be ever ready to embrace truth and to forsake falsehood, and that he should in all his dealings make justice the guiding principle. He held out as an object before the Arya Samaj to do good to humanity and to ameliorate its physical, intellectual and social condition. He asked the members of the Arya Samaj to be kind to all their brethren, and to diffuse knowledge and dispel ignorance. In becoming members of the Arya Samaj, he asked them to pledge themselves not to be content with the amelioration of their own condition, but to ameliorate the condition of others also. Lastly, in the tenth principle, he required the members not to sacrifice individuality in personal matters, but in matters concerning the well-being of society to subordinate their private interests to the interests of others. It was a high ideal of a noble, a pure and religious life which Swami Dayanand sketched out in the ten principles of the Arya Samaj for its members. If a member can conform his conduct to the ten principles of the Arya Samaj, there is not the slightest doubt that he can become an enlightened, unselfish, just, virtuous and religious man and a true member of the Arya Samaj.

As the members of the Arya Samaj have failed to rise to the ideal of Swami Dayanand Saraswati, and to grasp his high and noble object in establishing the Arya Samaj, and have failed to cultivate the spirit of toleration, and have neglected to perform the duty of *Swādhyaya*, they have not been successful, in ameliorating the condition of the Hindus, and in extricating them from the low and abject condition into which they have fallen, and in teaching them to co-operate and work together.

If the members of the Arya Samaj persist in spending their energy in crushing the freedom of thought and liberty of speech, and continue to follow the path which has been leading them downwards, and go on studiously ignoring the spirit of toleration, which it was the life-mission of Swamiji to foster, there is danger of the Arya Samaj doing harm to the Hindu community.

I have stated already that when a person joined the Arya Samaj he, signed the application (form given in the footnote to Upniyama 3) in which he promised to act according to the *Uddeśya* of the Arya Samaj detailed in the ten Niyamas He did not bind himself to believe in any set of doctrines, theories or tenets; nor did he undertake to believe the writings of Swami Dayanand Saraswati to be infallible; nor did he agree to have faith in the *Mantavya* of Swami Dayanand, nor did he promise to sacrifice his freedom of thought in compliance with the opinions of the majority of the members of the Arya Samaj for the time being.

After 1877, Swami Dayanand was very busy from morning till evening; besides doing *Swadhyaya* and meditation, he had to see people, deliver lectures and hold discussions almost every day, and to attend to correspondence, and over and above all this to publish his voluminous works. He had Pandits in his employ. Sometimes he used to dictate to Pandits what he wanted to be published, and other times he used to give to the Pandits the substance of what he wanted to be written, and leave it to them to write it out in their own words. He used to read or hear what had been written by the Pandits and make corrections. He was constantly moving from place to place. It is on account of these circumstances that he could not always exercise the necessary amount of supervision over what was published under his name. It may not be generally known that he wrote very seldom with his hand, and that also little and that the Sanskrit portion of his commentaries on the Vedas was written to his dictation, and that the Hindi portion of the same was mainly written by the Pandits in his service, in their own words. The proceedings of the Paropakāriṇī Sabhā held on the 28th December, 1883, show that "the whole of the Yajurveda had been fully commented upon, though only a portion had been published by Swamiji", and Ṛig Veda upto 7 *mandala* had "been interpreted" and it was "resolved that the work of correcting the proofs, and translating Sanskrit commentary into Hindi be entrusted to Pandit Bhimsen and Jwala Datta on Rs. 25 a month each."

Thus it is not always easy to find out in the works of Swami Dayanand which were published after 1877, what words were uttered by Swamiji himself and which were inserted by the Pandits in his service.

He made the ten principles of the Arya Samaj very catholic, so as to include persons of all kinds of views about matters on which the ten principles are silent. But it will be seen that he took care to include in them all the principles which go to make men noble, virtuous and religious. He in his life time welcomed into the Arya Samaj, all men who agreed to conduct themselves in accordance with the ten principles, notwithstanding that their opinion on matters on which the ten principles are silent were different from his own. He had no hesitation in admitting into the Arya Samaj men who had not the same views with him on questions as to what articles of food should be eaten.

In the life time of Swamiji, the opinions expressed in his works were never confounded with the articles of faith of the Arya Samaj. The opinions expressed by him in his works were held up as the opinions of a great man, and his exposition of the Veda was looked upon as one coming from a very learned Sanskrit scholar. He however was not regarded as infallible.

LAHORE MULRAJ

REMINISCENCES

IN the beginning of January 1877, Swami Dayanand Saraswati was at Delhi. From there he came *via* Meerut to Ludhiana.

At Ludhiana he met Munshi Alakh Dhari. At the beginning of the summer of 1877, Swamiji was invited from Ludhiana to Lahore by some members of the Brahmo Samaj and other public-spirited men They secured for his residence, a part of a building in Rattan Chand Dhariwala's garden. When Swamiji began to deliver his lectures against idolatry, Diwan Bhagwan Das Darhiwala, proprietor of the garden, who was an orthodox Hindu, did not allow Swamiji to reside in his garden. Then the *kothi* of Khan Bahadur Rahim Khan, which was located between Chhajju Bhagat's Samādh and the Dissection Hall of King Edward Medical College, where now there is a lawn, was secured for the residence and lectures of Swami Dayanand. Here the draft of the Niyams and Upniyamas of the Arya Samaj were approved by Swamiji. Swamiji resided for sometime in a *kothi* of Nawab Nawazish Ali Khan outside Musti Gate of Lahore. The *kothi* is still in existence and is the property of a member of the family of the Nawab.

One morning I was sitting with Swamiji in the garden of the *kothi* on a mat in front of Swamji. Swamiji was sitting in a chair. Some women of Lahore came and sat on a mat facing Swamiji. Swamiji turned his back to the women. The women asked Swamiji to give them *Updesh*. Swamiji told them to come to the public meetings in which he delivered his lectures, hear his *Updesh* and asked them not to come to his residential place. He dismissed the women. When the women were gone, I asked Swamiji why he did not give *Updesh* to the women. He said he had observed *Brahmcharya* all his life that it was not desirable for many reasons to allow women to come and sit near him. From Lahore, Swamiji went to Amritsar and delivered lectures there. An Arya Samaj was established there.

Swamiji visited Ferozepur, Gujranwala, Rawalpindi and some other places in the Punjab and delivered lectures and established Arya Samajes there. He used to return from outstations to Lahore and put up in the *chaubārā* at Rai Mela Ram's tank near the railway station.

When the Arya Samaj, Lahore was organised, it was located in a house in Anarkali, where afterwards the *Tribune* Press was located for some years. Here also Swami Dayanand used to deliver his lectures.

My brother the late Lala Shiv Dayal told me that he saw Swami Dayanand at Agra, and had a talk with him about the occult powers of a Yogi. Swamiji said that the whole world was connected and that every motion was communicated to the whole world, and that words uttered did not perish, and so were called *akshar* (अक्षर), and the incidents which happened left their impressions on ether, that the Yogi's mind on account of concentration and abstraction could read the faint impressions on ether of words spoken and incidents which took place in the past, which ordinary men could not perceive on account of their minds not being sensitive and developed.

On one occasion in 1877, I, with some members of the Arya Samaj went to the railway station to see Swamiji off to some station to the North-west of Lahore. We had to wait for the train. There was no bench at the place. There were several bundles of Sanskrit books, including copies of the Veda which Swamiji carried with him. Swamiji sat on one of the bundles. One of the persons present remarked that there were copies of Vedas in the bundle. Swamiji observed on this that there was no disrespect to the Vedas by sitting on a bundle of papers on which the Vedas were printed.

In 1891, I visited Udaipur. I put up there with the late P. Mohanlal Vishnulal Pandya. He took me to the garden in which Swami Dayanand Saraswati resided for sometime and pointed out to me a small plot of land in which *Manduk Parni* (Hydro-cotyle Asiatica used in place of *Brahmi* outside Bengal) was growing. He told me that the *Manduk Parni* was planted when Swamiji was residing in the garden, at the desire of Swamiji as he was in the habit of taking it every day. He also told me that Maharana Sajjan Singhji used to come to Swamiji everyday to read with him Dharma Śastra.

In November, 1879, I received a letter at Lahore from Swami Dayanand asking me to see him at Delhi. I went to Delhi and saw him in a garden where he was putting up. He had a talk with me about the Theosophical Society. It was decided that Arya Samaj should have no connection with the Theosophical Society. The same evening, I went with Swamiji to a house in the heart of the town, where he delivered his discourse. That was the last occasion on which I saw Swamiji.

SIMLA — MULRAJ

ARYA SAMAJ AS A NATIONAL INSTITUTION

NATIONAL life in India at the advent of the nineteenth century was in a dormant condition. Students of history familiar with the conditions prevailing in the eighteenth century know well the confusion that arose in India on the break-up of the Mughal empire. Following on the anarchical condition national life was at its lowest ebb. It was only in the beginning of the nineteenth century that with settled government and the impact of a new civilisation, intellectual and social activities were renewed. This revival could no longer be on the old lines nor be isolated in its outlook, for an alien but vigorous force had been installed by the introduction of Western ideas and methods.

It was only natural that with intellectual revival, the uncritical mind of the time would attribute the past disaster and misfortune to indigenous institutions and ideals. Rapid success came to those who had been imbued and saturated with Western ideas. Also naturally these came to be looked upon as in themselves superior and efficient. Thus we see that for over half a century imitation of the new ideas was the goal of educated India. Our foreign masters knew little of Indian civilisation and Christian missionaries abused all national institutions. The educated Indian followed the lead and was happy in attributing his country's misery to its past and was gladly ashamed of every thing Indian. The depth of this degradation in the revival period cannot be imagined now, except by those who have specially studied the social history of Bengal in the first half of the nineteenth century. For in those days what Bengal thought one year the rest of India did the next year.

This state of things was due to the glamour of the Western civilisation which brought its ideas of personal freedom and individual initiative at a time when there was little of either.

The distracted nation was overwhelmed and opened its arms wide to the new "faith," for it came with the force of religious fervour. The first stage was of utter confusion, of mad uprooting of whatever was indigenous. Destruction followed, and in religion, lack of any faith was the faith of youth. Even those who embraced Christianity did so less as a matter of conviction than as a convert to the Western style.

There can be no doubt that this could only be a passing stage in the onrush of national activities and that the revival movement would soon take the aspect of reform in the various departments of national life. This reformation was manifest everywhere, but we must here confine ourselves to the sphere of religion only. The first reform movement was the Brahmo Samaj. In spite of the extraordinary activities of its founder, Rājā Ram Mohan Roy, the Samaj was a failure so long as it kept to the originator's idea of a theistic association of all religions. It gained force and popularity after it had been reorganised as a separate church and especially because of its zeal for social reform and its emphasis on the individual conscience. In spite of the present insignificance of the branch founded by him the outstanding figure—the dynamic force—of the movement was Keshab Chandra Sen. His credal inspiration was dominantly Christian. There is little wonder, therefore, that as a religious order the Brahmo Samaj has receded to the background before the surging tide of twentieth-century nationalism. This should not make us blind to the services or the importance of Brahmo Samaj in the second half of the nineteenth century.

If we may borrow expressions from the history of the sixteenth century Europe, this reform movement naturally led to a counter-reform movement—one that would cling to the old, changing and modifying but essentially founded on the past. As the Brahmo Samaj was the most forceful manifestation of the reform movement, so was the Arya Samaj the earliest and most powerful factor in the counter-reform movement. Later, the orthodox party gathered force and probably the Bhārata Dharma Mahāmaṇḍala and Jamiat-ul-Ulemā have to-day a larger following than Arya Samaj. But like the Jesuit movement, the Arya Samaj came first on the field and was for a time the strongest revivalist movement of Hinduism. Like the Jesuit movement, again, it has specially worked for the education of the youth and made that an important plank of the rising nationalist feeling which has grown during the last half a century. From this point of view, in Northern India, it is even now ahead of all the other movements of reform and counter-reform.

The present writer is not competent to judge of the credal reform advocated by the great founder of Arya Samaj. But as a student of history, one should be able to realise the force of the movement which began as a reaction and has brought back national life to its natural and historical groove. It is here that a people's life-force can find scope for its inherent genius. But for the Brahmo and Arya Samajes and the greater reactions of a later age, Indian nationalism would have grown more slowly and in a more distorted fashion, out of touch and out of contact with the indigenous civilisation, and therefore at variance with the race-consciousness and spiritual inheritance of the land.

The life and achievements of Swami Dayanand Saraswati are too well known to need any recapitulation here. The steady growth of the Arya Samaj is proof of the enduring work of the Swami. It has been helped by the course of development of Indian national life, for the present position of the Arya Samaj, the Bhārata Dharma Mahāmaṇḍala and Jamiat-ul-Ulemā on the one hand, and Brahmo Samaj on the other, does point out the finger of fate and should be read as a moral and a portent. In the strife and controversy of a particularly heated atmosphere, especially with the double-edged fight that the Swami had to undertake with the Christian and Brahmo movements on the one side and the more extreme reactionary movements of orthodox Hinduism and Islām on the other, many doctrines had to be formulated and many strategic positions defended which may be considered as of doubtful validity at the present time. If the Swami were living to-day, an original mind like his would have had time to recover the perennial from the temporary, the essential from the accidental.

Let not the great work of the Swami be clouded by our greater reverence for what he said than for the spirit which inspired it. He condemned many things which were in the air at the time as also in the murky atmosphere inherited from the past. If the same zeal for truth, for reform, for love of this ancient land and its people inspire his followers to-day, the Arya Samaj will yet have a long life of usefulness and, may be, great achievement at the present crisis of India's social and religious life. On the occasion of the Nirvāṇa Ardha Shatābdī of the great Swami, if we can recover the spirit, the zeal, the love, and the determination which characterised him when he was on earth, we shall have amply justified our claim to deserve the privilege of celebrating the occasion that we shall be doing to-day.

INDORE

P. BASU

SWAMI DAYANAND AND THE CASTE SYSTEM

LIKE Raja Ram Mohan Roy, Swami Dayanand was also one of the greatest reformers of his time. A man of great religious zeal and reformist activities he directed his stupendous energies chiefly against the deep-rooted institution of caste system among the Hindus. He had the far-sighted vision to see that the institution was an anachronism that had long outlived its usefulness, a force that was working for the disruption of Hindu society and a cancer that was slowly poisoning the very life-blood of the nation. All the fantastic stories about the origin of the castes as propounded in religious text-books and the Purāṇas, he rightly held up to ridicule as utterly unworthy of reliance. According to him, it was based not on heredity or birth-right, but on inherent qualities and actions of an individual, "गुणकर्मविभागशः", as the Gītā says.

Jainism too owes its origin as a reaction to the over-emphasis laid on the *Varṇāśrama-Dharma* and its consequent disintegrating and demoralising influences, as well as to over-ritualistic tendencies resulting in the slaughter of animals in the name of religion. And Swamiji, though he severely criticised Jainism along with other Indian systems of thought, did not fail to utilize such Jain doctrines as he found to conform to his own ideas and principles.

In order to propagate these ideas he travelled far and wide over the country holding religious meetings and addressing learned gatherings on this subject and ultimately succeeded, by defeating the arguments advanced by the supporters of *Varṇāśrama-Dharma*, in convincing a considerable section of his co-religionists of the inequity and injustice involved in the system. This difference of opinion however resulted in a sharp split among the ranks of the Hindus and in the end led to the founding of a new social order called the '**Arya Samaj**'. The ideas let loose by

Swami Dayanand have steadily been growing in strength and to-day within half a century since the death of the illustrious Swami, the Samaj has assumed such an enormous form that it counts within its fold a considerable number of our educated and enlightened countrymen. Born of an orthodox Brahmin family belonging to the *Śaiva* sect at Morvi in Kathiawar and educated strictly according to the Brahmanical tradition, Dayanand showed signs of an inner revolt even at an early age and it is said of him that while still in his teens, he was worshipping the family idol *Śivalingam* on a *Śiva Chaturdaśī* night when a rat quickly ran over the body of *lingam* several times. This incident, however trivial in itself, marked a significant and turning point in the life of Dayanand and led him to meditate deeply over the really representative character of numerous idols and deities worshipped among the Hindus and to enquire about the validity and reasonableness of image-worship in course of which he became thoroughly convinced of its utter unreasonableness. Thereafter, he gave up the habit of idol-worship himself and preached the doctrine of unity and formlessness of the Godhead.

A born reformer, an erudite scholar well-versed in the lore of Sanskrit Śāstras in almost all branches, Dayanand combined in himself the burning zeal of a reformer, the independence of a free thinker and the devotion of a spiritual realiser. His brilliant commentary on the Ṛigveda and his relentless exposition of the institution of caste distinction recognised as unknown among the Hindus of the Vedic age have undoubtedly earned for him a luminous position among the galaxy of social and religious reformers of whom Hindu society may justly be proud.

CALCUTTA

PURANCHAND NAHAR

THE SŪTRA OF DAYANAND'S LIFE

यो विद्यात् सूत्रं विततं यस्मिन्नोताः प्रजा इमाः ।
सूत्रं सूत्रस्य यो विद्यात् स विद्याद् ब्राह्मणं महत् ॥ अथर्व० १० । ८ । ३७ ॥

The man who knows the extended Sūtra
Which passes through these numerous creatures,
The man who knows this Sūtra's Sūtra
He verily knows the mighty Brāhmaṇa.

Dayanand was a mighty Brahmin, a perfect representative of the ancient Arya Ṛishis. He had caught a full vision of the hoary *Brahma* culture, and it was the one extended thread of his life to strive in diverse ways for the resuscitation of that *Brahma* culture. An adequate understanding of Dayanand's life signifies one's capability to visualise the glory of ancient Aryan society when the *Brahma-vettā* stood at the apex of the social structure. We walk in harmony with the message of this great seer in so far as we successfully strive to reinstate Brahma in the lofty position from which He has been dislodged by our present philosophy of soul-negation.

Brahma is the central subject propounded in the Vedas. Dayanand understood Brahma and His divine wisdom to be identical. This found expression in his uncompromising advocacy of the Vedic Swādhyāya. The Vedas formed an inalienable part of his life and he owed his strength to them The Veda had made him what he was, and though attempts were made by individuals less staunch in faith to divert him from his fidelity to Vedic wisdom, he showed himself unshakable on this one point. Any one wishing to catch the spark of Dayanand's inspiration should meditate on the following five sūtras which constituted the rafters of his life. They are:—

1. Tapas,
2. Satya,

3. Brahma,
4. Dīkshā,
5. Yajña.

These principles comprehend all that was noble and good in the life of a Vedic Ṛishi, and hence in the life of Swami Dayanand. Like the five Prāṇas integrated to invest the human body with an all-round activity, they entered into him as the basic atoms of his mighty being His *Brahmacharya* was an expression of his *Tapas*, his devotion to Veda of his *Brahma*, his rationalism of his *Satya*, his life-long consecrated services to society and nation of his *Dikshā*, and his complete renunciation of material gain for the sake of the spirit was an expression of his *Yajña*. But let us not look at these five as isolated factors in the life of Dayanand. They converge at the çentre of a single cultural consciousness which he typified in his own person. That was the *Brahma* or Vedic culture alluded to in the beginning of this article. Vedic wisdom must find expression in Vedic life, hence it was that Dayanand hammered incessantly to make the Aryan society conform to Vedic principles, in other words, to laws of cosmic harmony. This philosophy underlies the secret of his life and work. If we love Dayanand, we must love the Vedas. Dayanand found the Vedas as an instrument of freedom. With their help he sharpened the intellect of his countrymen to cleave through thick palls of age-long ignorance. Let us not to-day feel them as fetters round our feeble hands.

Let the whole Aryan fraternity assembled at Ajmer understand this one truth clearly that the Vedas constitute our strength and not our weakness, and that consequently the mission of the Arya Samaj is the re-establishment of Vedic culture by employing all its available resources.

MUTTRA VASUDEVA ANGIRASA

DAYANAND AND THE REGENERATION OF INDIA

DAYANAND was a mighty creative genius. The importance of a genius lies in the fact that a certain characteristic of human nature is developed in him in the highest degree. He towers above the ordinary run of mankind. A genius is a great intellectual force lending a social upheaval a new line of advance or creating something of permanent value to society.

Dayanand's contributions to religious, philosophical, cultural, social and political thought form a great treasure to the world's literature. He has given a new meaning to human existence, and created new ideals for human achievements.

Swami Dayanand did his best to revive the old cultural system of India which had enriched the world and given rise to many a new cultural ideal. It may rightly be termed and interpreted as the mother of the present day cultures of the world. For sometime past there had, however, been a distinct deterioration of Indian culture. There were two reasons for this decay. Firstly, India had been a prey to foreign invaders, who had directly or indirectly tried to suppress her cultural ideals; and secondly, in the face of the more aggressive, dynamic, vitalizing cultures of the West, it had lost some of its beauties and lofty aims, and imitated others by the law of contact. Since the advent of Swami Dayanand on the cultural and religious field, India is gradually but surely reviving her cultural ideals. Swami Dayanand's clarion call of 'Back to the Vedas' served as a check to the fatal headlong wave of materialisation, and blind imitation of western civilization, which had caught hold of the educated youths of the country. An appeal to the lofty religion of the Vedas, the subtle but elevating philosophy of the Upanishads, the immortal verse of the *Bhagavadgītā*, the didactic teachings of Manu, the National and martial pleadings of the *Rāmāyaṇa*, the *Mahābhārata* and the art of the works of Kâlidâsa and Bhavabhûti, so forcibly made by Dayanand produced the desired effect on the plastic minds of the Indian youths. It was Dayanand who rid the Indians of the nightmare under which they had been degrading their little ones by labelling them with English names. It was he, too, who righted the perversion of the Indian mentality, that had led us to import as many English words as possible into our daily parlance. It was he, who revived the learning of Hindī and Sanskrit and their use in speaking and writing. The so-called 'dead language' of Sanskrit, the treasure, store and mine of ancient Indian lore, was placed by Dayanand on the high pedestal of fountain-head of all the modern languages of the world. Swami Dayanand is a pioneer in the renaissance movement in India. Nationalism, Swadeshi, widow-marriage, female education, care of the orphans, National education, spirit of proselytization, conversion of Non-Hindus to Hinduism, patriotism, the dissemination of Vedic principles, ideals and culture, all owe a great deal to him. His writings and his active participation in the process of regeneration and rejuvenation of India have become a source of inspiration to his countrymen in their struggles for national emancipation and cultural advancement. Swami Dayanand is in fact a leader of mankind; and his contribution to culture stands out as a great landmark in human progress.

Swami Dayanand was a relentless enemy of hypocrisy and untruth, and an implacable foe of superstition, irrationalism and everything dark, immoral and ignoble preached in the name, and under the cloak, of religion. He insisted in words of burning eloquence that India must be purged of all the putrefying accretions of her Dark Age, and Paurāṇic times. The deep pathos of his impassionate pleading for the submerged, for the untouchable, for the women-folk, the widows, orphans, and the illiterate, moved his countrymen to tears. He called upon his countrymen in his stentorian voice to abandon their ungodly attempts to turn India into Anglo-India. His burning love for his country, his erudition, indefatigable labour, physical strength, fearlessness, dauntless spirit, invincible faith in the grandeur and loftiness of the Vedic culture, passion for Swarajya and emancipation from intellectual, social and political bondage, love for truth and humanity, are traits, which serve as a model for the Indians in their onward path of resuscitation. Great is the debt we owe to Dayanand the *yogī*, thinker, seer, prophet, creator, reformer and philosopher. May his mission for the revivification of India, nay the unification of the universe, prosper! Following in the wake of Dayanand and his new school of thought ensuring human progress, India is bound to regain its pristine glory and greatness.

HOSHIARPUR DEVICHAND

DAYANAND SARASWATI

THE Arya Samaj is a standing memorial to the greatness of Swami Dayanand and will remain so for centuries to come.

Men like him are always needed to shake off the mental inertia, into which this unhappy land has a knack of relapsing. Dayanand stirred the Hindus of the Punjab to an abiding sense of their duty to the land of their birth, as no one had done before.

That the Arya Samaj is a living force which no other Samaj in India is, testifies to the hold he has on the hearts of the Hindus of the Punjab. The religious zeal of his followers is a matter to be reckoned with. Some of his followers have not only given their all to the cause at their heart, but have even risked their lives on its behalf. One may not agree with Swami Dayanand's interpretations of Vedic texts; but these same interpretations are gospel truths to millions.

SURAT V. K. RAJWADE

DAYANAND—FAR AHEAD OF HIS TIMES

I must express my sincere gratitude to the organisers of this celebration for the opportunity afforded to me for recording a few lines in appreciation of the life work of Maharshi Dayanand. As compared with Gujarat and the adjoining districts, Cutch and Kathiawar can lay claim to greater orthodoxy and more of conservatism. It is all the more wonderful, therefore, that a man born and brought up in the land which can be styled as the traditional home of orthodoxy could rise head and shoulders over the natural surroundings and family traditions, and successfully raise the standard of revolt throughout the length and breadth of India.

The death of his sister at quite a tender age made him meditate on the inevitability of death and the ways and means to avert or to delay it. Brahmacharya seemed to him to be the only sure remedy and he took a vow of permanent celibacy. He considered child-marriage as another fruitful source of degradation and decay and he became a social reformer for the rest of his life. Like Buddha he left his home to keep himself free from the shackles of matrimonial and family ties. He wandered from place to place in search of knowledge and worldly experience. He visited various places of pilgrimage and came in contact with different religious preceptors and learned pandits. From his boyhood he was taught to recite the Vedas which were represented to him to be the store-house of knowledge on all subjects. Not satisfied with the parrot-like recital of these holy books, he acquired a knowledge of higher Sanskrit grammar and literature, and thus equipped, he began a systematic study of the Vedas. He mastered various interpretations of obscure passages and the more he dived deep into this sacred lore, the more he was convinced of the hollowness of the exclusive right claimed by the Brahmins to study them. He saw no reason why such a store of universal knowledge should be a closed chapter to non-Brahmins. The Brahmin oligarchy not only disallowed the study of the Vedás to non-Brahmins, but considered it a sin for themselves to recite the Vedas in the presence of or even within the hearing of any member of the non-privileged class. He ventilated far and wide his reformed view on this subject and that was another shock to the orthodox and unprogressive section of his community.

These days in India there is a nation-wide agitation for the abolition of untouchability due partly to the cultural advance in the ideas and sentiments of the masses and partly as the result of preaching of the nationalist leaders. In spite of this, the Sanatanists are up in arms against the movement and are devising schemes for defending the stronghold of their orthodoxy. One can easily imagine the strength and vehemence of the opposition which the Maharshi experienced from his countrymen in those palmy days of Brahmin supremacy.

He was a staunch Hindu and deplored the dwindling down of the Hindu community. This he attributed to the exclusiveness of the present day Hindus who unlike their predecessors have closed the doors of Hinduism for fresh converts and defaulters. To remedy this evil he started the movement of Shuddhi and Sangathan by which such of the Hindus as had gone out or were turned out of the fold can be again taken into the fold after performing certain purificatory rites. He could not reconcile himself to the extreme rigidity of the Smṛitis and works on *prāyaśchita* which would not enjoin the same status and position which the sinner originally occupied even after the purificatory rites were performed. He thus became the pioneer of the Shuddhi and Sangathan movement which is at present the main plank in the programme of the Hindu Sabha.

His shrewd foresight made him realise that the present system of education patronised by the schools and colleges was not suitable to the Indian masses. That system hopelessly failed in training Indians in the right direction and it was futile to expect them to turn out ideal Indians such as would fulfill the future expectations of those who had the interest of India at heart. Relations existing between the teachers and the taught were merely of a contractual nature and the love and reverence which a *śishya* ought to feel for his *guru* were absolutely absent. To remedy this evil he recommended the revival of the Gurukula system of education throughout India. There are several such institutions existing at present in India. Students therein are made to live together in common brotherhood under the direct supervision of the Acharya in charge. Thus the students reap all the advantages which were enjoyed in olden times by the pupils of well-known Ṛishis and preceptors.

BOMBAY — G. V. ACHARYA

—:o:—

I have not had the privilege of coming into personal contact with Swami Dayanand Saraswati, but there can be no doubt that he was a great scholar and a reformer of very strong personality. His interpretation of the Vedas was apparently based on the views of the *ékavādi* School mentioned in Nirukta. Although being a follower of the Sanātana Dharma, I do not share his views on many subjects, nevertheless, I must say that broadly speaking he made it much easier for the educated people to follow the old religion under modern conditions and bearing in mind the trend of the times, tried to preserve the religion in a form adapted for cultured minds.

LAHORE — HARI KRISHNA KAUL

DAYANAND SARASWATI AND THE ARYA SAMAJ

HALF a century has gone since the death of Swami Dayanand Saraswati, the founder of the Arya Samaj. And it is proposed to celebrate the fiftieth year of his passing away in a befitting manner. We should all join in honouring the memory of this great son of India, one of her greatest reformers in recent times. And this tribute of respect should be tendered by the people of this country, irrespective of the narrow sectarian divisions which divide our ranks.

As we look back on the fifty years of India's life which followed the work and times of Swamiji, a little thought gives us an estimate of his remarkable influence. For North India (save Bengal where the Brahmo Samaj had anticipated Swamiji) he can be justly considered the father of modern progress. Swami Dayanand and the Arya Samaj have been, directly or indirectly, the motive force in bringing about the social awakening and even the political consciousness which have stirred the nation in recent years. He endeavoured essentially to effect a reform in the religious life of the Hindus. However, his radicalism, his rational outlook, his deep earnestness, his utter sincerity and above all his powerful personality united in giving a fresh thought, a new message to the community giving birth to a new Order. Its members distinguished themselves easily from the rest by their iconoclastic zeal, their puritanical outlook, their bold challenge to the tyranny of ritualism and the dead weight of traditions. This was no narrow religious reform in the sense of mere theological interpretation, although it was meant to be chiefly that. Its influence was comprehensive, and steadily reached every aspect and department of social and individual life. Thus, for instance, educational activity was greatly stimulated, the rigidity of caste-system, with its abhorent institution of untouchability, was sharply attacked, the inferiority of women and the custom of *purdah* were condemned. A new power was generated, as it were, from an old world. Naturally this produced notions of self respect, self esteem, self-consciousness and an aggressive faith in the whole community to regain its proper position in relation to other creeds and nations.

Arya Samaj has paved the way for the great Reformation which India is awaiting to-day in order to restore her to a position of moral and spiritual greatness. And Swami Dayanand, as its founder, is in the front rank of the makers of modern India.

Undoubtedly his work and thought have been in the direction of religious reform. But I do not purposely wish to refer to that aspect of his greatness. Others more intimately connected with the Arya Samaj and better qualified to do justice to that subject will write more authoritatively about it. I much prefer to estimate Swamiji and his contribution to our national progress, as a student of social history.

India's vastness and her antiquity are the two factors which make her great in the eyes of the world. For us to-day, however, they both constitute the greatest obstacles to the reform of our lives and the regeneration of our people. Truly this ancient Bharatvarsh requires the leadership of very big minds, of truly high souls to lift her from the depth of her present degradation. Swami Dayanand was admittedly one such leader. In him the nineteenth century found a true Ṛishi. In honouring such a person and in reminding ourselves of such greatness, we are really serving the nation and indeed advancing the cause of true progress.

UDAIPUR (RAJPUTANA) MOHAN SINHA MEHTA

RAM BILAS SARDA

SOME RECOLLECTIONS OF SWAMI DAYANAND SARASWATI

SWAMI DAYANAND Saraswati used to deliver a series of lectures in every town he visited. I had the privilege of hearing the lectures he delivered at Ajmer, on two or three occasions. On two occasions, he delivered them in the *Gajmalji-ka-Nohra* in the Nahar Mohalla, and I went with my father every evening to hear them. My revered father was a Sanskrit scholar, a religious-minded man, and a firm believer in the *Adwait* system of Vedanta. After attending to his official duties in the Government College, Ajmer, he used to spend his spare time in the company of learned *sannyasis*. He visited Swami Dayanand Saraswati every day when the latter came to Ajmer.

The earliest occasion when I remember to have had *darshan* of Swamiji was when my father took me with him to see the great man on a Sunday morning. We found Dayanand alone, standing in the eastern verandah of Seth Fatehmal Bhaḍaktiya's *Kothi*, which stands near the Nasiyān temple of Seth Mulchand Nemichand Soni. After salutating him we sat down. He stood a giant, his face beaming. He asked me what I was reading. I replied with a single word *siddha*. My father explained what *siddha* meant. Swamiji blessed me, and my father began to talk to him on philosophy.

Another occasion when I had his *darshan* was when he came to Pushkar in 1878 A.D. during the Great Fair annually held there during the last five days of the month of Kartik (October-November) when people from near and far go there to have a bath in the sacred waters of the Pushkar Lake. He was then staying in the Kotah Ghat. We saw him seated on a mat on the terrace, suffering from a cold in the head, his nose running, and a number of people sitting before him and asking him questions.

I will cite an instance of the witty way in which he would

sometimes expose the weaknesses of his opponents. Mir Shafi Husain, uncle of the Sajjada of the Durgah Khwaja Sahib, Pandit (later Mahamahopadhyaya) Shive Narain, and some other Hindus and Muslims were sitting one morning at P. Bhag Ram's house in Lakhan Kotri, at Ajmer, discussing the relative merits and demerits of Hinduism and Islam, the Muslim's pointing out the weaknesses and superstitions of Hinduism and the Hindus, the defects of Islam. Swamiji listened to them and then said:—"You (addressing Mir Shafi Husain) grow a beard and you (addressing P. Shive Narain) a *choti*: I would catch you by the beard and you by the *choti*.[1] I have neither; you can not catch me."

An incident which occurred during one of his lectures at Ajmer has impressed itself on my mind. One evening after listening to his lecture in the *Gajmalji-ka-Nohra*, people dispersed, but a few remained behind as usual to put questions to him and have their doubts removed. It was about eleven O'clock when he got up to return to the garden where he was staying. We were about fifteen or sixteen people. As we proceeded towards the gate we found it shut, with the wicket open. Some men advanced to open the gate but it would not open; a few more men lent their hands till only two or three of us remained with Swamiji. They tried their strength but, whether the doors got jammed or whatever else had happened, the doors remained shut. Seeing them all struggling with the door, Swamiji smiled and said:—"You are *chokras* of *chokras*,[2] step aside please." He shook the doors and planting his left foot and his left hand against the doors, and throwing his weight against them, he took the chain off the *kunda* and, with a jerk, opened the door, while we all stood reverentially silent, amazed at his physical strength.

Swami Dayanand breathed his last in Ajmer on 30, October, 1883 A.D. In September 1883, he went to Jodhpur as the guest

[1] It is the religious duty of Muslims to grow a beard and the Hindus, a *choti* (tuft of hair on the skull).

[2] He often called the present generation of *Hindus, children of children*, meaning thereby that they were weaklings, being the offspring of child-marriages. Dayanand condemned child-marriage as being inequitous and against the Sastras.

SWAMI ATMANAND SARASWATI

of the Maharaja there. Swamiji used to take a cup of milk before retiring. On the 29th of that month he began to feel unwell soon after taking his usual drink of milk. Foul play was suspected. Poison had been given to him several times in his life. The best medical advice available was secured, but the treatment did him no good. He was advised to go to a cool place, and he was taken on 16, October to Mount Abu. Not improving there, he left for Ajmer and arrived here at 3 a. m. on 27, October. He put up at the Bhinai House. When we heard of this, I and my friend Ram Gopal and my cousin Ram Bilas went to the Bhinai House in the afternoon to make enquiries. We were class mates reading for the matriculation in the Government College, Ajmer. I was a little over sixteen years: Ram Bilas, eighteen and Ram Gopal, twenty. We eagerly looked forward to hearing his discourses on his getting well. He was treated by one Dr. Lachhmandas, a Punjabi Sub-Assistant Surgeon in Government employ in Ajmer. No improvement occurred. On 29, October he became very weak and all hope of recovery was lost. The next day was the Diwali day. We went as usual to the Bhinai House but found the whole place plunged in gloom, as all hope had been given up. We were in the Bhinai House when Swamiji breathed his last at about 6 p.m. It was a sublime scene. He called Swami Atmānandji and Brahmchari Ramānand and blessed them and asked all present there to stand behind him. After blessing all present there, he recited the *Gayatri*, engaged himself in Samādhic meditation for a few minutes and then lay down. The last words he uttered were:—

"दयामय, सर्वशक्तिमन् ईश्वर तेरी यही इच्छा है तेरी इच्छा पूर्ण हो–अहा ! तूने अच्छी लीला की"

"Merciful Father! Almighty God! This is thy will! Let thy will be done! Wonderful are thy ways."

Saying this, he turned on his side, drew a long breath and threw it out. That was his last breath.

We three of us returned home weeping. The Diwali being the happiest and the most auspicious day of the year for the Hindus, my father surprised at seeing us in tears, enquired what the reason was. I sobbed and said, "The Sun of India had set". My father, who was aware of our visits to the Bhinai House, consoled us.

Next day Dayanand's bodily remains were cremated. Between 9 and 10 a. m. the *Viman* containing his body was taken in procession to the cremation ground. Entering the city through the Agra Gate, the procession passed the Naya Bazar, Kaḍka Chauk, Dhānmandi, Dargah Bazar, Ghaseti, Diggi, emerged at the Usri Gate and proceeded to the cremation ground at *Malusar*. The cremation ceremony was performed in strict accordance with the directions laid down by Swamiji in his *Svikārpatra*.

I was with the procession from the start, and had the privilege of putting my shoulder to his bier along with the other Arya Samajists. It was a big bier and while we were passing through the city I happened to count the men who were carrying it. I found the number to be sixteen. This later brought to my memory the remark I once heard him make during a public lecture at Ajmer when condemning the evil practice of child-marriage and extolling *Brahmacharya*. He had said that those who did not observe *Brahmacharya* and were the victims of child-marriage were weaklings, with diminutive bodies. Speaking of himself he said that he had observed perfect *Brahmacharya* all his life and would require sixteen men even to carry his body to the cremation ground.

Rai Bahadur Pt. Bhāgram, the Judicial Assistant Commissioner of Ajmer, who was a great admirer and supporter of the Swamiji and who had made arrangements for the funeral procession, walked with the procession to the cremation ground. Before the cremation, he delivered a short speech eulogizing Swamiji's services to mankind and asking those present to continue the work he had started for the good of the world.

AJMER — HAR BILAS SARDA

Site where Swamiji's Remains were Cremated

DAYANAND, THE TEACHER

THE history of India is marked by a unique succession of men who had experienced God, who lived in the consciousness of the Eternal, who judged the standard of national life by the standard of Divine righteousness and who spoke to their generation on the strength of the light within. They were the moving force in the spiritual progress of the Nation. One of the greatest amongst these luminaries of India was Maharshi Dayanand Saraswati. He was the embodiment of truth, love, service, sacrifice, grace and beauty. The spiritual splendour of his teachings based on truth alone can be judged by a reference to the Introduction to *The Light of Truth*. He had the consciousness of historic mission to the whole of humanity. His utterances show the most daring faith—faith in ancient wisdom, culture and the Vedas. His attention was drawn very early in life to the misery caused by ignorance and egoism, and his quest enabled him to solve the most knotty problems of life, not only for himself but for the world at large. His was a true renunciation caused by the poverty of the worldly objects to attract the soul. Search for a higher love made him forget worldly love. He obtained perfect bliss, because he placed himself entirely in the Divine hands and dedicated his mind, body and soul to the Divine Master. Faith in God gave him all the power, wisdom and joy that he needed for his great task. Perfect, unflinching faith in Him—an essential qualification of the seeker after Truth—is evidenced by innumerable incidents in his life. Faith conferred wisdom and enabled him to unravel the mystic mystery. He meditated on the splendour of the Divine Being which illumined his intellect, refreshed and strengthened his mind for the noble task of the regeneration of the down-trodden masses and heralding peace and solace for the world at large. Being a *Yogī*, he yoked his mind with God and by rendering it both open and obedient to Divine influence, he unfurled the flag of social and spiritual reform, raising the general ethical and moral standards, at the historic Kumbha fair at Hardwar.

Our generation in this country is profoundly troubled by the problems of reorganising Indian society on the lines that would enable her to win back her ancient all-round greatness. The most active interests of the serious-minded patriots in this country and those of all well-wishers and friends of this cradle of civilization of the world, are concentrated in finding a solution of such problems. We know we are in great need of moral light and spiritual inspiration in our gropings. There is an increasing realisation too that the salvation of Indian society lies in the direction of spirituality and the Vedas to which the torch-bearer, Dayanand, led us in the nineteenth century. He taught us that human life and personality in whatever form it may be is sacred. Every man has worth and sacredness as a man. Social justice demands equal treatment and equal opportunities for all. The deeper our insight into human destiny the more sacred does every individual human being seems to us. The consciousness of God-love reveals the beauty of man. The concept of life in ancient India was decidedly superior to the work-a-day ideas of modern life. The weak, the wicked and the unfit require greater constructive help than the other classes. Sympathy for the people is the acid test of greatness. The Rishi resented the exploitation of the so-called depressed classes. He inspired the people by removing social ailments from the body-politic and proclaiming glad news of the Vedas—the only revealed work of God and of true knowledge to all. For him it made no difference whether a man was born in a good or a bad family. He wanted to knit the world in ties of common brotherhood. The Arya Samaj and its democratic constitution grew out of the feelings of Dayanand for the common people. Even the problem of international peace is the problem of expanding the era of love and social unity. The principle of वसुधैव कुटुम्बकम्, of the consciousness of humanity and internationalism in its practical aspect, is one of the Ṛishi's greatest contributions to modern thought.

By interpreting the Vedas in their true light, he exhorted the educated and the learned to develop arts, crafts, industries and sciences, and raise ethical and moral standards by making a strong and bold stand for the weak, by dispelling their fears and misgivings, and above all, by enabling the people to develop their spiritual nature and reach the goal of emancipation. The learned, he said, are not judged by their dogmas and creeds, but by the reality of their social feeling and by the selfless services rendered to the lowly. The right social order is the one which is conducive to the highest good of all the social classes. Swami Dayanand, a man of action, looked upon life as a combat, faced opposition steadfastly, hated mere talk, praised energetic action, and gave an impetus to the people which is visible in so many departments of national life to-day. A collective moral ideal is a necessity for the individual and the race and this is what is furnished by the Arya Samaj founded by the Ṛishi. He tried to discover the best social order laid down by the Vedas and then did his best to establish it. Now it is the business of the Arya Samajists to realise their responsibilities, and achieve the ideal.

The death of the Swami at Ajmer and his parting words are the key, which unlocks the meaning of his life. His death was really the highest demonstration of a permanent law of human life. He approached death and faced it as a free spirit. He was fighting the forces of organised evil in society, and the poison administered to him at Jodhpur was the effective culmination of his work. The social principle of sacrifice and pain enunciated by the great Ṛishi and by his disciples like Swami Shraddhanand and others is a challenge to all who are conscious of the qualities of leadership.

My homage to the great Ṛishi, the great teacher, social reformer and fighter of organised evil!

R. K. KUMAR

MOGA, PUNJAB

A TRIBUTE

SWAMI Dayanand Saraswati was the greatest reformer of the nineteenth century as well as the saviour of the Hindu India. He opened the doors of the Vedic Dharma to mankind without any distinction of creed and colour. But for him there would have been no resurrection of the Vedic civilization. The great men of to-day are preaching what the Maharshi preached in the nineteenth century and are supplementing his work. In his private life he was as kind and loving as fearless, undaunting and heroic in his public life. He was uncompromising in his principles.

Had the institution of Brahmacharya as preached by him been established in this land of Ṛishis, Bharat would have reached the zenith of her glory. To his students he looks great from every point of view. In religion he has revolutionised the thought of the whole world. In politics his principles are sound and practical. Had the present day political leaders received light from the writings of the great Ṛishi, their line of action would have been quite different and would have not met with so many sad disappointments to-day.

The spirit of Dayanand's teachings is the spirit of freedom. Let the youth of the country imbibe it and they shall have their long cherished salvation, social, economic and political.

JULLUNDUR — MEHR CHAND

DAYANAND AND HINDUISM

THE Ardha Shatabdi of Swami Dayanand Saraswati will be celebrated in Ajmer in October next. It is in contemplation to publish a Commemoration Volume on the occasion and I am asked to contribute a short article. While I recognize my duty to pay my homage to the sacred memory of the great man on this auspicious occasion, I do so with hesitation and diffidence. It is not easy for me to do justice to the task in a manner worthy of the name and fame of the founder of the latest school of Hindu religious thought. Such a duty is moreover best discharged by one who knew the Swamiji personally and at close quarters. I had not the privilege of a personal acquaintance with him. He passed away in 1883 before the Indian National Congress, which provided the first means of inter-provincial intercourse in our large country, was born. What I know of the very valuable service the Swamiji has rendered in the cause of Hindu religious reform has been gathered from my intimate acquaintance and friendship with several of his prominent and devoted disciples and from books. Of the former, I would mention Lala Lajpatrai and Shraddhanand Sannyasi. Swami Shraddhanand who died a martyr to the cause of Arya Samaj, was a towering intellect and a man of lofty character and intense patriotism. It is to him chiefly, alike to his conversation and example, that I owe such understanding as I possess of the principles and doctrines of the great founder.

To think of Swami Dayanand Saraswati as merely the founder of a sect of Hindus is to do him absolute injustice. He was in every sense a full-blooded all round Hindu who fought down disruption and materially helped to consolidate the Hindu religion against inroads, numerical and moral. Let it not be forgotten that Hinduism is the one religion that can, consistently with the increasing achievements of science, maintain its claim that it was by God revealed to man. Proof more and more conclusive is being afforded by science that man has been evolved from lower forms of life and that he became rational and capable of articulate speech more than a million years ago, and that he is continuously in a state of development intellectually and morally. Atheists and agnostics excepted, we cannot but believe that if merciful God intended to instruct him in view to enable him to make the best of himself with his then capacity and resources, not only revelation was necessary but also means should be provided to expound its principles and doctrines from time to time. Hence Avatars and divinely appointed appearances are bestowed upon us. It must be remembered that Hinduism, being as old as rational man, was revealed to him before writing was invented. The Hindu scriptures, the Vedas, were preserved and handed down orally. Hence too arose the necessity for a special full-time class to be reciting and preserving and teaching the same. Naturally enough among the mass of people, ill-educated and illiterate, practices, conventions and even superstitions in the name of religion arose from imperfect knowledge of all its principles and doctrines. We can now understand the great phenomena of Hinduism, the advent of Avatars, that God should, at long intervals, become incarnate for the purpose of renovating the religion and that distinguished interpreters appeared from time to time. We have a glorious series of such interpreters beginning with Gautama Buddha and ending with Swami Dayanand Saraswati. This fact is responsible for schisms in Hinduism. Buddhism with Jainism, Sikhism, Brahmo Samaj and Arya Samaj are the chief of these schisms. But it is necessary to observe here that the last is the nearest to the parent religion. Indeed if Swami Dayanand Saraswati had not given a distinctive name to his school of thought while really it is a truly Vedic and Hindu cult, he would be regarded and honoured exactly as Sri Śankarâchārya and Sri Ramanujacharya and Sri Madhvacharya, as one of the

Alwars[1] and philosophers within its pale.

The Hindus owe a vast debt of gratitude to this great product of their religion, who resuscitated our faith in the revelation of the Vedas and our loyalty to its leading doctrines and principles, of which the divinest is the doctrine of *ahimsa*. In his own conduct the saintly reformer proved his faith in this noble doctrine and thereby rendered his invaluable service to the cultural thought of humanity. For, the last glorious act of his mortal existence was to forgive his assassin and enable him to escape his punishment, shewing that he was one of the supermen sent down by God here below to shew the right path to mankind and which will stand out as a moral beacon.

Like some other greatmen throughout the world, Swami Dayanand Saraswati has had his detractors and it was my unpleasant experience to read, quite by chance, a little book, ferociously hostile, attacking him from cradle to his death, detecting in him nothing but fraud and hypocricy throughout his career. Ye, Gods and the little fishes, what are we coming to? We honoured Kapila the agnostic and Charvaka the atheist, and ranked them among Munis or Ṛishis. But for Dayanand, the biggest prop of Hinduism in modern times, an educated Sanatani Hindu fellow countryman has nothing but rank abuse! May the light and leading of this great soul be the solace and guide of millions of my fellow Hindus, resurrecting their weakening faith in the cosmopolitan and divine flow of his evangel. May his great soul eternally rest in the peace Narayana!

SALEM C. VIJIARAGHAVACHARIAR

[1] A South Indian term meaning "Teacher."

KAUSAMBI

SWAMI DAYANAND SARASWATI was a learned Vedic scholar and grammarian. I have chosen Kauśāmbi as the theme of this little note as it was the birth-place of Kâtyāyana, the celebrated author of *Vārttikas* on Pāṇini's *Ashṭādhāyī*. There is no means of ascertaining when the city of Kauśāmbī was first founded. So much, however, is known that it was the capital of the kingdom of Kauśâmbī and is mentioned in such early books as the *Śatapatha Brāhmaṇa*, the *Rāmāyaṇa*, etc. The Sanskrit drama, *Ratnāvalī* recites the glories of the city and its inhabitants. According to the Chinese pilgrim Hiuen Tsiang, Gautama Buddha preached at Kauśāmbī for several years, but scholars doubt whether he ever went so far west as this region.

This city has been conclusively identified with the ancient remains near the village of Kosam on the Jumna river, some 30 miles above the city of Allahabad (*vide* my article entitled Kauśāmbī in the Journal of the Royal Asiatic Society, 1927, pages 989 *seq.*) Two inscriptions described in that article revealed the fact that in the first half of the eleventh century, Kauśāmbī formed part of the territory of a ruler named Yaśaḥpala and at the end of the twelfth century A.D. of the kingdom of Jayachchandradeva, Gaharwar king of Kanauj. There was nothing else known about its ancient history from monumental records. Five inscriptions emanating from the ruins at Kosam and acquired in recent years establish the existence of a feudatory family of Mahārājas in Kauśāmbī about the third century A.D. A sixth epigraph of this dynasty also found at Kosam is described in Dr. Fleet's *Gupta Inscriptions*, pp. 266-67 and reproduced in Plate XXXIX, C. All these epigraphs are inscribed in Brāhmī characters of the pre-Gupta period and in a language which is a mixture of Prākṛit and Sanskrit usually employed in the inscriptions of the Kushān period. They are all dated and the method of recording the date is also similar to that employed in the inscriptions of the pre-Gupta period, thus:—"(In the Government) of the Mahārāja, the illustrious Bhadramegha, in the year eightyseven, 87, in the third fortnight of the rainy season, on the 5th day, on this occasion as specified". Such being the case, Dr. Fleet's view that Mahārāja Bhīmavarmaṇ mentioned in the inscriptions dealt with by him was a feudatory chief of the early Gupta king, Skandagupta, must be discarded. Of the remaining five inscriptions, two were brought to light by myself in the villages in the vicinity of Kosam, when I was engaged in the re-erecting of the Aśoka pillar at Kosam in 1921-22 and published in the *Epigraphia Indica*, Vol. XVIII, pp. 158-60 and plate. They state respectively that in the reigns of the Mahārājas Śrī Śivamegha and Bhadramegha certain pious acts were performed by certain individuals. The date of the former inscription is only partially preserved; the other is dated in the year 88, in the third fortnight of the rainy season, on the 5th day. The remaining three inscriptions were discovered last year, two by Mr. B. M. Vyas, Executive Officer, Allahabad Municipal Board, and the third by Mr. Kshatresa Chandra Chatterji of the Allahabad University and are now preserved in the Municipal Museum at Allahabad. One of the former and the one discovered by Mr. Chatterji pertain to the reign of Bhadramegha and were both engraved on the same date, namely, in the year 87, in the third fortnight of the rainy season, on the 5th day and their object is to record the installation of seating slabs (*asanapaṭṭa*) in honour of the noble goddess (*Bhagavatī*) by the sons of a certain Śapara along with certain other persons. The last inscription is engraved on a fragment of a Buddhist railing post, and may be rendered thus:—"(In the Government) of Śrī Bhīmavarmaṇ in the year one hundred and thirty, 130, in the first fortnight of the summer season on the........day".

These inscriptions supply names of three rulers, namely:—

1. Bhadramegha.
2. Bhīmavarmaṇ.
3. Śivamegha.

We have the dates of 87 and 88 for No. 1; 130 and 139 for No. 2 and none for Śivamegha. It is not possible as yet to say how these three rulers were related to each other. It is, however, interesting to observe that the family to which they belonged was not unknown to the Purāṇas. Several versions of the *Brahmāṇḍa* and *Vāyu Purāṇas* tell us that "In Kośala there will be nine very powerful and wise kings celebrated as Meghas" (Pargiter, *Dynasties of the Kali Age*, p. 51), and I have no doubt that the three Mahārājās mentioned above belonged to this very family of Meghas inspite of the fact that the name of one of them has the cognomen "varman". The readings *Medyā* and *Medhātithi* in place of *Meghā tti* in some of the manuscripts of the *Vāyu Purāna* are no doubt corruptions of the original reading due to the ignorance of the scribes. It may be hoped that the names of the remaining six rulers of this family will some day be revealed by further epigraphical discoveries on this site.

The era in which the dates of the inscriptions discussed above are recorded is unfortunately not specified. To judge from the nature of the characters employed and other reasons cited above, it seems very likely that it was the era of Kanishka and this fits in well enough with the third century A. D. assigned to this family of the Meghas by Mr. Pargiter.

The extensive remains at Kosam call for early exploration. Many interesting objects including terracotta figurines, seals including one of the third century B. C. and other objects of interest have been found among them by the villagers and systematic excavations whenever they may be undertaken may be expected to reveal even more valuable objects in the way of sculptures, inscriptions, etc.

SIMLA

DAYA RAM SAHNI

AN INDUSTRY WITH A HISTORIC PAST

SWAMI DAYANAND SARASWATI was one of the greatest men of India. He was the first great Indian to advocate the revival of Indian industries, of which the hand-loom industry was the most important.

The beginnings of the hand-loom industry go back to the hoary past, when cotton clothing was unknown to most parts of the world, and men and women covered themselves with garments made of the rudest materials. Some scholars trace the history actually to the period of the Ṛigveda. However that may be, there is no doubt that the industry has a very ancient origin, and by common consent, India is regarded as the birthplace of cotton manufactures. As early as the period of Alexander the Great's conquest of the Punjab, Indian textiles were enjoying supremacy in the markets of the world. For over 2,000 years this pre-eminence was maintained, and travellers and historians in all ages and climes have praised the excellence of India's handicraft. The famous Dacca Muslin was the high-water-mark of the hand-loom weaver's art. It is said that out of one pound of cotton, a thread 250 miles long was spun and went to the making of this wonderful fabric. The art was not confined to any particular part of the country, and places as far scattered as Surat, Benares and Masulipatam plied a large export trade with the countries of the West.

In the early years of the British connection, India was sending large quantities of muslins, prints and calicos to the British market. When England became the pioneer of the industrial age, and the genius of Hargreaves, Arkwright and others laid the foundations of the spinning and weaving industry, her manufacturers found it difficult to compete with the products of India, and by a series of enactments of a fiscal and penal character India's export trade was crippled. From that time onwards the hand-loom industry suffered a progressive decline. That was accelerated when power factories were established in India towards the middle of the last century. It is a remarkable circumstance, however, that in this unequal struggle, the hand-loom weaver has by no means been crushed out of existence, and manages still to hold an important place in the economic life of the country.

It has been estimated that nearly two million people are engaged at one time or another in the industry, and that they produce something like 1,500 million yards. Not all the looms are at work throughout the year, as quite a number of the people engaged in the industry devote themselves to agriculture during the cultivation season. For all that, the industry is strongly entrenched, and whole families and villages subsist on it. The use of artificial silk yarn, which began to be imported into this country in appreciable quantities from 1925, gave a real impetus to the industry, as it helped to turn out very attractive designs which found ready favour with large sections of the population.

The position to-day is that Japanese competition is as much a menace to the hand-loom weaver as it is to the manufacturer. The mill-made cloth does not enter into direct competition to any extent with the products of the hand-loom, but the same cannot be said of Japanese imports which are penetrating every nook and corner of India, and which by their cheapness are seriously affecting the demand for the indigenous article. As regards the future, the hand-loom industry, like every other industry, is passing through a period of unexampled difficulty, but the vitality it has shown for centuries in the face of tremendous odds may be taken as an indication that it has got its roots deep down in the social habits of the people, and that, with sympathetic watchfulness, this most important of Indian industries might be expected to hold its own even in the machine age in which we are living.

BOMBAY

H. P. MODY

DAYANAND ASHRAM, AJMER.

SWAMI DAYANAND SARASWATI

A man's character is revealed in nothing so much as in the petty incidents of his life, when he is off his guard, when he is away from the public gaze, or, when he is faced by dangers and difficulties; when he receives provocation from others, when he has to deal with his enemies, and when he has temptations placed in his way. We have culled the following incidents from Dayanand's eventful life because they reveal him to us as he really was. We find him a man of unusually strong physique, born of his constant and unflinching observance of *Brahmacharya,* fearless, possessed of great courage and fortitude, ready to lay down his life for his convictions, tolerant to a degree, kind even to his deadly enemies, a strict devotee of truth, a man of great ready wit and presence of mind, possessed of an inexhaustible store of learning, a skilful debater, an eloquent speaker, a powerful writer, a patriot of no mean order, uncompromising in his principles, able to resist the strongest temptations, keen of intellect, broad in his views, a philosopher of the highest order, a sworn enemy of evil customs and irreligious rites, a merciless exposer of absurdities and enormities sanctioned by antiquity, a great *Yogi*, a staunch monotheist unshaken in his faith in God and His Word, the Vedas. Dayanand was a reformer through and through. His reforms were not confined to religion alone. They embraced every sphere of life. He was a social reformer, an educationalist, an advocate of physical culture and a political seer, a moralist. He did not know any European language and yet his views were most enlightened and liberal. Such was Dayanand, and it would be a happy day for India when Indians try to study and understand him and to follow in his footsteps.

Demonstration of a Brahmachari's Strength

I. Dayanand was holding a conversazione and delivering public lectures at Jullundur. One day at one of the private meetings he was exchanging thoughts on various topics with those present. Sardar Vikram Singh of Ahluwalia, the premier *rais* of the locality, was among the audience. He asked Dayanand as to whether all that was claimed for *brahmacharya* was true. The latter replied that that was the verdict of the Śastras. The Sardar said that it was difficult to prove the truth of the Śastric sayings and taunted Dayanand that he also was a *brahmachari*, but in him there were no signs which showed that he possessed any extraordinary strength.

Dayanand did not reply to this taunt at the time. When, however, the meeting broke up and the Sardar took his seat in his carriage and pair, Dayanand slipped silently out and took hold of one of the hind wheels of the Sardar's carriage. The driver took up the reins and shook them with a view to make the powerful and sturdy wheelers start. The horses did in vain try to start, but they were unable to move even one step forward. The Sardar put his head out of the window and cast a look behind in order to find out what it was that was acting as a brake to his horse locomotive. To his great chagrin he saw Dayanand holding one of the wheels. The latter told him with a smile that he was simply demonstrating the strength of a *brahmachari* and so saying let go his hold. The spirited horses then started with a bound and the carriage rattled swiftly away.

II. One evening, Dayanand was sitting at the edge of the waters of the Ganges at Benares. His mode of sitting was what is known by the name of *Padmásan* (sitting erect, cross-legged with soles of both feet turned upwards and the palms turned upwards resting on knee-caps). A band of Muhammadans chanced to pass by him. Some of them recognised him as the *fakir* who a few days ago had severely criticised Islām. They at once flew into a rage and two of them, who perhaps thought themselves to be the strongest of all, advanced towards him and passing one arm under each of his armpits and the other over his shoulders, gripped him with both hands. They swung him with a view to gain momentum for throwing him into the river. Dayanand at once divined their evil intention and stuck his arms to his sides so that their arms were caught as it were in a vice. Then he stood up and dragging them after him plunged into the river and left them in mid-stream to take a ducking to their hearts' content. He himself dived under the water and swam away to a safe distance. His assailants were completely outwitted. They had never thought that the *fakir* would turn the tables on them in so strange a manner. They somehow managed to reach the bank. They and their companions, to avenge their discomfiture, remained standing on the bank with brick-bats and clods of earth in their hands, so that they might pelt the *fakir* with those missiles as soon as he popped his head above water. But here too they counted without the host; for Dayanand was too astute to be caught in this trap. They had imagined that Dayanand was still under water and would not be able to remain there for long. They waited for a sufficiently long time, but when they did not see his head popping out, they concluded that he had been drowned and left the place in great vexation. When the shades of evening had fallen, Dayanand returned to his place none the worse for this adventure.

Fearlessness

I. Dayanand was absolutely unacquainted with fear. No danger, however great, could unman him. Once when he was travelling to find the source of the Narbada river, he found himself in a thick and impenetrable forest. He was trying to find a way out of it when suddenly he found himself face to face with a ferocious black bear standing on his hind legs, uttering a fearful roar and advancing towards him with open jaws.

Dayanand did not lose his presence of mind. He had no other weapon with him than a small cudgel. Nothing daunted he thrust it into the gaping mouth of the beast. The beast was so much cowed down that it at once turned its back upon him and ran as fast as it could with the air of a whipped cur.

His firm faith in what he preached

Revd. J. J. Lucas gives the following account of his interview with Dayanand at Farrukhabad in 1877:

"He spoke so strongly and with such evident conviction against idolatry that I was surprised at the hearty reception the people of Farrukhabad gave him. I remember his saying that if he were marched up to the mouth of a cannon and told that unless he prostrated himself before an idol he would be blown to pieces, he would reply 'Blow away'. I went away from the interview feeling that he was a strong man, strong and sincere in his hatred of idolatry."

Resistance to Temptations

Maharana Sajjan Singh, the ruler of Mewar, was a great admirer and devoted follower of Dayanand. The kingdom of Mewar is supposed to be the gift of *Eklinga Mahadeva* and the banner of Udaipur bears the emblem of that deity on it. In fact, the Maharanas of Udaipur profess to rule as his agents only. One day the Maharana, proposed to him that if he would give up preaching against idolatry he would be installed as the chief priest of the temple of *Eklingji* and would practically become the owner of the great estate valued at several lacs of rupees that was attached to it. Dayanand was not a little annoyed at this and with the air of a man who had been touched to the quick, replied in an angry tone:—

"By placing this temptation before me you want me to break the command of God. Your small kingdom, the boundaries of which I can cross in one run and its temple cannot make me break God's commands. Lacs of people are guided in matters of faith by me and I have always to be on my guard that I act rightly." The Maharana was more than ever convinced of Dayanand's sincerity.

His Ready Wit

I. Dayanand was a man of ready wit and genuine humour. He would often silence his adversaries simply by a flash of wit or biting sarcasm. But he made use of these weapons against those only who were not really learned but only pretended to be so and were big in their own conceit.

In the famous religious controversy with the learned Pandits of Benares on the 2nd November 1869 A.D. he non-plussed two of his opponents Swami Vishuddhanand and Pt. Bālśastri, who professed to be omniscient in Dharma Śastra, by his wit alone.

Swami Vishuddhanand quoting an aphorism of Vyasa asked Dayanand to quote a Vedic text in its support. The latter said that it had nothing to do with the subject under discussion and was irrelevant. Swami Vishuddhanand however pressed Dayanand to quote the Vedic text if he knew it. Dayanand said that if one did not have a text by heart one could quote it by seeing the book. Swami Vishuddhanand then taunted Dayanand by saying that if he did not know everything by heart why had he dared engage in a controversy in the city of Kāshi.

Dayanand : Have you everything by heart?

Vishuddhanand : Yes I have everything by heart.

Dayanand : Please say what is the own form of Dharma?

Vishuddhanand : (said in his own Sanskrit that that) which was sanctioned by the Vedas and had some purpose of its own was Dharma.

Dayanand : This is your own Sanskrit. It has no probative value. Please quote from the Vedas and Smritis.

Vishuddhanand : The differentium of Dharma is impulsion.

This is an aphorism of Jaimini.

Dayanand : This is an aphorism. Why do you not quote from the Vedas and Smritis from memory. As regards impulsion also you should quote a text of the Vedas or the Smritis which give that impulsion.

Vishuddhanand: did not say anything in reply.

Dayanand : Very well you have not given the own form of Dharma, now please say how many differentia there are of Dharma.

Vishuddhanand: There is only one differentium of Dharma.

Dayanand : What is it?

Vishuddhanand kept silent.

Dayanand : There are ten differentia of Dharma. How do you say that there is only one differentium.

Vishuddhanand: What are they?

Dayanand : Fortitute, forbearance, control of the passions, non-stealing, cleanliness, control of the senses, intellect, knowledge, truthfulness, freedom from anger—these are the differentia of Dharma according to Manu, how then do you say there is only one differentium of Dharma.

Vishuddhanands' lips were sealed. Balśastri then stepped forward and said—Yes I have read all the Dharma Śastras.

Dayanand : Very well, you please give me the differentia of Adharma.

At this, Balśastri also was dumb-founded and could not utter a word in reply.

II. The observance of the rule that a *Sannyasi* is not to touch metal is enjoined upon all modern *Sannyasis*. Dayanand regarded the rule as absurd and did not observe it. He used freely to handle money and utensils of metal. One day a brother *Sannyasi* taunted him for this. The objector happened to have his crown shaved that very day. Dayanand was ready with his answer to the taunt. He said, "Brother, it seems that your crown has been shaved not with a razor, but with cloth or leather." The man did not know how to meet this trenchant sarcasm of Dayanand.

III. Dayanand was a master of the art of playing upon words. When in a jocular mood he would take up the name of a visitor and by analysing and recompounding it would assign such an absurd meaning to it that its owner would become the laughing stock of all present. But he never indulged in a frivolity like this for its own sake. He did so when he found a man with an ugly name with a view to teach people to give beautiful names to their children. Once a person of the name of Gayadin happened to visit him. The name simply meant the gift (*din*) of Gaya (the famous Hindu place of pilgrimage) but Dayanand took it to be a hybrid composed of the Hindi word *gāyá* (the past tense of the verb *jánā*, to go) and the Arabic word *din* meaning religion. He said to the owner of the name My dear sir, your name means that your religion is gone. What then is left to you if you have lost your religion ?

Dayanand as a Yogi

It is a well-known fact that Dayanand bade adieu to the parental roof with the sole object of finding out the way of triumphing over death. His uncle's and young sister's death produced such a deep impression on his boyish mind that he lost all interest in the affairs of the world and the unravelling of the mystery of death became the question of questions for him. After leaving his home he wandered in jungles infested with bears, lions and tigers, ascended the inaccessible mountain-tops and crossed and recrossed icy rivers in search of Yogis, for he was told that *yoga* was the only means of conquering death. He passed months and months in practising it and acquired a great proficiency in that art—the peculiar heritage of Indians. We give below an extract from a letter of the late B. Jyoti Swarup pleader of Meerut and afterwards of Dehra Dun whose munificence and exertions brought into existence the famous Mahadevi Kanya Pathshala, Dehra Dun and who had the unique honour of sitting at the feet of Dayanand. This will clearly show that Dayanand was a *yogi* and that too of no mean order. The letter was addressed to the late B. Devendranath Mukerji the Bengali biographer of Dayanand. The conversation referred to in it took place in B. Jyoti Swarupa's presence.

"One evening at Meerut in 1879, Colonel Olcott said that he and Madame Blavatsky had doubts whether it could be true that Swami Śaṅkarāchārya transferred his soul from his own body to that of a prince who had died that very day. Swamiji said that it was strange that one versed in *yoga* like the Madame could entertain a doubt on a point like the above. For his part, he said, he had none. He was not a first class *yogi*; his accomplishments, however, never went beyond those of a middle class *yogi* and yet he could concentrate his life to any one part of his own body and withdraw it from all others, that is to say, his body would be dead to all intents and purposes except in that part of it where he (had) collected all his vital forces. This he said he could demonstrate to them whenever they liked. If he a middle class *yogi* could do so much, he thought (it) within the pale of possibility that an adept in *yoga* might go a step further and transfer his life from his own body to another." We have it on the authority of such a reliable person as the late Rai Bahadur Pandit Sunder Lal, Superintendent, Postal Workshops U.P., that Dayanand could enter the state of *Samadhi* (trance) and remain absorbed in deep meditation for twelve hours at a stretch.

MEERUT — GHASI RAM

SWAMI DAYANAND AND ARYA SAMAJ

"THE world is fettered by the chain forged by superstition and ignorance. I have come to snap asunder that chain and to set slaves at liberty."—Swami Dayanand.

The Arya Samaj is a society of Aryas ('Arya', means "the virtuous and learned"), started for the revival and propagation of the oldest religion in the world, the Vedic Dharma[1]. It is the belief of the Arya Samaj that from the beginning of the creation uptil 5,000 years back, the religion of the world was Vedic, and that after the war of Mahâbhârata, in which most of the learned and the brave of the world took part, different sects and religions which we now find upon earth, came into existence. It was after the Great War that the dark ages of India began. In those ages were introduced the worship of idols, caste restrictions, animal sacrifice, licentious rites, the multiplicity of deities and other accretions with which frail humanity, to use the euphuistic phraseology of Mr. Nevinson, "has surrounded the stern purity of the Vedic revelation." The whole country became priest-ridden. Individuality was lost. The most important problems of life and death were considered and the sacred rites performed by the priests for the people. The astrologers were the masters of the situation; and the 'Brahmin priests' of India became 'gatekeepers' of Heaven.

Happily a picture of the times just before the advent of the Arya Samaj is preserved for us. It is from the pen of a master mind. Keshab Chander Sen, the great Brahmo leader says:— "Look at yourselves, enchained to customs, deprived of freedom, lorded over by an ignorant and crafty priesthood, your better

[1] "That which is devoid of partiality, which inculcates justice and equality, which teaches truthfulness of thought, speech and deed, in a word, that which is in conformity with the will of God as embodied in the Vedas, even that I call *dharma*."—*Swami Dayanand.*

sense and better feelings all smothered, under the crushing weight of custom. Look at your homes, your wives and sisters, your mothers and daughters, immured within the dungeon of the *zenānā*, ignorant of the outside world little better than slaves, whose character of liberty of thought and action has been ignored. Look at your social constitution and customs, the mass of enervating, demoralising and degrading curses they are working. Watch your daily life, where almost at every turn you meet with some demand for the sacrifice of your conscience, some temptation to hypocrisy, some obstacle to your improvement and true happiness. Say, from your own experience, whether you are not hemmed in on all sides by a system of things which you cannot but hate and abhor, denounce and curse; whether the spiritual government under which you live is not despotism of the most galling and revolting type, oppressive to the body, injurious to the mind, and deadly to the soul? Are you not yoked to some horrid customs of which you feel ashamed, and which to say the least are a scandal to reason and have you not often sighed and panted for immediate deliverance? Are you not required to pass through a daily routine of social and domestic concerns against which your educated ideas and cultivated tastes perpetually protest? And considering the sum total of mischief and misery caused religiously, socially, and physically, have you not often wept bitterly in solitude for your hard lot and that of your countrymen?"

It was at such a time as this, that a great man, a celibate after a life of wide study and deep contemplation for forty years, came to the rescue of the people. After a most successful struggle with the orthodox Pandits, Swami Dayanand Saraswati—that was the name of the great Reformer and Revivalist—established the first Arya Samaj at Bombay in 1875, to restore the ancient Dharma and as a strong protest against the later day Hinduism and other religions. Thus the Arya Samaj had its origin in the vigorous protest against superstitious ideas and impious and irreligious acts of the selfish priests, maulvis, and the deceitful missionaries. It was also an act of revivalism. Mr. A. J. Davis of America, says:—"I behold a *fire* that is universal, the fire of infinite love, which burneth to destroy all hate, which dissolveth all things to their purification. Over the fair fields of America—over the great land of Africa—over the everlasting mountains of Asia—over the wide empires and kingdoms of Europe, I behold the kindling flame of the all-consuming, all purifying fire. Beholding this infinite fire—which is certain to melt the kingdoms and empires and governmental evils of the whole earth, I rejoice exceedingly and I take hold of life with an enkindling enthusiasm, "To restore primitive Aryan religion to its first pure state was the *fire* in the furnace called "Arya Samaj" which started and burnt brightly in the bosom of that inspired son of God in India, Dayanand Saraswati. From him the fire of inspiration was transferred to many noble and inflaming souls in the land of Eastern Dreams............Hindus and Muslims ran together to extinguish the consuming fire, which was flaming on all sides with a fierceness that was never dreamed of by the first kindler Dayanand. And Christians too, whose altar fires and sacred candles were originally lighted in the dreamy East, joined the Muslims and the Hindus in their efforts to extinguish the new Light of Asia. But the heavenly fire increased and propagated itself."[1]

Here we may say a word or two regarding some of the basic doctrines of the Vedic Dharma. The first is the doctrine of eternal Trinity. God, souls[2] (innumerable of course) *Prakṛiti* (the material cause of the Universe) are the eternal substrata. Being eternal their essential nature, their attributes, and their characteristics are also eternal. They contain germs of every science. Then the doctrine of concatenation of Creations and Dissolutions of the Universe. Creations and

[1] "*Beyond the Valley*," p. 382.

[2] "The immortal, eternal principle which is endowed with attraction and repulsion, feelings of pleasure and pain, and consciousness and whose capacity for knowledge is limited —even that I believe to be the soul."—Swami Dayanand.

Dissolutions have eternally followed each other in succession. It is the belief of the Arya Samaj that the primitive man cannot instruct himself without another's help. For this purpose and to afford as a sort of text-book on geography to explain the map of the Universe, the Vedas—the word of God—were given in the beginning of every Creation. The Arya Samaj believes that 'the Vedas are the books of true knowledge'.

Now, the Vedas[1] are meant for the whole Universe and not for the people of India only. God says in the Vedas: "As I have given this word (i. e., the four Vedas), which is the word of salvation (happiness here and hereafter) for all mankind—Brahmins, Kshattriyas, Vaiśyas, Śūdras, women, servants, aye, even the lowest of the low,—so should you all do, i. e., teach and preach the Veda".[2] "Brahmins, Kshattriyas, Vaiśyas, and Śūdras" spoken of in the scripture are the four natural divisions of human society, namely the priestly class, the warrior class, the mercantile class, and the labouring class respectively. But unlike the teaching of the Vedas and that of the Arya Samaj, the present day Hinduism considers these classes (castes) to be based on birth, to remain water-tight compartments, hereditary prisons, "from which there is no exit and into which no outsider may enter".

But that is not the case. Swami Dayanand teaches that the so-called 'castes' ought to be based on personal qualifications.

[1] The Arya Samaj lays down the following tests of true Revelation :

"I. It must be as old as the creation of man.

II. It must give a true description of God, soul and matter ; with their relations to one another, sufficient for the guidance of man.

III. The laws laid down therein must be eternal and immutable.

From the above the following corollaries may be deduced.

IV. It must not contain stories or histories of past events ; for such matter would prove that it was composed after these events had taken place.

V. It should not contain contradictions or a repeal of its own laws, for these would point to its imperfect origin." *Handbook of the Arya Samaj*, 27.

[2] यथेमां वाचं कल्याणीमावदानि जनेभ्यः ।

ब्रह्मराजन्याभ्याᳫं शूद्राय चार्य्याय च स्वाय चारणाय ॥ *Yajurveda, XXVI, 2*

Says the great Reformer: " The class and order of an individual should be determined by his merits". A short anecdote from his biography would give a more comprehensive idea of Swami Dayanand's belief on the subject. " One day when Rev. Dr. Hooper sat in a chair opposite Swamiji (on the day set apart for discussion), the Reverend gentleman put two questions to Swamiji in Sanskrit the second of which was as regards the 'caste, system' in the Vedas. Swamiji replied that in the Vedas division of classes was according to *guṇa* (qualities) and *karma* (actions). The Reverend gentleman: If my qualities and actions be good, can I then be called a Brahmin? Swamiji: "Certainly, if your qualities and actions be that of a Brahmin you also can be called a Brahmin."[1]

The great work of Swami Dayanand is the *Satyārth Prakāsh* or " Light of Truth" as it is called. It has been chiefly instrumental in stimulating the reasoning faculty to work in the field of theology. Unlike other religions it is the claim of the Arya Samaj that the *Dharma* based on the Vedas can withstand the fiercest inroads made by the highest intellect. In fact, the Arya Samajists believe that science is the hand-maid of religion, and that wherever knowledge would go, the Vedic Dharma would follow in its wake. Thus, the *Light of Truth* has been a powerful cause of the emancipation of man's intellect.

The teaching of the great Swami made men use their own minds in thinking out the problems of life and death. " For the first time," to use the picturesque phrase of M. Taine, " men opened their eyes and saw". In India it is the result of Swami Dayanand's teaching that " the right of thinking freely and acting independently, of using our minds without excessive awe of authority, and shaping our lives without unquestioning obedience, is now a finally accepted principle in some sense or other with every school of thought that has the smallest chance of commanding the future."

MEERUT MADAN MOHAN SETH

EAST LONDONERS AND HINDUS

WHEN grave-faced ambassadors come over to London to represent some Foreign Power at Court or Conference, they always lodge in the WEST END among the rich and great, West End people entertain them, exchange views with them and try to interpret to them the character and aspirations of the British people. When it is time for the visitors to return to their own land, they go back ignorant of our country, because they have had no opportunity of getting into touch with the people, the real people, the working people, who form the great majority of the inhabitants of this island.

This has always seemed to me a tremendous disadvantage, blocking the way to real good will and understanding between the Nations. I have longed for many years that representatives of foreign powers should stay in our part of London—the East End—as guests of the working people, learning from them what conditions of life are. Here, among the common people is to be found the ground of unity and understanding for lack of which so many conferences, pacts and promises prove abortive.

When I heard, therefore, that five Hindu friends were coming to London at the invitation of the King to attend a conference, I wrote post-haste to Mr. Gandhi to say that we longed for the honour of entertaining them here in Bow. The best we had would be put at their disposal, not only for the love we bore towards India, nor for the personal friendship we felt for himself, but chiefly because we were convinced that now was the appointed time to break away from the age-old habit of entertaining statesmen in gilded halls, rather than in the homes of the populace. It seemed a matter of political principle to me. Mr. Gandhi saw it in the same light. So in due course, East Londoners turned out to line the streets to welcome a plenipotentiary from a foreign country, who for the first time in the history of our country, had chosen to take up his abode among the humblest and poorest of its citizens.

Humble and poor! yes, the words are relevant. Wise and far-seeing! these words are equally true of the East Ender. He is not educated in any academic sense of the term, but he acquires tolerance, patience and wisdom through the necessity of facing every day anew, the stark realities of life and death, pain and want, hunger and fear.

So in their characteristic manner, they accepted Mr. Gandhi as one of themselves. They treated him with the directness and spontaneity which is the finest flower of courtesy. They joined in his prayers. They welcomed him at theirs. They brought their children up to him and pressed them into his arms. They cracked jokes with him. Some even got up in the freezing cold at unearthly hours, to go walking with him. They entertained him in their homes. A blind man, a hospital inmate, sent him a message, would he visit his ward? Next day at 6 a.m., Mahatmaji was by his bedside. A cripple who could not leave his room longed to see him. Next morning he was enjoying his company, as they sat chatting by his kitchen fire.

These little two-roomed homes were badly shaken during the war by bombardment. Night after night, the Zeppelins went over Bow. The first Kingsley Hall was bombed, a nearby school was hit and twenty-two children killed and wounded.

Seven nights in succession, Bow had to suffer the terrors of War in the air.

The people might be expected to show over-wrought bitterness, yet what many of them felt about it all was several times expressed by one or another of the women, as we sat side by side in their little kitchen.

"After all, miss, the Germans, you can't blame them. They're made to do it, just like our men. They're only some poor mother's son."

This spirit of tolerance and understanding has developed more and more since the days of war.

We glory in the hope and prayer that, translated into action, it may spread all over the world and make an end of misery and famines and want.

Good-will manifested in service, courage, patience in suffering, unquenchable hope, these attributes are the only stable and reliable basis of unity between race and race, nation and nation, sect and sect. These attributes are to be found in every corner of the world, among the common people. Wherever I travel, as far East as Assam and as far West as Chicago, I have found them in full fruition. They are of the spirit of God, creative and trustworthy, and must eventually triumph.

This deep fundamental ground of unity is the only hope for civilization in its present state of incipient disintegration.

God has made of one blood all Nations under heaven.

Our highest honour and privilege is to be allowed to co-operate with God in helping to produce food, clothing, fuel and shelter for the satisfaction of the needs of the other members of His family, of whatever race or creed.

KINGSLEY HALL, LONDON — MURIEL LESTER

SWAMI DAYANAND

I am glad to be able to pay my tribute to Swami Dayanand on the present occasion. The Arya Samaj, founded by him, cannot be said to have flourished in Maharashtra. But all the same, even we of the Maharashtra have always regarded him as a great personage, especially a personage to whom the whole Hindu India must feel grateful for the successful manner in which he rallied the decaying forces of Hinduism in Northern India, and made the Hindu Nationality stand on its feet and fight with inimical forces.

It is a great achievement for one whose mother tongue was Gujarati, whose classical language was Sanskrit, and yet who by dint of study and practice acquired such a mastery over the Hindi language that he accomplished his whole life-work as an author and propagandist in the Hindi Language itself. I make this special reference to his original ignorance and subsequent mastery over the Hindi Language, because the want of knowledge of other provincial languages than our own has proved a great impediment to the exchange of cultural thoughts and ideas, which alone can knit together the different nationalities in India into one whole. A native of Gujarat, Swamiji ultimately became a native, as it were, of Rajputana, and northern India. This could not be, unless he possessed the propagandist or evangelistic spirit in an uncommon degree. It could not be, unless he was moved by a powerful urge to give his message of spiritual hope and enlightenment to people outside his own province who were obviously in distress for want of a spiritual guide and would have been swallowed up in sheer despair by non-Hindu religions, whose strength lay in unscrupulousness, energy and resources of wealth.

The work of the ruin of Hinduism commenced in the early days of the Mughal invaders was being completed under the aegis of

British rule by plausible Christian Missionaries. The whole edifice of Hindu Society was being pulled down, stone by stone, owing to the callous indifference of the Hindus themselves.

The strength of Hinduism is found to be greater and greater as we proceed southwards. But that strength cannot be said to be due to any organised effort or rational reconstruction on the part of Hindu society. The strength was due rather to the weakness of the non-Hindu forces, at least Muhammadan forces, though even Maharashtra and southern India cannot be said to have been entirely free from their ravages. Hindu learning and culture were strong in these parts and the homogeneity of the Hindu society was not so much disturbed as in upper India. It was upper India, therefore, that required a rallying centre, and this evidently was furnished by the great personality and the learning of Swami Dayanand. Maharashtra and southern India are dominated by Brahmanical learning and theology. Both the doctrines of Advaitism and Dvaitism strongly held their grounds in their own way. Both the Advaitis and Dvaitis had found the spiritual solace they wanted in idol-worship which was accepted and understood under only rational manner. It was, therefore, to be expected that the preachings of Swami Dayanand were regarded and opposed as iconoclast, and notwithstanding the common element of the sense of sanctity for Vedas much scope was naturally to be found in difference of opinion in the matters of textual interpretation of the Vedas and Vedic literature.

As for Swamiji's scholarship and learning, his monumental book, "The Light of Truth" or "*Satyarth Prakash*" bears ample testimony to it.

I am glad that a great festival is undertaken at Ajmer to celebrate the memory of the founder of the Arya Samaj and I can assure the leading members of this festival that even those of us who may not be able to attend it will be present there in spirit.

POONA

N. C. KELKAR

SWAMI DAYANAND AND THE POSITION OF WOMEN IN INDIA

THE debt that the present day India owes to men like Swami Dayanand can hardly be reckoned in any measure. Only a man of fearless courage, sterling honesty and the highest and noblest of instincts for humanity, could achieve what Swami Dayanand did, and thus disturb the slumbers of India in those early days. It was he who laid the foundation of the present day reform movement in India, and it is from within that India's renaissance has to come.

His followers of the Arya Samaj have been carrying on his great work, and it is their reform regarding the status of the women of India that has enabled the women of to-day to come forward and do the little that they can. We women who are striving to improve present day conditions in India owe a deep debt of gratitude to men like Swami Dayanand, and the only way in which we can return this is to carry on the work initiated by him with full vigour and with the one idea of service only.

The work that Swami Dayanand did in starting the Arya Samaj has within these few years proved its worth. The women of the Arya Samaj are able to hold their own, and the fearless way in which they carry out the work undertaken by them shows an inward strength born of their belief in sex-equality which cannot be equalled or surpassed by those still holding orthodox views. If his advice that women should discard purdah, that girls should be taught equally with boys and should not be married before the age of sixteen, had been carried out fully within the last fifty years, conditions in India would have been different now. He advocated the complete emancipation of women. India is a crippled nation at present, as all her work of citizenship is being done with half its strength. The power created by God, of Man and Woman, Woman and Man, is not utilized to its full extent. The chariot is trying to move on with only one wheel greased and turning.

India to-day needs the services of every son and daughter. The immensity of the work to be done in so many different directions and different forms is overwhelming; but I feel certain that if every individual made up his mind to give one hour a week regularly to the service of the country, the existing conditions will soon be changed.

I consider it a great honour to have been asked by this kind friend of the women of India, Dewan Bahadur Har Bilas Sarda, to contribute a few words to this Commemoration Volume, and I am most deeply grateful to him for it. My prayer and request is that this powerful Association will devote even greater energy and funds during the next ten years to the improvement of the education of girls even more than of boys, and so bring about the necessary equality between the two sexes, which alone will help the country. I wish these Arya Samaj workers every success in their undertaking.

SIMLA

MRS. RUSTOMJI FARIDOONJI

THE VEDA AND THE SYSTEMS OF PHILOSOPHY

THE Vedas have been declared to be divine knowledge by the six systems of Hindu philosophy. For instance:—

1. The Atomists recognize the Vedas to be authoritative as they are the word of God. Vaiśeshik 1. 1. 3; 10. 2. 90.
2. According to the Logicians, the Vedas are authoritative like the fruits of the *Mantras* and the Medical Science. 2. 1 69.
3. The *Sankhyas* have gone so far as to say that the hater of the Vedas cannot obtain the knowledge of the self, as he is fond of illogical reasoning (VI. 3. 4). In their opinion there can be no avoidance of the doctrines of the Vedas. I. 147.
4. The Yoga system holds that the Vedas contain the seeds of the knowledge of the Omniscient. I. 24.
5. The Vedanta insistently propagates the doctrine that the Vedas teach the knowledge of Brahma. 3. 3. 1.
6. Saint Jaimini begins his system with the investigation of Dharma which means any matter enjoined by the Veda with a view to obtaining a beneficial result. He believed the Veda to be eternal. Even the omniscient God remembers the Veda in the beginning of this world-cycle from past world-cycles and makes it known. It was not composed by any person with the usual means of knowledge. In other words, even God is not an author of the Vedas, but merely a revealer of the eternal word of the Veda. Thus each and every system of philosophy started with the hypothesis of the divinity of the Vedas, sometimes proved the divine character of this knowledge and invariably bowed to it as the final authority.

Secondly, the Veda was looked upon as the fountain-head of all knowledge. It is a settled principle that in cases of conflict between the Vedas and *Smriti*, Vedas and *Nyaya*, Vedas and *Purana*, Vedas and the injunctions of the wise, the former are to be preferred. The writers of law-books, logic, history and economics—all these bow before the authority of the Vedas like the seers of the Upanishads. The sacred lore was recognized as the source of all Dharma or duty, and of all branches of knowledge. Even medicine, mathematics, music, astronomy, politics, economics trace their source from the Vedas.

The ancients went so far as to say that the Veda was the root of all Dharma, that it can make clear what has been, what is, what is to be, what is near and what is afar off.

चोदना हि भूतं भवन्तं भविष्यतं
सूक्ष्मं व्यवहितं विप्रकृष्टमित्येवं जातीयमर्थं शक्नोति ॥

Thus scholars look upon the Veda as the fountain from which streams of knowledge have flowed to water different lands. Max Muller, however, found many hymns as utterly unmeaning and insipid, nay, a large part of the Veda as childish and foolish. This opinion is shared by many European writers, and yet it is contradicted by the accumulated evidence of saints, seers, and sages, prophets and philosophers of ancient India, who themselves are held in the highest estimation by European scholars.

The third feature was the universality of the Veda—It must be remembered that the Veda was not a sealed book to the masses of India, but it formed the most widely studied work in the world. There were one thousand schools of the *Samaveda*, one hundred schools of the *Yajurveda*, twenty-one schools of the *Rigveda* and nine schools of the *Atharva* Veda. Thus 1,130 branches of the four Vedas were studied in thousands of seminaries and universities by men of all classes. Half the population of the Hindus was directly and indirectly studying the Veda. The intelligentia of the country was busy night and day in encouraging the Vedic studies in the thousands of schools existent in India. At the time of the compilation of the Shaunaka's *Charan Vyuha* and Patanjali's *Mahābhāshya*, more than

1,000 branches of the Veda were studied on this continent. Millions of educated people could not blindly pin their faith to meaningless rhymes or to the primitive songs of their ancestors, but must have stimulated research in a variety of ways.

The fourth feature was the healthy rivalry in the rational criticism of the Veda:—About 500 B.C. there existed schools of etymologists, grammarians, ritualists, historians and Naidanas. The views of these have been quoted and criticised by Yāska in his *Nirukta.* Similarly, he criticized the views of many commentators of the Vedas and took pains to prove the revealed character of this ancient lore. Yaska's explanations are pervaded with a rationalistic spirit, yet he was not the final authority. His opinions and etymologies have been challenged by authors like Shaunaka in his *Brihaddevata.*[1] Any one who runs through the latter may see the numerous differences in the derivations of words between Yaska and Shaunaka. The latter too quotes the opinions of many authors for criticising these or in confirmation of his view. Sandilya, Aśvalayana, Kaushitaki, Kraushtuki, Shaktayana, Gargya, Rathitara, Lomakayana, Mudhuka, Shvetaketu, Galava, Mathara, Bashkalas, Aurnavabha, Aupamanyava, Shakauni, Bhaguri, Mudgala, etc. were famous Vedic professors. Some of these were also quoted by Yaska. The latter mentions a few more ancient writers like Agrayana, Ágrayana, Aundumbrayana, Kautsa, Kraustuki, Charmashiras, Taitiki, Varshyayani, Satabalaksha, Sthaulashtlini, Haridravikam, etc.[2]

Yāska cannot be put later than 500 B.C. and Shaunaka not later than 400 B. C. It is evident that in the sixth century B.C. there were numerous schools and distinguished professors engaged in Vedic interpretation. The works of many have been lost now, but a remarkable ingenuity was shown in the preservation of the text.

The fifth feature was research by lady philosophers:—The study of the Veda was not limited to men, but ladies too

[1] II. 111—113 ; II. 137—143 ; VI. 107 ; VII. 153 ; VIII. 65—67.

[2] L. Sarup—Nighantu and Nirukta.

took a keen interest in investigating the meanings of the hymns. The names of women seers deserve mention here. Ghosha, Godha, Vishvavara, Apala, Upanishad, Nishad, Brahmajaya, Juhu Aditi, Indrani, Indramata, Sarama, Romasha, Urvashi, Lopamudra, Yami, Shasvati, Shri, Laksha, Sarparajni, Vac, Sraddha, Medha, Dakshina, Ratri, Surya, Savitri are the well-known Brahmavadinis. Thus scholars of both the sexes vied with each other in interpreting the Vedic hymns, even earlier than a thousand years before Christ.

The extraordinary preservation of the Veda text forms the sixth feature of Vedic studies :—It is also remarkable that no nation on earth can compare with the Hindus in the preservation of their sacred lore through numerous catastrophies and revolutions. Every verse of the Veda was learnt by heart in various ways to preserve the purity of the text. Thousands of Brahmins spent all their lives in safeguarding the oral transmission of this treasure, so that the profane hand of the vandal would not get an opportunity to destroy the books.

A collection of primitive songs can not be conceived to have been preserved with the superhuman effort made in India for milleniums against elemental fury, accidental loss, political revolution and religious persecutions.

The seventh feature was the penalty of being outlawed for neglect of Vedic studies. There are numerous texts in the Dharmasutras and Smrities to the effect that a Brahmin by not studying the Vedas, becomes a Śūdra even in this life with all his family. योऽनधीत्य द्विजो वेदमन्यत्र कुरुते श्रमम्। स जीवन्नेव शूद्रत्वमाशु गच्छति सान्वयः॥ With such penalties of being outlawed from one's caste, the highest section of the society was devoted to the study of the Veda. Such a universal study must have stimulated research in the true import of the texts.

The eighth feature was the study of many supplementary sciences for the proper understanding of the Veda. It could not be studied without the aid of the six branches of knowledge. It is said that "*Chhandas* is the feet of the Veda, and *Kalpa* is declared to be its hands: *Jyotisha* is called its eye, and the *Nirukta* its ear. *Śiksha* is the Veda's nose; Grammar they call its face: therefore, he who studies the Veda along with these its limbs will be great in heaven".[1]

The Upavedas, Upangas, Purānas and History were also the necessary adjuncts of Vedic study.

Deep learning essential:—It was a general rule that a period of twelve years should be spent in mastering a Veda. Celibacy extending over a period of thirty-six or forty-eight years was enjoined for the completion of the Vedic studies. A few injunctions from the Vedas and other ancient works on the investigation of true meanings will clear up the issue.

> 1. "He is a mere post holding up a weight who learns the Veda but does not understand the interpretation thereof: he who knows the meaning of the Veda, wins every good thing; his sins are destroyed by that knowledge, and he goes to heaven. "The Veda learnt and recited but not understood is dry fuel thrown upon ashes; it will never blaze up."[2]
>
> 2. "Wisdom came to the Brahmin and said, protect me, for I am your treasure: do not teach me to the scornful or the knavish or the sensual man; so shall I be strong."[3]

[1] छंदः पादौ तु वेदस्य हस्तौ कल्पोऽथ पठ्यते ।
ज्योतिषामयनं चक्षुर्निरुक्तं श्रोत्रमुच्यते ॥
शिक्षा घ्राणं तु वेदस्य मुखं व्याकरणं स्मृतम् ।
तस्मात्सांगमधीत्यैव ब्रह्मलोके महीयते ॥

[2] स्थाणुरयं भारहारः किलाभूदधीत्य वेदं न विजानाति योऽर्थम् ।
योऽर्थज्ञ इत्सकलं भद्रमश्नुते नाकमेति ज्ञानविधूतपाप्मा ॥
यद् गृहीतमविज्ञातं निगदेनैव शब्द्यते ।
अनग्नाविव शुष्कैधो न तज्ज्वलति कर्हिचित् ॥

[3] विद्या ह वै ब्राह्मणमाजगाम गोपाय मा शेवधिष्टेऽहमस्मि ।
असूयकायानृजवेऽयताय न मा ब्रूया वीर्यवती तथा स्याम् ॥

3. "But if there be one whom you know to be pure, eager to hear, intelligent, and chaste, who will never do you harm, teach me to him. Oh Brahmin: he will protect me, your treasure.[1]

4. "An ignorant man, seeing speech, does not see her, and hearing her does not hear her. She unfolds her body or reveals herself (the true meaning) to another, as does a wife to the husband of her choice, clothed in beautiful raiment."[2] In short, a man versed in all the fourteen sciences, has full vision of the secret of the meanings of the Veda. Such a man standing firmly in the friendship of the Veda, has drunk of the nectar of the meaning of the Veda. Sitting in the assemblies of scholars, such a man can not be defeated by any one. But the other man, engaged in learning the recitation of the Veda only, is a bearer of the work stripped of its flower (Dharma) and fruit (Brahma). A reciter of the Veda walks with an illusion. The word is not a cow but a deceptive vision[3] to him. Mere recitation was of no higher use than the croaking of the frogs in the rainy season.

The Pauranik Age:—The revival of Hinduism from the fourth century gave a special impetus to the Vedic studies. These were encouraged by the patronage of the Hindu kings of northern as well as southern India. Numerous commentaries were written from the Augustan age of the Guptas up to the decline of the Vijyanagar Empire. The works of Bhavaswamin, Guhadeva, and Shri Nivasa have been completely lost. The commentaries of

[1] यमेव विद्याः शुचिमप्रमत्तं मेधाविनं ब्रह्मचर्योपपन्नम् ।
यस्ते न द्रुह्येत्कतमच्चनाह तस्मै मा ब्रूया निधिपाय ब्रह्मन् ॥

[2] उत त्वः पश्यन्न ददर्श वाचमुत त्वः शृण्वन्न शृणोत्येनाम् ।
उतो त्वस्मै तन्वं विसस्रे जायेव पत्य उशती सुवासाः ॥

[3] उत त्वं सख्ये स्थिर पीतमाहुर्नैनं हिन्वंत्यपि वाजिनेषु ।
अधेन्वा चरति माययैष वाचं शुश्रुवाँ अफलामपुष्पाम् ॥

Madhava, Skandswamin, Bharatswamin, Madhavadeva, Uvata, Bhatta Bhaskar, Udgitha, Narayana, Gomati, Hastamalakar, Atmananda, Ravana, Dhanushkayajvan, Lakshmana, Mudgal, Anandtirtha, Haradatta, Mahidhar, Hariswami, and many more may be mentioned here. Thus an unbroken tradition of strengthening Hinduism on the foundation of the Vedas and later law-books was maintained for a thousand years. The climax of this effort was reached in the comprehensive commentary by Sayana.

Defects of Sayana's work:—His interpretation of the Veda, though a monument of erudition and industry suffers from several defects. His sole purpose to write the commentary was to rejuvenate Pauranik Hinduism on the foundation of the Vedas, to replace Jainism and its iconography by Hinduism and Pauranik iconography. For that purpose he imported Pauranik mythology into the Veda. (2) He took his stand on the doctrines of the Ritualists, and thus presented a liturgical interpretation of every verse to revive Brahmanic ritual and capture the imagination of the masses by ritual practices. (3) He preferred to give to the oldest Vedic words, the meanings accepted in later Sanskrit. (4) Following the etymologists, he sometimes indulged in curious etymological explanations. (5) Then he brought in legends which were conclusively contradictory to the spirit of the Veda. (6) He created a hierarchy of gods from insentient and insignificant things which could never have been intended as names of divine beings.

In short, Sayana was obsessed with the dominating idea of reviving Hinduism with the help of the Vedas. To achieve that end, he imported Pauranik mythology, legends and rituals into the interpretation of the Vedic hymns.

Dayanand's contribution:—Dayanand condemned this system of exegesis. He brought rationalism into Vedic interpretation (2) He depended upon the ancient literature like the Brahmanas, Upanishads, Aranyaks, Nirukta, Panini's grammar for finding out the meanings of the words. (3) Dayanand started with the age-long belief that the Vedas were revealed books. This did not put a seal on criticism but aroused a vehement desire for proving the divine origin of the verses. These must be perfect and universal in their application. They should have eternal truths which can stand the test of acute reason and searching science. (4) He consequently took the ancient motto—"Logic is our preceptor and our saint." Every verse was to fulfil the twofold test of conforming with logic and science. This hypothesis excluded territorialism, communalism, ritualism, mythology, iconography, history, legends, even good or bad stories of men and gods from the Vedas. They were not a historical record of the ancestors of the Aryans, they did not present a social, political and ethical picture of the ancient Aryan society, but they were beyond the limitations of space and time as eternal verities. His irrevocable faith in the sacred character of the Vedas, led him to purge this lore from Pauranik myths and historical descriptions. He raised them to the highest status of being the fountain-head of all true knowledge and the repository of Brahma Vidya. Aurobindo Ghosh has aptly remarked that immediately the whole character of the Veda is fixed in the sense Dayanand gave to it, "the merely ritual, mythological, polytheistic interpretation of Sayana collapses, the merely meteorological and naturalistic European interpretation collapses. We have instead a real scripture, one of the world's sacred books and the divine word of a lofty and noble religion".

One may not accept his interpretation of this or that verse, but the rationalistic spirit of research brought to bear upon the exegesis of the Veda forms the most important contribution of Dayanand. It is his commentary alone which attempted to give rational meaning of each verse. In looking upon the Veda as the word of God, he was in the good company of all the saints, seers and sages of ancient India. He gave to the Hindu society the bedrock of the Veda instead of the shifting sands of mythological Puranas and contradictory Smritis. He saved the oldest book in the library of man from the oblivion and slur of being collection of songs of primitive shepherds and cultivators. He gave a crushing reply to the oriental and occidental people who called the authors of the Vedas as "buffoons, knaves, and spirits of darkness," and the Vedas as 'incoherent rhapsodies of knaves'. He alone by his sharp criticism of the Buddhist, Charvaka and Arhata systems made the ground slip from under their very feet. He established the supremacy of the Veda against the onslaughts of the Muslims, Christians, scientists, evolutionists and atheists. We should not mind the defects if any, of Dayanand's commentary of the Vedas, as the Ṛishi had very little time to devote to this difficult task in days when a sufficient number of books were not available to him.

The work ahead:—The Arya Samaj has not been able to bring out any authoritative interpretation of the Vedas during half a century that has elapsed since the death of the Swami. Attempts have been made by Pandits Arya Muni, Tulsiram, Satyavalekar and Jaideva, but the Arya Samaj has not put the seal of authority on any one of these commentaries. It shows the difficulty of the task. The Gurukulas were expected to perform this work, but it is a pity that the study of European languages and comparative philology is not introduced in the Gurukulas. The result is that the modern works of German, French, and Russian authors cannot be utilized by the scholars of the Arya Samaj. The latter have no access to Assyriology and Egyptology, nor to the ancient literature of Persia and China. The study of archæology too is conspicuous by its absence. Hence there is no competent scholar to carry on Vedic research on modern lines in the circle of the Arya Samaj.

The need of the moment is to establish chairs for the study of such languages as German, French, Russian, Greek, Latin, and Zend, for comparative philology and religion, as well as for archæology, ethnology, and ancient civilizations of the East and the West. If this is not possible, scholars should be sent to various universities for specializing in the preceding branches of study, so that the Gurukula can really become a centre of oriental research.

A note of warning must frankly be given here. The Arya Samaj has begun to suffer from conservatism and fanaticism. Some of its leaders are not ready to give freedom of thought to its scholars. Every word of Swami Dayanand is taken to be the truth. None is permitted to differ from the Swamiji in the interpretation of a Vedic verse. His was the only and the final word on the subject.

Public opinion is excited against those who dare to differ from the Swamiji by a coterie of persons who are not competent to speak on the Vedas. Free expression of thought has been practically muzzled by these misguided soldiers of the Samaj.

Hence it has ceased to be a progressive body. Will it be content to live on the crumbs of Dayanand and unwilling to accept light from new sources? If it shuts itself up in the dark chambers of conservatism and persecution, it shall have sentenced itself to death. Let us hope that this lamentable condition of atrophy and inanition will not last long. The Samaj will be true to its founder by following the principle that "Reason alone shall be the guiding preceptor." One of the ten principles of the Samaj is to accept truth and to abandon untruth at all costs. The test of truth is its acceptance by an individual conscience, and not by the masses, by this preceptor or that saint. Every one has the right to proclaim the truth as he realizes it. It is certain that freedom of thought and speech in the sphere of Vedic interpretation will let loose such mighty forces as will bring in floods of light, energy and knowledge in the Samaj.

KOLHAPUR — BAL KRISHNA

FOLK DANCE AND FOLK SONG IN INDIAN SCHOOLS

MAHARSHI DAYANAND SARASWATI was such a vital force in educational reform in India that the celebration of the bi-centenary of his decease affords an appropriate opportunity for dealing with a new factor which has come into being to revitalise the whole sphere of Indian education in the twentieth century. This factor is the movement for the introduction of folk dance and folk song into schools which has been set on foot in Bengal for the last three years, and from Bengal bids fare to spread to other provinces of India.

Hitherto the folk dances of India which have been conserved and handed down by the illiterate village folk have been treated with neglect and contempt by the educated classes of modern India whose mis-education has entirely blinded them to their great cultural value The time has now come to correct the dire results of this miseducation and to engraft the living traditions of art, particularly of folk dance and folk song which still survive among the village folk in various provinces of India into our educational and social systems

No system of education is either rational or complete unless it included in its scope the folk dances and songs of the country. The place of folk dance and song in education has been recognised in the advanced countries of Europe and America and educationists in those countries are slowly beginning to realise the importance of these dances and songs.

Being impressed with the national importance of the matter I had the honour of inaugurating a movement for the revival of the practice of folk dance and folk song in Bengal in the year 1929 and in February, 1931 established the Rural Heritage Preservation Society of Bengal of which I was elected the Founder-President. The object of the Society is the revival and conservation not only of the ancient folk dances and songs of the country but also of folk literature and of rural games and sports and rural fine arts. I was fortunate in discovering in the villages of Bengal three fine types of manly dance indigenous to the province:—

The Raibeshe dance, the Dhali dance and the Kathi dance. The first two of these were the war dances of Bengali troops in ancient times. Since January, 1931 a systematic attempt has been made to introduce these dances and other suitable folk dances as well as folk songs into the schools of all grades in Bengal.

My plea has been accepted by the Department of Education in Bengal; the University of Calcutta invited me to deliver a lecture on the importance of folk dances and folk songs from the educational point of view; and the recent Educational Conference at Lahore invited me to read a paper on this subject. The question has assumed an All India character and it is necessary that all those who are interested in educational reform in the country should realise what this Folk Dance movement stands for.

In the first place, the folk dances and songs of a country constitute a national heritage. In the folk dances and folk songs the simple joys and sorrows of a nation have found expression; in them the unsophisticated masses have recorded their experience and their philosophy of life. As a vehicle of self-expression these dances and songs are simple, natural and spontaneous and each race has evolved a mode of self expression according to its genius and its culture. Education to be a real and vital force in life, must be native to the genius of the soil and must maintain a touch with its cultural past. Folk dances and folk songs provide a living link with a nation's cultural past and as such are indispensable elements of a truly national education.

Our present day education represents a system which is over intellectualised, and in which the spirit is continually being stunted. The pent up emotions of the youth of the nation constitute a potent source of danger for the emotions and when repressed, find vent in undesirable channels. Dances and songs afford a means of artistic self-expression and maintain that balance between the body and mind and brain which is the *sine qua non* of true development. What is true of dances and songs generally, is true of folk dances and folk songs, being free from all voluptuous associations, are particularly suitable for inclusion in a system of education for youths.

Folk dances and songs have another feature which is very essential from the educational point of view. A system of education in order to be fruitful must be in touch with the realities of life or it becomes unreal and artificial. Our present system of education seems to have created for itself a groove of its own where the factors which govern life do not enter and within which the students become secluded from those every day experiences which envigorate life and constitute a literal education in themselves. The result is that the products of this system of education often find themselves alien to the conditions of actual life and unequal to the task of coping with the growing struggle for existence. Folk dances and folk songs help to break this insulation and to restore the vital bonds between the learners and the world they live in, and put them in touch with the realities of life.

The value of folk dances and songs from the physical point of view is great; other forms of physical exercise develop muscles. But just as an over-intellectualised educational system ignores the mind and the body and is therefore incomplete, so systems of physical culture like Callisthenic drills and gymnastics ignore the mind and are, on that ground, unsuitable for complete body and mind building. Dances and songs on account of their rhythm and music, conduce to the harmonious development of the body and the mind and thus constitute the most rational form of physical exercise. No other system of physical culture combines with it the same amount of recreational effect as dances and songs do.

These aspects of the question have been stressed by me on

various occasions and the importance of folk dances and folk songs has received recognition in enlightened quarters. A Folk Dance Society has been recently formed at Delhi and a few demonstrations of folk dances and songs were given there in April last by traditional folk dancers and a batch of school boys from Bengal, trained under my personal guidance. These demonstrations included the Raibeshe—the ancient war dance of Bengal, the Jari dance and song of East Bengal and Baul Dances and songs. The vigour and manliness of Raibeshe, the exquisite melody of the Jari songs and the spiritual abandon of the Baul dances and songs created a deep impression and these demonstrations took Delhi by storm.

As a result of these demonstrations great interest was aroused among representative men from all parts of India then assembled at Delhi who became aware of the unique value of the ancient traditions of folk dances and folk songs which still preserve a neglected existence in the various provinces of India and many leading members of the Indian Legislative Assembly have constituted themselves into an All India Folk Dance and Folk Song Society and have honoured me by electing me its President.

It is gratifying to note that the educational authorities in Bengal have recently included several Bengali folk dances discovered and revived by me in the syllabus for physical education in secondary schools and it is to be hoped that the lead thus given by the Bengal Education Department will be followed by educational authorities in other provinces.

CALCUTTA

G. S. DUTT

SWAMI DAYANAND
AND
THE RENAISSANCE OF VEDIC CULTURE

ALL that India can give to the world proceeds from her religion and culture. The greatest service a man can render to his country and humanity at large is to be a hero whose name and memory will be like a mile-stone in human history, to guide and inspire individuals and nations in their progress. Such heroes are seldom admired in their life-time, for their motives are misunderstood. Like other great heroes of human history, Swami Dayanand was not only depreciated but mocked at and stoned by his own generation and fellow-beings. But during only three or four decades, the mentality of the world has changed. Now he is looked upon by his countrymen as one standing upon a glorious pedestal, far above the ordinary leaders and reformers, as one of those who are born after centuries to arrest the downward course of human history and to uplift fallen humanity. Though he is no longer with us in flesh and blood, the spirit that he breathed into India survives, to accomplish the great object for which it was designed. To us of the younger generation, to whom he entrusted the glorious work of India's regeneration, he is the great light-house, to guide us in our way of progress—cultural, moral, spiritual, physical, economical and industrial. To reflect upon his teachings and his work is an arduous task; the coming generation will comprehend the full greatness of the Seer.

The golden era of Indian culture existed till the Mahābhārata period when the Upanishads were composed by the Ṛishis of yore; their sublime and subtle ideas soared above the firmament. Thus India produced splendid literature, the highest philosophic and scientific writings, before which the lessons of Pythagoras and Bacon pale into insignificance. Von Schelgel, the German philosopher, rightly remarked, "The loftiest European philosophy compared with oriental realism is like a feeble Promethean spark in the full flood of a heavenly galaxy. Not only this but their marvellous intellectual genius found an avenue in drama, poetry, science and medicine". But with the advent of Muhammadans into India all freedom was stifled, life and liberty became insecure. A slave nation could not produce any literature worthy of its ancient tradition. With the advent of the Europeans into India as a commercial class, the missionaries began to pour in India and finding Indian culture sublime and beautiful, not only commenced its study in India, but even created Sanskrit chairs in the various universities of Europe.

This revival reached the climax in India under Swami Dayanand who accomplished more than any of his predecessors in popularising and propagating Indian culture. When the British Raj was firmly established in India there was a great influx of Europeans of every class in India. They introduced their culture and literature into India. Indian culture began to be contemptuously spoken of by the Indian youths. At this stage, Swami Dayanand appeared as a divine champion of Aryan civilization and Vedic culture. He proclaimed that the new light was not to replace ancient civilization, and the ancient Hindu culture was not to be supplanted by the dazzling superficial culture of the West. He however, wanted to work out a unity of the two cultures and thus make our civilization grander and richer than the European.

We could not build up a purer, nobler and higher Hinduism, a rational and scientific Hinduism, by an appeal in the name of Western culture to the average Hindu mind. The most authoritative arguments are those based on old scriptures and Śāstras. To cure our social evils we require the revival of our ancient culture.

This is why the mission of Swami Dayanand has succeeded where the Brahmo Samaj and other reforming bodies have failed. The revival of our Vedic culture was essential and preliminary to the work of Hindu reformation. We have to make our contribution to the world culture, and Swami Dayanand has laid the foundation.

Swami Dayanand while giving the true interpretation of Vedas, declared that before an attempt is made to interpret the Vedas, one must master the Brāhmaṇas, Upa-Vedas six systems of Indian Philosophy, Upanishads, Nirukta (philology), Grammar, Astronomy and many other branches of learning. Swami Dayanand has been supported by the late Pandit Satyavrata Sāmaśramī, a Sanskrit research scholar and professor, Calcutta University, who says:—"The study of certain portions of the Vedas leads to the conclusion that certain scientific researches had been carried on in this country to such perfection that even America, the constant source of scientific discoveries, and advanced countries of Europe have not yet attained. In fact, a full and satisfactory explanation of the Vedas requires perfect familiarity with all the lores on the part of the expositors."

Swami Dayanand, by interpretating the Vedas in their true sense, has resuscitated the whole ancient Indian culture, glorified and made bright the name of India before the eminent and research scholars of modern days. His interpretation of the Vedas and the revival of Indian culture have opened the eyes of the West and led them to admit the superiority and sublimity of Indian culture. The President, International Religious Congress held in London, paid a tribute to India in the following glowing terms. "The East formerly a land of dreams, fables and fairies has become to us a land of unmistakable realities. The curtain between East and West has been lifted up and our old forgotten home stands before us again in bright colours and definite outlines. Two worlds separated for thousands of years have been reunited as by a magic wand and we feel the rich impact that may be the pride of our noble race. We say no longer vaguely, "Ex orient Lux," but we know that all the elements of our knowledge and civilization, our language, our habits, figures, weights, arts, religion, traditions, even nursery tales, came to us from the East and we must confess that but for the Eastern light that called forth the hidden gems of the dark and dreary East, Europe, now the very light of the world, might have remained for ever a barren and forgotten promontory of the primeval Asiatic continent. We live indeed in a new World; the barrier between the East and the West that seemed insurmountable has been removed.

"The East is ours and we are its heirs. I do not say that the East cannot teach us new things, but it can place before us old things and leave us to draw from them lessons more strange and startling than anything dreamt of in our philosophy. To my mind, the great epochs of the world's history are marked not by destruction or foundation of empires or by revolutions; all this is outward history made up of events that seem gigantic and overpowering to those only who cannot see beyond and beneath."

"The real history of man is the history of religion, the wonderful way by which different families of the human race have advanced towards the true knowledge and deeper love of God. It is the light, the soul and life of history."

The oldest, the most simple, form of faith finds its expression in the Vedas. The Zendavestā represents in its language and thought a branching off-shoot of that most ancient stem. Without the Vedas, neither the reforms of Zarthushtra nor the new teachings of Lord Buddha would have been possible. The Veda by its language and thought supplies that distant background in the history of all the religions of the world which was missed by every careful observer. According to Mr. Rath (*History and Literature of the Vedas*) "the most ancient record of human civilization, literature and religion are the Vedas. This claim cannot be disputed by the Egyptian papyrus roll, monumental records or cuniform inscriptions, tablets, libraries or the long literature of Assyrians, now brought into light. They are fragments while the Vedas are complete records." In the same way, Max Muller in his book, *Science of Language* : says:—"The founders of the ancient religions of the world were minds of high stamp, full of noble aspiration, yearning for truth, examples of purity and unselfishness. If new light is to be thrown on the most ancient and interesting period in the history of the human mind, the period in which names were given and myths formed, that light must come from the Vedas. How Zeus and the Olympic Gods came to be what they are in the minds of Homer, or how such beings as Jupiter and Mars came to be worshipped by Italian peasants, all these questions which used to yield material for baseless speculation, can now be answered by a simple reference to the hymns of the Vedas. Sanskrit is the earliest deposit of the Aryan speech, while the Veda is the earliest deposit of the Aryan faith."

Max Muller, who called the Vedas pastoral songs in 1873, after studying Dayanand's *Introduction to the study of Rig Veda* in 1878, changed his views and in his book, *India: What Can It Teach Us*; he speaks of Vedic culture as follows:—

> "Vedic literature opens to us a chamber in the education of humane race to which we can find no parallel anywhere else. Whoever cares for the historical growth of our language and thoughts; whoever cares for the first intelligible development of religion and mythology; whoever cares for the first foundation of science, astronomy, grammar, and etymology; whoever cares for the first intimation of the philosophical thoughts, for the first attempt at regulating family life as founded on religion, ceremonials, traditions and contract must in future pay full attention to the study of Vedic literature."
>
> "In the study of the history of the human mind, in the study of ourself, India occupies a place second to no other country. Whatever sphere of human mind you may select for your study, whether it be religion, mythology or philosophy, whether it be laws or customs, primitive art or science, you have to go to India because some of the most valuable and instructive materials in the history of men are treasured up in India and India only......... I maintain that for the study of the human being, rather Aryan life, there is nothing in

the world equal in importance to the Vedas. I maintain that everybody who cares for himself, for his ancestors, for his history, or for his intellectual development, the study of Vedic literature is indispensable."

Towards the end of his life he published another book called, *Six Systems of Indian Philosophy,* wherein he says, "Whatever may be the date of the Vedic hymns, they have their own unique place and stand by themselves in the literature of the world. They tell us something of the early growth of the human mind of which we find no trace anywhere else. Whatever æsthetic judgment may be pronounced on them, they will always retain their peculiar value, far superior to the chronology and far superior to the ancient inscriptions. Because every verse, nay, every word, in them is an authentic document in the history of the greatest empire—empire of the human mind as established in India in the second millennium B. C."

Thus Swami Dayanand is the pioneer of Vedic literature, the resuscitator of ancient Indian culture, the explorer of the minds and the wisdom of the ancient Ṛishis, the excavator of the subterranean fields of Vedic culture. He has opened and given a treasure of knowledge to the world which the human mind was in need of. Swami Dayanand will be commemorated in the world, and posterity will perpetuate his name for the heritage of India which he has distributed far and wide, to the humanity at large, irrespective of caste, colour and creed. Such was Dayanand, the reviver of the Vedic culture, the propagator of Divine Wisdom—the heir-loom of our forefathers.

ZANZIBAR, EAST AFRICA JAIMINI

SWAMI DAYANAND SARASWATI
WITH
RAMANAND BRAHAMCHARI

RISHI DAYANAND—THE MAKER OF MODERN INDIA

RISHI DAYANAND can easily be counted among the greatest and mightiest Masters who have successfully shaped and moulded the destinies of countless generations of human beings. The sacred land of India is fertile in the matter of producing such world-teachers. All who have carefully studied the cultural history of this land of sages know full well that world-teachers have incarnated here according to a periodic law operating recurrently, in obedience to the supervention of certain well-defined social phenomena possessing salient common features. When the founts of inspiration had been corrupted and polluted and the lofty morality and impeccable courses of conduct embodied in the scriptures had degenerated into lifeless forms and perverted symbolism, the great Buddha was born at the psychological moment to revive the ancient teachings in their pristine purity.

Buddha was not an exponent of a philosophy of pure negation and philosophical Nihilism as some occidental scholars represent him to be. To quote Arthur Lillie, the Buddhist movement "was the result of the higher Brahminism against the lower". In fact, Bhagwan Buddha himself declared :—"The true Dharma being lost, the world was plunged into sensuality, caste disputes and animal sacrifices". That lost Dharma, it was the mission of Buddha to hold up once more "as an oil lamp so that those who have eyes may see."

Again in the "*Tvegga Sutta*" Buddha declares in unequivocal terms :—"Brahma I know, Vasethha, and the world of Brahma, and the path leading to it." Certainly Buddha knew Brahma, for he was pure in heart and his psychic powers were fully developed.

The scribes of his age "learned in the three Vedas" were afflicted with knowledge without illumination and, he, with the true insight of a seer, set himself to the Herculean task of improving morals and refrained from talking to those who could not understand what could only be experienced. In this matter, he followed the ancient sages of the Upanishads who taught the highest truths of mysticism and *yoga* only to initiates and neophytes. The initiate was subjected to a rigid moral and spiritual test before he could be indoctrinated into the mysteries of Being and Thought. In the lifetime of the Buddha, this very spirit of reverence and exclusiveness, was successfully maintained. When the most celebrated Bhikuni was asked a question about the existence of the soul, she most appropriately replied "Follow the eight-fold path and then you will know all these things." The Buddha scrupulously avoided metaphysical logomachies and devoted himself exclusively to purifying the morals of his compatriots. Perhaps, this was a mistake. From a world-teacher a complete and comprehensive system of philosophy is demanded. The later Bhikhus are responsible for the system of philosophic Nihilism which is what is popularly understood as Buddhist philosophy.

This Bhikuism, masqueraded as Buddhism, plunged India once again in gross materialism. The natural instincts of worship found gratification in homage to images. The denial of soul and consequently of life after death led to the attrition of all motives for altruistic activity, and artificial horror of all war led to political downfall. It was for this reason that the great empire founded by Chandragupta and consolidated by Asoka the Great before he became a Buddhist, began to crumble with his death, and India did not rise again to political greatness till the revival of Vedicism in the time of Samudragupta. Japan has risen on account of Shintoism and the Bushido and in spite of Buddhism. In China, Buddhism never completely dethroned Taoism and Confucianism. Tibet is predominently Buddhistic and therefore, does not seriously aspire to independence. The hoary land of Ind had to be rescued from soul-withering atheism and Śaṅkara the mighty was born to redeem his ancient race. He opposed thorough-going idealism to through-going materialism and drove out Buddhism from India.

But what was good enough as a weapon of controversy failed as a soul-satisfying and vitalising system of thought. Śaṅkara's idealism degenerated into gross pantheism and pantheism led to universal slothfulness and to the undermining of the very bases of morality. The Law of *karma*, if an omnipresent, omnipotent and all-righteous supersoul that rewards and punishes the human souls according to their deeds is denied, always degenerates into fatalism.

This fatalistic attitude led the bulk of our ancestors in the Muslim period to submit to a tyrannical foreign yoke without effective protest, because it was the decree of Fate. Nanak, Kabir, Namdeva, Chaitanya and a large number of other saints raised their potent voice against fatalism and achieved a fair measure of success. If the tornado of Islam which had swept over the landmarks of ancient culture, wherever it had blown over, was successfully turned back by the invincible rock of Aryan culture, it was due to these great men.

The impact of the aggressive civilization of the West with passive, submissive and meek, degenerate Hinduism, which had its roots in the immemorial past but had lost all its vitality and therefore became hollow, was producing its inevitable results. The old was gradually giving way before the forced marches of the new. This was another critical period in the history of the race. Though it hung between life and death, still it was profoundly influencing the mightiest minds of Europe and bewildering its most colossal intellects. Schopenhaur had exclaimed in a flush of ecstasy.—

"In India our religion will now and never strike root......... ......The primitive wisdom of the human race will never be pushed aside by the events of Galilee. On the contrary, Indian wisdom will flow back upon Europe and produce a thorough change in our knowing and thinking."

In spite of this, Christianity was more than a match for degenerate and lifeless Hinduism which alone was preached and enforced by the priest. It seemed that the most ancient religion and social polity of the world, which had survived so many social cataclysms and political vicissitudes, was in imminent danger.

Just at this moment, the genius of our race, which brought about the miraculous survival of the Divine Wisdom—just when it was about to perish—asserted itself through the instrumentality of its most perfect embodiment, Dayanand Saraswati. No mere saint like Buddha could save the race when the diseases from which it suffered were not merely moral; nor could a mere philosopher like Śaṅkara save it, for the time needed a revolution not only in thought but in the sphere of conduct as well. What a stupendous and bewildering mass of work lay before him. He had to fight single-handed the forces of unrighteousness, inane superstition, blind respect for authority without any intellectual sanction. The success that attended was nothing short of a miracle. He worked for a short period of ten years and won all along the line. Pandit Bishen Narayan Dar who presided over the Indian National Congress in 1912, said:—"But in Upper India a great man was born whose career cut short in its prime, was destined to give a new lease of life to Hinduism which seemed to be dying everywhere, by placing it upon the nationalism of the Vedas. To him more than to any other Indian of this century belongs the credit of having breathed a new life into the inert mass of Hindu society, by inspiring it with the sentiment of nationality. The Arya Samaj is in one sense a greater achievement than the Brahmo Samaj; because it is more national, and because it has communicated the impetus of reform and progress to those classes of Indians who have not yet been sufficiently influenced by English education and English modes of thought. Swami Dayanand is therefore the most original Hindu of this age—the one great Indian reformer who owes practically nothing to western culture. If in Upper India, the Punjab and Rajputana, Hindus, even such Hindus as do not know a word of English, openly repudiate caste and idol-worship, are able to take pride in the purity of their ancient faith without accepting the morbid over-growths of later ages, if they are zealous advocates of widow-marriage and female education and sea-voyage, if they have a better organization than before, both for offensive and defensive purposes, and are imbued with a strong national sentiment which is at the bottom of their present political revival it is due to the mighty genius of Dayanand."

Yes, Dayanand's cause has prevailed and is prevailing. He is not only the Maker of New India but is also the inaugurator of a new era in the world of thought.

Swami Dayanand was the first to declare that the Vedas contain the germs of all sciences. Mark what many Vedic scholars of indigenous birth, who have received the highest English education on modern lines say. Mr. Parmasiva Aiyar, author of the "Riks" says :—

"A full and accurate exposition of the Vedas and the Brahminical literature based on the Vedas will demand the aid of a plastic intellect, *scientific imagination, expert knowledge, practical and theoretical, of Geology, Mining, Organic Chemistry, Agriculture, and Astronomy as well as close familiarity with high mountains and the petroliferous regions.*"

Mr. Pangee, M.A., author of the 'Vedic Fathers of Geology' says:—

> "There are ample materials, abundant stray notes and fragmentary details, scattered here and there, and probably throughout the vast field of Vedic literature, from which inference can be reasonably drawn, that our Vedic Ṛishis of the hoary past, not to say of the tertiary period, as I shall presently show, had deep knowledge of the subject Geology."

Professor Bhim Chandra Chatterji of the National Council of Education, in his "Economic Botany of India", traces in the Ṛigveda (VIII-47-9, & II, 1-14) the knowledge of photosynthesis and the action of light and storage of energy on plants. "The fact that the sun is the source of the energy in the fuel and that it is the setting sun, i.e, having less refractive rays whence the energy is transformed and rapt in potential form in the fuel, and that this potential energy is manifested as fire or heat, were also known"—Prof. Benoykumar Sarkar's article on Hindu Botany in the "Collegian" of Calcutta for December, 1913.

Dr. Rele of Bombay has recently (in 1931) brought out a book called "The Vedic Gods as Figures of Biology." Forewords have been written by Edward J. Thomas, M.A., D.Litt., the English Orientalist and V. G. Nadgir, M.Sc. One quotation from the book will suffice:—

"My conviction as a whole leads me to believe that the Vedas are books on the Physiology of the Nervous System written by different Vedic seers. They describe its structure and function in a language which is full of metaphors taken from the natural phenomena connected with the place inhabited by the authors. (page xi).

The leaven of Dayanand's potent thought is working in the brains of the great philosophers of the West also. Says Edward Carpenter in his "Art of Creation":—"A new philosophy we can hardly expect or wish for since indeed the same germinal thought of the Vedic authors comes all the way down history even to Schopenhaur and Whitman, inspiring philosophy after philosophy and religion after religion.........and it is only to-day that science, with its huge conquest in the material plane, is able to provide—for these world-old principles—somewhat of a new form and so wonderful a garment of illustration and expression as it does." (page vii).

It is therefore, clear that Dayanand's teachings are shaping the destinies of the human race; and the Veda, in the words of the French savant Edward Schure, like a beautiful rock-crystal reflects the sun of eternal truth, and in the brilliant prism shine all the beams of a world-wide theosophy."

GURUKULA KANGRI — RAM DEVA

SWAMI DAYANAND AND REFORM

TWO movements in India, the Arya Samaj and the Theosophical Society, will undoubtedly be specially noticed by the future historian, because both have done a similar kind of work in awakening the memories of the past glories of India. Both were organised in the same year of 1875, one in India, the other in the city of New York in America. All know well that the aim of the Arya Samaj was to purify Hinduism by emphasizing the earliest teachings represented by the Vedas. It was the same ideal which animated the Theosophists of New York, though they sought the earliest teachings of Hinduism less for the sake of India and more for the sake of the whole world. These two movements for a while joined hands. Though they later separated, their work has run in many ways along parallel lines.

The work of Swami Dayanand Saraswati has made a profound impression on the Indian consciousness, particularly the peoples of North India. It was indeed a bold attempt on his part, while upholding the Vedas, to try to proclaim as non-Vedic child-marriage, the caste-system, seclusion of women, and other reforms. The battle waged by him and by those who came after him, for a nobler life for the Indian people, has of course been denounced by those who were not able to accept the idea that Hinduism has been encrusted again and again by many teachings which are not from the Ṛishis, but from commentators and from a priestly class that was narrow-minded and thought more of strengthening its own position than of adapting the ancient teachings to the needs of the changing times.

It is not without interest to note that while the work of the Arya Samaj is particularly strong in North India, that of the Theosophical Society has been strong in South India. In the field of social reform the necessary work has been done by both these bodies, so that in some ways there has been no need to duplicate the efforts of either. While the name of Swami Dayanand is associated with "militant Hinduism", that of the Theosophists is more identified with Brotherhood, and the bringing within the pale of the Divine Life other revelations of the Sanātana Dharma which are not found in India.

The history of a people is mostly the history of its great men, and among the greatest, because of his profound and lasting influence, is that of Swami Dayanand. His personality has permeated the consciousness of North India.

It is necessary that the names of great workers should be kept before the imagination of the young, so that youth may be inspired by their sacrifices, and particularly may dream of the greatness of India as these leaders dreamed.

ADYAR, MADRAS C. JINARĀJADĀSA

SWAMI DAYANAND SARASWATI

OF all the distinguished Indians of the last century, Swami Dayanand Saraswati, by common consent, was one of the most remarkable. It may be permissible to differ from some of his religious conceptions, but it is impossible to deny either his courage or greatness. A Sanskritist brought up in the old school, unaffected by western education or influence, he caught the glimpse of liberated Hinduism and of a virile and progressive Hindu race. In face of virulent opposition he strove with all his might for the realization of his dream. He achieved wonderful success in his campaign against unreasoning and unmoving orthodoxy and he may truly be described as the saviour of Hinduism and Hindus, especially in the north. For every thoughtful Hindu therefore it must be a pious duty to pay the grateful tribute of respect and admiration to the memory of the great Swamiji.

We who are enjoying the fruits of his fearless and relentless advocacy of social reform cannot vividly realise the difficulties he must have had to encounter in battering the citadel of orthodoxy in the last century. They were great, nay, staggering. But, by his heroic and untiring efforts, Swamiji has made our task easier and our path smoother and has thereby earned the gratitude of generations yet unborn.

By his unique personality Mahatma Gandhi has made the uplift of Harijans a question of transcendental importance but let us not forget that for well-nigh half a century, Arya Samajists, the followers of Swamiji, have been striving to abolish untouchability. They have initiated *Shuddhi*, advocated widow-marriage, condemned child marriage and indeed have thrown their weight in favour of every beneficient measure of social reform under the inspiration of their illustrious leader and have thereby demonstrated to the world that Hinduism is not a bundle of superstitions and cramping rules and regulations but on the other hand is a growing system which has to deliver a message for humanity. The services of Swamiji to our race, only blind partisanship can afford to ignore or minimize.

In this hour of gloom and despondency the thought gives hope and courage that as long as India continues to produce a Dayanand, a Gandhi, a Tagore so long there is no reason to despair of its future.

ALLAHABAD — ISWAR SARAN

DAYANAND SARASWATI

SWAMI DAYANAND SARASWATI was a great seer, a great thinker and a great man of action. He was a born leader of men. He came to this world to uplift mankind, to save humanity from moral destruction. God revealed Divine Wisdom through the Arya Ṛishis, and had chosen our great forefathers as the agents through whom He showed the right path of life to the peoples of the world; and when the descendants of those Ṛishis and the people of Aryavarta left that path and became degraded and degenerate, Swami Dayanand Saraswati came not only to rescue them, but to show anew to humanity the right path to follow, and to teach mankind, Truth. As he declared, he came to break the chains of superstition, ignorance and error and to make men free. He devoted himself to pointing out the evils of the faiths they were following and teaching them the simple, pure and sublime principles, by following which men would secure happiness in this world and salvation hereafter. He went round the country carrying the nectar of immortality to the homes of the people.

The last few days of his life were spent in Rajputana, but he did not live long enough to complete the work he had begun. He had to work against heavy odds. He gave up his life in defence of Truth, by telling Truth and by acting Truth. He showed us the way and then left us. It is now our duty to follow the way he showed us and prove ourselves worthy of the descendants of those who first brought Light to the world. He has set us on our feet, let us now stand up and do our work. Dayanand wished us all to do our duty.

NAWABGANJ, ETAH — NAND KISOR SINGH

MY IMPRESSIONS OF SWAMI DAYANAND SARASWATI

IT was in 1875 that I had the honour— or, I should rather say the blessing—of hearing the popular discourses of Swami Dayanand Saraswati in the spacious hall of the Normal School then located in the Kothi of Amin-ud-daula in Lucknow.

I felt that a great soul was speaking in him. He seemed to me something greater than a patriot, one whose mission was to cut down the chains of fraud and superstition. My heart yearned to hear something more from his lips.

It was, however, in 1879 that I found an opportunity of a private conversation with the great Swami in the beautiful garden, the Ananda Bagh, belonging to the Mahārājā of Viziānagram, in Benares. I was requested by the then District Magistrate of Benares to translate into English the notice and counter-notices issued in Sanskrit by and against the Swami, and found the utter futility of the opposition to him. The Swami's literary onset was terrible, and all the learning of Benares had to degenerate itself into vituperation. In his private conversations, I have hardly ever seen during my pretty long life, a personage so earnest in his convictions and yet so perfectly calm and serene.

When I saw him he was dictating to a scribe, what appeared to be a book in Sanskrit and Hindi. I inquired of him if he was writing a *Bhāshya* (commentary) of the Ṛigveda. He said :—" No, I am compiling a set of books on Sanskrit grammar."

Swami Dayanand Saraswati is the brightest luminary in the galaxy of patriots and reformers which the last century has produced and he has done more for the social, moral and intellectual uplift of the country than all the other reformers put together.

ALLAHABAD SITARAM

DAYANAND SARASWATI

(Romain Rolland)

INDIAN religious thought raised a purely Indian Samaj against Keshab's Brahmo Samaj and against all attempt at Westernization, even during his lifetime, and at its head was a personality of the highest order, Dayanand Saraswati (1824-1883).

This man with the nature of a lion is one of those, whom Europe is too apt to forget when she judges India, but whom she will probably be forced to remember to her cost; for he was that rare combination, a thinker of action with a genius for leadership.

For fifteen years this son of a rich Brahmin, despoiled of everything and subsisting on alms, wandered as a *Sadhu* clad in the saffron robe along the roads of India. At length about 1860 he found at Muttra an old Guru even more implacable than himself in his condemnation of all weakness and his hatred of superstition, a *sannyasi* blind from infancy and from the age of eleven quite alone in the world, a learned man, a terrible man, Swami Virjanand Saraswati. Dayanand put himself under his "discipline", which in its old literal seventeenth century sense scarred his flesh as well as his spirit. Dayanand served this untamable and indomitable man for two and a half years as his pupil. It is therefore mere justice to remember that his subsequent course of action was simply the fulfilment of the will of the stern blind man When they separated Virjanand extracted from him the promise that he would consecrate his life to the annihilation of the heresies that had crept into the Pauranic (old) faith to re-establish the ancient religious methods of the age before Buddha, and to disseminate the truth.

Dayanand immediately began to preach in Northern India, but unlike the benign men of God who open all heaven before the eyes of their hearers he was a hero of the *Iliad* or of the *Gita* with the athletic strength of a Hercules, who thundered against all forms of thought other than his own, the only true one. He was so successful that in five years Northern India was completely changed. During these five years his life was attempted four or five times—sometimes by poison. Once a fanatic threw a cobra at his face in the name of Shiva, but he caught it and crushed it. It was impossible to get the better of him; for he possessed an unrivalled knowledge of Sanskrit and the Vedas, while the burning vehemence of his words brought his adversaries to naught They likened him to a flood Never since Śaṅkara had such a prophet of Vedism appeared. The orthodox Brahmins, completely overwhelmed, appealed from him to Benares, their Rome. Dayanand went there fearlessly, and undertook in November, 1869, a Homeric contest. Before millions of assailants, all eager to bring him to his knees, he argued for hours together alone against three hundred pandits—the whole front line and the reserve of Hindu orthodoxy. He proved that the Vedant as practised was diametrically opposed to the primitive Vedas. He claimed that he was going back to the true Word, the pure Law of two thousand years earlier. They had not the patience to hear him out. He was hooted down and excommunicated. A void was created round him, but the echo of such a combat in the style of the *Mahabharata* spread throughout the country, so that his name became famous over the whole of India. Dayanand was not a man to come to an understanding with religious philosophers imbued with Western ideas. His national Indian theism, its steel faith forged from the pure metal of the Vedas alone, had nothing in common with theirs, tinged as it was with modern doubt, which denied the infallibility of the Vedas and the doctrine of transmigration. Its (Arya Samaj's) spontaneous and impassioned success in contrast to the slight reverberations of Keshab's Brahmo Samaj, shows the degree to which Dayanand's stern teachings corresponded to the thought of his country and to the first stirrings of Indian nationalism, to which he contributed.

The enthusiastic reception accorded to the thunderous champion of the Vedas, a Vedist belonging to a great race and penetrated with the sacred writings of ancient India and with her heroic spirit, is then easily explained. He alone hurled the defiance of India against her invaders. Dayanand declared war on Christianity and his heavy masssive sword cleft it asunder with scant reference to the scope or exactitude of his blows.

Dayanand had no greater regard for the Koran and the Puranas, and trampled under-foot the body of Brahmin orthodoxy. He had no pity for any of his fellow countrymen, past or present, who had contributed in any way to the thousand-year decadence of India, at one time the mistress of the world. He was a ruthless critic of all who, according to him, had falsified or profaned the true Vedic religion. He was a Luther fighting against his own misled and misguided Church of Rome; and his first care was to throw open the wells of the holy books, so that for the first time his people could come to them and drink for themselves. He wrote commentaries on the Vedas in the vernacular—it was in truth an epoch-making date for India when a Brahmin not only acknowledged that all human beings have the right to know the Vedas, whose study had been previously prohibited by orthodox Brahmins, but insisted that their study and propaganda was the duty of every Arya.

Dayanand transfused into the languid body of India his own formidable energy, his certainty, his lion's blood. His words rang with heroic power. He reminded the secular passivity of a people, too prone to bow to fate, that the soul is free and that action is the generator of destiny. He set the example of a complete clearance of all the encumbering growth of privilege and prejudice by a series of hatchet blows. With regard to questions of fact he went further than the Brahmo Samaj, and even further than the Ramkrishna Mission ventures to-day.

His creation, the Arya Samaj, postulates in principle equal

justice for all men and all nations, together with equality of the sexes. It repudiates a hereditary caste-sytem, and only recognises professions or guilds, suitable to the complementary aptitudes of men in society; religion was to have no part in these divisions, but only the service of the state, which assesses the tasks to be performed. The State alone, if it considers it for the good of the community, can raise or degrade a man from one caste to another by way of reward or punishment. Dayanand wished every man to have the opportunity to acquire as much knowledge as would enable him to raise himself in the social scale as high as he was able. Above all he would not tolerate the abominable injustice of the existence of untouchables, and nobody has been a more ardent champion of their outraged rights. They were admitted to the Arya Samaj on a basis of equality; for the Aryas are not a caste. "The Aryas are all men of superior principles; and the Dasyus are they who lead a life of wickedness and sin."

Dayanand was no less generous and no less bold in his crusade to improve the condition of women, a deplorable one in India. He revolted against the abuses from which they suffered, recalling that in the heroic age they occupied in the home and in society a position at least equal to men. They ought to have equal education, according to him, and supreme control in marriage over household matters including the finances. Dayanand in fact claimed equal rights in marriage for men and women and though he regarded marriage as indissoluble, he admitted the marriage of widows.

I have said enough about this rough *Sannyasi* with the soul of a leader, to show how great an uplifter of the peoples he was—in fact the most vigorous force of the immediate and present action in India at the moment of the rebirth and reawakening of the national consciousness. He was one of the most ardent prophets of reconstruction and of national organization. I feel that it was he who kept the vigil.[1]

[1] *The Life of Ramakrishna.*

DAYANAND

The man and his work

(Sriyut Aurobindo Ghosh)

AMONG the great company of remarkable figures that will appear to the eye of posterity at the head of the Indian Renaissance, one stands out by himself with peculiar and solitary distinctness, one unique in his type as he is unique in his work. It is as if one were to walk for a long time amid a range of hills rising to a greater or lesser altitude, but all with sweeping contours, greenclad, flattering the eye even in their most bold and striking elevation. But amidst them all one hill stands apart, piled up in sheer strength, a mass of bare and puissant granite, with verdure on its summit, a solitary pine jutting out into the blue, a great cascade of pure, vigorous and fertilising water gushing out from its strength as a very fountain of life and health to the valley. Such is the impression created on my mind by Dayanand.

It was Kathiawar that gave birth to this puissant renovator and new-creator. And something of the very soul and temperament of that peculiar land entered into his spirit, something of Girnar and the rocks and hill, something of the voice and puissance of the sea that flings itself upon those coasts, something of that humanity which seems to be made of the virgin and unspoilt stuff of Nature, fair and robust in body, instinct with a fresh and primal vigour, crude in the crude, but in a developed nature capable of becoming a great force of genial creation.

When I seek to give an account to myself of my sentiment and put into precise form the impression I have received, I find myself starting from two great salient characteristics of this man's life and work which mark him off from his contemporaries and compeers. Other great Indians have helped to make India of to-day by a sort of self-pouring into the psychological material of the race, a spiritual infusion of themselves into the fluent and indeterminate mass which will one day settle into consistency and appear as a great formal birth of Nature. They have entered in as a sort of leaven, a power of unformed stir and ferment out of which forms must result. One remembers them as great souls and great influences who live on in the soul of India. They are in us and we would not be what we are without them. But of no precise form can we say that this was what the man meant, still less that this form was the very body of that spirit.

The example of Mahadeva Govind Ranade presents itself to my mind as the very type of this peculiar action so necessary to a period of large and complex formation. If a foreigner were to ask us what this Maharatta economist, reformer, patriot precisely did that we give him so high a place in our memory we should find it a little difficult to answer. We should have to point to those activities of a mass of men in which his soul and thought were present, as a formless former of things, to the great figures of present day Indian life who received the breath of his spirit. And in the end we should have to reply by a counter question, "What would Maharastra of to-day have been without Mahadeva Govind Ranade and what would India of to-day be without Maharastra"? But even with those who were less amorphous and diffusive in their pressure on men and things, even with workers of a more distinct energy and action, I arrive fundamentally at the same impression. Vivekananda was a soul of puissance if ever there was one, a very lion among men, but the definite work he has left behind is quite incommensurate with our impression of his creative might and energy. We perceive his influence still working gigantically. We know not well how, know not well where in something that is not yet formed, something leonine, grand, intuitive, upheaving that has entered the soul of India and we say, "Behold Vivekananda still lives in the soul of his Mother and in the souls of her children". So it is with all. Not only are the men greater than their definite works but their influence is so wide and formless that it has little relation of any formal work that they have left behind them:

Very different was the manner of working of Dayanand. Here was one who did not infuse himself informally into the indeterminate soul of things, but stamped his figure indelibly as in bronze on men and things. Here was one whose formal works are the very children of his spiritual body, children fair and robust and full of vitality, the image of their creator. Here was one who knew definitely and clearly the work he was sent to do, chose his materials, determined his condition with a sovereign clairvoyance of the spirit and executed his conception with the puissant mastery of the born worker. As I regard the figure of this formidable artisan in God's workshop, images crowd on me which are all of battle and work and conquest and triumphant labour. Here, I say to myself, was a very soldier of Light, a warrior in God's world, a sculptor of men and institutions, a bold and rugged victor of the difficulties which matter presents to spirit. And the whole sums itself up to me in a powerful impression of *spiritual practicality.* The combination of these two words, usually so divorced from each other in our conceptions, seems to me the very definition of Dayanand.

Even if we leave out of account the actual nature of the work he did, the mere fact that he did it in this spirit and to this effect would give him a unique place among our great Founders. He brings back an old Aryan element into the national character. This element gives us the second of the differentia I observe and it is the secret of the first. We others live in a stream of influences; we allow them to pour through us and mould us; there is something shaped and out of it a modicum of work results; the rest is spilt out again in a stream of influence. We are indeterminate in our lives, we accommodate ourselves to circumstance and environment. Even when we would fain be militant and intransigent, we are really fluid and opportunist. Dayanand seized on all that entered into him, held it in himself, masterfully shaped into the form that he saw to be right. That which strikes us in him as militant and aggressive, was a part of his strength of self-definition.

He was not only plastic to the great hand of Nature, but asserted his own right and power to use Life and Nature as plastic material. We can imagine his soul crying still to us with our insufficient spring of manhood and action. "Be not content, O Indian, only to be infinitely and grow vaguely, but see what God intends thee to be, determine in the light of his inspiration to what thou shalt grow. Seeing, hew out of thyself, hew that out of Life. Be a thinker but be also a doer; be a soul, but be also a man; be a servant of God, but be also a master of Nature!" For this was what he himself was; a man with God in his soul, vision in his eyes and power in his hands to hew out of life an image according to his vision. Hew is the right word. Granite himself, he smote out a shape of things with great blows as in granite.

In Dayanand's life we see always the puissant jet of this spiritual practicality. A spontaneous power and decisiveness is stamped everywhere on his work. And to begin with, what a master-glance of practical intuition was this to go back trenchantly to the very root of Indian life and culture, to derive from the flower of its first birth the seed for a radical new birth! And what an act of grandiose intellectual courage to lay hold upon this Scripture, defaced by ignorant comment and oblivion of its spirit, degraded by misunderstanding to the level of an ancient document of barbarism, and to perceive in it its real worth as a Scripture which conceals in itself the deep and energetic spirit of the forefathers who made this country and nation—a Scripture of divine knowledge, divine worship, divine action. I know not whether Dayanand's powerful and original commentary will be widely accepted as the definite word on the Veda. I think myself some delicate work is still called for to bring out other aspects of this profound and astonishing Revelation. But this matters little.

The essential is that he seized justly on the Veda as India's Rock of Ages and had the daring conception to build on what his penetrating glance perceived in it a whole nation-hood. Rammohan Roy, that other great soul and puissant worker who laid his hand in Bengal and shook her—to what mighty issues? —out of her long indolent sleep by her rivers and rice fields—Rammohan Roy stopped short at the Upanishads. Dayanand looked beyond and perceived that our true original seed was the Veda. He had the national instinct and he was able to make it luminous—an intuition in place of an instinct. Therefore the works that derive from him, however they depart from received traditions, must needs be profoundly national.

To be national is not to stand still. Rather, to seize on a vital thing out of the past and throw it into the stream of modern life, is really the most powerful means of renovation and new creation. Dayanand's work brings back such a principle and spirit of the past to vivify a modern mould. And observe that in the work as in the life it is the Past caught in the first jet of its virgin vigour, pure from its sources, near to its root principle and therefore to something eternal and always renewable.

And in the work as in the man we find that faculty of spontaneous definite labour and vigorous formation which proceeds from an inner principle of perfect clearness, truth and sincerity. To be clear in one's own mind, entirely true and plain with one's self and with others, wholly honest with the conditions and materials of one's labour, is a rare gift in our crooked, complex and faltering humanity. It is the spirit of the Aryan worker and a sure secret of vigorous success. For always Nature recognises a clear, honest and recognisable knock at her door and gives the result with an answering scrupulosity and diligence. And it is good that the spirit of the Master should leave its trace in his followers, that somewhere in India there should be a body of whom it can be said that when a work is seen to be necessary and right, the men will be forthcoming, the means forthcoming and that work will, surely, be done.

Truth seems a simple thing and is yet most difficult. Truth was the master-word of the Vedic teaching, truth in the soul, truth in the vision, truth in the intention, truth in the act. Practical truth, *Aryatva*, an inner candour and a strong sincerity, clearness and open honour in the world and deed was the temperament of the old Aryan morals. It is the secret of a pure unspoilt energy, the sign that a man has not travelled far from Nature. It is the bar dexter of the son of Heaven, Devasputra. This was the stamp that Dayanand left behind him and it should be the mark and effigy of himself by which the parentage of his work can be recognised. May his spirit act in India, pure, unspoilt, unmodified and help to give us back that of which our life stands especially in need, pure energy, high clearness, the penetrating eye, the masterful hand, the noble and dominant sincerity.[1]

SWAMI DAYANAND SARASWATI

(Rev. C. F. Andrews)

"FOR Dayanand's personality and character there may well be almost unqualified admiration. He was a puritan to the backbone, and lived up to his creed. He was a fighter, strong, virile, independent, if somewhat imperious in behaviour... His courage in facing his own countrymen through years of contumely and persecution was nothing less than heroic. *He was a passionate lover of truth.*"[2]

[1] *The Arya*, Pondicherry.
[2] *The Indian Renaissance.*

SWAMI DAYANAND SARASWATI
at the Hardwar Kumbha Fair, March 1867 A.D.

DAYANAND SARASWATI

(Madame Blavatsky)

ONE is inclined to think that this wonderful Hindu bears a charmed life, so careless is he of raising the worst human passions, which are so dangerous in India. At Benares, a worshipper of the Shiva, feeling sure that his cobra, trained purposely for the mysteries of a Shivaite pagoda, would at once make an end of the offender's life, triumphantly exclaimed: 'Let the god Vasuki (the snake god) himself show which of us is right!'

"Dayanand jerked off the cobra twisting round his leg, and with a single vigorous movement crushed the reptile's head. 'Let him do so,' he quietly assented, 'your god has been too slow. It is I who have decided the dispute. Now go,' added he, addressing the crowd, 'and tell every one how easily perish all false gods'. Truly, a marble statue could not be less moved by the raging wrath of the crowd. We saw him once at work. He sent away all his faithful followers, and forbade them either to watch over him or to defend him, and stood alone before the infuriated crowd, facing calmly the monster, ready to spring upon him and tear him to pieces."

* * * * *

"It is perfectly certain that India never saw a more learned Sanskrit scholar, a deeper metaphysician, a more wonderful orator, and a more fearless denunciator of any evil, than Dayanand, since the time of Śaṅkarāchārya."[1]

[1] *The Caves and Jungles of Hindustan.*

SWAMI DAYANAND SARASWATI

(Colonel H. S. Olcott, President, Theosophical Society)

"A master spirit has passed away from India. Pandit Dayanand Saraswati......is gone; the irrepressible, energetic Reformer, whose mighty voice and passionate eloquence for the last few years raised thousands of people in India from lethargic indifference and stupor into active patriotism, is no more.

"De mortuis nil nisi bonum. All our differences have been burnt with the body.........We remember only the grand virtues and noble qualities of our former colleague and *teacher*, and late antagonist. We bear in mind but his life-long devotion to the cause of Aryan regeneration; his ardent love for the grand philosophy of his forefathers; his relentless, untiring zeal in the work of the projected social and religious reforms; and it is with unfeigned sorrow that we now hasten to join the ranks of his many mourners. In him, India has lost one of her noblest sons. A patriot in the true sense of the word, Swami Dayanand laboured from his earliest years for the recovery of the lost treasures of Indian intellect. His zeal for the Reformation of his mother-land was exceeded only by his unbounded learning. There can be but one opinion as to his knowledge of Sanskrit, and the impetus to the study of both received at his hands. There are few towns and but one province we believe—namely, Madras—that Pandit Dayanand did not visit in furtherance of his missionary work, and fewer still where he has not left the impress of his remarkable mind behind him. He threw, as it were, a bomb-shell in the midst of the stagnant masses of degenerated Hinduism, and fired with love for the teachings of the Rishis and Vedic learning the hearts of all who were drawn within the influence of his eloquent oratory. Certainly there was no better or grander orator in Hindi and Sanskrit than Dayanand throughout the length and breadth of this land."[1]

[1] *The Theosophist.*

Dayanand's parental home at Tankara in which he was born.

AUTOBIOGRAPHY OF SWAMI DAYANAND SARASWATI

(**Fragment**)

IT was in a Brahmin family of the Oudichya caste, in a town belonging to the Rajah of Morvi, in the province of Kathiawar, that in the year 1881, of Vicrama Samvat, I, now known as Dayanand Saraswati, was born. If I have from the first refrained from giving the names of my father and of the town in which my family resides, it is because I have been prevented from doing so by my duty. Had any of my relatives heard again of me, they would have sought me out. And then, once more face to face with them, it would have become incumbent upon me to follow them. I would have to touch money again, serve them, and attend to their wants. And thus the holy work of the Reform to which I have wedded my whole life, would have irretrievably suffered through my forced withdrawal from it.

I was hardly five years of age when I began to study the Devanagari characters, and my parents and all the elders commenced training me in the ways and practices of my caste and family, making me learn by rote the long series of religious hymns, mantrams, stanzas and commentaries. And I was but eight when I was invested with the sacred Brahminical cord (triple thread) and taught the Gayatri Sandhya with its practices, and Yajur Veda Sanhita preceded by the study of the *Rudrādhyaya*. As my family belonged to the Siva sect, their greatest aim was to get me initiated into its religious mysteries; and thus I was early taught to worship the uncouth piece of clay representing Siva's emblem, known as the *Pārthiva Lingam*. But as there is a good deal of fasting and various hardships connected with this worship, and I had the habit of taking early meals, my mother, fearing for my health, opposed my daily practising of it. But my father sternly insisted upon its necessity, and this question finally became a source of everlasting quarrels between them. Meanwhile, I studied Sanskrit grammar, learned the Vedas by heart, and accompanied my father to the shrines, temples, and places of Siva worship. His conversation ran invariably upon one topic; the highest devotion and reverence must be paid to Siva, his worship being the most divine of all religions. It went on thus till I had reached my fourteenth year, when, having learned by heart the whole of the Yajur Veda Sanhita, parts of other Vedas, of the Shabda Rupavali and grammar, my studies were completed.

As my father's was a banking house and held, moreover, the office hereditary in my family of a Jamadar, we were far from being poor, and things, so far, had gone on very pleasantly. Wherever there was a Siva Puran to be read and explained, there my father was sure to take me along with him; and finally unmindful of my mother's remonstrances, he imperatively demanded that I should begin practising *Pārthiwa Puja*. When the great day of gloom and fasting called Sivaratri had arrived, this day following on the 13th of Magh Vadi, my father, regardless of the protest that my strength might fail, commanded me to fast, adding that I had to be initiated on that night into the sacred legend, and participate in that night's long vigil in the temple of Siva. Accordingly, I followed him, along with other young men, who accompanied their parents. This vigil is divided into four parts called *praharas*, consisting of three hours each. Having completed my task, namely, having sat up for first two *praharas*, till the hour of midnight, I remarked that the Pujaries, or temple servants, and some of the lay devotees, after having left the inner temple had fallen asleep outside. Having been taught for years that by sleeping on that particular night, the worshipper lost all the good effect of his devotion, I tried to refrain from drowsiness by bathing my eyes now and then, with cold water. But my father was less fortunate. Unable to resist fatigue he was the first to fall asleep, leaving me to watch alone.

Thoughts upon thoughts crowded upon me and one question

arose after the other in my disturbed mind. Is it possible—I asked myself—that the semblance of man, the idol of a *personal* God, that I see bestriding his bull before me, and who, according to all religious accounts, walks about, eats, sleeps, and drinks: who can hold a trident in his hand, beat upon his *dumroo* (drum), and pronounce curses upon men—is it possible that he can be the Mahadeva, the great Deity? The same who is invoked as the Lord of Kailasa, the Supreme Being and the divine hero of all the stories we read of him in his Puranas (Scriptures)? Unable to resist such thoughts any longer, I awoke my father, abruptly asking him to enlighten me, to tell me whether this hideous emblem of Siva in the temple was identical with the Mahadeva (great god) of the Scriptures or something else. "Why do you ask?" said my father. "Because," I answered "I feel it impossible to reconcile the idea of an Omnipotent, living God, with this idol, which allows the mice to run over his body and thus suffers his image to be polluted without the slightest protest". Then my father tried to explain to me that this stone representation of the Mahadeva of Kailasa, having been consecrated by the holy Brahmins, became, in consequence the god himself, and is worshipped and regarded as such; adding that as Siva cannot be perceived personally in this Kali-Yug—the age of mental darkness—hence we have the idol in which the Mahadeva of Kailasa is imagined by his votaries; this kind of worship pleasing the great deity as much as if, instead of the emblem, he were there himself. But the explanation fell short of satisfying me. I could not, young as I was, help suspecting misinterpretation and sophistry in all this. Feeling faint with hunger and fatigue, I begged to be allowed to go home. My father consented to it, and sent me away with a sepoy only reiterating once more his command that I should not eat. But when, once home, I had told my mother of my hunger, she fed me with sweetmeats, and I fell into a profound sleep.

In the morning, when my father had returned and learned

that I had broken my fast, he felt very angry. He tried to impress me with the enormity of my sin; but do what he could, I could not bring myself to believe that that idol and Mahadeva were one and the same god, and, therefore, could not comprehend why I should be made to fast for and worship the former. I had, however, to conceal my lack of faith, and bring forward as an excuse for abstaining from regular worship my ordinary study, which really left me little or rather no time for anything else. In this I was strongly supported by my mother, and even my uncle, who pleaded my cause so well that my father had to yield at last and allow me to devote my whole attention to my studies. In consequence of this, I extended them to "Nighantu", "Nirukta" "Purvamimansa", and other Shastras, as well as to "Karmakand" or the Ritual.

There were besides myself in the family two younger sisters and two brothers, the youngest of whom was born when I was already sixteen. On one memorable night, as we were attending a *nautch* festival at the house of a friend, a servant was dispatched after us from home, with the terrible news that my sister, a girl of fourteen, had been just taken sick with a mortal disease. Notwithstanding every medical assistance, my poor sister expired within four *ghatkas* after we had returned. It was my first bereavement, and the shock my heart received was great. While friends and relatives were sobbing and lamenting around me, I stood like one petrified, and plunged in a profound revery. It resulted in a series of long and sad meditations upon the instability of human life. 'Not one of the beings that ever lived in this world could escape the cold hand of death'—I thought; 'I, too, may be snatched away at any time, and die. Whither then shall I turn for an expedient to alleviate this human misery, connected with our death-bed; where shall I find the assurance of, and means of attaining Mukti, the final bliss... It was there, and then, that I came to the determination that I would find it, cost whatever it might, and thus save myself from the untold miseries of the dying moments of an unbeliever. The ultimate result of such meditations was to make me violently break, and for ever, with the mummeries of external mortification and penances, and the more to appreciate the inward efforts of the soul. But I kept my determination secret, and allowed no one to fathom my innermost thoughts. I was just eighteen then. Soon after, an uncle, a very learned man and full of divine qualities—one who had shown for me the greatest tenderness, and whose favourite I had been from my birth, expired also; his death leaving me in a state of utter dejection, and with a still profounder conviction settled in my mind that there was nothing stable in this world, nothing worth living for or caring for in a wordly life.

Although I had never allowed my parents to perceive what was the real state of my mind, I yet had been imprudent enough to confess to some friends how repulsive seemed to me the bare idea of a married life. This was reported to my parents, and they immediately determined that I should be betrothed at once, and the marriage solemnity performed as soon as I should be twenty.

Having discovered this intention, I did my utmost to thwart their plans, I caused my friends to intercede on my behalf and pleaded my cause so earnestly with my father, that he promised to postpone my betrothal till the end of that year. I then began entreating him to send me to Benares, where I might complete my knowledge of Sanskrit grammar, and study astronomy and physics, until I had attained full proficiency in these difficult sciences. But this time, it was my mother who opposed herself violently my desire. She declared that I should not go to Benares, as whatever I might feel inclined to study could be learned at home, as well as abroad: that I knew enough as it was, and had to be married anyhow before the coming year, as young people through an excess of learning were apt to become too liberal and free sometimes in their ideas.

I had no better success in that matter with my father. On the contrary, for no sooner had I reiterated the favour I begged of him and asked that my betrothal should be postponed until I had returned from Benares a scholar, proficient in arts and sciences, than my mother declared that in such a case she would not consent even to wait till the end of the year, but would see that my marriage was celebrated immediately. Perceiving, at last, that my persistence only made things worse, I desisted, and declared myself satisfied with being allowed to pursue my studies at home, provided I was allowed to go to an old friend, a learned pandit who resided about six miles from our town in a village belonging to our Jamadaree. Thither then, with my parent's sanction I proceeded, and placing myself under his tuition, continued for some time quietly with my study. But while there, I was again forced into a confession of the insurmountable aversion I had for marriage. This went home again. I was summoned back at once, and found upon returning that everything had been prepared for my marriage ceremony. I had entered upon my twenty-first year, and had no more excuses to offer. I fully realized now, that I would neither be allowed to pursue any longer my studies, nor would my parents ever make themselves consenting parties to my celibacy. It was when driven to the last extremity that I resolved to place an eternal barrier between myself and marriage.

On an evening of the year Samvat 1903, without letting any one this time into my confidence, I secretly left my home, as I hoped for ever. Passing that first night in the vicinity of a village about eight miles from my home, I arose three hours before dawn, and before night had again set in I had walked over thirty miles; carefully avoiding the public thoroughfare, villages and localities in which I might have been recognized. These precautions proved useful to me, as on the third day after I had absconded, I learned from a Government officer that a large party of men including many horsemen, were diligently roving about in search of a young man from the town of——who had fled from his home. I hastened further on, to meet with other adventures. A party of begging Brahmins had kindly relieved me of all the money I had on me, and made me part even with my gold and silver ornaments, rings, bracelets, and other jewels, on the plea that the more I gave away in charities, the more my self-denial would benefit me in the after life. Thus, having parted with all I had, I hastened on to the place of residence of a learned scholar, a man named Lala Bhagat, of whom I had heard much on my way, from wandering Sannyasis and Bairagees (religious mendicants). He lived in the town of Sayale, where I met with a Brahmachari who advised me to join at once their holy order, which I did.

After initiating me into his order and conferring upon me the name of Shuddha Chaitanya, he made me exchange my clothes for the dress worn by them—a reddish-yellow garment. From thence, and in this new attire, I proceeded to the small principality of Kouthagangadh, situated near Ahmedabad, where, to my misfortune I met with a Bairagi, the resident of a village in the vicinity of my native town, and well acquainted with my family. His astonishment was as great as my perplexity. Having naturally enquired how I came to be there, and in such an attire, and learned of my desire to travel and see the world, he ridiculed my dress and blamed me for leaving my home for such an object. In my embarrassment he succeeded in getting himself informed of my future intentions. I told him of my desire to join in the Mela of Kartik, held at that year in Siddhpore, and that I was on my way to it. Having parted with him, I proceeded immediately to that place, and taking my abode in the temple of Mahadeva at Neelkantha, where Daradi Swami and other Brahmacharis, already resided. For a time, I enjoyed their society unmolested, visiting a number of learned scholars and professors of divinity who had come to the Mela, (Fair) and associating with a number of holy men.

Meanwhile, the Bairagi, whom I had met at Kouthagangadh had proved treacherous. He had despatched a letter to my family informing them of my intentions and pointing to my whereabouts. In consequence of this, my father had come down to Siddhpore with his sepoys, traced me step by step in the Mela, learning something of me wherever I had sat among the learned pandits, and finally one fine morning appeared suddenly before me. His wrath was terrible to behold. He reproached me violently, accusing me of bringing eternal disgrace upon my family. No sooner had I met his glance, I thought, knowing well that there would be no use in trying to resist him, I suddenly made up my mind how to act. Falling at his feet with joined hands, and supplicating tones, I entreated him to appease his anger. I had left home through bad advice, I said; I felt miserable and was just on the point of returning home, when he had providentially arrived; and now I was willing to follow him home again. Notwithstanding such humility, in a fit of rage he tore my yellow robe into shreds, snatched at my *tumba*, and wresting it violently from my hand flung it far away; pouring upon my head at the same time a volley of bitter reproaches, and going so far as to call me a matricide. Regardless of my promises to follow him, he gave me in the charge of his sepoys, commanding them to watch me night and day, and never leave me out of their sight for a moment.

But my determination was as firm as his own. I was bent on my purpose and closely watched for an opportunity of escaping. I found it on the same night. It was three in the morning, and the sepoy whose turn it was to watch me believing me asleep, fell asleep in his turn. All was still; and so, softly rising and taking along with me a *tumba* full of water, I crept out, and must have run over a mile before my absence was noticed. On my way I espied a large tree, whose branches were overhanging the roof of a pagoda; on it I eagerly climbed, and hiding myself among its thick foliage upon the dome, awaited what fate had in store for me. About four in the morning, I heard and saw through the apertures of the dome, the sepoys enquiring after me, and making a diligent search for me inside as well as outside the temple. I held my breath and remained motionless, until finally, believing they were on the wrong track, my pursuers reluctantly retired. Fearing a new encounter, I remained concealed on the dome the whole day, and it was not till darkness had again set in that, alighting, I fled in an opposite direction. More than ever I avoided the public thoroughfares, asking my way of people as rarely as I could, until I had again reached Ahmedabad, from whence I at once proceeded to Baroda. There I settled for some time; and at Chetan Math (temple), I held several discourses with Brahmanand and a number of Brahmacharis and Sannyasis, upon the Vedanta philosophy. It was Brahmanand and other holy men who established to my entire satisfaction that Brahma, the deity, was no other than my own self— my *Ego*. I am Brahma, a portion of Brahma; *Jiva* (Soul) and Brahma, the deity, being one. Formerly, while studying the Vedanta, I had come to this opinion to a certain extent, but now the important problem was solved, and I had gained the certainty that I was Brahma.

At Baroda hearing from a Benares woman that a meeting composed of the most learned scholars was to be held at a certain locality, I repaired thither at once, visiting a personage known as Satchidanand Paramahansa, with whom I was permitted to discuss various scientific and metaphysical subjects. From him I learned also, that there were a number of great Sannyasis and Brahmacharis who resided at Chanoda, Kanyali. In consequence of this I repaired to that place of sanctity, on the banks of Narbada and there at last met for the first time with real Dikshits, or, initiated Yogis, and such Sannyasis as Chidashrama and several other Brahmacharis. After some discussion, I was placed under the tuition of one Parmanand Paramahansa, and for several months studied "Vedantsar", "Arya Harimide Totak", "Vedant

Paribhasha", and other philosophical treatises. During this time, as a Brahmachari I had to prepare my own meals, which proved a great impediment to my studies. To get rid of it, I therefore concluded to enter, if possible, into the fourth order of the Sannyasis. Fearing, moreover, to be known under my own name, on account of my family's pride, and well aware that once received in this order I was safe, I begged of a Deccani pandit friend of mine, to intercede on my behalf with a Dikshit, the most learned among them that I might be initiated into that order at once He refused, however, point-blank to initiate me, urging my extreme youth. But I did not despair. Several months later, two holy men, a Swami and a Brahmachari came from the Deccan, and took up their abode in a solitary, ruined building, in the midst of a jungle near Chanoda, and about two miles distant from us. Profoundly versed in the Vedanta philosophy, my friend, the Deccani Pandit, went to visit them, taking me along with him. A metaphysical discussion following, brought them to recognize in each other Dikshits of vast learning. They informed us that they had arrived from "Shrangiri Math", the principal monastery of Śhaṅkarāchārya in the South, and were on their way to Dwarka. To one of them, Purananand Saraswati, I got my Deccani friend to recommend me particularly, and state at the same time, the object I was so desirous to attain and my difficulties. He told him that I was a young Brahmachari, who was very desirous to pursue his studies in metaphysics unimpeded; that I was quite free from any vice or bad habits, for which fact he vouchsafed; and that, therefore, he believed me worthy of being accepted in this highest probationary degree, and initiated into the fourth order of the Sannyasis; adding that thus I might be materially helped to free myself from all worldly obligations, and proceed untrammelled in the course of my metaphysical studies. But this Swami also declined at first. I was too young he said. Besides, he was himself a Maharashtra, and so he advised me to appeal to a Gujarati Swami. It was only when fervently urged on by my friend, who reminded him that Deccani Sannyasis can initiate even Gowdas, and that there could exist no such objection in my case, as I had already been accepted and was one of the five Dravids, that he consented. And on the third day following he consecrated me into the order, delivering unto me a *Dand*, and naming me Dayanand Saraswati. By the order of my initiator though, and my proper desire, I had to lay aside the emblematical bamboo the *Dand*, renouncing it for a while, as the ceremonial performances connected with it would only interfere with, and impede the progress of, my studies.

After the ceremony of initiation was over, they left us, and proceeded to Dwarka. For some time, I lived at Chanoda Kanyali as a simple Sannyasi. But upon hearing that at Vyasashram there lived a Swami whom they called Yoganand, a man thoroughly versed in Yoga, to him I addressed myself as a humble student, and began learning from him the theory as well as one of the practical modes of the science of Yoga (or Yoga Vidya). When my preliminary tuition was completed, I proceeded to Chhinour, as on the outskirts of this town lived Krishna Śhastri, under whose guidance I perfected myself in Sanskrit grammar, and again returned to Chanoda where I remained for some time longer. Meeting there two Yogis, Jwalanand Puri and Shivanand Giri, I practised Yoga with them also, and we all three held together many a dissertation upon the exalted science of Yoga; until finally, by their advice, a month after their departure I went to meet them in the temple of Doodheswar, near Āhmedabad, at which place they had promised to impart to me the final secrets and modes of attaining Yoga Vidya. They kept their promise, and it is to them that I am indebted for the acquirement of the practical portion of that great science. Still later, it was divulged to me that there were many far higher and more learned Yogis than those I had hitherto met, yet still *not* the highest who resided on the peaks of the mountain of Abu, in Rajputana. Thither then, I travelled again to visit such noted places of sanctity as the *Arvada Bhawani* and others, encountering at last, those whom I so eagerly sought for, on the peak of Bhawani Giri, and learning from them various other systems and modes of Yoga. It was in the year of Samvat 1911, that I first joined in the Kumbha Mela at Hardwar, where so many sages and divine philosophers meet, often unperceived. So long as the Mela congregation of pilgrims lasted, I kept practising that science in the solitude of the jungle of Chandi; and after the pilgrims had separated I went to Rishikesh, where, sometimes in the company of good and pure Yogis and Sannyasis, oftener alone, I continued in the study and practice of Yoga.

After passing a certain time in solitude, at Rishikesh, a Brahmachari and two mountain ascetics joined me, and we all three went to Tehri. The place was full of ascetics and Raj (Royal) pandits so-called on account of their great learning. One of them invited me to come and have dinner with him at his house. At the appointed hour he sent a man to conduct me safely to his place, and both the Brahmachari and myself followed the messenger. But what was our dismay upon entering the house, to first see a Brahmin preparing and cutting meat, and then proceeding further into the interior apartments, to find a large company of pandits seated with a pyramid of flesh, rumpsteaks, and dressed up heads of animals before them! The master of the house cordially invited me in; but, with a few brief words begging them to proceed with their 'good work' and not to disturb themselves on my account, I left the house and returned to my own quarters. A few minutes later, the beef-eating pandit was at my side, praying me to return, and trying to excuse himself by saying that it was *on my account* that the sumptuous viands had been prepared. I then firmly declared to him that it was all useless. They were carnivorous, flesh-eating men, and myself a strict vegetarian, who felt sick at the very sight of meat. If he would insist upon providing me with food he might do so by sending me a few provisions of grain and vegetables which my Brahmachari would prepare for me. This he promised to do, and then, very much confused, retired.

Staying at Tehri for some time, I enquired of the same pandit about some books and learned treatises I wanted to get for my instruction; what books and manuscripts could be procured at that place, and where? He mentioned some works on Sanskrit grammar, classics, lexicographies, books on astrology and the *Tantras* or ritualistics. Finding that the latter were the only ones unknown to me, I asked him to procure the same for me. Thereupon the learned man brought to me several works upon this subject. But no sooner had I opened them, than my eye fell upon such an amount of incredible obscenities, mistranslations of text and absurdity, that I felt perfectly horrified. In this Ritual I found that incest was permitted with mothers, daughters, and sisters (of the shoemaker's caste), as well as among the *Pariahs* or the outcastes, and worship was performed in a perfectly nude state. Spirituous liquors, fish, and all kinds of animal food, and *Mudra* (exhibition of indecent images)......were allowed, from Brahmin down to *Mang*. And it was explicitly stated that all those five things of which the name commences with the nasal, *M*, as for instance, *Madya* (intoxicating liquor); *Meen* (fish); *Maons* (flesh); *Mudra*......and *Maithoon*......were so many means of reaching Mukti (salvation). By actually reading the whole contents of the *Tantras*, I fully assured myself of the craft and viciousness of the authors of this disgusting literature which is regarded as RELIGIOUS. I left the place and went to Śrinagar.

Taking up my quarters at a temple, on Kedar Ghat, I used these Tantras as weapons against the local pandits, whenever there was an opportunity for discussion. While there, I became acquainted with a *Sadhu*, named Gangagiri, who by day never left his mountain where he resided in a jungle. Our acquaintance resulted in friendship, as I soon learned how entirely worthy he was of respect. While together, we discussed Yoga and other sacred subjects, and through close questioning and answering became fully and mutually satisfied that we were fit for each other. So attractive was his society for me, that I stayed over two months with him. It was only at the expiration of this time, and when autumn was setting in, that I, with my companions, the Brahmachari and the two ascetics, left Kedar Ghat for other places. We visited Rudra Prayag and other cities, until we reached the shrine at Agastamuni. Further to the north, there is a mountain peak known as the Shivpuri (town of Shiva) where I spent the four months of the cold season; when, finally parting from the Brahmachari and the two ascetics, I proceeded back to Kedar, this time alone and unimpeded in my intentions, and reached *Gupta Kashi* (the Secret Benares)......

I stayed but few days there, and went thence to the *Triyugi Narayan* shrine, visiting on my way Gaurikund tank, and the cave of Bheemgupha. Returning in a few days to Kedar, my favourite place of residence, I there finally rested, a number of ascetic Brahmin worshippers—called Pandas, and the devotees of the temple of Kedar, of the Jangam sect, keeping my company until my previous companions, the Brahmachari with his two ascetics, returned. I closely watched their ceremonies and doings, and observed all that was going on with a determined object of learning all that was to be known about these sects. But once that my object was fulfilled, I felt a strong desire to visit the surrounding mountains with their eternal snows and glaciers, in quest of those true ascetics I had heard of, but as yet had never met, the *Mahatmas*. I was determined—come what might—to ascertain whether some of them did or did not live there as rumoured. But the tremendous difficulties of this mountanious journey and the excessive cold forced me, unhappily, first to make enquiries among the hill-tribes and learn what they knew of such men. Everywhere I encountered either a profound ignorance upon the subject or a ridiculous superstition. Having wandered in vain for about twenty days, disheartened, I retraced my steps, as lonely as before, my companions who had at first accompanied me, having left me two days after we had started, through dread of the great cold. I then ascended the Tunganath Peak. There, I found a temple full of idols and officiating priests, and hastened to descend the peak on the same day. Before me were two paths, one leading west and the other south-west. I chose at random that which led towards the jungle, and ascended it. Soon after, the path led me into a dense jungle, with rugged rocks and a dried up waterless brook. The path stopped abruptly there. Seeing myself thus arrested, I had to make my choice to either climb up still higher, or to descend. Reflecting what a height there was to the summit, the tremendous difficulties of climbing that rough and steep hill, and that the night would come before I could ascend it, I concluded that to reach the summit that night was an impossibility. With much difficulty, however, catching at the grass and the bushes, I succeeded in attaining the higher bank of the *nulla* (the dry brook), and standing on a rock, surveyed the environs. I saw nothing but tormented hillocks, high land, and a dense, pathless jungle covering the whole, where no man could pass. Meanwhile the sun was rapidly descending towards the horizon. Darkness would soon set in, and then, without water or any means for kindling a fire, what would be my position in the dreary solitude of that jungle.

By dint of tremendous exertion, though, and after an acute suffering from thorns, which tore my clothes to shreds, wounded my whole body, and lamed my feet, I managed to cross the jungle, and at last reached the foot of the hill and found myself on the high-way. All was darkness around and over me, and I had to pickup my way at random, trying only to keep to the road. Finally I reached a cluster of huts, and learning from the people that that road led to Okhee Math, I directed my steps to that place, and passed the night there. In the morning, feeling sufficiently rested I returned to the *Gupta Kashi* (the Secret Benares), from whence I had started on my northward journey.

But that journey attracted me, and soon again I repaired to Okhee Math, under the pretext of examining that hermitage and observing the way of living of its inmates. There I had time to examine at leisure, the ado of that rich and famous monastery, so full of pious pretences and a show of asceticism. The high priest (or Chief Hermit), called *Mahant*, tried hard to induce me to remain and live there with him, becoming his disciple. He even held before me the prospect, which he thought quite dazzling, of inheriting some day his lacs of rupees, his splendour and power, and finally succeeding him in his *Mahantship* or supreme rank. I frankly answered him that had I ever craved any such riches or glory, I would not have secretly left the house of my father, which was not less sumptuous or attractive than his monastery with all its riches.—"The object which induced me to do away with all these worldly blessings" I added, "I find you neither strive for, nor possess the knowledge of." He then enquired what was that object for which I so strived. "That object", I answered "is the secret knowledge, the *Vidya*, or true erudition of a *genuine* Yogi: the *Mukti* which is reached only by the purity of one's soul and *certain attainments* and unattainable without them. Meanwhile, the performance of all the duties of man towards his fellow-men, and the elevation of humanity thereby."

The *Mahant* remarked that it was very good, and asked me to remain with him for some time at least. But I kept silent and returned no reply: I had not yet found what I sought. Rising on the following morning very early, I left this rich dwelling and went to Joshi Math. There, in the company of Dakshani or Maharashtra Śhastris and Sannyasis, the true ascetics of the fourth order—I rested for a while. [1]

[1] *From the Theosophist.*

NARAIN SWAMI

स्वामी दयानन्द सरस्वती

स्वामी दयानन्द १९वीं शताब्दी के सबसे बड़े वेद के विद्वान्, धर्मप्रचारक, समाज-संशोधक, देशोद्धारक और सर्वतोमुख सुधारक थे। उनकी विशेषताएं यह थीं—

धार्मिक सुधार

(१) वे वेद को सत्यविद्याओं का ग्रंथ मानते थे। उनकी दृष्टि में वेद के सभी शब्द यौगिक, और इसीलिये मानवी इतिहासशून्य, और उनकी सभी शिक्षाएं नित्योपयोगी हैं। इसी दृष्टिकोण से उनकी प्रचारित वेदार्थ-शैली ने उन्हें सायण आदि वेदभाष्यकारों की कोटि से पृथक् कर यास्काचार्य आदि नैरुक्तों की श्रेणी में पहुँचा दिया था।

(२) उन्होंने शंकर, रामानुज आदि प्रायः सभी मध्यकालीन आचार्यों के संकोच की अवहेलना करते हुए वेद का द्वार मनुष्य-मात्र के लिये खोल दिया और 'यथेमां वाचं कल्याणीमावदानि जनेभ्यः ××× (यजुर्वेद २। ६२)' की घोषणा करते हुए स्त्रियों, शूद्रों और अतिशूद्रों को भी वेदाध्ययन का अधिकारी ठहराया।

(३) उन्होंने वेदमात्र को स्वतः प्रमाण और वेदेतर सभी ग्रंथों को परतः प्रमाण बतलाते हुए मूर्तिपूजा, मृतक-श्राद्धादि पौराणिक प्रथाओं को अवैदिक प्रकट करते हुए हेय ठहराया और घोषणा की कि वेद केवल निराकार ईश्वर की पूजा का विधान करते हैं।

(४) स्वामी दयानन्द के प्रादुर्भाव के समय देशवासी वेद के नाममात्र से परिचित थे, उन्हें यह मालूम नहीं था कि वेद की शिक्षा क्या है? इसी कारण यह संभव हो सका कि एक पोर्चुगीज[1] पादरी ने एक संस्कृत पुस्तक वेद के नाम से गढ़कर उसमें ईसाई-मत की शिक्षा अंकित की और उसके द्वारा मद्रास प्रान्त में अनेक लोगों को ईसाई बनाया, परन्तु स्वामीजी ने इतने बल से वेदप्रतिपादित धर्म

[1] उस पादरी का नाम रोबर्टो डि नोबली (Roberto De Noblee) था और वह सन् १६०६ ई० में मदुरा पहुँचा था। इसका गढ़ा हुआ वेद पेरिस के अद्भुतालय से सम्बंधित पुस्तकालय में अब भी मौजूद है।

का प्रचार किया और उनकी शिक्षा के प्रकट करने के लिये ऋग्वेदादि-भाष्य-भूमिका, सत्यार्थप्रकाश आदि ग्रन्थों की रचना की, जिससे भविष्य में धोखे से हिन्दुओं को विधर्मी बनाना सुगम काम नहीं रहा।

(५) जो लोग उपर्युक्त भाँति या अन्य प्रकार से धर्मभ्रष्ट किये गये थे उनके लिये शुद्धि का द्वार खोलकर उन्हें फिर हिन्दू बनने की शिक्षा दी[1] और एक जन्म के मुसलमान को देहरादून में शुद्ध करके शुद्धि का क्रियात्मक रूप भी जनता के सामने रख दिया।

(६) देश में अंग्रेज़ी शिक्षा के प्रचार और ईसाई तथा मुसलमानों द्वारा उपस्थित किये हुए हिन्दू-धर्म के विरुद्ध साहित्य से वैदिक सभ्यता का मान घट रहा था और उसका स्थान अनेक उत्पातों की मूल पश्चिमी सभ्यता ले रही थी; प्राचीन संस्कृत साहित्य निकम्मा और वेद गड़रियों के गीत कहे जाने लगे थे और देशवासी, विशेषकर अंग्रेज़ी शिक्षित पुरुष, आँखें बन्द कर अंग्रेज़ी साहित्य और पश्चिमी रस्म-रिवाज पर मोहित होकर, पश्चिमी लोगों के पीछे चलने में गौरव मानने लगे थे; इस परिस्थिति और देश में उपस्थित ऐसे वातावरण को बदलकर प्राचीन सभ्यता का मान उत्पन्न करके, "वेद की ओर चलो" (Back to the Vedas) की ध्वनि को प्रतिध्वनित कर देना स्वामी दयानन्द के विशाल व्यक्तित्व, उनके अखंड ब्रह्मचर्य्य, उनके त्याग और तपस्या और उनके अपूर्व पाण्डित्य एवं निर्भीकतापूर्ण सत्य उपदेशों का ही फल था।

हिन्दी-प्रचार

(७) देश के नवयुवक मातृ(हिन्दी)भाषा को अंग्रेज़ी की वेदी पर बलिदान कर चुके थे और हिन्दी गंदी कहलाने लगी थी; हिन्दी पुस्तक या हिन्दी अख़बार पढ़ना फ़ैशन के विरुद्ध समझा जाने लगा था, परन्तु स्वामी दयानन्द ने अपने जगत्-प्रसिद्ध ग्रंथों को हिन्दी में लिखकर, जब कि उनकी मातृभाषा गुजराती थी, इस बेढंगी चाल को भी बदल दिया। अब सभी जानते हैं कि हिन्दी राष्ट्र-भाषा (Lingua Franca) समझी और मानी जाने लगी है और उसका प्रचार तथा साहित्य दिन-दूनी और रात-चौगुनी उन्नति कर रहा है। युनिवर्सिटियों (Universities) में भी उसका मान नित्यप्रति बढ़ रहा है।

[1] १९२० ई० के अन्त तक लगभग ४ लाख स्त्री-पुरुष शुद्ध होकर हिंदू बन चुके हैं।

सामाजिक सुधार

(८) सामाजिक सुधार के सम्बन्ध में भी ऋषि दयानन्द का हृदय बड़ा विशाल था और उन्होंने कुरीतियों को समाज से निकाल देने का प्रशंसनीय प्रयत्न किया। उदाहरण के लिये कतिपय सुधारों का यहाँ उल्लेख किया जाता है—

(क) बालविवाह का प्रचार और ब्रह्मचर्य का लोप हो जाने से शारीरिक बल का ह्रास हो रहा था, इसीलिये दूसरों की अपेक्षा हिन्दू जाति निर्बल समझी जाने लगी थी; इसी कारण उसे समय-समय पर अपमानित भी होना पड़ता था। स्वामी दयानन्द ने इसके विरुद्ध प्रबल आवाज़ उठाई और ब्रह्मचर्य की महिमा अपने उपदेशों और अपने क्रियात्मक जीवन से प्रकट कर ब्रह्मचर्य का सिक्का लोगों के हृदय में जमा दिया। उसी का फल है कि देश में जगह-जगह ब्रह्मचर्याश्रम खुले, सरकारी विश्वविद्यालयों ने भी अनेक जगह नियम बना दिये कि हाई-स्कूलों में विवाहित विद्यार्थियों का प्रवेश न हो और शारदा एक्ट भी बना।

(ख) इसी बाल-विवाह में वृद्ध-विवाह ने भी योग दे रक्खा था और दोनों का दुष्परिणाम यह था कि जाति में करोड़ों विधवाएं हो गई थीं, जिनमें लाखों बाल-विधवाएं भी थीं और उनमें हज़ारों ऐसी भी विधवाएं थीं जिनकी आयु एक-एक दो-दो वर्ष की थी। भ्रूणहत्या, गर्भपात, नवजात-बालवध आदि अनेक पातक हिन्दू जाति के लिये कलंक का टीका बन रहे थे। इन दुःखित विधवाओं का दुःख ऋषि दयानन्द का दयालु हृदय किस प्रकार सह सकता था, इसलिये उन्होंने बाल-विधवा-विवाह को प्रचलित करके इनके दुःखों को दूर करने की भी चेष्टा की।

(ग) मातृशक्ति होते हुए भी स्त्रियों का जाति में अपमान था, वे शिक्षा से वंचित करके परदे में रक्खी जाती थीं; उनके लिये वेद का द्वार बन्द था। उनको यदि श्रीमत् शंकराचार्य ने नरक का द्वार बतला रक्खा था[1], तो दूसरी ओर गोस्वामी तुलसीदासजी "ढोल गँवार शूद्र पशु नारी, ये सब ताड़न के अधिकारी" का ढोल पीट रहे थे; परन्तु ऋषि दयानन्द ने उनके

[1] देखो शङ्कराचार्य-कृत प्रश्नोत्तरी—"द्वारं किमेकं नरकस्य स्त्री"।

लिये भी वेद का द्वार खोला, उन्हें शिक्षा की अधिकारिणी ठहराया, पर्दे से निकाला, उन्हें मातृशक्ति के रूप में देखा और उनका इतना अधिक मान किया कि हम ऋषि दयानन्द को एक छोटी बालिका के आगे उदयपुर में नतमस्तक देखते हैं[1]। उसी का फल है कि आप्त कथाओं की ऊँची-से-ऊँची शिक्षा का प्रबन्ध हो रहा है।

(घ) जन्म की जाति प्रचलित हो जाने से चार वर्णों की जगह हिन्दू जाति हज़ारों कल्पित जातियों और उपजातियों में विभक्त हो रही थी। प्रत्येक का खान-पान, शादी-ब्याह पृथक्-पृथक् था। इन मामलों में एक जाति या उपजाति का पारस्परिक सम्बंध न होने से हिन्दू जाति एक जाति नहीं थी और न उसका कोई सम्मिलित उद्देश्य बाक़ी रहा था, न उस उद्देश्य की पूर्ति के सम्मिलित साधन उसके अधिकार में थे। ऋषि दयानन्द ने इस जन्म की जाति को समूल नष्ट करने की शिक्षा दी, क्योंकि यह सर्वथा वेद-विरुद्ध थी। उसी के फल-स्वरूप अब हिन्दुओं में अन्तर्जातीय सहभोज और अन्तर्जातीय विवाह होने लगे और इनके प्रचारार्थ अनेक संस्थाएं बन गई।

(च) दलित जातियों के साथ उच्च जातियों का व्यवहार अत्यन्त आक्षेप के योग्य और उनके लिये असह्य भी था; उसी के दुष्परिणाम-रूप बहुसंख्या में दलित भाई ईसाई और मुसलमान बन रहे थे। ऋषि दयानन्द ने इसके भी विरुद्ध आवाज़ उठाई और उन्हें खान-पान आदि सहित उन सभी अधिकारों के देने का निर्देश किया जो उच्च जातियों को प्राप्त हैं। देश-भर में ऋषि के इस निर्देश की पूर्ति के लिये जद्दोजहद हो रहा है और हिन्दुओं के मध्य से छूत-अछूत का भेद तथा छुआछूत का विचार ढीला पड़ रहा है।

(छ) दान की अव्यवस्था की ओर भी स्वामी दयानन्द ने ध्यान दिया; मनुष्य को निकम्मा बनाने के लिये जो दान देने की कुप्रथा प्रचलित थी उसका बलपूर्वक खंडन किया और उसके स्थान पर देश, काल तथा पात्र को देख-कर सात्त्विक दान देने की प्रथा प्रचलित की।

[1] देखो पं० लेखराम-कृत स्वामी दयानन्द का जीवनचरित्र—"उदयपुर का हाल"।

राजनैतिक सुधार

(९) राजनैतिक सुधार की ओर भी ऋषि दयानन्द ने देशवासियों का ध्यान खींचा और उस समय, जब देश में किसी राजनीतिक संस्था का अस्तित्व तक नहीं था, ऋषि दयानन्द का इस सम्बन्ध में दृष्टिकोण क्या था, यह बतलाने के लिये उनके जगत्-प्रसिद्ध ग्रंथ 'सत्यार्थप्रकाश' से कुछ वाक्य यहाँ उद्धृत किये जाते हैं—

(क) "अब अभाग्योदय से और आर्य्यों के आलस्य, प्रमाद, परस्पर के विरोध से अन्य देशों के राज्य करने की तो कथा ही क्या कहनी, किन्तु आर्य्यावर्त में भी आर्य्यों का अखंड, स्वतन्त्र, स्वाधीन, निर्भय राज्य इस समय नहीं है। जो कुछ है सो भी विदेशियों के पादाक्रान्त हो रहा है।"
(सत्यार्थप्रकाश; अष्टम समुल्लास, पृष्ठ २३७, बारहवाँ संस्करण)

(ख) हिन्दुओं में प्रचलित छूत-छात का खंडन करते हुए ऋषि दयानन्द ने लिखा है कि "इसी मूढ़ता से इन लोगों ने चौका लगाते-लगाते विरोध करते-कराते सब स्वातन्त्र्य, आनन्द, धन, राज्य, विद्या और पुरुषार्थ पर चौका लगाकर हाथ पर हाथ धरे बैठे हैं" (सत्यार्थप्रकाश; दशम समुल्लास, पृष्ठ २७८)।

(ग) "उसी दुष्ट दुर्योधन गोत्रहत्यारे, स्वदेशविनाशक, नीच के दुष्ट मार्ग में आर्य्य लोग अब तक भी चलकर दुःख बढ़ा रहे हैं। परमेश्वर कृपा करे कि यह राज-रोग हम आर्य्यों में से नष्ट हो जाय" (सत्यार्थप्रकाश; दशम समुल्लास, पृष्ठ २८०)।

(घ) "सृष्टि से लेकर महाभारत पर्यन्त चक्रवर्ती सार्वभौम राजा आर्य कुल ही में हुए थे। अब इनके सन्तानों का अभाग्योदय होने से राजभ्रष्ट होकर विदेशियों के पादाक्रान्त हो रहे हैं" (सत्यार्थप्रकाश; ११ समुल्लास, पृष्ठ २९०–२९१)।

(च) "कोई कितना ही करे परन्तु जो स्वदेशीय राज्य होता है वह सर्वोपरि उत्तम होता है……मतमतान्तर के आग्रह रहित……पक्षपात शून्य प्रजा पर पिता माता के समान कृपा, न्याय और दया के साथ विदेशियों का राज्य भी पूर्ण सुखदायक नहीं है" (सत्यार्थप्रकाश; अष्टम समुल्लास, पृष्ठ २३८)।

स्वदेशी वस्तु-प्रेम

(१०) स्वदेशी वस्तुओं के प्रयोग की भी ऋषि दयानन्द ने अपने ग्रन्थों में जगह-जगह

शिक्षा दी है। उसी का फल यह है कि वर्तमान आन्दोलन के बहुत पहले से आर्य्यसमाज के अनेक सदस्य नियम से देशी वस्त्रादि का प्रयोग करते हैं।

सहिष्णुता

(११) ऋषि दयानन्द में सहिष्णुता कमाल की थी। उन्हें जब अनूपशहर में एक व्यक्ति ने पान में रखकर विष दिया और सैयद मुहम्मद मजिस्ट्रेट ने इस अपराध में विष देनेवाले को पकड़वाकर हवालात में बन्द करा दिया, तो स्वामी दयानन्द ने उसे छुड़वा दिया और कहा कि "मैं दुनिया को क़ैद कराने नहीं किन्तु क़ैद से छुड़ाने आया हूँ।"

ब्रह्मचर्य्य

(१२) ऋषि दयानन्द ब्रह्मचर्य्य की मर्यादा का कितना ध्यान रखते थे उसका कुछ अनुमान इस घटना से किया जा सकता है कि एक दिन जब वे मथुरा में यमुना-तट के विश्रान्त घाट पर समाधिस्थ थे, उस समय एक देवी ने श्रद्धा से अपना सिर उनके पाँव पर रख दिया तब उन्होंने प्रायश्चित्त-रूप में तीन दिन तक उपवास रक्खा था।

वीरता

(१३) कर्णवास में स्वामी दयानन्द एक दिन गंगा-तट पर उपदेश दे रहे थे। बरोली के राव कर्णसिंह कुछ हथियारबन्द साथियों के साथ वहाँ आये और कुछ बात-चीत करते-करते वे इतने क्रोध में आ गये कि उन्होंने तलवार खींचकर स्वामीजी पर आक्रमण कर दिया। स्वामीजी ने तलवार छीनकर दो टुकड़े कर दिये और राव साहिब को पकड़कर कहा कि "मैं तुम्हारे साथ इस समय वही सलूक कर सकता हूँ जो किसी आततायी के साथ किया जा सकता है; परन्तु मैं संन्यासी हूँ, इसलिये छोड़ देता हूँ, जाओ ईश्वर तुम्हें सुमति देवे"।

निर्भीकता

(१४) एक दिन बरेली में स्वामीजी को व्याख्यान देना था; उससे पहिले दिन वे ईसाई-मत का खंडन कर चुके थे। उनसे कहा गया कि आज आप ईसाई-मत का खंडन न करें, क्योंकि इससे वहाँ के उच्च राज्यकर्मचारी अप्रसन्न होंगे। व्याख्यान में कमिश्नर आदि उपस्थित थे। स्वामीजी ने गरजकर कहा—"लोग कहते हैं कि

असत्य का खंडन न कीजिये, इससे कमिश्नर अप्रसन्न होगा, कलेक्टर नाराज़ होगा; परन्तु चाहे चक्रवर्ती राजा भी अप्रसन्न क्यों न हो, हम तो सत्य ही कहेंगे"।

योग की विभूति

(१५) प्रयाग में एक दिन स्वामीजी सभा में विराजमान थे । पं० सुन्दरलालजी आदि अनेक प्रतिष्ठित सज्जन भी उपस्थित थे । स्वामीजी यकायक हँस पड़े । कारण पूछने पर प्रकट किया कि एक पुरुष मेरे पास आ रहा है उसके आने पर एक कौतुक दिखाई देगा । थोड़ी देर के बाद ही एक आदमी स्वामीजी के लिये मिठाई लाया और कहा कि महाराज, इसमें से कुछ भोग लगावें । स्वामीजी थोड़ीसी मिठाई लानेवाले को देने लगे, परन्तु उसने लेने और खाने से इन्कार कर दिया। इस पर स्वामीजी हँस पड़े । थोड़ी मिठाई एक कुत्ते को खिलाई गई; वह फ़ौरन मर गया, क्योंकि मिठाई में विष मिला हुआ था । जब उस मिठाई लानेवाले को पुलिस के हवाले करने लगे, तो स्वामीजी ने यह कहकर छुड़वा दिया कि यह स्वयं अपने पाप के कारण लज्जित है और काँप रहा है ।

अपूर्व विद्वत्ता

(१६) कर्णवास में अनूपशहर के पं० हीरावल्लभजी एक धुरंधर संस्कृतज्ञ कतिपय साथियों के साथ स्वामीजी के पास आये और शास्त्रार्थ के लिये सभा संगठित हुई । पं० हीरावल्लभजी ने बीच में ठाकुरजी का सिंहासन रख दिया, जिसपर शालिग्रामादि की मूर्तियाँ थीं और प्रतिज्ञा की कि स्वामीजी से इन्हें भोग लगवाकर उठूँगा । छः दिन तक बराबर धाराप्रवाह संस्कृत में शास्त्रार्थ होता रहा । सातवें दिन हीरावल्लभजी ने सभा में प्रकट कर दिया कि जो कुछ स्वामीजी कहते हैं वही ठीक है और सिंहासन से मूर्तियों को उठाकर गंगा में प्रवाहित कर दिया और सिंहासन पर वेद की स्थापना की ।

विश्वप्रेम

(१७) ऋषि दयानन्द का दृष्टिकोण वेद की शिक्षानुकूल संकुचित जातीयता-पूर्ण (Nationalistic) नहीं था, किन्तु विश्वप्रेम-पूर्ण (Humanistic) था; इसीलिये उनके ग्रन्थों में जगह-जगह यही भावना आदर्श रूप में मिलती है । वास्तव में वर्तमान संकुचित जातीयता का विचार संसार में शान्ति स्थापित नहीं कर सकता।

आत्म-निरीक्षण

(१८) आत्म-निरीक्षण ऋषि दयानन्द के दैनिक कार्यक्रम में सम्मिलित था। हरद्वार में कुंभ के मेले के अवसर पर जब उन्होंने पाखंडखंडिनी पताका लगाकर धर्म-प्रचार किया, तो उन्हें ज्ञात हुआ कि प्रचार का जितना प्रभाव होना चाहिये था उतना नहीं हुआ। उन्हें इसका कारण अपने तप की न्यूनता जान पड़ी, तभी से उन्होंने सर्वमेध यज्ञ करके केवल एक लंगोटी पहनकर गंगा के तट पर विचरना शुरू किया और अनेक वर्ष इसी प्रकार व्यतीत किये।

अन्त-समय मृत्यु का अद्भुत दृश्य

(१९) स्वामीजी का अन्त-समय आया और अजमेर में अनेक सज्जन उनके अन्तिम दर्शन करने पहुँचे। उनमें लाहौर के प्रसिद्ध विद्वान् पं० गुरुदत्त विद्यार्थी, एम्० ए० भी थे। गुरुदत्त को ईश्वर की सत्ता में विश्वास नहीं था, परन्तु स्वामीजी के लिये बड़ी श्रद्धा थी। स्वामीजी ने सबसे बातचीत करके उन्हें रुख़सत कर दिया। अब वे जिस शय्या पर थे उसपर बैठ गये और बैठकर उन्होंने कुछ प्राणायाम किया। प्राणायाम के बाद कुछ वेदमंत्रों का उच्च स्वर से उच्चारण किया। मंत्रोच्चारण करते-करते उनके मुख पर मुसकराहट आई। गुरुदत्त सोचने लगे कि मौत का नाम सुनकर लोग काँप जाया करते हैं, परन्तु इस मृत्यु का स्वामी दयानन्द पर कुछ प्रभाव नहीं, वे दुःखी होने की जगह मुसकरा रहे हैं। स्वामी दयानन्द की यह मुसकराहट एक विद्युत् थी, जिसने गुरुदत्त के हृदय में जाकर वहाँ नास्तिकता का जो कूड़ा-करकट जमा था उसे भस्म करके गुरुदत्त को उच्च कोटि का आस्तिक बना दिया। अस्तु। स्वामी दयानन्द मुसकराते हुए ही बोले— "प्रभो! आपने अच्छी लीला की, आपकी इच्छा पूर्ण हो"। इन शब्दों के साथ ही उन्होंने अन्तिम श्वास खींचा और दुनिया से रुख़सत हो गये। मृत्यु के इस अद्भुत दृश्य ने प्रकट कर दिया कि जो महान् पुरुष ईश्वरविश्वासी होते हैं, जिनके हृदय में परोपकार के भाव भरे रहते हैं और जिनका संसार में किसी से ईर्ष्या-द्वेष नहीं होता, वे इस प्रकार प्रसन्नवदन, मुसकराते और ईश्वर को स्मरण करते हुए ही संसार से कूच किया करते हैं।

दिल्ली

नारायण स्वामी

H. H. MAHARANA SAJJAN SINGHJI

महर्षि दयानन्द सरस्वती और महाराणा सज्जनसिंह

महर्षि दयानन्द सरस्वती का नाम सारे संसार में प्रसिद्ध है। वे वैदिक धर्म के संस्थापक और वर्तमान हिन्दू-धर्म की प्रचलित मूर्ति-पूजा आदि कई बातों के खंडन-कर्ता माने जाते हैं। महर्षि ने प्रचलित हिन्दू-धर्म की कई बातों की उपेक्षा कर उनके विरुद्ध खंडन का बीड़ा क्यों उठाया ? इसका कोई गूढ़ कारण होना चाहिए, क्योंकि उनको धन एकत्र कर सुख-भोग की इच्छा नहीं और न किसी धर्म के आचार्य होकर मठाधीश बनने की लालसा थी।

वे यह मानते थे कि प्राचीन वैदिक धर्म शुद्ध, आडम्बर-शून्य और जीवमात्र के हित के लिये था, परन्तु पीछे से उसमें बहुत-कुछ परिवर्तन होकर विद्या का अभाव, मत-मतान्तर, रीति-रिवाज़ और भेद-भावरूपी अनेक कीड़े लग गये, जो समग्र हिन्दू-जाति को नाश की ओर ले जा रहे हैं। वर्णाश्रम-व्यवस्था लुप्त हो जाने से सैकड़ों जातियाँ और उपजातियाँ बनकर भेद-भाव और ऊँच-नीच की भावना बढ़ते-बढ़ते पारस्परिक वैमनस्य का कारण हो गई। तीर्थस्थल, मंदिर और मठ, जो शान्ति प्राप्त करने के लिये बनाए गए थे, विलासिता के केन्द्र बन गए। पंडे, पुजारी और मठाधीश पीड़ित हिन्दू-जनता का रक्त-शोषण कर उसे निर्धन बनाने के साथ ही द्रव्य का दुरुपयोग करते रहे। विद्या का अभाव होने से मनुष्य-जीवन के महत्त्व को भूलकर वे शास्त्रों के गूढ़ रहस्य को जानने से वंचित रह गये। कला-कौशल का नाश होने से पराश्रय में रहकर जीवन व्यतीत करना पड़ता और बेकारों की संख्या बढ़ती जा रही है। बाल-विवाह, वृद्ध-विवाह और बहु-विवाह की प्रथा से देश को महान् क्षति पहुँचती है और आश्रम-धर्म उठता जा रहा है। विचारों की संकीर्णता के कारण प्रतिवर्ष हजारों हिन्दू दुःखी हो अन्य धर्मों का आश्रय लेते हैं और सामाजिक कुप्रथाओं के कारण विधवाओं की संख्या बढ़कर कई मारी-मारी फिरती हैं, जिससे अनाचार की वृद्धि होती और हिन्दू-जाति का ह्रास होता है। अखंड ब्रह्मचर्य का पालन करते हुए पन्द्रह वर्ष से चालीस वर्ष की आयु तक निरन्तर तपस्या और विद्याध्ययन के प्रभाव से महर्षि ने एकमात्र वैदिक धर्म के अभाव को इन सब बुराइयों की जड़ जानकर यह संकल्प किया कि

नष्टप्राय वैदिक धर्म को पुनः भारत में फैलाकर सोई हुई हिन्दू-जाति को जगाई जाय, तभी हिन्दू-जाति का अस्तित्व रहेगा। अपने इस संकल्प को सिद्ध करने के लिये महर्षि ने कौन-कौनसे कार्य किये, उनका इस लेख में संक्षेप से वर्णन किया जाता है, परन्तु इसके पहले थोड़े-से शब्दों में यह बतलाना आवश्यक है कि बौद्ध और जैन धर्म का विकास होने के पूर्व भारत में वैदिक धर्म की क्या स्थिति थी; बौद्ध और जैन धर्म की उन्नति के दिनों में उसकी कैसी दशा रही और फिर उसका रूपान्तर होते-होते वह किस दशा को पहुँचा।

वैदिक धर्म आर्य-जाति का सब से प्राचीन धर्म है। ईश्वर की उपासना, यज्ञ, वर्ण-व्यवस्था आदि इसके मुख्य अङ्ग थे। समस्त जनता ब्राह्मण, क्षत्रिय, वैश्य और शूद्र, इन चार वर्णों में विभक्त थी और इनमें परस्पर घनिष्ठ सम्बन्ध था और प्रत्येक वर्ण का पुरुष अपने तथा अपने से नीचे के वर्णवालों में विवाह भी कर सकता था। शूद्रों का सेवा-कार्य होने पर भी उनको पंचमहायज्ञ करने का अधिकार था, जैसा कि पतञ्जलि के महाभाष्य तथा कैयट की टीका से ज्ञात होता है। ईश्वर के भिन्न-भिन्न नामों के अनुसार उसकी उपासना पृथक्-पृथक् रूप में होती थी। अनार्य या विधर्मियों के लिये भी इस धर्म का द्वार खुला हुआ था। यज्ञों में पशु-हिंसा होती थी और मांस-भक्षण का प्रचार बढ़ा हुआ था। अहिंसा के समर्थक इसका विरोध भी किया करते थे। इस हिंसा-वृत्ति को रोकने के लिये ईसवी सन् पूर्व की छठी शताब्दी में क्षत्रिय-वंशी बुद्ध और महावीर ने क्रमशः बौद्ध और जैन धर्म का प्रचार आरंभ किया। इन दोनों धर्मों में अहिंसा की प्रधानता थी। ये दोनों धर्म, अनीश्वरवादी होने पर भी, दिन-दिन उन्नति करने लगे और राज्याश्रय मिलने पर उनके अनुयायी बहुत हो गये, जिससे वैदिक (ब्राह्मण) धर्म का प्रभाव घटने लगा।

ईसवी सन् पूर्व की तीसरी शताब्दी में मौर्यवंशी सम्राट् अशोक ने बौद्ध धर्म ग्रहण कर अपने राज्य-भर में उसकी बहुत उन्नति की। इतना ही नहीं, किन्तु भारत के बाहर सुदूर देशों में भी उसके प्रचार के लिये उसने उपदेशक भेजे। बौद्ध-धर्म के उपदेशकों ने शनैः-शनैः निःस्वार्थभाव से इस धर्म का प्रचार भारत के बाहर ब्रह्मदेश, स्याम, चीन, जापान आदि देशों में किया। साइबीरिया और मध्य एशिया भी इस धर्म के अनुयायी हो गये। ईसवी सन् पूर्व की दूसरी शताब्दी में मौर्य-साम्राज्य के अन्तिम

राजा बृहद्रथ को मारकर उसका सेनापति शुंगवंशी पुष्यमित्र उसके राज्य का स्वामी बन गया और उसने वैदिक धर्म का पक्ष लेकर फिर अश्वमेध यज्ञ जारी किया; परन्तु सौ वर्ष से कुछ अधिक रहकर वह वंश भी समाप्त हो गया। फिर भी बौद्ध धर्म का प्रचार बढ़ता गया, जिसके फलस्वरूप कई वैदिक-धर्मावलंबी ब्राह्मणों, क्षत्रियों, वैश्यों और शूद्रों ने भी बौद्ध धर्म को ग्रहण किया। वैश्यों ने अपने परंपरागत कृषि-कर्म को छोड़ दिया, तब शूद्रों ने उसे अङ्गीकार कर लिया।

ईसवी सन् पूर्व की दूसरी शताब्दी में जैन-धर्मावलंबी, प्रतापी एवं विजयी राजा खारवेल ने जैन धर्म के प्रचार के लिये बहुत-कुछ उद्योग किया। कुशानवंशी राजा कनिष्क ने ईसवी सन् की पहली शताब्दी में बौद्ध धर्म की और भी उन्नति की। इस प्रगति का वेग गुप्तों के राज्य के प्रारंभ-काल तक बना रहा। इसका परिणाम यह हुआ कि बौद्ध धर्म का प्रचार बढ़ने और वैदिक धर्म का ह्रास होने लगा। ब्राह्मणों की सत्ता दिन-दिन निर्बल होती गई और बौद्धों तथा ब्राह्मणों में पारस्परिक द्वेष बहुत बढ़ गया। ब्राह्मणों ने बौद्ध धर्म ग्रहण करनेवाले समस्त क्षत्रियों, वैश्यों आदि को 'वृषल' अर्थात् धर्मच्युत माना और बौद्ध-प्राय देशों में तीर्थयात्रा के बिना जानेवालों के लिये फिर से संस्कार कराने की विधि प्रचलित की।

कुछ समय पश्चात् ब्राह्मणों को अपनी भूल की सूझ पड़ी। उन्होंने बौद्ध और जैन-धर्मावलंबियों को फिर अपने (वैदिक) धर्म में लाने की चेष्टा की, इतना ही नहीं, किन्तु उनको अपने वैदिक धर्म में परिवर्तन भी करना पड़ा और एक नवीन साँचे में ढलकर वह पौराणिक धर्म बन गया। उसमें बौद्ध और जैनों से मिलती-जुलती धर्म-सम्बन्धी बहुतसी नई बातें जोड़ी गईं और बुद्ध तथा महावीर की गणना विष्णु के अवतारों में हुई। मांस-भक्षण का भी निषेध किया गया और मूर्ति-पूजा की प्रवृत्ति बढ़ी। उसमें अनेक देवी-देवताओं की कल्पना की गई। यह परिवर्तित धर्म इस समय 'सनातन धर्म' नाम से प्रसिद्ध है।

यह बात इतने ही से न रुकी, किन्तु सुदूरवर्ती दक्षिण (मद्रास प्रान्त) के ब्राह्मणों ने तो पुराणों के इस कथन—'शिशुनाग वंश के अंतिम राजा महानंदी के पीछे शूद्रप्राय राजा होंगे'—पर विश्वास कर केवल दो ही वर्ण मान लिये, जो ब्राह्मण और अब्राह्मण (शूद्र) नाम से प्रसिद्ध हुए। उनकी देखादेखी महाराष्ट्र के ब्राह्मणों ने भी ऐसा

ही किया। ईसवी सन् की तेरहवीं शताब्दी के कुछ पीछे तक के शिलालेखों, दानपत्रों और प्राचीन ऐतिहासिक पुस्तकों से ज्ञात होता है कि महाराष्ट्र के ही नहीं, किन्तु सुदूरवर्ती दक्षिण (मद्रास प्रान्त) के राजा अपने को बराबर क्षत्रिय मानते रहे, तो भी ब्राह्मणों की प्रबलता तथा प्रधानता के कारण उनका आदेश चल निकला और क्षत्रियों को भी शूद्र मानकर उन्होंने उनकी धार्मिक क्रियाएँ वैदिक रीति से नहीं, किन्तु पौराणिक पद्धति से कराना शुरू कर दिया। उनके यजमानों के अज्ञान के कारण यह पद्धति कुछ समय तक चलती रही। फिर कमलाकर पंडित ने 'शूद्र-कमलाकर' (शूद्र-धर्म-तत्त्व) नामक ग्रंथ लिखकर उनकी धर्म-क्रियाओं की पौराणिक विधि स्थिर कर दी। जब प्रसिद्ध राजा छत्रपति शिवाजी ने महाराष्ट्र में अपना राज्य स्थापित किया और अपना राज्याभिषेकोत्सव बड़ी धूमधाम से कराना चाहा, तब उनके पुरोहितों ने वेद-विधि से उनका राज्याभिषेक करना स्वीकार न किया। इसपर शिवाजी ने काशी से विश्वेश्वर भट्ट (उपनाम गागा भट्ट) नामक विद्वान् को, जो उस समय का वेदव्यास माना जाता था, बुलाकर अपना राज्याभिषेक वैदिक विधि से करवाया और उनके पूर्वज मेवाड़ के सूर्यवंशी सीसोदिया क्षत्रिय होने से उन्होंने अपनी राज्यमुद्रा में 'क्षत्रिय-कुलावतंस श्री राजा शिव छत्रपति' लेख खुदवाया। शिवाजी के पीछे यह भावना लुप्त हो गई। सद्भाग्य से उत्तर भारत के ब्राह्मणों ने इस प्रथा का अनुमोदन न किया; किन्तु बौद्धों के अवनति-काल में जो लोग फिर वैदिक धर्म में आना चाहते, उन्हें प्रारंभ में 'व्रात्यस्तोम' क्रिया से और पीछे से बिना किसी क्रिया के फिर उनके मूलवर्ण में मिलाने लगे।

ब्राह्मणों के इस परिवर्तित धर्म की गुप्त राजाओं के समय से उन्नति होने लगी और क्रमशः बौद्ध धर्म की अवनति होते-होते दसवीं शताब्दी के आसपास भारत के अधिकांश भाग से बौद्ध धर्म का अस्तित्व उठता गया। गुजरात के प्रतापी राजा कुमारपाल के पश्चात् उधर जैन धर्म का विकास भी रुक गया। इसके अनन्तर मुसलमानों का राज्य भारत में होने के समय से वे भी भारतवासियों को अपने धर्म में मिलाने लगे, जिससे मुसलमानों की संख्या में वृद्धि होती गई। ब्राह्मणों के धर्म में मत-मतान्तरों की संख्या बढ़ गई। क्षत्रिय (राजपूत) वर्ण को छोड़कर अन्य वर्णों में इतनी उपजातियाँ बन गईं कि एक-दूसरे के साथ का खान-पान और विवाह-सम्बन्ध छूट गया। इस प्रकार जो हिन्दू-जाति पहले सभ्यता के आदर्श पर रहकर केवल चार वर्णों में ही विभक्त थी,

वह हज़ारों जातियों और उपजातियों में विभक्त होकर इस समय मृतप्राय दशा को पहुँच गई। वैदिक काल की 'व्रात्यस्तोम' क्रिया का लोप होने से हिन्दुओं की जन-संख्या बराबर घटती ही गई। अंग्रेज़ी राज्य का अभ्युदय होने पर ईसाई-धर्म का भी यहाँ प्रचार होने लगा और जातिगत संकीर्णता बढ़ जाने से कई लोग उदासीन हो ईसाई-धर्म भी ग्रहण करने लगे। फिर पारस्परिक भेदभाव भी बढ़ता गया और ऊँच-नीच का प्रश्न उत्पन्न हो गया। इससे पारस्परिक प्रेम में न्यूनता होकर एक-दूसरे में बड़ा अन्तर पड़ गया। अपने इस संकुचित व्यवहार के कारण एक समय जो हिन्दू-जाति उच्च विचारों से भूषित होकर विशाल-हृदय कहलाती थी, वह पतनोन्मुख होकर मृतप्राय बन गई; परंतु फिर भी हमारे धर्माचार्यों का इस ओर ज़रा भी ध्यान आकृष्ट न हुआ और वे उल्टे पारस्परिक द्वेष को बढ़ाते ही गये।

जब अधोगति चरमसीमा तक पहुँच जाती है, तब उस जाति में कोई महान् पुरुष उत्पन्न होता है; यह प्राचीन सिद्धान्त है। तदनुसार जब हिन्दू-जाति पतन के समीप पहुँचने लगी, तब उन्नीसवीं शताब्दी के अन्त में वि० सं० १८८१ (ई० स० १८२४) में काठियावाड़ के मोरवी राज्य के टंकारा गाँव में एक औदीच्य ब्राह्मण के घर में बालक मूलशंकर का जन्म हुआ। बाल्यकाल से ही इस बालक में प्रतिभा दृष्टिगोचर होने लगी और चौदह वर्ष की आयु में उसने सारी शुक्ल यजुर्वेद-संहिता कंठस्थ कर ली। एक बार शिवरात्रि के दिन शिवलिंग का पूजन करते समय लिंग पर एक चूहा चढ़ गया और उसके ऊपर चढ़ाई हुई सामग्री को खाने लगा। यह देख बालक मूलशङ्कर के हृदय में एकदम महान् परिवर्तन हो गया और जड़वाद का नाश होकर उसमें सत्यान्वेषण की धुन पैदा हुई। उसकी अन्तरात्मा जाग उठी और उसमें जगत् के कल्याणकारी परमपिता परमेश्वर की प्राप्ति के लिए उत्कट इच्छा उत्पन्न हुई, हृदयस्थल में अन्तर्नाद होने लगा और उसे निश्चय हो गया कि मूर्तिपूजा ईश्वर-प्राप्ति का साधन नहीं है। बालक मूलशंकर के हृदय की इस उथल-पुथल में ही दो वर्ष के पश्चात् उसकी छोटी बहिन की मृत्यु हो गई और फिर चाचा का भी देहान्त हो गया, जिससे जिस भाँति गौतम बुद्ध को संसार से निराशा हो गई थी, उसी प्रकार उसका चित्त भी संसार से हट गया। आशावाद का अन्त हुआ और अमर फल पाने की लालसा जाग उठी। माता-पिता ने उसको विवाह द्वारा सांसारिक बन्धनों में जकड़ना चाहा; परन्तु दृढ़प्र-

तिज्ञ मूलशंकर ने उस ओर ध्यान नहीं दिया। वह बीस वर्ष की आयु में घर से निकल गया। उसने पूर्णानन्द सरस्वती नामक विद्वान् से संन्यास ग्रहण कर अपना नाम दयानन्द सरस्वती रक्खा। तदनन्तर स्वामीजी ने योग की क्रिया को सीखना आरम्भ किया और व्याकरण में अपनी गति बढ़ाई। इस प्रकार वि० सं० १६११ तक वे इधर-उधर फिरते हुए विद्वान्, महात्माओं और योगियों के सत्संग से लाभ उठाकर अपनी आत्मिक उन्नति करते रहे। फिर वे हिमालय की ओर गये, पर वहाँ भी उनके मानसिक परितोष का साधन न मिला। तत्पश्चात् वे नर्मदा-तट पर तीन वर्ष तक विचरते रहे और वहाँ से मथुरा जाकर प्रसिद्ध विद्वान् स्वामी विरजानन्दजी से वेद और आर्ष-ग्रन्थों का अध्ययन करने लगे। अष्टाध्यायी, महाभाष्य, वेदान्तसूत्र आदि कई ग्रन्थों का अध्ययन करने के पश्चात् अपने शिक्षा-गुरु की आज्ञा के अनुसार हिन्दू-जाति को मतमतान्तर के बन्धनों से छुड़ाकर सच्चे धर्म पर लाने के लिये उन्होंने अपना कार्य आरम्भ कर दिया।

सर्व-प्रथम महर्षि ने वि० सं० १६२० (ई० स० १८७३) में आगरे में उपदेश देना आरंभ किया और वहाँ से करौली, धौलपुर, ग्वालियर, जयपुर, कृष्णगढ़, अजमेर, पुष्कर, मथुरा, मेरठ, अनूपशहर, सोरों, शाहबाज़पुर, फ़र्रुख़ाबाद, कानपुर, बनारस, डुमराँव, पटना, मुंगेर, भागलपुर, वृंदावन, प्रयाग, जबलपुर, बम्बई, अहमदाबाद, राजकोट, पूना, लुधियाना, लाहौर, जालंधर, फ़ीरोज़पुर, रावलपिंडी, झेलम, गुजराँवाला, मुलतान, रुड़की, दिल्ली, देहरादून, मुरादाबाद, बदायूं, बरेली, लखनऊ आदि नगरों में जाकर उन्होंने प्राचीन वैदिक धर्म का प्रचार किया। उनको अनेक स्थानों में पंडितों से शास्त्रार्थ करना पड़ा, जिसमें महर्षि सदा विजयी होते रहे। उपर्युक्त स्थानों में से कुछ में महर्षि का कई बार जाना हुआ और प्रत्येक बार उन्हें सफलता मिली। उनके उपदेशों से अपूर्व जागृति उत्पन्न हुई और उनके व्याख्यान सुनने से लोगों की प्राचीन वैदिक धर्म की तरफ़ फिर श्रद्धा बढ़ने लगी। हिन्दू-धर्म को सार-हीन समझकर जो लोग अन्य धर्म ग्रहण करते थे, उन्हें जान पड़ा कि वैदिक धर्म में जो उत्तमता है वह अन्य धर्मों में नहीं। इसके अतिरिक्त बाल-विवाह, वृद्ध-विवाह तथा बहु-विवाह बंद करने और गुरुकुल, अनाथालय, विधवाश्रम, विद्यालय आदि संस्थाएँ खोलकर जनता का हित करने के विचारों का अंकुर लोगों के चित्त में उत्पन्न हुआ। नियमित रूप से उपदेश

होते रहने के लिये प्रत्येक जगह आर्यसमाज स्थापित होकर पंजाब आदि देशों में बड़ी जागृति हुई। हज़ारों मनुष्यों ने वैदिक धर्म ग्रहण किया, छूतछात का भूत मिटने लगा और वैदिक धर्म से च्युत होकर अन्य धर्मों में गए हुए व्यक्तियों की पुनः शुद्धि करा उन्हें वैदिक धर्म में मिलाने की ओर भी प्रवृत्ति बढ़ने लगी।

अब तक महर्षि का राजपूताने के अधिकांश प्रदेश में शुभागमन नहीं हुआ था। वहाँ प्रचार की अत्यन्त आवश्यकता थी, इसलिये वे जून सन् १८८१ ई० को मसूदे गये और वहाँ से रायपुर होते हुए ब्यावर पहुँचे। महर्षि वहाँ से बनेड़ा और चित्तोड़ होते हुए बम्बई जानेवाले थे। उस समय भारत के वाइसरॉय लॉर्ड रिपन चित्तोड़ जाकर मेवाड़ के महाराणा सज्जनसिंह को जी. सी. एस्. आई. का खिताब देनेवाले थे। उसके उपलक्ष्य में उक्त महाराणा ने वहाँ एक विशाल दरबार करने का आयोजन किया, जिसमें लगभग ९० हज़ार पुरुष एकत्र हुए। महर्षि ने तत्कालीन मेवाड़-पति महाराणा सज्जनसिंह का विद्याप्रेम, गुणग्राहकता, धर्माभिरुचि, कुलाभिमान, न्यायप्रियता, शासन-सुधार एवं सामाजिक सुधार आदि की प्रशंसा सुन रक्खी थी; जिससे उस समय वहाँ ठहरकर उपदेश द्वारा उनको अपना अनुयायी बनाने और वहाँ की जनता में प्राचीन वैदिक धर्म का प्रचार करने की इच्छा हुई; क्योंकि भारतवर्ष के हिन्दू-राजाओं में मेवाड़ के महाराणाओं का सर्वोपरि स्थान है। प्रत्येक हिन्दू मेवाड़ के महाराणा को बड़ी श्रद्धा से देखता और उन्हें अपना नेता मानता है, क्योंकि मुसलमानों के राजत्वकाल में, जब हिन्दू-धर्म की अवहेलना हो रही थी, मेवाड़ के महाराणा ही उसकी रक्षा कर रहे थे। अनेक वार रक्त-रंजित होने से मेवाड़ की वीर-भूमि तीर्थ-स्थल समझी जाती है, अतएव महर्षि ने भी इस अवसर पर वहाँ जाने का निश्चय किया।

महाराणा सज्जनसिंह का महर्षि से सम्बन्ध

ता० ६ अक्टोबर ई० स० १८८१ (वि० सं० १९३८) को महर्षि बनेड़े पहुँचे। वहाँ के स्वामी राजा गोविंदसिंह ने, जो संस्कृत के विद्वान् थे, महर्षि का अच्छा सत्कार किया। उनके दोनों राजकुमारों—अक्षयसिंह और रामसिंह—ने महर्षि को साम-गान सुनाया, जिससे उन्हें बड़ी प्रसन्नता हुई। वहाँ के पुस्तकालय से महर्षि ने वेद का निघंटु ग्रन्थ लेकर अपने पास की प्रति से उसका मिलान किया। वहाँ से बिदा होकर वे ता० २६

अक्टोबर सन् १८८१ ई० को चित्तोड़ पहुँचे। महाराणा की आज्ञा के अनुसार कविराजा श्यामलदास ने महर्षि के स्वागत का समुचित प्रवन्ध करवा दिया। नियमानुसार महर्षि ने वेदोक्त आर्य-धर्म का वहाँ प्रचार करना आरम्भ किया। उनके उपदेशों को सुन मेवाड़-वासी जग गये। विरोधियों ने विष उगलना आरम्भ किया, परन्तु उनकी एक न चली। महर्षि के उपदेशों को सुनने के लिये मेवाड़ के प्रतिष्ठित सरदारों में से देलवाड़े के राज फ़तहसिंह, कानोड़ के रावत उम्मेदसिंह, शाहपुरे के राजाधिराज नाहरसिंह, आसींद के रावत अर्जुनसिंह, शिवगढ़ के महाराज रायसिंह आदि प्रायः उनके पास जाया करते थे। महाराणा भी यथावकाश महर्षि के पास उपदेश सुनने जाते थे। इससे महर्षि के प्रति उनकी श्रद्धा बढ़ती गई और उन्होंने उदयपुर आने के लिये महर्षि से विनयपूर्वक आग्रह किया। इसपर महर्षि ने सूचित किया कि बंबई से लौटता हुआ मैं उदयपुर अवश्य आऊँगा।

अपनी पूर्व-प्रतिज्ञा के अनुसार बंबई से लौटते समय महर्षि का वि० सं० १९३९ के द्वितीय श्रावण (ता० ११ अगस्त ई० स० १८८२) को उदयपुर में आगमन हुआ। वहाँ सज्जन-निवास बाग़ के नौलक्खा नामक महल में उनका ठहरना हुआ। महाराणा द्वितीय श्रा० कृ० १४ को महर्षि से भेंट करने गये और तत्पश्चात् नियमपूर्वक महर्षि के पास जाया करते थे। महाराणा के सभी सरदार महर्षि के उपदेशों को बड़ी श्रद्धा से सुनते। उन(सरदारों)में आसींद के रावत अर्जुनसिंह, पारसोली के राव रतसिंह, शाहपुरे के राजाधिराज नाहरसिंह, शिवगढ़ के महाराज रायसिंह, मामा बख्तावरसिंह, कविराजा श्यामलदास, राय मेहता पन्नालाल, मेहता तख्तसिंह, पुरोहित पद्मनाथ और ढींकड्या जगन्नाथ आदि मुख्य थे।

महर्षि के सारगर्भित उपदेशों का महाराणा के जीवन पर बड़ा प्रभाव पड़ा। महाराणा का पहले से ही संस्कृत की ओर झुकाव तो था और इस सत्समागम से दर्शन-शास्त्रों की ओर भी उनका अनुराग बढ़ा। उन्होंने संस्कृत-शैली से सब राजकीय कार्यालयों के नाम रक्खे, जैसे महद्राज-सभा, शैलकान्तार-सम्बन्धिनी सभा, निज-सैन्य-सभा, शिल्प-सभा आदि। महाराणा के हृदय पर महर्षि की विद्वत्ता का सिक्का जम गया था, इसलिए वैशेषिक दर्शन, पातञ्जलयोगसूत्र और मनुस्मृति आदि ग्रंथों को महर्षि से सुना करते थे। उन(महाराणा)की स्मरण-शक्ति इतनी प्रबल थी कि वे एक घंटे में मनुस्मृति के २२ श्लोकों का आशय याद कर लेते थे। उन्होंने महर्षि से कुछ योग-

NAVA LAKHA PALACE

Swami Dayanand's Residence at Udaipur

संबन्धी क्रियाएँ भी सीखीं, परन्तु फिर बीमार रहने से वे उनमें विशेष उन्नति न कर सके।

महाराणा जवानसिंह के पश्चात् चार पीढ़ी तक बागोर की शाखा से गोद लिये जाकर महाराणा बनाए गए थे और उनमें से किसी के संतति न हुई। इस वर्ष महाराणा सज्जनसिंह की तीसरी महाराणी के, जो ईडर की थी, गर्भस्थिति के चिह्न दृष्टिगोचर होने लगे, तब प्राचीन रीति के अनुसार गर्भ-रक्षार्थ नाना प्रकार के अनुष्ठान, जप, याग आदि होने लगे। महर्षि ने भी यह वृत्तान्त सुना। हवनादि कार्यों में भाग लेने की प्रार्थना पर महर्षि ने भी, जो यज्ञादि के बड़े पक्षपाती थे और दैनिक कृत्यों में हवन को गृहस्थ का मुख्य कर्म समझते थे, वैदिक रीति से यज्ञ करवाया। यज्ञ का फल शुभ हुआ और माघ शु० २ (ता० ६ फ़रवरी सन् १८८२ ई०) को महाराणा के कुँवर का जन्म हुआ। इस शुभ अवसर पर उक्त महाराणा ने दस लाख रुपये व्यय करना निश्चय किया था, परन्तु उस नवजात राजकुमार का उसी रात्रि को परलोक-वास हो गया, जिससे सारा हर्ष शोक में परिणत हो गया, तो भी महाराणा ने राजकुमार की पुण्य-स्मृति में एक अच्छी रक़म फ़ीरोज़पुर के अनाथालय को भेज दी।

महर्षि के सत्संग से महाराणा की दिनचर्या में बड़ा परिवर्तन हुआ और वे प्रत्येक कार्य नियत समय पर करने लगे। लोकोपयोगी कार्यों में प्रतिदिन महाराणा की रुचि बढ़ने लगी। महर्षि ने महाराणा को परामर्श दिया कि क्षत्रियों के लिए पृथक् पाठशाला बनाई जाकर उन्हें शास्त्रोक्त विधि से हर तरह की शिक्षा देने के साथ शस्त्रास्त्र-शिक्षा की भी योजना की जाय। महाराणा ने इस बात को स्वीकार किया, किन्तु उनके अस्वस्थ रहने से वह कार्य स्थगित रहा। मेवाड़ में राजकीय भाषा हिन्दी थी, परन्तु उसमें फ़ारसी शब्दों का अधिक प्रयोग होता था। यह देख महर्षि ने महाराणा को राजकीय भाषा में शुद्ध नागरी को स्थान देने और साधारण लोगों के समझ में आ सके, ऐसी भाषा के रखने का आग्रह किया। स्वामीजी का आदेश स्वीकार कर महाराणा ने नागरी लिपि और सरल भाषा में कार्य होने की आज्ञा जारी की। महर्षि ने महाराणा को स्वदेशी वैद्यों द्वारा चिकित्सा कराने और देशी औषधालय जारी करने का भी परामर्श दिया था; परन्तु महाराणा का देहावसान हो जाने से वह कार्य पूरा न हो सका।

महर्षि ने उदयपुर में ही 'सत्यार्थप्रकाश' के द्वितीय संस्करण को समाप्त कर वि० सं० १९३९ भाद्रपद के शुक्ल पक्ष में उसकी भूमिका लिखी और वहीं रहते समय परोप-

कारिणी सभा की स्थापना कर महाराणा को उसका सभापति नियत किया। महाराणा ने भी उस सभा की सहायता के लिए दस हज़ार रुपये दिये और उनके सरदारों आदि ने भी इस कार्य में सहयोग दिया, जिससे एक अच्छी रक़म एकत्र हो गई। यद्यपि स्वामीजी के शरीर में व्याधि का लेशमात्र भी नहीं था, तो भी उन्होंने शरीर को अनित्य जान अपने संग्रह किये हुए ग्रंथ, धन और यन्त्रालय आदि को परोपकार में लगाने की आज्ञा देकर उदयपुर में ही उसका स्वीकार-पत्र तैयार किया और उसके २३ ट्रस्टियों में महाराणा के अतिरिक्त मेवाड़ से ही सात सदस्य (बेदला के राव तख्तसिंह, देलवाड़े के राज फ़तहसिंह, आसींद के रावत अर्जुनसिंह, शाहपुरे के राजाधिराज नाहर-सिंह, शिवरती के महाराज गजसिंह, कविराजा श्यामलदास और पं० मोहनलाल-विष्णु-लाल पंड्या) रक्खे गये। इससे निश्चय होता है कि महाराणा और उसके सरदारों के सम्मिलित होने से आर्यसमाज की अधिकाधिक उन्नति होने का महर्षि को विश्वास था।

महाराणा ने महर्षि से षड्दर्शनों का भाष्य छपवाने का अनुरोध किया और उसके लिये बीस हज़ार रुपये अपनी ओर से व्यय करने का वचन दिया। फाल्गुन वदि ६ (ता० २७ फ़रवरी ई० स० १८८२) को महाराणा से बिदा होकर महर्षि शाहपुरा गये। उस अवसर पर महाराणा ने स्वयं उनके पास जाकर बिदायगी के सम्मान-रूप दो सहस्र रुपये भेंट किये, परन्तु महर्षि ने उन्हें लेना मंज़ूर नहीं किया। फिर महाराणा ने वह द्रव्य परोपकारिणी सभा को दे दिया। महर्षि उदयपुर से शाह-पुरा और वहाँ से जोधपुर गये, जहाँ उन्होंने प्राचीन वैदिक धर्म की महत्ता बतलाते हुए अन्य प्रचलित धर्मों की कई बातों का खण्डन किया, जिससे वहाँ उनके बहुतसे शत्रु हो गये। अन्त में कुछ दुष्टों ने चिढ़कर उनके आहार में विष मिला दिया; जिसके प्रभाव से कई दिन पीड़ित रहकर वि० सं० १९४० कार्तिक वदि ३० (ता० ३० अक्टोबर ई० स० १८८३) को अजमेर में उनका निर्वाण हुआ।

महर्षि के बीमार होने की सूचना पाते ही महाराणा ने पं० मोहनलाल-विष्णुलाल पंड्या को यह आदेश देकर उनके पास भेजा कि यदि महर्षि के निर्वाण की संभावना हो, तो ऐसा प्रबन्ध करना कि मैं भी उनके अंतिम दर्शन कर सकूं, परन्तु समय थोड़ा रह जाने से महाराणा की यह अभिलाषा पूरी न हो सकी।

महाराणा ने महर्षि के निर्वाण का संवाद सुना, तब वे शोक-सागर में डूब गये

RAJA DHIRAJ SIR NAHAR SINGHJI BAHADUR, K.C.S.I.
OF SHAHPURA.

और उन्होंने उसी समय निम्नलिखित छन्द रचकर महर्षि के प्रति अपूर्व श्रद्धा के साथ शोकोद्‌गार प्रकट किया—

दोहा

नभ-चव-ग्रह-ससि दीप-दिन, दयानंद लह सत्व।
वय त्रेसठ वत्सर बिचै, पायो तन पंचत्व॥

कवित्त

जाके जीह-जोर तें प्रपंच फ़िलासिफ़न को,
अस्त सो समस्त आर्य्य-मंडल में मान्यो मैं।
वेद के विरुद्धी मत-मत के कुबुद्धि मंद,
भद्र-मद्र आदिन पै सिंह अनुमान्यो मैं॥
ज्ञाता षट्‌ग्रंथन को वेद को प्रणेता जेता,
आर्य-विद्या-अर्क हू को अस्ताचल जान्यो मैं।
स्वामी दयानंदजू के विष्णु-पद प्राप्त हू तें,
पारिजात को सो आज पतन प्रमान्यो मैं॥

देश का दुर्भाग्य है कि महाराणा सज्जनसिंह भी अधिक न जिये और वि० सं० १९४१ पौष सुदि ६ (ता० २३ दिसम्बर ई० स० १८८४) को इस असार संसार से बिदा हो गये। यदि वह कुछ वर्ष और जीवित रहते, तो आर्यसमाज का इतिहास किसी अन्य रूप में लिखा जाता।

पुण्य-भूमि मेवाड़ के प्रति महर्षि की अपूर्व श्रद्धा थी और चित्तोड़ को वे हिन्दू-जाति का पवित्र तीर्थ समझते थे। चित्तोड़ में रहते समय उन्होंने अपने शिष्यों से कहा था कि भारत में गुरुकुल के योग्य यदि कोई स्थल है, तो वह चित्तोड़ ही है; अतएव चित्तोड़ में गुरुकुल बनाने का प्रयत्न करना आवश्यक है। प्रसन्नता का विषय है कि अब कुछ वर्ष पूर्व महर्षि की यह आकांक्षा सफल होकर चित्तोड़ में गुरुकुल स्थापित हुआ है।

महर्षि के प्रयत्न से हिन्दू-समाज के विचारों में बहुत-कुछ परिवर्तन हुआ, अनेक नगरों में आर्यसमाज स्थापित हुए और लोगों में नवीन विचार तथा जागृति उत्पन्न हुई। जो लोग हिन्दू-धर्म को छोड़कर अन्य-धर्मावलम्बी बनते थे, उन्हें रोकने, और जो

अन्य धर्म ग्रहण कर चुके थे, उन्हें पुनः शुद्ध कर वैदिक धर्म में मिलाने के लिए शुद्धि का आयोजन किया गया। महर्षि ने अपने उपदेशों के समस्त ग्रन्थ हिन्दी भाषा में प्रकाशित किये, जिससे हिन्दी की बहुत-कुछ उन्नति हुई। पंजाब जैसे देश में, जहाँ हिन्दी भाषा का कुछ भी प्रचार न था, आर्यसमाज के अनवरत परिश्रम के फलस्वरूप हिन्दी का यथेष्ट प्रचार हुआ और हो रहा है। महर्षि के उपदेश से वैदिक धर्म की जागृति हुई, इतना ही नहीं, किन्तु हिन्दू-जाति में समाज-सुधार का काम चल निकला। कई स्थानों पर कन्या-पाठशालाएँ खुलीं। जालंधर के कन्या-महाविद्यालय में सैकड़ों बालिकाएँ हिन्दी के साथ उच्चकोटि की शिक्षा पा रही हैं। उनके सदुपदेशों के कारण स्थान-स्थान पर गुरुकुल खुले, जहाँ अनेक विद्यार्थी संस्कृत, हिन्दी, अंग्रेजी आदि में उच्च कोटि की शिक्षा प्राप्त कर अनेक लोकोपयोगी कार्यों में भाग ले रहे हैं। सारे भारत में इस समय जो जागृति देख पड़ती है, उसका मुख्य कारण महर्षि के उपदेश ही हैं।

इन पंक्तियों के लेखक को बंबई में रहते समय सन् १८८१ ई० के दिसंबर से सन् १८८२ ई० के मई मास तक महर्षि के अनेक व्याख्यान सुनने का सौभाग्य प्राप्त हुआ और उसका बहुत-कुछ प्रभाव उसके चित्त पर पड़ा। अतएव दयानन्द-निर्वाण-अर्द्धशताब्दी के सुअवसर पर उक्त आदरणीय महापुरुष, आदर्श विद्वान्, अपूर्व वेदज्ञ, निर्भीक धर्मप्रवर्त्तक, सच्चे समाज-सुधारक, आर्य-संस्कृति के सर्वश्रेष्ठ पुरस्कर्ता, विश्वप्रेमी महर्षि दयानन्द सरस्वती के चिरस्मरणीय जीवन-कार्य की स्मृति में लेखक की यह लेख-रूप श्रद्धाञ्जलि अर्पित है।

अजमेर — गौरीशंकर-हीराचंद ओझा

स्वामिनं तमहं वन्दे

सनातन धर्मावलम्बियों की सन्तति होने और देवी-देवताओं के सम्मुख सिर झुकाने पर भी मेरे हृदय में श्रीस्वामी दयानन्दजी सरस्वती पर अगाध श्रद्धा है। वे बहुत बड़े समाज-संस्कर्ता, वेदों के बहुत बड़े ज्ञाता तथा समयानुकूल भाष्यकर्ता और आर्य्य संस्कृति के बहुत बड़े पुरस्कर्ता थे। उन्होंने जिस समाज की संस्थापना की है उससे भी अपने देश, अपने धर्म और अपनी भाषा को बहुत लाभ पहुँच रहा है। मैं स्वामीजी की विद्वत्ता और उनके कार्य्य-कलाप को अभागे भारत के सौभाग्य का सूचक चिह्न समझता हूँ। उनका चित्र चिरकाल तक मेरे नेत्रों के सामने रहकर मेरी आत्मा को बल का, तथा मेरे बैठने के कमरे को शोभा का, दान देता रहा है। स्वामीजी के विषय में इससे अधिक लिखने की शक्ति इस समय मेरे जरा-जीर्ण शरीर में नहीं। अतएव—

धन्यञ्च प्राज्ञमूर्धन्यं दयानन्दं दयाधनम्।
स्वामिनं तमहं वन्दे वारं वारञ्च सादरम्॥

दौलतपुर

महावीरप्रसाद द्विवेदी

स्वामी दयानन्द सरस्वती

कहावत है—"अंधी पीसे कुत्ते खायँ"। स्वामी दयानन्द सरस्वतीजी का जन्म हुआ था, उस समय हिन्दू-जाति की ठीक यही दयनीय दशा थी। हिन्दू-जाति अपने उज्ज्वल अतीत को एकदम भूलकर ऐसी तीव्र गति से अधःपतन के गहरे गड़हे में गिर रही थी कि उसका अस्तित्व ही खतरे में था। उसको अपनी नित्यप्रति क्षीण होनेवाली दशा का वैसा ही ज्ञान था जैसा कि तपेदिक के किसी रोगी को अपनी दशा का। सम्भव है, बहुतसे विचारशील लोग इस दुःखद दशा को समझते रहे हों, परन्तु उसे प्रकट करने का साहस किसी में न था। स्वामी दयानन्द सरस्वती की दशा इससे विपरीत हुई। उन्होंने अपनी दूरदर्शी सूक्ष्म ज्ञानदृष्टि से समाज के अंग-प्रत्यंग की परीक्षा की और अपनी सहज निर्भीकता के साथ इस श्रुति-कटु सत्य को प्रकट करना आरम्भ किया। लकीर की फ़कीर अंधविश्वासी हिन्दू-जनता में खलबली-सी पैदा हो गई। चारों ओर से घोर विरोध की आवाज़ें आने लगीं, किन्तु साँच को आँच कहाँ। सत्य की सभी जगह विजय होती है, वही इनकी दशा में भी हुआ। स्वामीजी के अल्पकालीन जीवन ने "सत्यमेव जयति नानृतम्" की सचाई में पुनः लोगों का विश्वास स्थापित कर दिया। परिणाम यह हुआ कि थोड़े ही दिनों के बाद जिनमें समझने की शक्ति थी, जो साँच-झूँठ की पहिचान—चाहे दूसरे के दिखाने पर ही क्यों न हो—कर सकते थे, वे परिस्थितियों के वशीभूत होने के कारण स्वामीजी के कार्य में खुल्लमखुल्ला सहयोग न कर सकने पर भी उनके सुधार और उद्धार-संबंधी कार्य्यों से सहानुभूति रखने लगे और आज हम देख रहे हैं कि, जिन-जिन कार्यों का बीज श्रीस्वामी दयानन्द सरस्वती ने बोया था वही महात्मा गाँधी सरीखे महान् व्यक्तित्व रखनेवाले महापुरुषों तक के लिये जीवन-मरण के प्रश्न बन रहे हैं। भला कौन ऐसा व्यक्ति है जो इस निर्विवाद सत्य से इनकार करेगा कि हमारी इस महानिन्दनीय निर्बलता की ओर सर्वप्रथम जाति का ध्यान आकृष्ट करने का श्रेय स्वामीजी ही को है। वास्तव में स्वामीजी एक ऐसे वैद्य थे जिन्हें न केवल सामाजिक अधःपतन तथा उत्थान के वास्तविक कारणों का सच्चा ज्ञान ही था, बल्कि जो

सच्चे निदान के बाद रोगनिवारण के लिये उत्तमोत्तम ओषधि का प्रयोग भी करना जानते थे। श्रीस्वामीजी में हमें एक ऐसे महामना उदारचेता कलामर्मज्ञ इंजीनियर के दर्शन होते हैं जो सौन्दर्य का सच्चा पुजारी है, जिसका हृदय श्रेष्ठतम कला-मर्मज्ञों के जीवनप्रद सौन्दर्य को मानो अपना एक आश्रम समझता हो और उसमें रहनेवाले अज्ञानी लोगों की अपकीर्त्ति के कारण उसे नष्ट-भ्रष्ट होते देखकर टूक-टूक हो जाता है; और वह उस पागल की भाँति, जो सत्य की बूँटी छाने हो, चिल्ला-चिल्ला-कर कहना शुरू करता है—अपने पूर्व-पुरुषों की समुज्ज्वल कीर्ति पर कलंक का टीका लगानेवाले इस अनुपम भवन के योग्य (?) निवासियो ! तुम इसकी संगमरमर की फ़र्शों पर गऊ का गोबर क्यों पोत रहे हो ? इस आश्रम की सदैव रक्षा करनेवालों को उनकी साधारण-से-साधारण मानवी निर्बलताओं तथा त्रुटियों के दण्डस्वरूप इससे बहिष्कृत कर तुम उनको सदैव के लिये इसका जानी दुश्मन क्यों बना रहे हो और अपनी महान् अक्षम्य त्रुटियों पर फूटी आँख से भी नज़र नहीं डालते ? क्यों तुमने इसके उन दरवाज़ों को बन्द किया और अब भी कर रहे हो जिनसे इसकी अनुपम सुन्दरता पर मुग्ध होकर सत्य के पुजारी इसमें प्रवेश कर ज्ञानामृत पीकर जीवन-मुक्त होते थे और इस प्रकार इसको खंडहर या ऊजड़ गाँव बना रहे हो ? किन्तु उसकी इस सच्ची सलाह को न मानकर उस भवन के निवासी उसपर आक्रमण आरम्भ करते हैं। वह सत्य-बल के सहारे कुछ दिन उनका मुक़ाबला करता है। अन्त में उन्हीं के निन्दनीय षड्यंत्रों का शिकार बन जाता है, किन्तु वह मरकर भी आज तक इस प्रकार जीवित है कि अब भी हम उसके अद्वितीय व्यक्तित्व-जन्य सुखद प्रकाश के सहारे अविद्यारूपी अन्धकार से आच्छादित जीवन-रात्रि को बिताने का साहस कर सकते हैं। हम देख रहे हैं कि उसी महान् पुरुष के द्वारा निर्धारित मार्गों पर चलकर कितने कला-मर्मज्ञ इञ्जीनियर और कितने कलाहीन, किन्तु लगन के सच्चे, ओवरसियर, थवई, मिस्त्री, बढ़ई और कुली मिलकर उस विशाल भवन की टूटी-फूटी दीवारों, फटे दरवाज़ों, चटकी छतों, झुकी शहतीरों, गिरी कारनिशों इत्यादि की ऋषिकुलों और गुरुकुलों की ईंटों, विधवा-विवाह-प्रचारक तथा बाल-वृद्ध-विवाह-निवारक संस्थाओं के सीमेंट, अछूतोद्धार के गारे, स्वदेशी वस्त्रों तथा वस्तुओं के झाड़न तथा वसुलियों और कुरीति-निवारण-समितियों के चूने इत्यादि की मदद से मरम्मत करने में इस प्रकार तल्लीन हो गये हैं कि

वह दिन बहुत दूर नहीं मालूम होता, जब हम इसके प्रवेश-मार्गों पर सुनहले अक्षरों में लिखी हुई "सत्यं–शिवं–सुंदरम्" की पंक्तियाँ देखेंगे और इस विशाल मंदिर में प्रवेश कर आर्य-साहित्य और सभ्यता से निकले हुए शांति-रूपी अमृत का पान करेंगे।

कुर्री सिधौली — रामपालसिंह

पथ-प्रदर्शक दयानंद

कहते हैं कि किसी समय में देवताओं और दैत्यों ने मिलकर समुद्र मथन करके उसमें से चौदह रत्न निकाले थे। यह तो एक कहानी है, परन्तु आधुनिक युग में संस्कृत के प्राचीन तथा अर्वाचीन साहित्य का मथन अपने विद्या तथा बल के साथ करके ऋषि दयानन्द ने वैदिक धर्म का वास्तविक स्वरूप-रूपी रत्न निकालकर संसार के सम्मुख रक्खा, जिससे धर्म के मार्ग पर चलने वालों को, जो इधर-उधर भटक रहे और भूल-भूलैया में पड़े हुए थे, उन्हें शाही राह दिखा दी।

मैं कह नहीं सकता कि मुझे इस अमृत के पान करने का सुअवसर मिलता या नहीं, परन्तु मेरा सौभाग्य है कि मेरे पूज्य पितामह स्वर्गवासी राजाधिराज सर नाहरसिंहजी बहादुर, के. सी. आई. ई., को ऋषि के समीप शिक्षा व दीक्षा का सौभाग्य प्राप्त हुआ था और वे ऋषि के श्रद्धालु भक्त थे। अतः उन्होंने मेरे बाल्य-काल से ही मेरे अन्दर उन उत्तम संस्कारों के डालने का स्तुत्य प्रयत्न किया, जिसे मैं अपना अहोभाग्य समझता हूं। उन्हीं की कृपा से मुझमें ऋषि दयानन्द-कृत ग्रन्थों के प्रति श्रद्धा तथा प्रेम उत्पन्न हुआ। ऋषि द्वारा स्थापित आर्य्यसमाज आज भी धर्म-मार्ग का प्रदर्शन करनेवाली संस्था है। प्रभु उसके कार्य में सफलता प्रदान करे, ऐसी शुभ कामना है। इति।

बिजवा स्टेट (अवध) — शत्रुञ्जयदेव

RAJA SHATRUNJAYA DEV OF BIJWA

वेदार्थ में ऋषि दयानन्द की क्रान्ति

वेद प्रभु की पवित्र वाणी है, जो आदिसृष्टि में जीवों के कल्याणार्थ, संसार के अन्य भोग्य पदार्थों की भाँति कर्मों की यथार्थ व्यवस्था के ज्ञानार्थ, तदनुसार आचरण करने के लिये परम पवित्र ऋषियों द्वारा प्रदान की गई है। भावी कल्प-कल्पान्तरों में भी यही वाणी इसी प्रकार सदा प्रादुर्भूत होगी। यह किसी व्यक्ति या व्यक्ति-विशेषों की कृति नहीं, अपितु सम्पूर्ण विश्व के रचयिता परमपिता परमात्मा की ही रचना है। इसमें किसी प्रकार न्यूनाधिकता नहीं हो सकती। **"धाता यथापूर्वमकल्पयत्, ऋतञ्च सत्यञ्चाभीद्धात्तपसोऽध्यजायत"**—समग्र संसार तथा तत्संबंधी ज्ञान यह सब विधाता की यथापूर्व कृति है।

यह है सार (निचोड़) वेदसम्बन्ध में वैदिक धर्मावलम्बियों की धारणा का, जिसे सत्य के देवता, आप्त अर्थात् यथार्थवक्ता ऋषि दयानन्द ने अपने जीवनकाल में उपदेश-द्वारा तथा अपने ग्रन्थों में एक-एक पंक्ति-द्वारा दर्शाया। यथार्थता की कसौटी पर ठीक उतरने से वैदिक धर्मावलम्बियों ने इस धारणा को अङ्गीकार किया है और इसके पुनरुद्धार का भार अपने ऊपर लिया है।

वेद के इस स्वरूप को निर्धारित करने में वीतराग तपस्वी दयानन्द को कहाँ तक परिश्रम करना पड़ा और वह भी उस अवस्था में जब वेद का पठन-पाठन लुप्तप्राय ही हो रहा था, इसके कहने की आवश्यकता नहीं। मैं तो उस भयङ्कर तूफ़ान का ध्यान करके ही स्तब्ध हो जाता हूँ जब "दयानन्द" को शास्त्र-सम्बन्धी विविध रूढ़ियों, प्रचलित रीतियों, सब शास्त्रकारों के नाम पर परस्पर विरोध की काली घटाओं, विविध वादों के भँवर में, मत-मतान्तरों का तो कहना ही क्या, इस घोर तूफ़ान में चट्टान की तरह अविचल पाता हूँ। नहीं-नहीं, दयानन्द उस तूफ़ान में डिगे नहीं, अपने आप को केवल सँभाले रहे, इतना ही नहीं, अपितु उन्होंने एकदम इन सब परस्पर विरुद्ध रूढ़ियों और वादों के विरुद्ध घोषणा कर दी कि "वेद परमपिता परमात्मा की वाणी है", "नित्य", "स्वतः प्रमाण" है। "अन्य सब शास्त्र वेदानुकूलतया ही प्रमाण हैं"। "वेद में किसी व्यक्ति-विशेष का इतिहास नहीं", "वेदमन्त्रों का अर्थ आध्यात्मिक,

आधिदैविक, आधियाज्ञिकादि प्रक्रियाओं के आधार पर करना होगा", अर्थात् "अग्निमीळे पुरोहितम्" में अग्नि भौतिक अग्नि का ही वाचक है यह बात नहीं, अपितु यहाँ अग्नि से परमात्मा तथा विद्वान् का भी ग्रहण करना होगा।

दयानन्द की इस धारणा को मानने में लोग अब तक ननुनच करते (हिचकिचाते) हैं। यूरोपियन स्कॉलर स्वामीजी के अर्थ को Interpretation of his own Image मनमानी कल्पना कहते रहे, क्योंकि ऐसे लोगों के सामने अब तक केवल सायणाचार्य का ही वेदार्थ रहा।

स्वामीजी ने यह सब अपनी कल्पनामात्र से ही नहीं लिखा, अपितु सब प्रमाण और तर्क के आधार पर। "वेद ईश्वरीय ज्ञान है", इसमें तो अब तक समस्त ऋषि, महर्षि, विद्वान्, आचार्य, वेदभाष्यकार, सब-के-सब सहमत रहे हैं। ईश्वरीय होने से नित्य स्वयंसिद्ध है। "स्वतः प्रमाण", "अन्य शास्त्र सब वेदानुकूलतया ही प्रमाण हैं", इसमें ऋषि दयानन्द ने–

या वेदबाह्याः स्मृतयो याश्च काश्च कुदृष्टयः।
सर्वास्ता निष्फलाः प्रेत्य तमोनिष्ठा हि ताः स्मृताः॥ मनु० १२।९५॥
विरोधे त्वनपेक्ष्यं स्यादसति ह्यनुमानम्॥ मी०।१।३।३॥

जैमिनि, मनु आदि ऋषियों के इन वचनों के आधार पर ही लिखा। तर्कवादियों के लिये ऋग्वेदादिभाष्यभूमिका में तर्क द्वारा भी उपर्युक्त बातें सिद्ध कीं।

अब जब कि सायणाचार्य से प्राचीन अनेक वेदभाष्यकारों का पता लग गया है और लगभग बीस वेदभाष्य मिल भी रहे हैं, यथा–स्कन्दस्वामी, उद्गीथ, वेङ्कटमाधव, आत्मानन्द, देवस्वामी, मुद्गल, हरिस्वामी, आनन्दबोध, देवयाज्ञिक, देवपाल, भवस्वामी, भट्टभास्कर, भरतस्वामी इत्यादि सायणाचार्य से प्राचीन विद्वानों के वेदभाष्य मिल रहे हैं तथा हस्तामलकादि लगभग सौ वेदभाष्यकारों का पता लग रहा है, ऐसी अवस्था में सायण को ही वेद का प्रामाणिक भाष्यकार मानना नितान्त भूल है। हम विस्तारभय से केवल एक ही वेदभाष्यकार स्कन्दस्वामी का, जो सायण से लगभग ९०० वर्ष प्राचीन है, मत विज्ञ पाठकों के सम्मुख अति संक्षेप से रखते हैं—

सायणाचार्य ने अपने समय की प्रचलित याज्ञिक प्रक्रिया (Ritual system) से पराहत होकर मन्त्रों का केवल याज्ञिक अर्थ ही दर्शाया। आचार्य दयानन्द ने ऋग्वेदादिभाष्यभूमिका, पृ० २६३, प्रतिज्ञा विषय में–

"अथात्र यस्य यस्य मन्त्रस्य पारमार्थिकव्यवहारिकयोर्द्वयोरर्थयोः श्लेषालङ्कारादिना सप्रमाणः सम्भवोऽस्ति, तस्य तस्य द्वौ द्वावर्थौ विधास्येते, **परन्तु नैव परमेश्वरस्यैकस्मिन्नपि मन्त्रार्थेऽत्यन्तं त्यागो भवति**"

अर्थात् मन्त्रों के आध्यात्मिक, आधिदैविक, आधियाज्ञिकादि अर्थ होते हैं। साथ ही परमेश्वर का त्याग किसी भी मन्त्र में नहीं हो सकता।

आज तक एतद्देशीय तथा विदेशीय स्कॉलर कहलानेवाले महानुभाव दयानन्द की इस धारणा को कल्पनामात्र मानते और इसपर हँसी उड़ाते रहे, परन्तु सायण से इतना प्राचीन वेदभाष्यकार आचार्य स्कन्दस्वामी अपने निरुक्त-भाष्य[1] में आध्यात्मिक, नैरुक्त, याज्ञिक तथा शुद्ध याज्ञिक प्रक्रिया का निरूपण करके अन्त में लिखते हैं, पृ० ३६, Vo III

"**सर्वदर्शनेषु च सर्वे मन्त्रा** योजनीयाः। कुतः। **स्वयमेव भाष्यकारेण सर्वमन्त्राणां त्रिप्रकारस्य विषयस्य प्रदर्शनाय** 'अर्थं वाचः पुष्पफलमाह' निरु० १-२० इति यज्ञादीनां पुष्पफलत्वेन प्रतिज्ञानात्।"

अर्थात् सब दर्शनों (प्रक्रियाओं-दृष्टियों) में सब मन्त्रों की योजना करनी चाहिये; क्योंकि भाष्यकार (निरुक्त-भाष्यकार यास्क) ने "अर्थं वाचः पुष्पफलमाह" इत्यादि में यज्ञादि को पुष्प फल-रूप बताते हुए **वेद के सब मन्त्रों का तीन प्रकार का अर्थ होता है**, यह दर्शाया है।

स्कन्द का यह लेख यास्क को साथ लेता हुआ वैदिक संसार में एक अपूर्व क्रान्ति का हेतु है, यह बात विज्ञ वैदिक विद्वान् निष्पक्ष भाव से विचारें और देखें कि बीसवीं शताब्दी में दयानन्द वेदार्थ-क्रान्तिकर्त्ता के रूप में हैं या नहीं।

इसी प्रकार वृत्रासुर देवापि-शन्तनु आदि की कथाओं को स्वामी दयानन्दजी महाराज ने ऋ० भूमिका पृ० २९५ से ३१५ तक आलङ्कारिक सिद्ध किया है। आचार्य स्कन्दस्वामी ने भी देवापि को विद्युत् और शन्तनु को जल बताते हुए ऐतिहासिक प्रक्रिया का स्वरूप निम्न प्रकार दर्शाया है—निरु० भा०, पृ० ७८, Vo. II

"एवमाख्यानस्वरूपाणां मन्त्राणां यजमाने नित्येषु च पदार्थेषु योजना कर्त्तव्या। एष शास्त्रे सिद्धान्तः······**औपचारिको मन्त्रेष्वाख्यानसमयः**। परमार्थेन नित्यपक्ष इति सिद्धम्।"

[1] यह ग्रन्थ पंजाब युनिवर्सिटी में डॉ० लक्ष्मणस्वरूप, एम्० ए० द्वारा सम्पादित हुआ है।

(ii) वररुचि-कृत निरुक्त-समुच्चय[2] के Manuscript, पृ० १४४ (यह ग्रन्थ स्कन्द से भी प्राचीन है)—

"औपचारिको मन्त्रेष्वाख्यानसमय इति नैरुक्तानां सिद्धान्तः, नित्यत्वविरोधात्"

(iii) शतपथ ब्रा० के भाष्यकार हरिस्वामी[3] की भूमिका, पृ० १४।

"यद्यपि किञ्चिदनित्यार्थवचनमिव दृश्यमानं ततो वृत्रं······ग्रन्थस्यांशं कथयति ······वृत्रो ह वा इदं सर्वं वृत्वा······तदपि नैरुक्तदिशा प्रवाहनित्यं, एष विद्युदादि-व्यवहारवाचित्वेन। ऐतिहासिकदिशां वा सर्ववृत्तान्तानामेव शीतोष्णवर्षावर्त्तवद् (?) यथाकाल वर्त्तमानानां वेदेन कर्मकालेऽतीतरूपेण प्रतिपादनाद् अदोषः।"

क्या इन प्रमाणों से इस विषय में कुछ भी सन्देह रह जाता है ? इसीलिये जितना-जितना अधिक अध्ययन होगा, ऋषि दयानन्द की वेदविषयक धारणाओं में उतनी-उतनी अधिक निष्ठा बढ़ती जायगी। वेदार्थ के शुद्धस्वरूप का द्रष्टा होने से ही 'ऋषि' शब्द उनके लिये उपयुक्त ही लगाया गया है।

सुधार के अन्य कार्यों को हिन्दू-जनता बहुत-कुछ अपनाती जा रही है, अब आर्य महानुभावों का काम है कि स्वयं वेद का स्वाध्याय नित्यप्रति करें तथा वेद के विषय में कोई स्थायी और प्रौढ योजना की व्यवस्था इस पवित्र अवसर पर करें, तभी वैदिक धर्म-द्वारा देश की संस्कृति (culture) की रक्षा हो सकेगी।

ऋषि के हस्तलेखों के विषय में परोपकारिणी सभा ने पाँच सहस्र रु० की मशीन मँगवाकर उनका फ़ोटो उतारना आरम्भ कर दिया है। लगभग २० हज़ार पृष्ठों की सामग्री फ़ोटो करने योग्य है, जो सभा के पास बहुत सुरक्षित अवस्था में है। सब आर्य-प्रतिनिधि सभाओं, आर्यसमाजों तथा धनिक आर्य-पुरुषों का कर्त्तव्य है कि इस पवित्र कार्य में परोपकारिणी सभा को पूर्ण सहयोग दें।

यथा यथा हि पुरुषः शास्त्रं समधिगच्छति।
तथा तथा विजानाति विज्ञानं चास्य रोचते॥ मनु०॥

[2] यह हस्तलेख Mss. डी. ए. वी. कॉलेज-पुस्तकालय, लाहौर में है।

[3] यह हस्तलेख Mss. सरस्वती-भवन-पुस्तकालय, काशी में ही है।

विरजानन्द-आश्रम, अमृतसर — ब्रह्मदत्त जिज्ञासु

स्वामी दयानन्द

भारतवर्ष के आधुनिक इतिहास में स्वामी दयानन्द सरस्वती का स्थान अद्वितीय है। जब स्वामीजी ने अपने मत का प्रचार आरम्भ किया, तब सनातनी पंडित तथा धर्माचार्यों ने उनका घोर विरोध किया था। सनातनी पंडितों की दृष्टि से स्वामीजी हिन्दू-धर्म को रसातल में पहुँचानेवाले एक बड़े भारी नास्तिक थे। स्वामीजी का मूर्तिपूजा-विरोध, विधवा-विवाह का समर्थन, जातिभेद का निषेध आदि कई बातों से आर्य-समाज तथा स्वामीजी के सम्बन्ध में साधारण जन-समाज में भी इसी तरह का ख़याल हो गया था। आज ज़माना बदल गया है। हिन्दू-जनता आर्यसमाज के कुछ सिद्धान्तों को न मानते हुए भी आज उसको अन्य-धर्मियों के आक्रमणों से हिंदू-धर्म तथा समाज की रक्षा करनेवाले एक प्रबल एवं प्रभावशाली संगठन के रूप में गौरवपूर्ण दृष्टि से देखने लगी है। स्वामी दयानन्दजी धर्मद्रष्टा थे। जो बातें उन्हें ६० साल पहले स्पष्ट दिखाई देती थीं, उन्हें लोग अब ठीक तरह समझने लगे हैं।

अपने मतप्रचार के कार्य में स्वामीजी को बहुत कष्ट सहन करना पड़ा; अन्त में अपने प्राणों की भी भेंट चढ़ानी पड़ी। कहते हैं, महापुरुषों का जीवन मृत्यु के अनन्तर ही शुरू होता है। स्वामीजी के जीवनचरित्र में यह उक्ति चरितार्थ हुई जान पड़ती है। स्वामीजी का कार्य उनकी मृत्यु के पश्चात् तीव्रतर गति से फैलने लगा और फैल रहा है। समाज-सेवा का कार्य करनेवाले कार्यकर्ताओं को स्वामीजी के चरित्र से श्रद्धा तथा विश्वास का पाठ मिलता है।

आर्यसमाज की ओर हिंदू-जनता की दृष्टि के बदल जाने की बात ऊपर कही गई है, किन्तु आर्यसमाज की कार्यपद्धति में भी समयानुसार परिवर्तन होने की आवश्यकता जान पड़ती है। आर्यसमाज के धुरीण कार्यकर्ताओं को भी परिवर्तन की आवश्यकता प्रतीत हो रही है, यह सन्तोष की बात है। हिंदू-धर्म के संस्करण के कार्य को करते हुए आर्यसमाज तथा सनातन हिंदूधर्म एकरूप हो जायँगे, ऐसी मैं आशा रखता हूँ और इसी में स्वामीजी के कार्य की सच्ची विजय है।

वर्धा

जमनालाल बजाज

आर्यसमाज

मैं आर्य्यसमाज को पहले से ही हिन्दू-समाज का अग्रगामी मानता रहा हूँ। श्रीस्वामी दयानन्दजी महाराज ने आर्यसमाज को स्थापित कर, हिन्दू-समाज और धर्म पर उसकी अवनति के जमाने में जिन-जिन कुत्सित भावों का अध्यारोप हो गया था उनके विरुद्ध क्रान्ति का झण्डा खड़ा किया। इस क्रान्ति के लिये जितनी तपस्या, त्याग एवं निर्भीकता की जरूरत थी, उसे स्वामीजी महाराज ने अपने ज्वलन्त जीवन में पर्याप्त रूप से संचय किया था।

किसी स्थापित शासन या व्यवस्था के विरुद्ध जब बग़ावत खड़ी होती है, तब उसके दो परिणाम होते हैं। यदि उस शासन या व्यवस्था की नींव कच्ची और कमजोर होती है, अथवा मजबूत होने पर भी निर्जीव बन चुकी हो, तो वह समूल नष्ट हो जाती है और उसके स्थान में एक नया निर्माण होता है। परन्तु वह कच्ची या कमजोर न हो, अथवा निर्जीव न बन चुकी हो, तो उसमें समयानुसार आवश्यक सुधार हो जाते हैं और वह अपना संशोधित रूप धारण कर पुनः अधिकाधिक उपयोगी बन जाता है।

हिन्दू-धर्म और हिन्दू-समाज के अत्यंत दूरदर्शी और तपस्वी निर्माणकर्त्ताओं ने उसकी नींव इतनी मजबूत रक्खी थी कि उसका हिलना कठिन है।

वह न तो कच्ची ही थी और न निर्जीव बन चुकी थी, परन्तु कुरूढ़ियों से आक्रान्त जरूर हो गई थी और उनके कारण इसने भारी-से-भारी हानियाँ उठाईं; अतएव इस क्रान्ति के परिणाम-स्वरूप हिन्दू-समाज में आवश्यक सुधार होने लग गए और होते जा रहे हैं। परमेश्वर ने चाहा, तो वह शीघ्र ही इसके भीतर घुसी हुई कुरीतियों और बुराइयों को निकाल-कर असली रूप दिखाता हुआ हिन्दू-समाज ही नहीं प्रत्युत संसार-भर का कल्याण करेगा।

सामाजिक सुधार के जिस महान् कार्य को आर्यसमाज ने उठाया और जिसे अग्रसर करने में उसने कठिन-से-कठिन बाधाएँ और विपत्तियाँ झेलीं, उसकी सबसे बड़ी सफलता इसी से जानी जा सकती है कि आज प्रायः समस्त शिक्षित और विचारशील हिन्दू-समाज उसके अधिकांश को स्वीकार करने लग गया और कार्य्यरूप में परिणत करने की चेष्टा कर रहा है।

पटना जगतनारायणलाल

श्रद्धाञ्जलि

विक्रम की बीसवीं सदी के संसार के सर्वश्रेष्ठ महापुरुष की निर्वाण-अर्द्धशताब्दी के अवसर पर जब मुझे उनके प्रति हार्दिक कृतज्ञता तथा श्रद्धांजलि प्रकट करने का सुअवसर प्राप्त हुआ, तो मेरा हृदय हर्ष से पुलकित हो उठा। हम लोगों का यह परम सौभाग्य है कि हमारी क्षत्रिय जाति के लिये श्रद्धेय महर्षि ने अपने जीवन का महत्त्वपूर्ण भाग भेंट किया और कर्तव्यविमुख क्षत्रिय जाति को संजीवन-सन्देश देकर उसके उद्धार का उपाय बताया। अपने प्रचार-काल में महर्षि ने इस बात का भली भाँति निर्णय कर लिया था कि भारत की वर्त्तमान अधोगति से उसका उद्धार करने के लिये क्षत्रिय जाति का उन्नत होना सबसे प्रथम आवश्यक है। वे क्षत्रिय जाति को प्राचीन काल के क्षत्रियों के समान वीर, पराक्रमशाली एवं तेजस्वी रूप में देखना चाहते थे। वे भली प्रकार जानते थे कि क्षत्रियों की विलास-प्रियता तथा कर्तव्य-विमुखता के कारण ही देश की दुरवस्था हुई है और इसके उद्धार का एकमात्र उपाय यही है कि क्षत्रिय जाति का उद्धार हो। अपने राजपूताना के प्रोग्राम में महर्षि ने उदयपुर के महाराणा सज्जनसिंहजी, जोधपुर के महाराजा जसवन्तसिंहजी तथा शाहपुराधीश राजाधिराज सर नाहरसिंहजी को समय-समय पर क्षात्र धर्म का उपदेश दिया। आज भी महर्षि के सच्चे अनुयायी बनने के लिये क्षत्रिय जाति के व्यक्तिमात्र का यह कर्तव्य है कि वह राजनीति की महत्ता पर ध्यान देते हुए उसके महत्त्व को समझकर, देश के सच्चे रक्षक बनकर, क्षत्रिय शब्द को सार्थक करें और शाब्दिक क्षत्रिय न बनकर कर्मवीर क्षत्रिय बनें और सच्चे अर्थ में क्षात्र-धर्म का पालन करें। महर्षि दयानन्दजी महाराज एक क्षत्रिय जाति ही नहीं, अपितु प्राणिमात्र के शुभेच्छु थे। हिन्दू-जाति की सदियों की सामाजिक कुरीतियों को दूर करने के लिये उन्होंने बड़ा भारी प्रयत्न किया, और सुधार के प्रत्येक अंग पर प्रत्येक दृष्टि से विचार करने का आदर्श दिखाया। महिला-समाज की उन्नति तथा उसकी महत्ता के लिये महर्षि के विचार तथा कर्म अनुपम थे। यह महर्षि के कार्य का प्रभाव है कि आज हमारा देश समाज-सुधार तथा अन्य कार्यों में अग्रसर हो रहा है।

उस समय मेरी श्रद्धा महर्षि के प्रति और भी बढ़ जाती है, जब मैं उनके जीवन में स्थान-स्थान पर सिद्धान्तवाद का उच्च आदर्श पाता हूँ ।

महर्षि ने मानव-जाति को बुद्धि तथा तर्क से कार्य-सम्पादन करने का उपदेश दिया और उसे स्वयं कार्य्यरूप में परिणत कर दिखाया । उन्होंने अन्ध-विश्वास से भरी हुई जनता को व्यक्तिवाद की विनाशोन्मुखी प्रवृत्ति से हटाकर सिद्धान्तवाद-रूपी लोकोपकारक सुन्दर सोपान पर चढ़ने का आदेश दिया । वे भली प्रकार अनुभव कर चुके थे कि अन्धविश्वासपूर्ण व्यक्तिपूजन हमें पतन के गहरे गड्ढे में डाले हुए है; अतः महर्षि दयानन्द ने यह बीजमंत्र हमारे कानों में फूँका कि मनुष्य को ईश्वर ने सम्पूर्ण प्राणियों से अधिक बुद्धि दी है, वह इसी कारण कि इसका सदुपयोग हो और किसी काम को केवल किसी व्यक्ति के आधार पर न किया जाय । इस समय महर्षि के इस सुन्दर विचार का अधिकाधिक प्रचार करने की आवश्यकता है ।

आगरा — कुशलपालसिंह

वैदिक धर्म

यह सदा से नियम रहा है कि जब-जब धर्म की हानि होती है और अधर्म बढ़ जाता है, तो परमात्मा किसी महान् शक्तिसम्पन्न व्यक्ति को संसार में जन्म देकर लोगों को अधर्म से हटाकर धर्म की ओर लगाता है । भगवान् रामचन्द्र, कृष्णचन्द्र, बुद्ध भगवान् तथा शंकराचार्य आदि ऐसे ही व्यक्ति थे । आधुनिक युग में भगवान् दयानन्द इसी प्रकार के व्यक्तियों में से थे । इन्होंने हिन्दू-धर्म का सच्चा स्वरूप संसार के सामने रक्खा और दिखलाया कि वेद का आदर्श कितना ऊँचा और सारे संसार के लिये कल्याणकारी है । उसी आदर्श को सर्वसाधारण के सम्मुख रखने का कार्य्य आर्य्यसमाज कर रहा है । ईश्वर करे, लोग इसके महत्त्व को समझें और धर्म के नाम पर जो अनेक आडम्बरपूर्ण ढकोसले होते हैं, उन्हें छोड़कर वास्तविक धर्म के तत्त्व को ग्रहण करके आपस में भ्रातृभाव की स्थापना करें ।

धनोप (शाहपुरा राज्य) — सर्दारसिंह

Sirdarsingh
11th Nov 1923

राष्ट्र-निर्माता स्वामी दयानन्द

श्री स्वामीजी के जीवनकाल में भारतीय जनता उनको भिन्न-भिन्न दृष्टि से देखती रही है। उस समय वह यह भी निर्णय नहीं कर सकी थी कि स्वामीजी हैं क्या, और चाहते क्या हैं? किन्तु आज अर्द्धशताब्दी के पश्चात् संसार उनकी वास्तविकता को कुछ-कुछ समझने लगा है। पाश्चात्य विद्वानों की दृष्टि से स्वामीजी एक नवयुग-प्रवर्त्तक हैं, तो भारतीय जनता की दृष्टि से प्रबल एवं उच्च कोटि के धर्मप्रवर्त्तक अथवा धर्मोद्धारक हैं। स्वामीजी ने धर्म के मूल अविकृत स्वरूप को संसार के सम्मुख रक्खा, इसलिये जनता ने उनको वैसा समझा, तो कोई आश्चर्य की बात नहीं। स्वामीजी का जन्म हुआ था, तब भारत में पाश्चात्य सभ्यता का प्रवेश होने लगा था। जब स्वामीजी कार्यक्षेत्र में उतरे, तब उस सभ्यता ने अपने पैर अच्छी तरह जमाने प्रारंभ किये थे। उस समय पौरस्त्य सभ्यता के पैर उखड़ने लगे थे। उस सभ्यता के उपासक तो असंख्य थे, किन्तु उसके सच्चे रक्षक कोई नहीं थे। उस सभ्यता का रक्षक व पोषक साम्राज्य तो नष्ट-भ्रष्ट हो ही चुका था। पाश्चात्य सभ्यता की पीठ पर प्रबल साम्राज्य था। पाश्चात्य सभ्यता का पोषक विज्ञानयुग था। इस अवस्था में भारतवर्ष की वैसी दशा थी, जैसे—

प्रसुप्तमिव सर्वतः।

स्वामीजी कार्यक्षेत्र में उतरे, तब उनके सम्मुख दो प्रश्न थे—एक स्वधर्मरक्षा, दूसरा राष्ट्रनिर्माण। भारतीय तथा पाश्चात्य विद्वानों ने स्वामीजी को संकुचित दृष्टि से देखा था, इसलिये स्वामीजी को वे पूर्ण रूप से नहीं पहिचान सके, किन्तु अब जिस प्रकार स्वामीजी के विषय में चर्चा चल रही है, उससे स्पष्ट प्रतीत हो रहा है कि संसार का दृष्टिकोण बदलता जा रहा है। वर्त्तमान राष्ट्रीय आन्दोलन स्वामीजी की मृत्यु के पश्चात् की वस्तु है और आन्दोलन के आन्दोलक और उनके राष्ट्रनिर्माण के उपाय विशेष प्रकार के रहे हैं। स्वामीजी को राष्ट्र-निर्माण के साथ-साथ स्वसंस्कृति की रक्षा की भी प्रबल इच्छा थी। स्वसंस्कृति की रक्षा स्वधर्म के विना नहीं हो सकती। स्वामीजी भारतीय राष्ट्र-निर्माण का कार्य भी स्वसंस्कृति के आधार पर करना चाहते थे,

इसीलिये उनका प्रारम्भिक कार्यकाल स्वसंस्कृति के पुनरुज्जीवन में गया, जिसपर वे भारतीय भव्य भावनाओं का सुन्दर राष्ट्र-निर्माण देखना चाहते थे। पचास वर्ष पश्चात् आज स्वामी दयानन्द संसार के सम्मुख अन्य रूप में हैं। वर्त्तमान राष्ट्र-निर्माता भी अब स्वामीजी को राष्ट्र-निर्माता समझ रहे हैं और स्वामीजी की दूरदर्शिता को सराहते हैं। भारतीय राष्ट्र-निर्माण स्वसंस्कृति को छोड़कर नहीं हो सकता, इस तत्त्व को अब लोग समझने लगे हैं। व्यापक सार्वभौम धर्म का प्रसार, स्व-संस्कृति की रक्षा और स्वराष्ट्र-निर्माण—इन तीन पवित्र कार्यों की पूर्त्ति के लिये ही स्वामीजी का जन्म था। आज स्वामीजी जीवित होते, तो राष्ट्रीय आन्दोलन की प्रगति और ही प्रकार की होती। स्वामीजी भारतीय संस्कृति के पुनरुद्धार-द्वारा भारत को संसार का गुरु देखना चाहते थे। वे पहले भारत का भूमण्डल में Cultural Empire (सांस्कृतिक साम्राज्य) देखना चाहते थे और पश्चात् सर्वत्र भूमण्डल में वैदिक पद्धति का साम्राज्य, अधिराज्य अथवा महाराज्य बनाना चाहते थे। स्वसंस्कृति-विहीन राष्ट्र-निर्माण को वे कुछ भी महत्त्व नहीं देना चाहते थे। आज कवीन्द्र रवीन्द्र जिस सांस्कृतिक स्वराज्य का सुख-स्वप्न देख रहे हैं, पचास वर्ष पूर्व स्वामीजी उसी स्वराज्य—नहीं साम्राज्य—की आधार-शिला रख चुके थे। आज भारतीय राष्ट्र-नायक जिन उपायों को काम में ला रहे हैं, स्वामी दयानन्द उनके विषय में पहले ही लिख गये थे। इस प्रकार देखा जाय, तो स्वामीजी को भारतीय राष्ट्र-निर्माताओं का जनक कहना चाहिये। आधुनिक राष्ट्र-निर्माता नई ईंटों से नया राष्ट्र-भवन बनाना चाहते हैं। स्वामीजी कहते थे कि घर में ही प्रचुर मात्रा में पुराना पक्का मसाला पड़ा हुआ है, पुरानी पक्की बुनियाद पर ही उस मसाले से सुंदर राष्ट्र-भवन बन सकता है, इसीलिये नई ईंटों की, नये मसालों की, आवश्यकता नहीं है। पाश्चात्य सभ्यता के उपासक स्वामीजी का उपहास उड़ाते रहे, भारतीय जनता भी स्वामीजी का उपहास उड़ाती रही, किन्तु अब स्वामीजी अपने सुन्दर, सुडौल किन्तु भव्य रूप में दिखलाई पड़ रहे हैं और संसार चकित है कि उसने स्वामी दयानन्द को समझने में इतनी भूल क्यों की? उस समय संसार यदि स्वामी दयानन्द को न समझ सका, तो इतने आश्चर्य की बात नहीं है। सबसे बड़ा आश्चर्य यह है कि स्वामी दयानन्द के अनुयायी भी अब तक स्वामीजी के पूर्ण स्वरूप को नहीं समझ सके हैं। उनका वह दिव्य, तेजस्वी राष्ट्र-निर्माण-कार्य

ऐसे निस्तेज लोगों के हाथों में पड़ा है कि उसको देखकर कभी-कभी घोर निराशा होने लगती है, पर स्वामीजी के उस तेजस्वी कार्य को उनके अनुयायियों से भिन्न लोग अपना रहे हैं। यह भी कम आश्चर्य की बात नहीं है। स्वामीजी का भारतीय राष्ट्र-निर्माण-कार्य अथर्ववेद के निम्नलिखित मंत्र की पद्धति पर प्रचलित हुआ है—

भद्रमिच्छन्त ऋषयः स्वर्विदस्तपो दीक्षामुपनिषेदुरग्रे ।
ततो राष्ट्रं बलमोजश्च जातं तदस्मै देवा उपसंनमन्तु ॥

जब राष्ट्र छिन्न-भिन्न हो जाता है, उसकी मान-मर्यादा का रक्षक और पोषक कोई नहीं रहता, तब उसकी मानमर्यादा के रक्षक उस जाति और राष्ट्र के नायक ही होते हैं। वे राष्ट्रोद्धारार्थ तप की दीक्षा लेते हैं, तब छिन्न-भिन्न राष्ट्र में प्राण-संचार होता है, तब राष्ट्र में बल आता है, तब उसका ओज बढ़ता है, तब उसको पुनः गत वैभव प्राप्त होता है, तब उसकी मानमर्यादा ठिकाने आ जाती है; राष्ट्रोद्धार के लिये देवों को—नेताओं को—इसी उपाय का अवलम्बन करना चाहिये। राष्ट्र के पुरोहितों का यही धर्म है।

सत्यार्थप्रकाश में देश की दुर्दशा के विषय में स्वामीजी के जितने भी उद्गार मिलते हैं, उनसे स्पष्ट है कि स्वामीजी भारत को भव्य भारत बनाने के लिये कितने उत्कण्ठित थे, इस विषय में उनकी अन्तर्ज्वालाएँ कितनी प्रदीप्त थीं, उनकी हृदय-वेदनाएँ कितनी तीव्र थीं, उनका अन्तर्नाद किस प्रकार गूँज रहा था, उनकी बाह्य गर्जना भी कैसी डरावनी थी। उनका स्वराज्य आधुनिक स्वराज्य नहीं था, उनका स्वराज्य औपनिवेशिक स्वराज्य भी नहीं था। उनका स्वराज्य था, 'स्व' में अपना जो कुछ है उस सबको लेकर। इसीलिये यह कह सकते हैं कि उनका स्वराज्य सच्चे अर्थों में पूर्ण स्वराज्य था, सच्चे अर्थों में 'स्व'—'तन्त्र' अर्थात् पूर्ण रूप में अपने अधीन रहनेवाला सर्वाङ्गपरिपूर्ण स्वराज्य था। आजकल के 'स्वराज्य' शब्द के साथ जब तक 'कम्प्लीट' (पूर्ण) शब्द न लगे, तब तक उसका ठीक अर्थ ही नहीं बैठता। उसके साथ 'कम्प्लीट' शब्द लगाने पर भी वह अर्थ नहीं आता अथवा लगता जो स्वामी दयानन्द के स्वराज्य शब्द में है। इसलिये स्वामी दयानन्द न केवल सच्चे राष्ट्र-निर्माता हैं, अपितु राष्ट्र-निर्माताओं के जनक हैं। उनका राष्ट्र अथर्ववेद-वर्णित 'राष्ट्र' है, जो संपूर्ण दीप्ति का बोधक है, जिसमें यजुर्वेद-वर्णित (अष्टादशाध्याय) समस्त अर्थ का निवेश है—

सत्यं च मे श्रद्धा च मे जगच्च मे धनं च मे विश्वं च मे
महश्च मे क्रीडा च मे मोदश्च मे जातं च मे जनिष्यमाणं च मे

(यजुः–१८, ५)

स्वामीजी के 'स्वराज्य' शब्द में इतने व्यापक अर्थ का सन्निवेश था।

उनका विश्वबन्धुत्व भी–

देहि मे ददामि ते नि मे धेहि नि ते दधे।
निहारं च हरासि मे निहारन्निर्हराणि ते स्वाहा॥ (यजुः)

इस व्यापक अर्थ को लिये हुए था। आजकल का 'स्वराज्य' शब्द स्वधर्म की कल्पना को छोड़े हुए है, आजकल का 'स्वराज्य' स्वसंस्कृति की परवाह नहीं कर रहा है; आजकल का 'स्वराज्य', साम्राज्य, अधिराज्य अथवा महाराज्य सर्वथा नये रूप में नये अर्थ को धारण कर रहा है, जिसमें 'स्व' अत्यन्त संकुचित हो गया है। 'राज्य' शब्द वह भाव नहीं रख रहा है। स्वामीजी का "स्वराज्य" शब्द सोलह आने 'स्व' को रखता है। उसमें से एक पाई भी घटी कि उसका वह अर्थ नहीं रहता। स्वामी दयानन्द ऐसे सच्चे स्वराज्य व स्वराष्ट्र के निर्माता थे। उनको केवल धर्मोद्धारक, समाज-सुधारक, रिफ़ॉर्मर, देशोद्धारक, धर्माचार्य आदि कहना उनका अपमान करना है। प्रसुप्त भारत को प्रबुद्ध भारत बनाकर उसके द्वारा संसार को सुख, शान्ति और समृद्धि का आगार बनाने की प्रबल इच्छा रखनेवाले स्वामी दयानन्द की महत्ता को संसार अब जान गया है। इस मृत्युञ्जय अर्द्धशताब्दी के उपलक्ष्य में यह लेखक अपनी श्रद्धाञ्जलि को समर्पण करने के लिये ही इन पंक्तियों को लिख रहा है–**लेखक स्पष्ट अनुभव कर रहा है कि स्वामीजी का 'मिशन' सफल हो रहा है,** चाहे वह किसी द्वारा सफल क्यों न हो रहा हो। साथ ही वह करुणानिधान भगवान् से प्रार्थना कर रहा है कि स्वामीजी के अनुयायियों में उनके मिशन के योग्य तपोदीक्षा का प्रवेश हो, उनका हृदय उनके महान् उद्देश्य के अनुरूप ही विशाल हो। प्रतिध्वनि आरही है—"हाँ ऐसा ही हो"।

ज्वालापुर

नरदेव शास्त्री

ऋषि दयानन्द और स्त्री-जगत्

ऋषि दयानन्द के जन्म के पूर्व से ही भारतवर्ष पाश्चात्य सभ्यता के रंग में रँगा जा रहा था, पर वह सभ्यता स्वामीजी के इच्छानुकूल न थी। पाश्चात्य सभ्यता में स्त्री-स्वातन्त्र्य की बड़ी चर्चा और बड़ी स्थिति है। सभ्य पाश्चात्य देवियों के सामने भारतीय स्त्रियाँ कुछ भी न थीं। सुशिक्षा से ही मनुष्य सभ्य तथा उन्नत होता है। उस सुशिक्षा का भारतीय देवियों में अभाव था। उन्हें न अपने कर्तव्य का ज्ञान था, न अधिकार का। उनकी अपनी कोई स्वतंत्र सत्ता न थी। उनका कार्य्यक्षेत्र अत्यन्त संकुचित था। उनका कोई आदर्श अथवा उद्देश्य न था। यदि उनका कुछ मान था, तो इसलिये कि वह बच्चों की माताएँ थीं; पुरुष बच्चों को प्यार करते ही हैं, इसलिये उस नाते से उन्हें भी प्यार करते थे। यद्यपि वस्तुतः ऐसी बात न थी, क्योंकि पढ़ी-लिखी न होने अथवा थोड़ी पढ़ी-लिखी होने पर भी भारतीय देवियाँ सुशिक्षिता, गृह-कार्य्य-निपुणा, उदार-हृदया और सदाचारिणी थीं, तथापि अंग्रेज़ी पढ़े-लिखे भारतीय उनके इन गुणों के ग्राहक न थे। वे पाश्चात्य ढंग की सहचरी चाहते थे।

स्वामी दयानन्द ने समस्त वैदिक और आर्ष वाङ्मय का गम्भीर अध्ययन किया था। प्राचीन वैदिक सभ्यता और संस्कृति एवं आर्ष विज्ञान का पुनर्जीवन उनके जीवन का ध्येय था। वे स्त्री-स्वातन्त्र्य के प्रबल समर्थक थे, पर उनके स्त्री-स्वातन्त्र्य का आदर्श वैदिक ऋषिकाओं और कौशल्या, सीता, सावित्री पर था। "पत्युर्नो यज्ञसंयोगे" (अष्टाध्यायी ४-१-३३), इस व्याकरण-सूत्र में उन्होंने पत्नी की पवित्रता के महत्त्व का पाठ पढ़ा था। निन्दक चाहे कुछ कहें, परन्तु श्रीमती रमाबाई को उन्होंने बड़े सम्मान से सम्बोधित किया है। एक बार एक नंगी बालिका मार्ग में उनके सामने आ गई। स्वामीजी ने 'मा' कहकर उसका सादर अभिवादन किया और नंगी बालिका को देखने के पाप का मा-मंत्र द्वारा प्रायश्चित्त कर दिया। स्त्रियों के सम्बन्ध में उनके उदार तथा उपयुक्त विचार संस्कारविधि और सत्यार्थप्रकाश आदि उनके ग्रन्थों में भरे पड़े हैं।

पाश्चात्य देशों में स्त्रियों के नाम तक तो स्वतंत्र नहीं होते, परन्तु फिर भी बहुधा लोग उनकी स्वतंत्रता के गीत गाते नहीं थकते। मिस्टर टॉमसन की स्त्री को मिसेज

टॉमसन और पुत्री को मिस टॉमसन कहा जाता है, पर महाराज दशरथ के स्वर्गवास हो जाने पर जब महाराज श्रीराम ने अश्वमेध यज्ञ किया, तो "एका वीरा च कौशल्या" आदि द्वारा रामचन्द्रजी का परिचय वीरा कौशल्या का पुत्र कहकर दिया गया। मिसेज़ टॉमसन नाम नहीं है, परिचयसूचक विशेषण है।

ऋषि दयानन्द की शिक्षा और प्रेरणा से ही स्त्री-शिक्षा और स्त्री-संस्थाओं का प्रचार हुआ, स्त्रियों को तुच्छ समझने और उनकी उपेक्षा करने की दुर्मति पर दुर्मट पड़ा, उन्हें वेदादि शास्त्र पढ़ने का अधिकार हुआ और फिर से पत्नी-पूजा प्रारम्भ हुई। अब देवियाँ राजनैतिक कार्यों में भी भाग लेकर अपनी दिव्य शक्ति का प्रकाश कर रही हैं। महर्षि दयानन्द ने भारत की आँखों पर पड़ी हुई पाश्चात्य सभ्यता की चकाचौंध को दूर कर स्त्री-विषयक अनुचित आदर्श को धकेल दिया। भारत की आधी शक्ति पंगुता त्याग कर जीवन-संग्राम में पुरुष का साथ दे रही है। भारत की स्त्री-शक्ति की जागृति पर ही भारत की जागृति निर्भर है और इसका परिणाम भारत की स्वाधीनता है। भारत की स्वाधीनता का स्वाभाविक प्रभाव संसार की शान्ति है।

भारतीय स्त्रीत्व का आदर्श सच्ची मा बनना है। मा अपने दूध के साथ सन्तान में जो भाव संचार कर देती है वे प्राणों के साथ ही निकलें तो निकलें, अन्यथा नहीं। स्वामी दयानन्द की शिक्षा का आदर्श भी अच्छी माताएँ बनाना है। अच्छी माताओं के बिना राष्ट्रों का उद्धार नहीं हो सकता, क्योंकि कोई जाति अपनी माता की ऊँचाई से ऊँची नहीं उठ सकती।

किन्तु खेद है कि हम स्वामी दयानन्द के आदर्श पर नहीं चल रहे हैं। हम अपनी रुचि को ही सर्वेसर्वा मानते हैं। आर्यसमाज का आदर्श स्वामी दयानन्द का आदर्श नहीं, विल्सन-टॉमसन का आदर्श हो गया। हमारी देवियों का आदर्श सीता-सावित्री नहीं, यूरोपियन नाटकों, थियेटरों में भाग लेनेवाली नाट्य-पात्रियाँ हैं। हम भारतीय स्त्री-स्वातन्त्र्य की डींग तो अवश्य मारते हैं, परन्तु व्यवहार हमारा सर्वथा उल्टा होता है।

जालन्धर

शन्नोदेवी

स्वामी दयानंद

मनुष्यत्व ही मनुष्य का धर्म है। जितना अधिक उच्च उद्देशयुक्त मनुष्यत्व का पालन किया जाय, उतना ही अधिक धर्म का पालन होना कहा जा सकता है। इस पृथिवी पर मनुष्य ही एकमात्र ऐसा जीव है जो धर्माधर्म, कर्तव्याकर्तव्य, उचित-अनुचित को समझने में समर्थ है। ईश्वर, प्रकृति, जीव, अजीव, उत्पत्ति, स्थिति, प्रलय, ज्ञान, विज्ञान, भक्ति, उपासना, इहलोक, परलोक, सामाजिक, आर्थिक, राजनैतिक, शक्ति, सामर्थ्य, पराक्रम, व्यवस्था, नियम, मर्यादा, वर्णव्यवस्था, कर्म-व्यवस्था, देशहित, जातिहित, संगठन इत्यादि सारे ही विषयों पर विचार करके उचित मार्ग का अवलम्बन और अनुचित का त्याग ही मनुष्यत्व है। 'धर्म' शब्द की यही व्याख्या हमारे पूर्वज महर्षियों ने मानी है।

यूरोप में अर्थवाद या पूँजीवाद ही प्रधान है। यूरोप में ईश्वर का स्थान तो टका भगवान् ने ले लिया है और परलोक का स्थान सांसारिक सुख और भोगविलासिता ने ले लिया है।

भारतवर्ष की अवस्था यूरोप की अवस्था से सदा भिन्न रही है। भारतवर्ष में सदा से अवतार, ऋषि, मुनि, महात्मा और महान् पुरुष होते आए हैं, जिन्होंने पारलौकिक और इहलौकिक दोनों विषयों को साथ लिया है और दोनों ही विषयों के व्यवहार करने का समान उपदेश दिया और सच्चा मार्ग बताया है। जब तक उनके बताए हुए मार्ग पर चलता रहा, तब तक यह देश उन्नति के शिखर पर बना रहा। समय सदा एकसा नहीं रहता। जब उनके बताए मार्ग को भारतीय आर्य भूलने लगे, तब उसमें विकृति उत्पन्न हुई और देश गिरने लगा। ज्ञान-विज्ञान-मूलक उपासना, पूजा, अर्चना, वर्णव्यवस्था, आश्रमव्यवस्था, आर्थिक, सामाजिक, धार्मिक, राजनैतिक आर्यत्व के वास्तविक रूप को भूलकर मिथ्या विश्वास, अंधविश्वास, मिथ्याभिमान, संदेहशीलता और भ्रम ने स्थान ले लिया; वास्तविक बातों को लोग भूल गये और अनुचित मार्ग का अवलंबन कर पतन की ओर चल पड़े। ऐसे समय में भगवान् ने महर्षि दयानन्द को जन्म दिया। उन्होंने अपनी विद्या तथा बुद्धिबल से हिन्दू-जाति में धार्मिक और सामा-

जिक संशोधन का बड़ा आन्दोलन खड़ा कर दिया। उस वेग के सामने मिथ्या विश्वास, अंधविश्वास और मिथ्याभिमान न ठहर सके। उस वेग ने हमारी आर्य-जाति में धर्म के नाम से घुसे हुए अधर्म को उखेड़ दिया। मिथ्या विश्वास और भ्रम की नींद में पड़े हुए लोगों की आंखें खोलकर चेतन कर दिया और उनको धर्म और सामाजिक संशोधन के कार्य में लगा दिया। हिन्दू-जाति में आज जो धार्मिक तथा सामाजिक संशोधन नज़र आ रहा है वह महर्षि दयानन्दजी का ही आरंभ किया हुआ है। आज के ६० वर्ष पूर्व यदि स्वामीजी यह कार्य आरंभ ही न करते, तो हिन्दू-जाति में जो धार्मिक और सामाजिक संशोधन आज नज़र आ रहा है वह कभी नहीं आता। महर्षि दयानन्द ने जन्म लेकर यह सिद्ध कर दिया कि उच्च मनुष्यत्व का निभाना ही मनुष्य-धर्म है। अब भी हिन्दू-जाति में धर्म की ओट में अधर्म करनेवाले गुरु, आचार्यों और पण्डे-पुजारियों की कमी नहीं है, परन्तु स्वामीजी ही के प्रभाव से हिन्दू-जाति सचेत हो गई।

स्वामीजी के बनाए हुए सत्यार्थप्रकाश में पुरातन आर्य ऋषि-प्रणीत दार्शनिक, आध्यात्मिक विज्ञान विषय का अंश बहुत कम है, इससे यह न समझना चाहिये कि स्वामीजी इन विषयों से अविज्ञ थे। वास्तविक बात यह है कि इन उपर्युक्त विषयों की ओट में अधर्माचरण होने लग गया था। संशोधन करके इस अधर्म को निकाल देना स्वामीजी का उपदेश था, सो उन्होंने कर दिखाया।

श्रीरामकृष्ण परमहंस, स्वामी विवेकानन्द और स्वामी रामतीर्थ और विशेषतः ऋषि दयानन्द इस समय इस देश में जन्म न लेते, तो हमारी आर्यजाति अपना वास्तविक रूप भूलकर अंधकार से निकलकर प्रकाश में नहीं आ सकती थी।

खरवा

गोपालसिंह राष्ट्रकूट

The LATE R. B. TEJ NARAIN SINGH'S HOUSE AT BHAGALPUR
where Swami Dayanand Saraswati resided, and delivered public lectures in 20, October, 1872 A.D.

श्रद्धाञ्जलि

नवयुग के प्रवर्तक, संसार के सबसे महान् और सबसे पवित्र स्वातंत्र्य, ज्ञान, सत्य और प्रेम के प्रचारक, संसारोद्धारक, शुद्धि एवं दलितोद्धार के प्रबल प्रवर्तक, समाजसुधारक महर्षि दयानन्द सरस्वती की कीर्ति आज सारे संसार में फैल रही है। महर्षि ने २७ वर्ष तक भारत के बड़े-बड़े नगरों में घूमकर सच्चे वैदिक सिद्धान्तों का प्रचार कर निराश जनता को आशान्वित किया और कायरों को वीर बनाया। उनके दिव्य नाद से आज भी आर्य्यावर्त का कोना-कोना निनादित हो रहा है। उनके महान् उद्देश्यों को न समझकर मूर्ख लोगों ने उनका विरोध किया, उन्हें विष दिया, उनकी हत्या के लिये षड्यन्त्र रचे, कीचड़, ईंट, पत्थर फेंककर उन्हें अपमानित किया, परन्तु महर्षि दयानन्द इन सब अड़चनों से न घबराए। उस दयासिन्धु ने अपने शत्रुओं को क्षमा किया और धर्मप्रचार का कार्य्य अधिक तीव्रता से किया। उन्होंने आर्य्यसमाज स्थापित कर अमेरिका के परम विद्वान् 'एंड्रो जेक्सन डेविस' के शब्दों में रोग के स्थान में आरोग्य, झूठे विश्वास की जगह तर्क, वैर की जगह प्रेम, नरक के स्थान में स्वर्ग, दुःख के स्थान में सुख, पाप के स्थान में पुण्य और भूत-प्रेतों के स्थान में परमेश्वर की पूजा स्थापित की। आर्य्यसमाज का मिशन सारे संसार में सुख, शान्ति और आनन्द फैलानेवाला है। आर्य्यसमाज के दस नियमों में महर्षि ने अपने अपूर्व योगबल से सारे संसार के धर्मों की सर्वश्रेष्ठ बातें कूट-कूटकर भर दी हैं, ताकि सारे संसार के पुरुष आर्य्यसमाज के झंडे के नीचे आ सकें। अतः आर्य्यसमाज ही महर्षि का सच्चा स्मारक है और उसी की उत्तरोत्तर उन्नति से संसार का कल्याण होगा और महर्षि के उद्देश्यों की पूर्ति होगी। उनका संस्कृत का ज्ञान इतना गंभीर था कि न केवल भारत की पंडित-मंडली ने, बल्कि योरप के मोनियर विलियम्स, मैक्समूलर आदि विद्वानों ने उनकी विद्वत्ता की मुक्तकंठ से प्रशंसा की है। अब महर्षि के मिशन का देश-देशान्तरों और द्वीप-द्वीपान्तरों में प्रचार होगा और स्वतंत्र विचारों की वह लहर पैदा होगी जिससे दुःखी संसार की काया पलट कर संसार में सुख, शान्ति एवं सत्य का पूर्ण स्वराज्य स्थापित हो जायगा।

अजमेर

चांदकरण शारदा

स्वामी दयानंद

पूर्णता और प्राचीनता के विचार से शास्त्रों में वेद का स्थान सर्वोपरि है। इसी तरह धर्म और सभ्यता के विचार से भारत की आर्य-जाति का स्थान बहुत ऊँचा था; किन्तु मनुष्य प्रमाद, आलस्य या अपने अज्ञान के कारण धर्म से दूर चले जाते हैं। जब पाखंड या कपोल-कल्पित मत चलानेवाले स्वार्थियों के जाल में फँसकर धर्म को अधर्म मानने लग जाते हैं, तब संसार में दुःख और अशांति का ही साम्राज्य फैल जाता है, जैसा इस समय देखने में आ रहा है। अनुमान पाँच हज़ार वर्ष पहले भी जिस समय श्रीकृष्ण का जन्म हुआ, अत्याचारी और अभिमानी राजाओं के कारण धर्म में कुछ ग्लानि आ गई थी; उस समय उन्होंने अत्याचारियों का नाश करते हुए वेदों का सार श्रीभगवद्गीता के रूप में प्रकट किया था। उससे ढाई हज़ार वर्ष पश्चात् फिर अज्ञान-जन्य अंधभक्ति और विलासिता में फँसकर लोग पापाचार करने लग गये। तब भगवान् बुद्धदेव ने सच्चे आर्य-धर्म का प्रचार करने के लिये अंधभक्ति और विलासिता को दूर करने के लिये, विशेष प्रकार से अहिंसा, वैराग्य और प्रेम का उपदेश देते हुए लोगों को सन्मार्ग में लगाया था। उस समय तक भारतवर्ष तथा अन्य अधिकांश देशों में 'आर्य-धर्म' को ही माननेवाले रहते थे। भारत से ही आध्यात्मिक ज्ञान का स्रोत बहता रहता था। दूसरे देशों पर भी यहाँ की धार्मिक बातों का प्रभाव पड़ता था। इसलिये यहाँ पर जागृति होने पर अन्य देशों में भी एक प्रकार की नई लहर फैल जाती थी, जैसे भगवान् बुद्ध के पश्चात् भारत से बाहर अन्य देशों में भी उनके उपदेश शीघ्रता से फैल गये।

भगवान् श्रीकृष्ण और बुद्ध के समय की स्थिति भिन्न थी, इसलिये बुद्ध के उपदेश भी कुछ अंशों में भिन्न थे, किन्तु उन्होंने, आर्य सत्य बोलकर ही प्राकृत भाषा में उसी प्राचीन आर्य-धर्म का प्रचार किया था। भगवान् बुद्ध के पीछे अनुमान एक सहस्र वर्ष तक लोगों ने पर्याप्त सांसारिक और धार्मिक उन्नति की, किन्तु अति-दया और अति-वैराग्य की भावना बढ़ने से यहाँ का क्षात्र तेज लुप्त होता गया और भारत से बाहर दो नये पंथ उत्पन्न होने तथा किसी तरह उनका प्रभाव अनेक

देशों में पड़ने से स्थिति पलटती गई। वर्त्तमान समय की संसार की स्थिति बहुत पलट गई है। सच्चे धर्म की चर्चा नहीं के तुल्य रह गई है। भगवान् कृष्ण और बुद्ध के समय से भारतवर्ष बहुत अधोगति को चला गया है। बुद्ध के समय में देश बहुत संपन्न था, इसलिये भगवान् बुद्ध ने लोगों को मोक्ष, निर्वाण (जन्म-मरण, जरा-व्याधि के दुःखों से सदा के लिये छूटने) का ही उपदेश दिया था। ब्रह्मविद्या के दान से बढ़कर कोई दान नहीं, तब भी उस उपदेश के सभी अधिकारी नहीं होते; और इस समय तो लोगों को रोटी की इतनी चिंता है कि सब कुछ रोटी को ही समझने लग गये हैं। यद्यपि रोटी ही सब कुछ नहीं है, किन्तु "भूखे भक्ति न होइ गोपाला" वाली बात हो रही है। इन सब परिस्थितियों को विचारते हुए स्वामी दयानन्द ने पाखंड और अविद्या के नाश के लिये तथा इहलोक और परलोक की उन्नति के लिये वैदिक धर्म के आधार पर आर्यसमाजों की स्थापना की थी। धर्म की ग्लानि को मिटाने के लिये और आर्य हिन्दू-जाति को फिर से उन्नत करके संसार में धर्म का डंका बजाने के लिये आर्य्य-समाज की स्थापना हुई है। "यतो धर्मस्ततो जयः"। यदि आर्य्य लोग उत्साह और सचाई से धर्म की लगन से काम करते जायँ, तो निस्संदेह भारत में और संसार में सुख, शान्ति तथा धर्म के राज्य की स्थापना होगी। स्मरण रखना चाहिये कि आर्य-समाज का उत्तरदायित्व बहुत बड़ा है। यद्यपि अब तक आर्यसमाज ने जो कुछ सेवा की है, वह अच्छी है, किंतु जो गुरुतर कार्य हमें करना है वह बहुत बड़ा है। इसलिये इस अर्द्धशताब्दी के अवसर से लाभ उठाकर हमें कोई बड़ी योजना तैयार करनी चाहिये और लोगों को, विशेष त्याग की प्रतिज्ञा करते हुए, परमात्मा के भरोसे कार्य में जुट जाना चाहिये।

कलकत्ता

जुगलकिशोर बिड़ला

एकता का पोषक दयानन्द

हारनाक नामक एक जर्मन तत्त्ववेत्ता ने एक बार कहा था—"धर्म की शक्ति इस बात पर निर्भर नहीं है कि उसमें कितने सत्य का समावेश है, वह कितने सत्य का प्रचार करता है, वरन् इस बात पर कि उस धर्म में असत्य का कितना सम्मिश्रण है", अर्थात् वह धर्म ही धर्म है जिसमें असत्य का लेश भी न हो, और वह धर्म जिसमें सत्य की मात्रा अधिक होने पर भी असत्य कम नहीं है, धर्म नहीं कहा आ सकता। स्वामी दयानन्द ने इस तथ्य का अनुभव किया, और एकदम उस सम्पूर्ण धार्मिक साहित्य को, जिसका संदिग्ध मूल्य था और जो ऋषियों द्वारा प्रणीत न था, धार्मिक क्षेत्र से निकाल बाहर किया। इस विश्लेषण-क्रिया का फल यह हुआ कि केवल वेद ही धार्मिक ग्रंथ रह गये। इन वेदों में, उनका यह खुला चैलेंज था, कोई भी मिथ्यांश नहीं है। जॉन ने ईसा के विषय में कहा था कि अपने हाथ में पंखा लेकर उन्होंने गेहूं को भूसे से पृथक् कर दिया। यही काम स्वामी दयानन्द ने किया। उन्होंने वेद, शास्त्र, पुराणादि के ढेर से वे ग्रंथ-रत्न चुन लिये जिनमें उन्हें असत्य का आभास तक नहीं झलकता था। उन्हें आर्ष ग्रंथ कहकर प्रामाणिक माना और शेष को मानुषिक समझकर छोड़ दिया। हंस की तरह उन्होंने दूध को पानी से पृथक् कर दिया। ऋषि-महर्षि तो बहुतसे हुए हैं, किन्तु इस प्रकार का कार्य-संपादन कदाचित् ही किसी के द्वारा हुआ हो।

किन्तु यह किया क्यों ? केवल इसलिये कि हिन्दू-समाज की भित्ति ऐसे सिद्धांतों पर स्थिर हो जिनमें मिथ्यात्व का किंचित् भी सम्मिश्रण न हो। वे हिन्दुओं को एक केंद्र पर लाकर संगठित करना चाहते थे। अतः उन्होंने धार्मिक क्षेत्र में ऐसे अमूल्य सत्यपूर्ण ग्रंथ-रत्नों को चुना जिन्हें सब हिन्दू मानते अवश्य थे, किन्तु अन्य मनुष्यकृत ग्रंथ-जाल में फँसकर उनकी केवल मौखिक प्रशंसा किया करते थे। अतः उन्होंने मत-मतान्तर-रूपी भिन्न शाखा-प्रशाखाओं को सींचने का ध्यान छोड़ उनके मूल वैदिक सिद्धान्तों का सिंचन किया। किसी भी जाति की समष्टिरूप उन्नति के लिये प्रथम सैद्धांतिक एकता की आवश्यकता है। अतः यह उनका प्रथम मुख्य कार्य हुआ।

मूर्तिपूजा की ओर उनका ध्यान पहले से ही आकृष्ट हो चुका था। उनका विश्वास हो गया था कि मूर्तिपूजा जाति की विभिन्नता का स्रोत है। उन्होंने देखा कि विशाल-काय हिन्दू-समाज के अंगों का पारस्परिक सम्बन्ध शिथिल होता जा रहा है और एक ईश्वर को न मानकर नाना प्रकार के देवी-देवताओं की मूर्तियाँ स्थापित हो रही हैं। कुशल चितेरे भिन्न-भिन्न प्रकार के सुंदर चित्र बनाकर भोले-भाले हिन्दुओं से पुजवा रहे हैं। कहीं विष्णु की मूर्ति का पूजन है, तो कहीं शिव की। कहीं राम की मनोहर मूर्ति धनुष-बाण लिये खड़ी है, तो कहीं गिरिधारी कृष्ण की। कहीं पर्वत उठाए हनुमान चले जाते हैं, तो कहीं शेषशायी विष्णु लक्ष्मी सहित लेटे हुए हैं। भिन्न-भिन्न प्रकार की प्रतिमाएं मन्दिरों में स्थापित हो गईं और भिन्न-भिन्न समूहों में उन प्रतिमाओं के पुजारी विभक्त हो गये। हिन्दू-समाज के अंग-प्रत्यंग कट-कटकर गिरने लगे। एकेश्वर को भूलकर मनुष्य प्रतिमा-जाल में फँस गये। एक-दूसरे के प्रति इस कारण अश्रद्धा उत्पन्न होने लगी कि वे भिन्न मूर्ति के उपासक हैं। सब अपनी-अपनी डफली पीटने लगे। स्वामी दयानन्द ने देखा कि मूर्तिपूजा के वृक्ष पर फूट और अनेकता के फल लग रहे हैं। उन्होंने यह भी समझ लिया कि यह वृक्ष है बलवान्, और उसकी जड़ें बहुत नीचे तक पहुँची हुई हैं; पर इसकी उन्होंने कुछ भी परवाह न की और अपनी पूरी शक्ति से उसपर कुठाराघात करना प्रारम्भ कर दिया—मूर्ति-पूजा को धर्मविरुद्ध, वेदविरुद्ध और बुद्धिविरुद्ध बतलाकर हिन्दुओं में उसके प्रति अरुचि उत्पन्न करना आरम्भ कर दिया। साथ ही उनका निरंतर उद्योग रहा कि अमूर्त परमेश्वर ही उपास्य है। एक ईश्वर के नाते सम्पूर्ण जाति को एक सूत्र में बाँधने के लिये उन्होंने महान् प्रयत्न किया। समाज के संगठन का उनका यह दूसरा मुख्य कार्य था।

जातिगत वर्णव्यवस्था का आश्रय पाकर कितने ही उपवर्ण उत्पन्न हो गये थे। उनमें न तो अंतर्भोजन ही हो सकता था, और न अंतर्विवाह। एक उपजाति के मनुष्य दूसरी उपजाति के मनुष्यों से उस तरह प्रेमपूर्वक व्यवहार न करते थे, जिस तरह वह अपने जाति-बांधवों से मिलते थे। इसका फल यह हुआ है कि पारस्परिक प्रेम के स्थानापन्न ईर्ष्या और कलह हो गये। हिन्दुओं की संख्या अंतर्जातीय विवाह न होने के कारण बहुत कम होती जाती थी। योग्य वर और कन्याओं के न मिलने से विवाह

का फल अच्छा न होता था। स्वामी दयानन्द ने देखा कि इन सैकड़ों जाति-उपजातियों के चक्र में पड़कर हिन्दू-समाज नाशोन्मुख हुआ जा रहा है। अतः योग्य चिकित्सक की तरह उन्होंने जातिगत वर्णव्यवस्था के उच्छेद का बीड़ा उठाया। इस एक कार्य से उन्होंने समझा कि ऊँच-नीच और छूतछात के भाव स्वतः ही जाते रहेंगे और हिन्दू-समाज एक ऐसे दृढ़ चट्टान पर स्थिर हो जायगा कि वहाँ से उसे विचलित करना असंभव-सा होगा। यह स्वामीजी का हिन्दू-समाज में एकता लाने का तीसरा कार्य था।

देश में उस समय न तो कोई एक संस्कारपद्धति थी, न एक सन्ध्याविधि। न भाषा एक थी, न वेष। प्रत्येक बात में इतनी विभिन्नता देखकर उन्होंने सोचा कि किस प्रकार भारतीय राष्ट्र एक सूत्र में बँध सकता है। उन्होंने पर्याप्त परिश्रम किया और वेदों का मथन करके संस्कारविधि नामक विख्यात ग्रंथ तैयार किया। उन्होंने सब वर्णों के लिये एक संध्या बनाई, जिसे वेदों का संकर्ष कहा जाय, तो अत्युक्ति न होगी। उन्होंने प्रत्येक आर्य के लिये यज्ञोपवीत का विधान किया। गुजराती होते हुए भी उन्होंने हिन्दी भाषा को राष्ट्रभाषा का पद दिया। अपने सम्पूर्ण ग्रंथ हिन्दी भाषा में लिखकर उन्होंने हिन्दी का सम्मान किया। उन्होंने 'सीताराम', 'जयरामजी की', 'जय राधाकृष्ण', 'नमस्कार', पालागन' आदि विभिन्न अभिवादनों का खंडन कर एक अभिवादन–'नमस्ते'–की योजना की। इससे अधिक ऐक्य-स्थापन के लिये बाह्य और आभ्यन्तरिक साधन और क्या हो सकते थे? किस प्राचीन मंत्रद्रष्टा ऋषि ने, किस प्राचीन शक्तिशाली राजा ने, अथवा किस अर्वाचीन सामाजिक या धार्मिक नेता ने इस दिशा में किंचित् भी उल्लेखनीय कार्य किया है? भारत का दुर्भाग्य! उनका जीवन चिरस्थायी न हो सका।

ऐसे देश के अनन्य सेवक, धर्मतत्त्व-विज्ञाता, विभिन्नता के शत्रु, एकता के पोषक महर्षि दयानन्द के अनुयायी भी पग-पग पर यदि उनका क्रियात्मक अनुकरण करते, तो भारत के लिये कितना अच्छा होता।

अजमेर

देवकीनन्दन शर्मा

नवयुग का निर्माता

आज अर्द्ध-शताब्दी बीत रही है। आज के दिन नवयुग के निर्माता और भारतीय जागृति के जन्मदाता एक अवधूत संन्यासी ने देशोद्धार के यज्ञ-कुण्ड में अपने प्राणों की पूर्णाहुति दी थी। वह युग-प्रवर्तक महापुरुष था और उसके जीवन में कृष्ण के प्रेम और धैर्य्य का, बुद्ध की अहिंसा और संयम का तथा ईसा की दया और क्षमा का अद्भुत संयोग हुआ था। वह निर्बलों का बल, निर्धनों का धन, अनाथों का आश्रय, दासता का दुश्मन और मनुष्यता की विलक्षण शक्ति था। कभी वह हिमालय की चोटियों पर बर्फ़ों से टकराता, कभी वह आबू के जंगलों में विचरण करता और कभी गङ्गा की रेत पर टहलता हुआ सोचा करता कि इस महादेश का उद्धार कैसे होगा। वह अपनी आँखों से देखता कि आर्य्यावर्त की फुलवारी मुरझा गई है, मतलबी मनुष्यों ने उसे पैरों तले रौंद डाला है, कहीं पल्लव टूटे पड़े हैं, कहीं कलियाँ धूल में लोट रही हैं, कहीं कोई फूल दिखाई भी देते हैं, तो उनमें सुगन्ध नहीं; रस चखनेवाले भौंरे तड़फड़ा रहे हैं, पक्षियों के घोंसले उजड़ गये हैं, कोयलों की कुहुक में करुण क्रन्दन और मोरों की ध्वनि में अन्तर्वेदना है। जहाँ इन्द्रपुरी को मात करनेवाली नगरियाँ थीं, वहाँ आज खँडहर खड़े-खड़े रो रहे हैं, जहाँ ऋषियों के आश्रम थे वहाँ गिद्ध और सियारों के अड्डे हैं। हिमाचल और विन्ध्याचल यद्यपि वैसे ही सिर उठाए खड़े हैं; गंगा, यमुना और शोण की धाराएँ भी वैसी ही बह रही हैं, किन्तु वैदिक युग का वह आर्यावर्त कहाँ चला गया? शरीर तो वही है, पर रंग-रूप बिलकुल बदल गया है। इस अवस्था को देखकर उस महापुरुष के मुख से दर्दभरी आहें निकल पड़तीं। फिर वह सोचता कि संसार में ऐसे उथल-पुथल हुआ ही करते हैं, चीन की ऊँची-ऊँची दीवारें आज बड़े-बड़े नरेशों की समाधि पर चौकीदार का काम कर रहीं हैं, मिश्र की मीनारें आज वहाँ के बादशाहों के मसाले-भरे मृत-शरीरों को दबाये हुए खड़ी हैं; रोम, यूनान, बेबिलोनिया और स्कैंडिनेविया की पुरातन सभ्यताएँ आज कहाँ हैं? किन्तु अभी तक आँधी के अनेक झकोरे खाने पर भी वृद्ध आर्यावर्त किसी-न-किसी रूप में जीवित तो है और उसकी संस्कृति की रक्षा करना

मानो ईश्वरीय आदेश का पालन करना है। वह लँगोटधारी संन्यासी स्थान-स्थान पर जाता और निद्रित आर्य-जनता से कहता–उठो, अपने रूप को पहचानो। तुम उन्हीं ब्राह्मणों के वंशज हो जिनके तपोबल के सामने संसार सिर झुकाता था; उन्हीं क्षत्रियों के उत्तराधिकारी हो जिनके धनुष की टंकार से अधर्मी और अत्याचारी थरथर काँपते थे; उन्हीं वैश्यों के वारिस हो, जो सचाई, सरलता और ईमानदारी में अपना सानी नहीं रखते थे। आज तुम आत्म-विस्मृति के अन्धेरे में भटक रहे हो–तुम्हें न ओर सूझता है, न छोर। अब तुम्हें अपने हृदय को मज़बूत करके युद्ध-क्षेत्र में उतरना होगा और अत्याचारों से लड़ना होगा, वह चाहे अपना हो या पराया। अत्याचार सबसे बड़ा पातक है और पाप की निवृत्ति के विना देशोत्थान का कार्य सिद्ध नहीं हो सकता। पहले अपने ही अत्याचारों पर दृष्टि डालो, इसने तुमको इतना अन्धा बना दिया है कि तुम अपने ही शरीर के आधे अङ्ग पर ज़ुल्म ढा रहे हो। तुम्हारा हृदय न-जाने किस धातु का बना हुआ है, जो उनकी दुर्दशा को देखकर ज़रा भी नहीं पसीजता! तुमने अपने करोड़ों भाइयों को अछूत कहकर दुरदुराया और वह पाप कमाया, जिसका दूसरा दृष्टान्त मनुष्य-जाति के इतिहास में मिलना मुश्किल है। वह संन्यासी कहता–न ज़ुल्म करो और न ज़ुल्म से डरो। सदियों से ग़ुलामी के पलने में पले हुए मनुष्य उसका यह पैग़ाम सुनकर घबड़ा जाते और कहते–यह तो नया मत है, नवीन विचार है, हम इसे कैसे मानें? वह जवाब देता–यह कोई मेरा अभिमत नहीं है; यह तो वेदों की आज्ञा है, शास्त्रों का आदेश है, ऋषियों का वचन है। लोग उसे गाली देते, पत्थर मारते, अपमान करते, किन्तु वह किसी पर क्रोध न करता, दुर्वचन नहीं कहता, शाप नहीं देता, प्रत्युत देता था मङ्गलमय आशीर्वाद। उसके ललाट पर रेखाङ्कित था–"नवीन भारत का निर्माता" और उसका नाम था "महर्षि दयानन्द"।

सदियों के बाद आर्य माता को एक सपूत मिला था। उसके उठ जाने से मातृ-भूमि पर मानो वज्र टूट पड़ा। ऋषि दयानन्द के जीवन का यही उद्देश्य था कि वैदिक धर्म और आर्य-संस्कृति के प्रचार द्वारा आर्यावर्त का वर्त्तमान मानचित्र बदल दिया जाय और उसे दासता एवं परवशता के बंधन से छुड़ाया जाय, फिर चाहे वह धर्म के रूप में हो, सामाजिक रूढ़ियों के रूप में हो अथवा चाहे किसी अन्य रूप में हो। केवल इतना ही नहीं, प्रत्युत ऋषि की यह भी अभिलाषा थी कि संसार के कोने-कोने में वैदिक

धर्म और आर्य-संस्कृति का सन्देश पहुँचा दिया जाय । मैं देखता हूँ कि ऋषि की यह मनोकामना पूर्ण हो रही है । आर्यावर्त में आज आत्म-विस्मृति-रूप यामिनी का चतुर्थ प्रहर बीत रहा है और आत्म-विश्वास, आत्म-सम्मान एवं आत्मोत्सर्ग का उषाकाल प्राची दिशा में दृष्टिगोचर हो रहा है । अब यह विश्वासपूर्वक कहा जा सकता है कि आर्य्यावर्त का भविष्य आशाजनक, उज्ज्वल और मंगलमय है ।

जिस प्रकार बौद्ध भिक्षुओं ने जावा, सुमात्रा, बाली, लम्बक, कम्बोडिया, सिंहल, श्याम, बर्मा, लङ्का, चीन, जापान आदि देशों में आर्य-संस्कृति का प्रचार कर प्राचीन विशाल भारत की स्थापना की थी, उसी तरह दयानन्द के भक्तों ने नेटाल, ट्रांसवाल, पोर्चुगीज़, ईस्ट अफ्रीका, टंगेनिका, ज़ंज़िबार, यूगांडा, केनिया, मोरिशस, फिजी, ट्रिनीडाड, डेमरारा, सुरीनाम आदि देशों में वैदिक धर्म और आर्य-संस्कृति का सन्देश पहुँचाकर नवीन विराट् भारत की बुनियाद डाल दी है । अखिल भारतवर्षीय आर्य-कुमारपरिषद् के ग्यारहवें अधिवेशन के लिये दीन-बंधु सी. एफ़. एण्ड्रूज़ ने जो सन्देश भेजा था वह मेरे दावे का समर्थक है । आपने लिखा था–

"पृथ्वी के हर भाग में मुझे ऐसे नवयुवक और नवयुवतियाँ मिले, जिन्होंने श्रद्धा-पूर्वक आर्यधर्म में शिक्षा पाई है–ऐसे पुरुष और स्त्रियाँ जिन्होंने स्वामी दयानन्द के जीवन से ईश्वरीय प्रेरणा ग्रहण की है । मैं उनसे स्वयं मिला हूँ और अपने ज्ञान से लिखता हूँ । इस पत्र द्वारा मैं साक्षी देना चाहता हूँ कि उनका धर्म उनके लिये एक जीता-जागता ईश्वरीय ज्ञान रहा है। अपनी मातृभूमि से सहस्रों मील दूर रहकर भी इन युवा स्त्री-पुरुषों ने मनुष्य-जाति के प्रति अपने कर्तव्य को नहीं भुलाया, किन्तु लगातार अगणित प्रलोभनों के होते हुए भी अपने आर्यधर्म पर अटल रहे । यह मुझे एक विचित्र बात प्रतीत हुई, क्योंकि इन दूर देशों में जो कुछ मैंने अपनी आँखों से देखा, उससे मुझे ज्ञात हुआ कि कितने कम लोग अपनी बाल्यावस्था की धार्मिक शिक्षा पर दृढ़ रहते हैं और कितने अधिक लोग अपने धर्म को परित्याग कर अनात्मवादी हो जाते हैं, धन और सम्पत्ति की पूजा करते और बहुधा भ्रष्ट मार्ग के पथिक बन जाते हैं; परन्तु, जैसा मैंने ऊपर कहा है, आर्यसमाज के सभासदों ने इन प्रलोभनों का डटकर मुक़ाबला किया है।"

दक्षिण अफ़्रीका — भवानीदयाल संन्यासी

मेरे पूज्य पिता और महर्षि दयानन्द

मेरे पूज्यपाद पिताजी अपनी बाल्यावस्था से ही धार्मिक विषयों में अद्‌भुत वृत्ति रखते थे। बाल्य-काल में जब वे अपने दादा के मंदिर में जाते, तब अवसर पाकर मंदिर में घुस जाते और ठाकुरजी का खिलौना बनाकर खेला करते। कभी-कभी शालिग्राम को मंदिर के बाहर ले आते और लोगों के मना करने पर पूछते कि मंदिर से बाहर निकलकर भगवान् नाराज़ क्यों होते हैं ?

वंशपरंपरागत नियमों के अनुसार उनको कई आचार्यों से नाम सुनना पड़ा, कंठी बँधानी पड़ी और राज्यारूढ़ होने के अनन्तर बहुतसे सांप्रदायिक संस्कार, जो उस समय आवश्यक समझे जाते थे, कराने पड़े।

इस संस्कार-संघर्ष से उनकी आत्मतुष्टि तो नहीं हुई, किन्तु उनमें सत्य-धर्म की खोज करने की प्रवृत्ति पैदा हो गई। वे हिन्दू-मत-मतान्तरों में मूल सिद्धान्त और तत्त्व की खोज करने लगे। उन्होंने ईसाई-धर्म के सिद्धान्तों को भी जानना चाहा। इस प्रकार मत-मतान्तरों के विभिन्न भावों को सुनकर और जानकर उनके हृदय में नास्तिकता के भाव उत्पन्न होने लगे थे।

वि० संवत् १९३८ में चित्तोड़ में महर्षि दयानन्द सरस्वतीजी से उनकी भेंट हुई। यह बात अक्षरशः सत्य है कि जो जिसकी सच्ची लगन रखता है वह उसे अवश्य प्राप्त होता है। पिताश्री की धार्मिक जिज्ञासा बहुत प्रबल थी और वे सत्य-मार्ग ढूँढने को बहुत व्यग्र थे। उनकी वह इच्छा पूर्ण हुई।

महर्षि स्वामी दयानन्द चित्तोड़ के एक शिवालय में ठहरे हुए थे। जिज्ञासु ने पता लगा लिया। पहले ही दिन के सत्संग में स्वामीजी ने अपने सत्य-सिद्धान्त सुनाकर राजाधिराज को प्रभावित किया। पिताजी को भी आशा हो गई कि यह महात्मा मेरे संशयों को मिटाने का सामर्थ्य रखते हैं। फिर तो जबतक वहां ठहरना हुआ, नित्य सत्संग होने लगा। स्वामीजी के उपदेश में सत्य-ज्ञान की आभा नज़र आई। मन का भ्रम दूर होने लगा। तब पिताश्री के मन में इच्छा हुई कि महर्षि शाहपुरा में ठहरकर धर्मोपदेश द्वारा सत्य-मार्ग बताएं। महर्षि ने अधिकारी शिष्य की प्रार्थना स्वीकार कर ली।

RAJA DHIRAJ UMED SINGHJI BAHADUR
OF SHAHPURA

श्रीमहाराणा सज्जनसिंहजी बड़े गुणग्राही और धर्मनिष्ठ नरेश थे। महर्षि से उनकी भेंट भी चित्तोड़ में हुई। इस कथन में अतिशयोक्ति न होगी कि चित्तोड़ से ही पुरातन आर्य्य-विद्या का पुनः संस्करण हुआ।

वि० संवत् १९३९ में महर्षि ने अपने चरणों से शाहपुरा राज्य को पवित्र कर पिताश्री को वैदिक धर्म में दीक्षित किया। उनको योगसूत्र पढ़ाया, सांख्य की कारिकाएं सुनाईं और संसार के विविध मार्गों और वैदिक धर्म का अन्तर समझाया। पिताजी नित्य तीसरे पहर महर्षिजी के पास जाते, वार्तालाप करते और पढ़ते थे। फल यह हुआ कि नास्तिकवाद की तरफ़ झुकता हुआ उनका मन आस्तिकता की ओर आया और वे दृढ़ वैदिक धर्मानुयायी बन गए। तभी से उन्होंने अग्निहोत्र ग्रहण किया और उसे आजीवन निभाया।

महर्षि बालकों पर अत्यन्त स्नेह दिखलाया करते थे। उनके वात्सल्यभाव से मैं, जो उस समय बालक था, यह समझता कि मुझसे प्यार करनेवाला उन महात्मा से बढ़कर कोई नहीं है। पिताजी के रोकने पर भी स्वामीजी महाराज मेरा हाथ पकड़कर मुझे अपने पास बिठा लेते और बच्चों के समझने योग्य सरल तथा मीठे शब्दों में मुझे कहते—'खूब पढ़ना, धर्मात्मा बनना, न्याय करना' इत्यादि।

स्वामीजी क़रीब पौने तीन मास यहाँ रहे। रवानगी के समय महर्षि ने प्रसाद-रूपेण पिताजी को एक दुशाला दिया, वह अब तक मौजूद है। यह वस्तु मेरे लिये महर्षि की पुण्य-स्मृति है। इसको देखकर बाल्यकाल की वह सारी घटना, जिसे मैं महर्षि के समीप बैठकर देखा-सुना करता था, पुनः स्मरण हो आती है।

आर्य-बन्धुत्व के नाते पिताजी ने आप सब आर्य्य भाइयों को धर्मभ्राता समझा है। आप सब निकट ही के होकर रहे हैं। अतः आप उनके कार्यों से भली भाँति परिचित हैं। आप जो कुछ जानते हैं, मैं भी उतना ही जानता हूँ। इसपर भी कुछ विशेष कहना चाहूँ, तो यह कि मेरे पूज्य पिताजी ने अपने बैठने और सोने के कमरे में स्वामीजी के चित्र के सिवा और कुछ नहीं रक्खा। वे सदा उस चित्र को देखा करते, उनकी दी हुई पुस्तकें पढ़ते रहते और वैदिक स्वाध्याय करते। अपने जीवन-काल में उन्होंने बड़े-छोटे, खानदानी और बेखानदानी का कोई भाव नहीं रक्खा। 'वसुधैव कुटुम्बकम्' के सिद्धान्तानुसार वे सबको अपना कुटुम्बी समझते थे।

शाहपुरा

उम्मेदसिंह

श्रीस्वामी दयानन्द सरस्वती
और
हिन्दू-समाज के प्रति उनके उपकार

सामाजिक विप्लव-प्रेरकों में स्वामी दयानन्द सरस्वती के नाम का विशेष महत्त्व है। इस देश में जब धर्म के नाम पर कुरीतियों का और श्रद्धा एवं भक्ति के नाम पर पाखंड का पोषण किया जाता था, उस समय नवशिक्षा-प्राप्त नवयुवकों की स्थिति बड़ी डाँवाडोल थी। सामाजिक बहुमत और प्रचलित धर्म के आचार्य जिन कुरीतियों को मानने की शिक्षा देते आ रहे थे, वे सब कुरीतियाँ, नवशिक्षित युवकों की दृष्टि में, एक ऐसा बेहूदापन था जिसे दूर किये बिना उन लोगों की दृष्टि में हिन्दू-समाज का पतन अवश्यम्भावी था। कई एक नई रोशनीवाले, जो धर्म के नाम पर चलनेवाले पाखंड में श्रद्धा खो बैठे थे, येन केन प्रकारेण इस मायाजाल से निकलना चाहते थे, उनके लिये तो केवल एक ही मार्ग था, वह था धर्मान्तर होना। ऐसे समय में स्वामीजी का आविर्भाव हिन्दू-समाज के लिये महौषध का काम दे गया। राजा राममोहन राय ने भी ब्रह्म-समाज का प्रादुर्भाव करके नवशिक्षित हिन्दू-युवकों के लिये हिन्दू-समाज में टिके रहने की गुंजाइश कर दी थी, किन्तु राजा राममोहन राय ने अपना आधार केवल हिन्दू-संस्कृति को ही नहीं बनाया। उसके विपरीत स्वामीजी ने अपना झंडा केवल वेदों पर ही गाड़ा था। परिणाम यह हुआ कि ब्रह्म-समाज कुछ शहरी व्यक्तियों तक ही परिमित रह गया। आर्यसमाज ग्रामों तक भी पहुँच गया। स्वामी दयानन्दजी की तसवीर अशिक्षित ग्रामीणों के घरों में भी मिल सकती है। "आर्य-पंथी" शब्द गाँवों में घरेलू-सा बन गया है।

हिन्दू रीति-रस्मों की कुछ ऐसी विचित्रता है कि आवश्यकतानुसार इनका परिवर्तन होता रहा है। इसी खूबी ने हिन्दू-धर्म को आज तक जिंदा रक्खा। असल बात तो यह है कि हिन्दू-धर्म अन्य पंथों की तरह कोई पन्थ नहीं है। रूढ़ियों को चाहे भ्रम से आज लोगों ने धर्म मान रक्खा हो, किन्तु हिन्दू-धर्म का वस्तुतः रूढ़ियों से कोई सम्बन्ध नहीं है। बे-चोटी का बङ्गाली उतना ही हिन्दू है, जितना लम्बी-चोटी-वाला दक्षिणी ब्राह्मण। धर्म तो असल में "सत्य", "अस्तेय" आदि सदाचार पर

निर्भर रहा है, इसलिये समयानुसार रूढ़ियों के परिवर्तन करने में महापुरुषों को कभी मोह नहीं हुआ। ऐसे ही परिवर्तन-कर्त्ताओं में से एक स्वामी दयानन्द थे।

यह नहीं समझना चाहिये कि स्वामीजी के पूर्व-परिवर्तक क्रांतिकारी नहीं थे। बुद्ध से लेकर स्वामी दयानन्द तक जितने महापुरुष हुए, वे सभी क्रांतिकारी थे; किन्तु जब समय पलटता है, तो कल के क्रान्तिकारी आज के "सनातनी" बन जाते हैं। बात यह है कि मसीह या आचार्य का जीवन उसकी मृत्यु के बाद ही घड़ा जाता है और वह इस रद्दोबदल के साथ घड़ा जाता है कि कई एक अंशों में तो मसीह यदि कुछ शताब्दियों के बाद लौटकर आवे और अपना जीवन-चरित्र पढ़े, तो अपने असली और घड़े हुए जीवन-चरित्र में उसे पर्याप्त अन्तर मिल सकता है। न केवल जीवन-चरित्र में, किन्तु मसीह के नाम पर प्रचार किये जानेवाले विचारों में भी इतना परिवर्तन कर दिया जाता है कि उसके असली और प्रचार किये हुए विचारों में कोसों का अन्तर पड़ जाता है। इसके यह मानी नहीं कि यह परिवर्तन भद्दा ही होता है। प्रस्तुत कथन इतना ही है कि अनुयायी लोग अपने विचारों के अनुकूल एवं समय की गति के अनुकूल मसीह को लोकप्रिय बनाने का उद्योग करते रहते हैं और इसी सिलसिले में उसके जीवन और विचारों में भी अपने मनोनुकूल परिवर्तन कर डालते हैं। रामकृष्ण इस काटछाँट से न बचने पाए, बुद्ध का यही हाल हुआ। स्वामी रामानुज, जो अछूतों के सर्वश्रेष्ठ पक्षपाती थे और जिन्होंने अस्पृश्यों के सम्बन्ध में शायद सब आचार्यों से अधिक क्रांतिकारी आचरण किया, आज "छू मत"-पंथियों के भी (सत्यशोधक लोगों के तो हैं ही) परम आराध्य देव बन गये हैं। मानव-स्वभाव की यह विलक्षण प्रवृत्ति अवश्य ही दिलचस्प है। सौ वर्ष के बाद गान्धीजी का जीवनचरित्र किस रूप में होगा और अहिंसावाद का क्या रूप दिया जायगा, इसका तर्क बड़ा मनोरंजक मालूम पड़ता है।

आज के सनातनी समाज-सुधारक और नवयुवक आर्य-समाजियों में कुछ अन्तर नहीं रह गया है। नवयुवक आर्यसमाजी हवन और "संस्कारविधि" के विधि-निषेध के उतने पाबंद नहीं हैं, जितने उनके बाप-दादा थे, और न मूर्तिपूजा के खंडन में अपना समय नष्ट करते हैं। "शुद्धि" की चहल-पहल में महामना पं० मालवीयजी और श्रद्धेय स्वामी श्रद्धानन्दजी दोनों ही कन्धे जुटाकर चलते थे। ऐसी हालत में यह भेद कब तक निभेगा ?

आर्यसमाज और सुधारक-रूपी दो नाले साथ-साथ बह रहे हैं। बीच में एक पतली-सी भीत है, जो शीघ्र ही गिरना चाहती है । जहाँ वह गिरी, कि दोनों नाले गंगा बनकर साथ बहने लगेंगे और वह गंगा बृहत् हिन्दू-समाज-रूपी सागर में गिरी कि सब कुछ विलीन हुआ । यह बृहत् हिन्दूसमाज न-जाने कितनी गंगाओं को अपने में समाये बैठा है और इसको भी समा लेगा, इसमें कोई शङ्का नहीं । यही तो इसकी महत्ता है। इतिहास यही बताता है और वेद इसके साक्षी हैं—"सूर्याचन्द्रमसौ धाता यथापूर्वमकल्पयत्" । संसार का इतिहास कितना अद्भुत है !

नई दिल्ली — घनश्यामदास बिरला

ऋषि दयानन्द क्या चाहते थे ?

ऋषि दयानन्द ने, ब्रह्मचर्य्य का अखंड व्रत पालन करते हुए, उच्च स्वर से घोषणा की थी कि आर्य्यो ! यदि संसार में जीना है, तो ब्रह्मचर्य्य का आश्रय लो । ब्रह्मचर्य्य के बिना विश्वव्यापी जीवन-संग्राम में तुम विजेता न बन सकोगे ।

ब्रह्मचर्य्य एक यज्ञ है, जिसका पालन अत्यन्त ज्ञानवान् होकर ही किया जा सकता है । इस यज्ञ का पालन करने में ब्रह्मचारी के लिए आचार्य्य का आश्रय आवश्यक है। ब्रह्मचर्य्य का पालन कराने के लिये आचार्य ब्रह्मचारी से नियमपूर्वक ब्रह्मयज्ञ और देवयज्ञ करवाता है । ठीक उसी प्रकार राष्ट्र की विजय-कामना के इच्छुक हमारे पूर्वज आचार्य परमात्मा का आश्रय लेकर बड़े-बड़े यज्ञ किया करते थे, जिनमें अनेक दूर देशों से बड़े-बड़े विद्वान् आकर राष्ट्र को विजयी बनाने अथवा राष्ट्र के दोष मिटाने के प्रण किया करते थे ।

दूरदर्शी दयानन्द वही प्राचीन समय देखना चाहते थे । वे चाहते थे कि राष्ट्र का प्रत्येक व्यक्ति देवयज्ञ एवं ब्रह्मयज्ञ करता हुआ जीवन-संग्राम में विजयी बने और आर्य-राष्ट्र समय-समय पर बड़े-बड़े यज्ञों को करके अपने दोषों को भस्म करता हुआ कभी अवनत न हो । आर्य लोगों को चाहिये कि व्यष्टि और समष्टि-रूप में ब्रह्मचर्य्य का पालन करते हुए बड़े-बड़े यज्ञ करें, जिससे उनके देह या राष्ट्र को बिगाड़नेवाले दोष समूल नष्ट हो जायँ ।

अजमेर — कन्हैयालाल

PAROPKARINI SABHA'S GARDEN AT AJMER

Where Swamiji's Ashes were deposited

ہم نے خیال کیا مختصر طور پر گفتگو کرکے اجازت رخصت طلب کروں۔ کچہری بھی جانا ہے۔ اگر ممکن ہوا تو دوسرے وقت پھر آؤنگا۔ یہ سوچکر مینے عرض کیا کہ کیا جناب نے تاہل اختیار کیا۔ یعنی شادی کرلی۔ فرمایا تمنے کس اصول پر سمجھا کہ مینے شادی کرلی۔ مینے عرض کیا کہ آپ کپڑے سر سے پاؤں تک پہنے ہوئے گھرگرستیونکی صورت میں ہیں آگے تو آپ ایک لنگوٹ باندہے رہتے تھے اور بہت تیار تھے۔ اب دیکھتا ہوں کہ آپ بہت دبلے ہوگئے ہیں۔

سنکر کچھ خموش سے ہوگئے۔ اور فرمایا۔ مینے دنیاداری کی طرف توجہ نہیں کی ہے۔ اے امداد حسین جواب سنکر تمکو افسوس ہوگا۔ مجھکو تین بار زہر دیا گیا۔ بدن میرا بہت کمزور ہوگیا ہے۔ اسوجہ سے بدن کی حفاظت کرنیکے لئے مجبور ہوں۔ میں افسوس کرتے ہوئے بے اختیار تاسفانہ لہجہ کے ساتھ بول اٹھا۔ بس۔ اسی گاؤکشی کے لیکچر کا یہ نتیجہ ہوا۔ یہ مسلمانوں نے زہر دیا۔ فرمایا۔ ہرگز نہیں۔ ہندوؤں نے۔ مینے پوچھا کہاں۔ جہانتک یاد ہے فرمایا اسٹیٹ میں۔ میں پوچھنا چاہتا تھا کہ کس اسٹیٹ میں کہ آپ نے فرمایا کہ ایکبار تلوار سے بچ گیا مینے بے اختیار پوچھا۔ یہ کیونکر۔ آپنے کسی مقام کا نام لیا۔ جسکو میں بھولتا ہوں۔ فرمایا کہ بضرورت یعنی پاخانہ کیلئے کسی کھلے مقام میں گیا تھا۔ پاخانہ پھر رہا تھا۔ دیکھا کہ ایک شخص برہنہ تلوار لئے ہوئے میرے قتل پر آمادہ ہے مینے اوسے اشارتاً کہا کہ ٹھہر جا میں آبدست کرلوں تو میری گردن کاٹ لینا چنانچہ اوسنے موقع دیا اور میں نے نجاست کو پاک کیا۔ بعد طہارت کے مینے اپنا سر اوسکے سامنے جھکا دیا اور کہا لو سر کاٹ لو۔ وہ شخص خموش سا ہوگیا مینے دیکھا کہ اوسکا بدن کانپ رہا ہے۔ میں اپنا سر نیہوڑائے تھا۔ یکایک وہ ایک جانب کو بھاگ گیا۔

اسکے بعد میں چاہتا تھا کہ وہ تینوں ماجرے زہر دہی کے سنوں۔ لیکن وقت کچہری کا قریب آگیا تھا۔ سائیس نے آکر عرض کیا کہ سرکار نو بج گئے۔ خیال کیا کہ یہاں سے شہر دور ہے۔ مکان پر جاکر کھانا کھانا ہے اور کچہری حاضر ہونا۔ اجازت رخصت کی طلب کی۔ اجازت پاکر روانہ ہوگیا۔ پھر دوبارہ ملنے کی نوبت نہ آئی۔ سوامی جی صاحب رخصت ہوگئے۔ یہ زہر دینے والے قصے جسکو معلوم ہونگے وہ آپ سے ہربلاس جی صاحب مفصل کہیں گے۔ میں تو یہ کہتا ہوں کہ سوامی دیانند جی متعصب نہیں تھے جسطرح اونکے مقلد سمجھے ہوئے ہیں۔ والسلام۔ فقط۔ یکم جون ۱۹۳۳ء

نیک بندوں کو تہہ چرخ نہ آرام ملا + کیا دیانند سوامی بھی ستائے نہ گئے
ہائے افسوس کئی بار تمہیں زہر دیا + بت پرستوں سے ترے ناز اٹھائے نہ گئے

امداد حسین عفی عنہ

رمضانی بھیا سمجھ گئے۔ گائے کو لے لیا۔ پنڈت جی صاحب اپنے گھر تشریف لے گئے۔

رمضانی غریب بوڑھی گائے کو لیکر قربان کے یہاں پہونچے جو قصائی تھا۔ اوس نے گائے کو دیکھکر منہ بنایا کہ بہت دبلی ہے۔ رمضانی نے تمام قصہ بیان کیا اور کہا کہ تین روپیہ کی ہے۔ قربان نے کہا کہ دو روپیہ سے زیادہ ہم نہ دینگے۔ رمضانی نے کہا کہ دو روپیہ تو پنڈت ہی لے لیں گے۔ قربان نے مسکرا کر ۴/ اور دیا المختصر چار آنے رمضانی نے لئے۔ دو روپیہ پنڈت جی صاحب نے اور غریب بوڑھی گائے ذبح ہوگئی کیا معلوم قصہ مصنوعی ہے یا اسکی کوئی اصلیت ہے۔ جیسا کہ مینے عرض کیا۔ بیکار اور بوڑھی گائے کی حفاظت کیجائے۔ اگر ایسا کیا جائے تو قصائی کہاں سے ایسی گائے پائیں گے اور ذبح کرینگے۔ مینے اُن لوگوں سے یہ بھی کہا کہ کیا ہمارے ہندو بھائیوں میں ایک یہ بھی رسم ہے جیسا کہ قصہ میں ظاہر کیا گیا کہ مرتے وقت گئو دان کرتے ہیں۔ مینے نہیں دیکھا کہ عمدہ و قیمتی گائیں گاؤ دان میں دیجاتی ہوں۔ کم قیمت گائیں گاؤ دان پر برہمنوں کو دیتے ہیں۔ اور کون سا برہمن گاؤ دان کی سب گائیں رکھے ہوئے ہے۔ پھر وہ گائیں کیا ہوئیں۔ یہ تقریر میری سنکر بعض ہندو دوست میرے بے اختیار کہنے لگے کہ مولوی صاحب بہت صحیح فرماتے ہیں کوئی شک نہیں اسمیں ہماری غفلت شامل ہے اور ضرور ہم لوگ ہی قصوروار ہیں۔ جو تعصبی بھائی تھے وہ اون سے لڑنے لگے۔ تو وہ جھنجھلا کر کہنے لگے کہ اچھا بتاؤ تمہارے باپ دادے کے وقت کی گائیں جو بوڑھی ہوگئیں وہ سب کیا ہوئیں۔ غرض یہ کہ یہ سب تقریریں ہوتی رہیں۔ جبکہ گھر ملتا گیا وہ لوگ اپنے اپنے گھر چلے گئے۔ ہم بھی اپنے گھر گئے۔ کھا پی کر سو رہے۔ صبح ہی نماز پڑھکر سوامی جی صاحب کے پاس جس باغ میں وہ مقیم تھے جا پہونچے۔ کوئی پہرہ چوکی نہ تھی۔ بیدھڑک میں سوامی جی صاحب کی خدمت میں پہونچ گیا۔ مجھکو دیکھا۔ صورت سے ظاہر تھا کہ مجھکو دیکھکر خوش ہیں لیکن پہچان رہے ہیں۔ مینے خود عرض کیا کہ آپ مجھے پہچان رہے ہیں۔ میں امداد حسین ہوں جو نرائن کالج میں اوس وقت پڑھتا تھا اور درگا کنڈ جناب کی خدمت میں حاضر ہوا کرتا تھا۔ خوش ہوگئے۔ آؤ امداد حسین آؤ۔ تمکو دیکھکر دل خوش ہوگیا رہے اچھے۔ عرض کیا شکر ہے۔

اگرچہ میں علی الصباح گیا تھا مگر دیکھا کہ لوگ آنے لگے اور ہر شخص آرزومند تھا کہ ہم دو بات کریں۔ اسلئے

ہمارے گھر سے جدا ہوئیں۔ جہانتک یاد ہے وہ ہندوؤں کے ہاتھ فروخت ہوئیں چاہے وہ حرام زادہ قصائی رہا ہو یا ہندو بنا رہا ہو یا کسی نالایق ہندو کے ذریعہ سے قصائی خرید لے گیا ہو۔ اسمیں ہمپر کیا الزام ہو سکتا ہے۔

اب ہم اون سے پوچھیں کہ آپ نے بیچی کیوں۔ آپ نے خیال نہیں کیا کہ وہ دونوں گائے اب دودھ تو دیتی نہ تھی تو خریدنے والا کس غرض سے خرید رہا ہے۔ ہمارے سوامی جی صاحب کا لیکچر تو دودھ دینے والی گائے پر تھا۔ اونہوں نے ثابت کیا تھا کہ اگر معقول پرورش ایک گائے کی کیجائے تو اسقدر اشخاص اسقدر زمانے تک اوسکے دودھ سے نفع اُٹھا سکتے ہیں۔ بوڑھی کمزور بیکار گائے کے بیچنے کا ذکر تو اونہوں نے نہیں کیا کون زیادہ بیچتا ہے۔ مسلمان زیادہ بیچتے ہیں یا ہندو زیادہ بیچتے ہیں۔ ہندو مجھکو معاف فرمائیں۔ اونکی گائیں بہ نسبت مسلمانوں کے زیادہ قصائی کے ہاتھ میں جاتی ہیں۔ آخر کہاں سے آتی ہیں یہ مسلمان اسقدر گائے پالتے ہیں اور جب وہ ضعیف ہو جاتی ہیں تو قصابوں کو دیا کرتے ہیں؟ ہندوؤں کو اتنی توفیق نہیں ہوتی کہ ہر بستی میں ایک جگہ ایسی قرار دیں۔ جہاں جب کسی کی گائے ضعیف ہو جائے لیجاکر پہونچا دیں۔ اونکی پرورش عام چندہ دہندوں کے ذریعہ سے کیجاوے۔ چندہ دہندہ جو کوئی ہو۔ ہندو ہو یا مسلمان ہو انگریز ہو۔ اون سے لےلیویں اور پرورش کریں۔

میری تقریر جب اس موقع تک پہونچی۔ ایک ہندو صاحب بول اُٹھے۔ مولویصاحب بہت صحیح فرماتے ہیں۔ ہم الزام سے بری نہیں ہو سکتے۔

میں نے اونکو اپنا موئید پاکر عرض کیا کہ ایک شخص نے مجھسے بیان کیا کہ کسی ہندو کے گھر میں ایک شخص بیمار تھا۔ لوگوں نے اوسکے بیٹے سے کہا کہ باپ تمھارا جاں بلب ہے تم اسوقت ہو سکے تو گاؤدان کرادو۔ اُس نے اپنی غریبی کا اظہار کرکے مشورہ دینے والوں سے عرض کیا کہ میری حثیت کے مطابق فوراً کوئی گائے ملجائے تو دلوادو۔ کسی شخص کے یہاں محلہ میں ایک ضعیف گائے تھی تین روپیہ میں مل گئی۔ منگا کر سنکلپ کرادی گئی اور برہمن کو دیدی گئی۔ برہمن نے جو پایا تو وہ سمجھا کہ یہ تو میرے سر اچھی چپٹ لگی۔ انہوں نے اپنے گاؤں کے ایک جولاہے کو بلایا اور کہا کہ رمضانی بھیا ہمارے پاس جگہ نہیں ہے دیکھو یہ گائے ہمکو فلاں جگہ سے ملی ہے تین روپیہ کی ہے۔ تمہارے یہاں اگر جگہ ہو تو رکھ لو۔ ہم احسانمند ہونگے۔

جلسہ برخاست ہوا۔ گروہ گروہ جدا ہوئے۔ سوامی جی صاحب کے لیکچر کی بابت اپنے اپنے خیالات کا اظہار کرتے ہوئے اپنے اپنے گھر چلے۔ مسلمان اس لیکچر کو مذہبی لیکچر سمجھے۔ پھر کیا تھا میرے سر ہوئے۔ کیونکہ مینے جب بہ تحقیق سنا تھا کہ سوامی جی صاحب مرزاپور ضرور تشریف لاتے ہیں تو مینے اپنے احباب میں اونکی بیحد تعریف کی تھی۔ یہ کہا تھا کہ وہ بت پرستی کے خلاف ہیں اور مذہبی تعصب اونکو مطلق نہیں ہے۔ ایک صاحب نے مجھکو مخصوص مخاطب فرمایا اور مجھ سے سوال کیا کہ جناب تو فرماتے تھے کہ اونکو تعصب مذہبی مطلق نہیں ہے بلکہ برعکس اسکے وہ بت پرستی کو ناجائز قرار دیتے ہیں۔ جناب مولوی صاحب ارشاد فرمائیے یہ لیکچر کیا تھا۔

مینے عرض کیا کہ یہ لیکچر بابت حفاظت و پرورش ایسی گائے کے تھا کہ جو دودھ دینے والی ہے۔ اور نصیحت واسطے دونوں گروہ کے ہے چاہے وہ مسلمان ہو اور چاہے وہ ہندو ہو۔ مان لو کہ آپ فرماتے ہیں کہ گائے ذبح نہ کرو یا ذبح نہ کراؤ تو اس نصیحت میں دونوں شامل ہیں۔ مان لو بنارس میں گائے بہت گھروں میں پلی ہوئی ہے۔ غور کروگے تو معلوم ہوگا کہ ہندؤں کے گھر میں قریب قریب ۹۵ فیصدی گھر میں گائے ہوگی تو مسلمانوں کے ۵ گھروں میں گائے ہوگی۔ فرض کرلو کہ اونہیں بنارس والوں کو نصیحت فرماتے ہیں کہ گائے کو پرورش کرو۔ گائے ذبح نہو۔ تو اس کے یہ معنے ہوئے کہ وہ پانچ مسلمان اور پچانوے ہندؤں کو نصیحت فرماتے ہیں۔ فرض کرلو کہ بنارس میں ۲۰ گائے ذبح ایک مہینے میں ہوتی ہے تو مسلمان اگر ایک گائے کے ذمہ وار ہیں تو ہندو ۱۹ گائے کے۔ بتاؤ قصابوں نے کہاں سے ۲۰ گائے پائیں جنکو اون لوگوں نے ایک ماہ میں ذبح کیا۔

بات یہ ہے کہ جس گھر میں جاکر آپ دیکھیں گے گائے جوان اور دودھ دیتی ہوئی پائیں گے۔ تو اُن گھروں کی وہ غریب گائے جو دودھ دینے سے معذور ہوگئیں وہ کیا ہوئیں۔ یہ وہی معذور گائے مسلمانوں اور ہندؤں کی ہیں جو قصائی ذبح کرتے ہیں اور نیچے کلاس کے مسلمان خرید کرکے کھاتے ہیں۔ کیونکہ اُن غریب ضعیف گایوں کا گوشت سستا بکتا ہے۔ بس گائے کے ذبح کئے جانیکا الزام ہندو اور مسلمان دونوں پر عاید ہوتا ہے۔ مسلمانوں پر کم اور ہندؤں پر زیادہ ہے۔ اگر کسی ہندو سے ہم سوال کریں کہ آپکے گھر کی بوڑھی گائیں کیا ہوئیں۔ وہ ناراض ہو جائیگا۔ لڑنے کو تیار ہوگا۔ جواب دیگا کہ مرگئیں یا یہ کہیگا کہ دو گائیں

ہم اونکے ایسے معتقد تھے کہ حسب ارشاد تعمیل کرتے اور اس کے فائدے سے مستفید ہوتے۔

اب وہ زمانہ آیا کہ مہاتماجی نے بنارس چھوڑ دیا اور باہر چلے گئے۔ کہاں کہاں گئے اور کیا کیا۔ ہمکو کچھ خبر قابلِ اعتبار نہیں ملتی تھی۔ میرا طالب علمی کا زمانہ گذر گیا اور میں گورنمنٹ کی ملازمت میں آگیا اور آب ودانہ مجھکو شہر مرزاپور میں لے گیا وہیں رہتا تھا۔

مجھے یاد ہے کہ بنارس ترک کرنے سے پہلے مجھکو کچھ دئے ہوئے بغیر نہیں گئے۔ تاکید کے ساتھ نصیحت فرمائی کہ امداد حسین جبتک تمہاری پچیس برس تک کی عمر نہو جائے شادی نہ کرنا۔ اور شرط یہ ہے کہ پچیس برس تک کے زمانہ کو خوش اطواری کے ساتھ گذارنا۔ چنانچہ میں نے تعمیل حکم کیا۔

ایک مدت کثیر کے بعد یکایک خبر مسرت اثر شہر مرزاپور میں پھیلی کہ سوامی جی صاحب مرزاپور آنے والے ہیں۔ اب میری خوشی کا اندازہ ذریعہ تحریر کے میں نہیں کرسکتا۔ زیادہ انتظار نہیں کرنا پڑا معلوم ہوا کہ فلاں تاریخ فلاں دن۔ فلاں وقت تشریف لائیں گے۔ ایک مہاجن نے اپنے خام مکان کو خالی کیا جو اصطبل کرکے مشہور تھا مگر جگہ اوسمیں کم نہ تھی۔ شب میں ایک جلسہ قرار پایا لیکن لوگ تیسرے پہر ہی سے آنے لگے اور کافی مجمع ہوگیا۔ سرِ شام سوامی دیانندجی صاحب تشریف لائے۔ ایک تخت پر قالین کا فرش تھا۔ گاؤ تکیہ لگا ہوا تھا اوسپر بیٹھ گئے۔ ہندوؤں کیلئے فرش تھا۔ مسلمانوں کی تعداد کم تھی اونکے لئے کرسیاں تھیں۔ میں اپنی کرسی سے بیچین ہوکر سوامی جی کو دیکھتا تھا۔ بالکل وضع بدلی ہوئی تھی۔ سر سے پیر تک کپڑے پہنے ہوئے تھے اور نہایت دُبلے ہوگئے تھے۔ میں دل میں کہہ رہا تھا کہ یاالٰہی یہ وہی سوامی جی ہیں یا کوئی دوسرے ہیں۔

الغرض سوامی جی صاحب کا لیکچر شروع ہوا۔ آواز نے مجھکو یقین دلایا کہ یہ وہی سوامی جی صاحب ہیں جو ہمپر شفقت فرماتے تھے۔

لیکچر آپکا انحفاظِ گاؤ پر تھا۔ آپ نے ہر طرح اپنے بیان کی تائید کی کہ اگر گائے کی حفاظت کیجائے تو ایک گائے اپنے دودھ سے اسقدر آدمیوں کو اتنے زمانہ تک نفع پہونچا سکتی ہے۔ اسلئے گائے کی حفاظت از روئے فائدہ ہمپر لازم ہے۔ دس بجے رات تک یہ بیان ختم ہوا۔ بیان ایسا تھا کہ ہر شخص ساتھ اشتیاق کے سن رہا تھا۔

تو آپ انکو لوٹا شاہ یا تھریا شاہ فرمادیتے تھے - اوّل تو آپ کا ادب کبھی اجازت نہ دیتا تھا کہ ہر موقع پر کچھ دریافت کرسکوں مگر ہاں جب خوش مزاج پاکر ایسے موقع پر دریافت کیا تو فرماتے تھے کہ یہ پنڈت جی ہیں مگر اپنے مذہب سے بالکل بے بہرہ ہیں - ہمارے مذہب میں کہیں وید وغیرہ میں بت پرستی جائز نہیں ہے - یہ پنڈت خود بھی کرتے ہیں اور دوسروں سے بھی بت پرستی کراتے ہیں - بنارس میں اُس زمانے میں بہت سے مشہور پنڈت تھے کوئی آپ کے مقابل نہیں آتا تھا - مسلمانوں کو کوئی کد اون سے نہ تھی - صرف ذی علم برہمن برا مانتے تھے - کیونکہ وہ بت پرستی کے سخت مخالف تھے -

میں نے سنا کہ ایک روز ایک مجمع سوامی جی کی مخالفت میں مجتمع ہوا - (اوسمیں میں موجود نہ تھا اسلیئے ممکن ہے کہ میرا بیان حسب حال نہو -) اور نوبت بحث کی ہوئی - اصرار ہوا کہ گفتگو ذات خاص سوامی جی صاحب کی طرف سے شروع ہووے -

سوامی جی صاحب نے فرمایا - وید میں کہاں لکھا ہے کہ بت پرستی کرو - مخالف جماعت نے جواباً یہ کہا کہ - وید میں کہاں لکھا ہے کہ مت کرو - سوامی جی صاحب خاموش رہ گئے - غالباً انھوں نے اس قول پر عمل کیا کہ "جواب جاہلاں باشد خموشی" آپکا خموش ہوجانا تھا کہ تھپوی پٹ گئی کہ سوامی جی صاحب ہار گئے - میں جب دوسرے روز حضور میں حاضر ہوا - یہ قصہ معلوم ہوا لیکن سوامی جی صاحب نے اپنی زبان سے کچھ نہ فرمایا گویا اونکو یہ مباحثہ ایک فعل عبث معلوم ہوا اور اوسکا تذکرہ باعث تضیع اوقات محسوس ہوا -

اس زمانہ تک آپکی جو کچھ شہرت تھی وہ اسقدر تھی کہ آپ ایک مجرد درویش ہیں اور سنسکرت کے بڑے لاثانی عالم ہیں اور بت پرستی کے مخالف ہیں - مسلمانوں کو اوں سے کوئی وجہ مخالفت اوسوقت تک نہ تھی اور نہ کوئی مسلمانوں سے اونکو بحث مذہبی تھی - میں لکھ چکا ہوں کہ آپ لباس وغیرہ کے شوقین نہ تھے - شوقین کیسے کوئی کپڑا بجز لنگوٹ کے اُس زمانہ میں آپ پہنتے نہ تھے - بدن میں جابجا اور ماتھے پر کوئی خوشبودار شئے مثل صندل وغیرہ کے کچھ لگائے رہتے تھے - میں نہیں کہہ سکتا کہ کیا لگاتے تھے اور نہ کوئی موقع آیا کہ ہم دریافت کرتے اگر دریافت کرتے تو فوراً اُس شئے کا نام بتلا دیتے اور اوسکا فائدہ بتلاتے اور نصیحت فرماتے کہ استعمال کرو

توجہ فرمائے من ساردا جی صاحب زاد عنایتہٗ

جناب کا عنایت نامہ ۱۸ اپریل ۱۹۳۳ء موصول ہوا۔ سخت حیرت ہے کہ آپکو یہ علم کہاں سے ہوا کہ مجھکو سوامی جی صاحب کی ملازمت کا شرف حاصل ہے

اسوقت سوامی جی صاحب کی تصویر میرے زیر نگاہ ہے۔ میں خیال کرتا ہوں کہ عرصہ تخمیناً پچاس سال گذرا کہ آپ درگا کنڈ بنارس میں ایک باغ میں قیام فرماتے تھے۔ اُسوقت آپکی وضع یہ تھی کہ لنگوٹ باندھتے تھے اور تمام بدن کھلا رہتا تھا کرسی پر بیٹھتے تھے۔ اور جو لوگ آپ کی ملاقات کو آتے تھے وہ بھی کرسی پر بیٹھتے تھے۔ نہایت تندرست تھے اور خوش مزاج تھے۔ دو ایک شخص لکھے پڑھے قریب فرش پر بیٹھے رہتے تھے۔ جو کچھ آپ فرما دیتے تھے وہ لوگ لکھ لیا کرتے تھے۔ تعصبِ مذہبی بالکل نہ تھا۔ ایک لوہے کے چولہے پر کچھ پکتا رہتا تھا۔ آپ کرسی سے اُٹھکر دیکھ لیا کرتے تھے۔ میرا طالب علمی کا زمانہ تھا۔ جے نرائن کالج میں پڑھتا تھا۔ بعد برخاستِ مدرسہ میں روز جناب کی خدمت میں جایا کرتا تھا۔ روز کی حاضری کا یہ اثر ہو گیا تھا کہ آپ مجھ ایسے طالب علم کا انتظار فرماتے تھے اور جب سامنے سے آتے ہوئے دیکھتے تھے۔ خوش ہوکر فرماتے تھے۔ آؤ۔ بیٹھو۔ جہانتک مجھکو یاد ہے تعصبانہ مذہبی گفتگو سوامی جی صاحب نے مجھ سے نہیں کی بلکہ اتحادِ مذہب کی طرف اشارہ فرماتے تھے۔ کہ امداد حسین تمہارے یہاں خدا کے اسمِ صفات بہت ہیں۔ میں عرض کرتا تھا۔ بجا فرماتے ہیں۔ فرماتے تھے دو چار نام لو۔ میں عرض کرتا تھا۔ مثلاً رحیم کریم غفور۔ تو بجنسہٖ اوسی معنی کے الفاظ سنسکرت کے آپ فرماتے تھے اور ارشاد ہوتا تھا کہ دیکھو ہمارے یہاں یہ الفاظ ہیں جو تلفظ میں بھی کسیقدر مشابہ ہیں اور معنی میں بھی ہم معنی ہیں۔

ہاں اگر مذہبی خیال آپکا مجھکو کبھی محسوس ہوتا تھا تو اوسوقت جب کوئی پنڈت جی آجاتے تھے

مختصر حالات

سوامی دیانند سرسوتی

از احقر امداد حسین

حسب فرمائش

دیوان بہادر ہرملاس سارداصاحب

ایم۔ ایل۔ اے

***

FOUNDER SUBSCRIBERS

1. ALAKHDHARI, Foreign Secretary, Alwar.
2. AMARNATHA JHA, M.A., Professor of English, Allahabad University.
3. ANAND RAJ SURANA, P. P. Indo-Europa Trading Co., Delhi.
4. THE ARYA SAMAJ, Bhawanipur, 16 Paddapukur Road, Calcutta.
5. ATMA RAM, Chief Parcel Clerk, Burma Railway, Rangoon.
6. RAJA AUDHESH SINGH, Kalakankar, Oudh.

7. DR. BAL KRISHNA, PH.D., Principal, Rajaram College, Kolhapur.
8. RAI BAHADUR BELI RAM DHAWAN, M.A., Advocate, Peshawar.
9. BELI RAM, President, Arya Samaj, Rampura, Peshawar Cantt.
10. DR. BIHARI LAL TREHUN, Medical Officer, Attock Oil Company, President, Arya Samaj, Khaur, Distt. Attock.
11. RAO BAHADUR THAKUR BIJAI SINGH, Masuda.
12. RAI BAHADUR SETH BIRADH MAL LODHA, Banker and Rais, Ajmer.
13. RAI BAHADUR BRAJA NANDAN SINGH, Mithapur, Patna (B. & O.).
14. BUDHINI DEVIJI, Net Ram Pande, Rabha, P. Pihani, Hardoi.

15. D. M. COLLEGE, Moga, through R. K. KUMAR, M.A., Principal.
16. DAMODER SOONDERDAS Merchant & Commission Agent, Bombay.
17. DEVI DAYAL CHANDHOKE, of Bhera (Chairman U. I. T. Co., Ltd.,) Agent Oriental Life Office, Jodhpur.
18. DEVI CHAND M.A., President, Dayanand Dalit Uddhar Mandal Punjab, Hoshiarpur.
19. RAI SAHIB DR. DEVI DITTA c/o President, Arya Samaj, Rampura.
20. PROF. DIWAN CHAND SHARMA, D. A. V. College, Lahore.
21. DIRECTOR GENERAL OF ARCHÆOLOGY in India, Simla.
22. CAPTAIN RAJA DURGA NARAYAN SINGH, Tirwa, Farrukhabad.
23. DR. DWARKA PRASAD AIRANIA, In-charge Police Hospital, Ajmer.

24. GAJADHAR PRASAD, Senior Auditor, L. F. Accounts, Allahabad.
25 GANGA PRASAD, M.A., Chief Judge, Tehri.
26. GAURI SHANKAR PRASAD, Advocate, Bulanala, Benares City.
27. GAURI SHANKER G. VERMA, BAR-AT-LAW, Ajmer.

28. MAHAMAHOPADHYAYA, RAI BAHADUR GAURI SHANKAR HIRACHAND OJHA, Curator, Rajputana Museum, Ajmer.
29. GHANSHAM DASS BIRLA, Birla House, New Delhi.
30. GHASI RAM M.A., LL.B., Advocate, Meerut City.
31. PROF. GHISOO LAL, M.A., LL.B., Advocate, Ajmer.
32. DR. GOKAL CHAND NARANG, M.A., PH.D., Minister, Punjab Govt., Simla.
33. SWAMI GOPAL DASS, Churuwala, Central Jail, Bikaner.
34 GOVIND SINGH BHAVAN SINGH, MANSABDAR, PATUR, Akola.
35. DR GUR DAYAL KASHYAP, Jalalpur Bhattian, Distt. Gujranwala.
36. GYAN CHAND, Contractor, No. 17, Bara khamba Road, New Delhi.

37. DEWAN BAHADUR HAR BILAS SARDA, M.L.A., Ajmer.
38. HANMANT DASS, B.A., LL.B., President, Kangra Valley Ved Prachar and Trust Society, Dharmsala, District Kangra.
39. H. P. MODY, M.L A., Chairman, Millowners' Association, Bombay.
40. HARDWARI MAL SULEKH CHAND, Mahajan, Sonipat, Rohtak.
41. HARI PRASAD, Vice-Principal, Government College, Ajmer.

42. JAGAN NATH, M.L.A., President, Bar Association, Lahore.
43. JAINARAIN RAM CHANDER, 18 Mullick Street, Calcutta.
44. JAWAHAR LAL, B.A., Head Master, Oswal High School, Ajmer.
45. SAHIB SIHAJI JOOWAN SIHAJI Thakur Sahib, Gangod State, District Ahmedabad.

46. KANHYA LAL, B.A., L.T., Late Head Master, Normal School, Ajmer.
47. DR. KARTIK PRASAD, L.M.S., Health officer, Nepal.
48. KESHAV DEO MAHESHWARI, Cashier, Shri Mathra Prasad Gulabdevi Arya Kanya Pathshala, Babu Mohalla, Ajmer.
49. KHUBI RAM SARAF, c/o Sasta Sahitya Mandal, Ajmer.
50. KHUSHAL CHAND KHURSAND, Proprietor Daily "*Milap*", Lahore.
51. KHUSHI RAM, Retired Sub-Engineer, Ajmer.
52. KISHAN CHAND, Chief Engineer, P. W. D., Srinagar, Kashmir.
53. RAI BAHADUR KISHAN LAL, Retired E. A. C., Masuda, Ajmer.
54. KRIPA RAM, Head Master, Labhu Ram, Doaba High School, Jullundur City.
55. RAJA BAHADUR KUSHALPAL SINGH, Ex-Minister, U.P. Govt., Agra.

56. LAKSHMAN PRASAD, M.A., Principal, D. A. V. College, Dehra Dun.

57. DR. LAKSHMAN SARUP, M.A., PH.D., Professor, Punjab University, 33, Lodge Road, Lahore.
58. RAI SAHIB LAL CHAND, Sub-Divisional Officer, M.E.S., Mir Ali Camp, Via Bannu.

59. M. C. DHIMAN, Director, Steel Equipment & Construction Ltd., 113, Benares Road, Salkia, Howrah.
60. RAI SAHEB MADAN MOHAN SETH, M.A., LL.B., Assistant Sessions Judge, Meerut.
61. MAHADEORAO VISHNU GANU, Signal and Interlocking Inspector, B. B. & C. I. Ry., Ajmer.
62. PROF. MAHENDRA PRATAP SHASTRI, M.A., M.O.L., D. A. V. College, Dehra Dun.
63. MAHENDRA SINHA RANAWAT of Kaharwa (Mewar,) Revenue Commissioner, Bundi.
64. MAMRAJ of Khatoli, Manager Book Depot, Research Department, D. A. V. College, Lahore.
65. DR. MANKARAN SARDA, B.SC., M.B., B.S., Ajmer.
66. RAI BAHADUR DR. MATHRADAS, Hon. Assistant Surgeon to the Viceroy, Moga.
67. MAYADEVI KASHYAP, Jalalpur Bhattian, Distt. Gujranwala.
68. MOHAN LAL c/o President, Arya Samaj, Rampura.

69. NAU NIHAL, RAIS, Govt. Contractor, Benlay-Estate, Murree.
70. NAND KISOR SINGH, Ex-Secretary, State Council, Jaipur, Narai, Etah.

71. DR. P. BASU, M.A., PH.D., Principal, Holkar College, Indore.
72. P. SESHADRI M.A., Principal, Government College, Ajmer.

73. RAO RAJA RAGHUNATH SINGHJI, of Jiwand (Marwar).
74. RAJ NARAIN BRAHMWAR, Retired Deputy Collector, Proprietor Rajputana Electric Works, Ajmer.
75. RAJ ROOP, son of MEHTA SUNDAR DAS GADHOK, Bhaun, District Jhelum.
76. RAM CHANDRA OJHA, Manager Bijwa Estate, Lakhimpur, Kheri.
77. RAM DASS, Principal, D. A. V. College, Hoshiarpur
78. RAM GOPAL, BAR-AT-LAW, Bangalore.
79. RAMESHWAR BAJPAI c/o HANUMAN SAH Rameshwar, No. 7, Varda Thakur Lane, Bara Bazar, Calcutta.
80. RAMJIBAI C/o L. MEHAR CHAND, Forest officer, Shahpur.

81. THE HON'BLE RAJA SIR RAMPAL SINGH, K.C.I.E., Member, Council of State, Kurri Sudauli Raj, District Rai Barelli.
82. KUMAR RANANJAYA SINGH, Ex-M.L.A., of Amethi Raj, Oudh.
83. THAKUR SAJJAN SINGH, Istimrardar of Junia Estate, Ajmer District.
84. SATYA BHUSHAN ARYA, B.A., LL.B., Pleader, Dera Ghazikhan.
85. RAI BAHADUR DR. SURJU PRASAD TIWARI, 12, Tukaganj, Indore.
86. KUMARI SAVITRI DHAWAN B.A., c/o Rai Bahadur Beli Ram Dhawan, M.A., Advocate, Peshawar Cantonment.
87. THE SECRETARY, NAGAR ARYA SAMAJ, Phulati Bazar, Agra.
88. RAJA SHATRUNJAIDEV of Bijwa, Lakhimpur, District Kheri.
89. RAI BAHADUR BAKSHI SOHAN LAL, Advocate, High Court, Lahore.
90. SIR SUKHDEV PRASAD, KT., C.I.E., Prime Minister, Udaipur.
91. T. S. KASHIVE, Genl. Merchant and Coal Supplier, Lajpatgunj, Damoh City, C. P.
92. THAKUR DUTT, Proprietor, Amritdhara Pharmacy, Lahore.
93. RAI BAHADUR TRILOKI NATH SHARMA, City Magistrate, Ajmer.
94. RAJADHIRAJ SHRI UMED SINGHJI BAHADUR of Shahpura.
95. V. N. MEHTA I.C.S., Revenue Minister, Jammu & Kashmir State, Srinagar.
96. V. PARASHURAM MUDALIAR, Retired District Excise officer, Shegaon (Berar).
97. VARJANG VISHRAM CHOWHAN, Contractor & Rice-Mill owner P. O. Durg (C. P.).
98. VISHAMBAR DUTT (Batala Nivasi) Head Master, Middle School, Nagrota Bagnan, District Kangri
99. SETH JAGAN NATH, BANKER, Phulera Junction, B. B. & C. I. Ry.
100. GULRAJ GOPAL GUPTA, Assistant Engineer, B. B. & C. I. Ry., Delhi.
101. MANAGER, Student Book Depot, Shraddhanand Road, Bhiwani
102. GANGA SAHAI Sharma, P. O. Didwana, Marwar.
103. MAHASHYA KRISHNA, Proprietor The Daily "Pratap" Lahore.
104. GURDASS RAM BHANDARI, c/o Chief Accountant's office, Kenya & Uganda Railways, Nairobi, Kenya Colony, B. E. Africa.
105. RAM LAL BAHL, c/o Chief Accountant's office, Kenya & Uganda Railways, Nairobi, Kenya Colony, B. E. Africa.